THE
LITERATURE OF
ANCIENT SUMER

D1518464

THE
LITERATURE OF
ANCIENT SUMER

Translated and Introduced by

JEREMY BLACK

GRAHAM CUNNINGHAM

ELEANOR ROBSON

and

GÁBOR ZÓLYOMI

OXFORD
UNIVERSITY PRESS

OXFORD
UNIVERSITY PRESS

Great Clarendon Street, Oxford OX2 6DP

Oxford University Press is a department of the University of Oxford.
It furthers the University's objective of excellence in research, scholarship,
and education by publishing worldwide in

Oxford New York

Auckland Cape Town Dar es Salaam Hong Kong Karachi
Kuala Lumpur Madrid Melbourne Mexico City Nairobi
New Delhi Shanghai Taipei Toronto

With offices in

Argentina Austria Brazil Chile Czech Republic France Greece
Guatemala Hungary Italy Japan Poland Portugal Singapore
South Korea Switzerland Thailand Turkey Ukraine Vietnam

Oxford is a registered trade mark of Oxford University Press
in the UK and in certain other countries

Published in the United States
by Oxford University Press Inc., New York

First published 2004
First published in paperback 2006

British Library Cataloguing in Publication Data

Data available

Library of Congress Cataloging in Publication Data

Data available

Typeset by Regent Typesetting, London
Printed in Great Britain
on acid-free paper by
Biddles Ltd, King's Lynn, Norfolk

ISBN 0–19–926311–6   978–0–19–926311–0
ISBN 0–19–929633–2 (pbk.)   978–0–19–929633–0 (pbk.)

1 3 5 7 9 10 8 6 4 2

ACKNOWLEDGEMENTS

This volume of translations has grown out of the Electronic Text Corpus of Sumerian Literature (ETCSL) project. The project, founded by Jeremy Black, is based at the Oriental Institute of the University of Oxford. It has received funding from the following bodies: the University of Oxford (1997), the Leverhulme Trust (1997–2000), and the Arts and Humanities Research Board (2001–6). Graham Cunningham has worked full time for the project, as an editor and then senior editor, since 1997. Eleanor Robson worked full time for the ETCSL pilot project in the first nine months of 1997. She was supported in 1997–2000 by a British Academy Postdoctoral Fellowship and thereafter by a fellowship at All Souls College, Oxford. During both fellowships she acted as part-time technical developer for the project. Gábor Zólyomi worked full time for the ETCSL project as an editor in 1997–2000. Since then he has been supported by the Hungarian Scientific Research Fund (OTKA) and by a János Bolyai Research Scholarship of the Hungarian Academy of Sciences. He was supported by a Humboldt Research Fellowship in 2003–4.

We are extremely grateful to all those who have contributed source material to the project: in particular Miguel Civil, but also Bendt Alster, Antoine Cavigneaux, Gertrud Farber, Andrew George, Geerd Haayer, Bram Jagersma, Joachim Krecher, Marie-Christine Ludwig, Piotr Michalowski, Martha Roth, Yitschak Sefati, Steve Tinney, Herman Vanstiphout, Niek Veldhuis, Konrad Volk, Christopher Walker, Claus Wilcke, and Annette Zgoll.

Images of UM 55-21-327 = 3N-T 436 are reproduced with the permission of the curators of the Babylonian Section, University of Pennsylvania Museum, and with the kind assistance of Kevin Danti. Figures 8, 10, and 20 are reproduced from J. Boese, *Altmesopotamische Weihplatten: Eine sumerische Denkmalsgattung des 3. Jahrtausends v. Chr* (Berlin, New York: De Gruyter, 1971) and Figure 19 from J. V. Canby, *The Ur-nammu Stela* (Philadelphia: University of Pennsylvania Museum of Archaeology and Anthropology, 2001), pl. 40 (detail), with the permission of the publishers; all others were drawn by the authors. The maps were produced by Vuk Trifkovic.

We warmly thank our colleagues on the ETCSL project who joined us later—Esther Flückiger-Hawker (editor, 2001), Jon Taylor (editor, 2001–2), and Jarle Ebeling (technical developer, 2003–)—as well as other colleagues and students in Oxford and elsewhere who have contributed directly or indirectly to its success. We owe a particular debt of thanks to Tim Potts and Niek Veldhuis, who read the manuscript with great care and thought at very short notice. While we did not always agree with their comments they were always useful in helping us to clarify what we meant and how we said it. Naturally, we take full responsibility for all errors and infelicities that remain. As many as possible were corrected for this paperback edition.

The other editors dedicate this book to Jeremy Black—our teacher, colleague, and friend—who died while the hardback edition was in press.

CONTENTS

LIST OF ILLUSTRATIONS

HOW TO USE THIS BOOK

In this book are new translations of seventy Sumerian literary works—about a fifth of the known corpus as counted by lines or words. We have chosen the most complete and the most interesting (to us) which we edited as part of the Electronic Text Corpus of Sumerian Literature <http://etcsl.orinst.ox.ac.uk>.

THE TRANSLATIONS

In choosing which works to include here, a number of different criteria have been used. First, we wanted them to be representative. We have picked as widely as possible from across the corpus to include a range of styles and genres (ancient and modern). Some of these works have been anthologized before; others are known only through scholarly editions in specialist journals. But we also wanted them to be readable, so translations of the works which are currently known only in a very fragmentary state have been excluded.

Nevertheless, you will still encounter many passages encumbered with ellipses (. . .) marking broken or incomprehensible passages in the original text. Longer passages are indicated like this: (*10 lines unclear, fragmentary, or missing*). Likewise, there are a number of Sumerian words which cannot yet be translated but in each case it will be clear from the context what sort of object is being named. Three modified alphabetic characters have been used within Sumerian words and names: ĝ stands for *ng* as in 'sing'; ḫ represents the sound *ch* as in 'loch', š means *sh* as in 'ship'. Very little is known about Sumerian vowel length, but Akkadian distinguishes long vowels, which are marked like this: Rīm-Sîn. We have chosen to use Sumerian place-names although other versions may be more familiar: Nibru instead of Nippur, Unug for Uruk, and Urim for Ur. We also use Zimbir (Sippar) and Eridug (Eridu).

Our translations are all in English prose—we have not attempted to capture the poetics of Sumerian but rather to aim for comprehensibility. Numbers in the left-hand margin at the beginning of each paragraph—1–14—indicate the line numbers of the Sumerian composite text to which they relate. Most compositions are attested on more than one tablet, as explained in the Introduction. Some manuscript sources of some compositions use variant words or phrases; deviations from the main text are signalled like this: ° and are given in the notes at the end of each translation. Each translation is prefaced by a short introduction, outlining the plot or structure of the narrative and drawing attention to particular features of the work. Sumerian names, which are sometimes complicated and confusing, are explained in a Glossary at the back.

THE BOOK AND THE WEBSITE

It seemed a hopeless and wrong-headed task to organize the translations according to modern or ancient criteria of genre, or by geography, chronology, or any other formal system of classification. Instead the translations have been arranged thematically into ten different groups according to the themes they address, the deities they feature, or the functions they served. There are groups about heroes and kings (A), love and sex (F), the natural order (G), and scribes and learning (I). There are groups featuring the deities Inana and Dumuzid (B), Enlil and Ninlil (C), the moon-god Nanna-Suen (D) and various warrior gods (E). These groups are not in themselves meaningful, except perhaps one concerning ancient genre categories (H) and another containing an ancient curricular sequence (J). All of the works chosen inevitably deal with several themes, so at the end of the introduction to each group further relevant compositions from the other groups are listed. Similarly, at the back of the book we have given lists of other themes to follow. There are as many paths through the book, and as many connections between the compositions, as there are ways of reading Sumerian literature.

In the index on page 358 the title of each work is given an ETCSL catalogue number like this: 4.16.1, which you can use to locate it on the ETCSL website <http://etcsl.orinst.ox.ac.uk>. For each composition the website gives the Sumerian text on which our translation is based, a bibliography of scholarly literature on the work, a list of manuscript sources and their places of publication, as well as the translation itself. Sometimes the web translations differ in small details from those published in the book, which have been lightly edited for a stylistic consistency that was not an aim of the website. More significantly, about a fifth of the compositions pre-sented in this book are known in two or more different versions, only the best preserved of which is included here. The other versions are all given on the website. Even more importantly, you will also find translations and editions of over three hundred more Sumerian literary works—an estimated 70 per cent of the total corpus, edited and unedited, as it is known today.

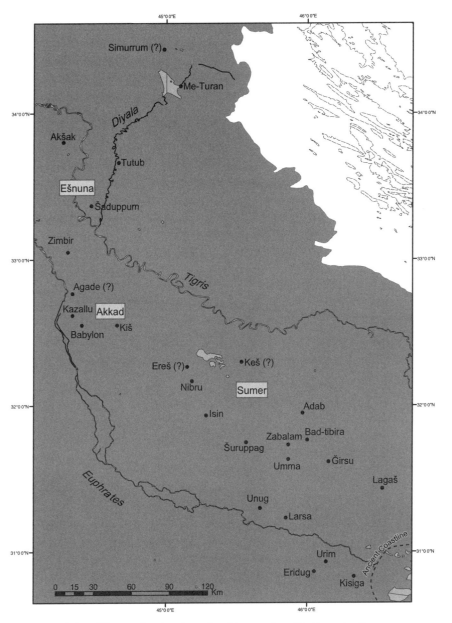

FIG. I. Map of Sumer, showing the major cities mentioned in Sumerian literature

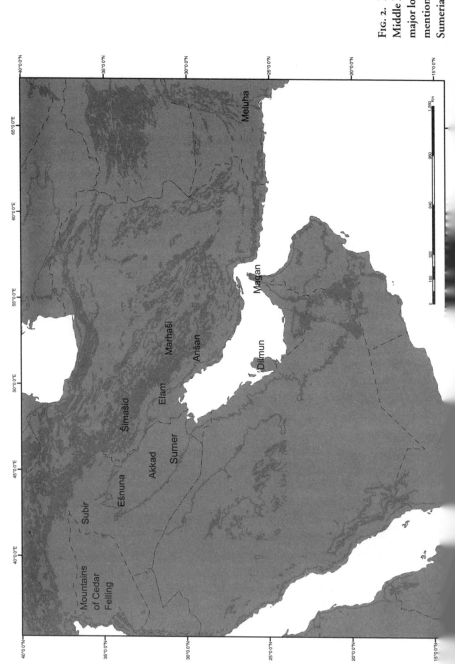

Fig. 2. Map of the Middle East, showing major locations mentioned in Sumerian literature

CHRONOLOGICAL TABLE

Period/Dynasty	Approximate dates BCE	
Ubaid	5000–4000	First settlements in southern Iraq
Uruk	4000–3000	Development of urban living and cuneiform writing in southern Iraq
Early Dynastic	3000–2350	Interdependent, sometimes conflicting Sumerian city states
Old Akkadian or Sargonic	2350–2230	First territorial empire, based at Agade to the north of Sumer. Kings Sargon and Naram-Suen; priestess En-ḫedu-ana; first widespread writing of Akkadian language
Third Dynasty of Urim (Ur III)	2112–2004	Bureaucratic empire, sponsor of Sumerian royal praise poetry. Kings Ur-Namma, Šulgi, Šu-Suen, Ibbi-Suen
Old Babylonian	2000–1600	Successor states to the Third Dynasty of Urim; Akkadian gradually replaces Sumerian as the literary language
Isin	2017–1794	Kings Šu-ilišu, Iddin-Dagan, Išme-Dagan, Lipit-Eštar, Ur-Ninurta
Larsa	2025–1763	Kings Sîn-iqīšam, Rīm-Sîn
Babylon	1894–1595	Kings Ḫammurabi, Samsu-iluna

INTRODUCTION

Sumerian literature is the oldest readable poetry in the world. It was written down on clay tablets in the cuneiform script by scribes in southern Iraq some 4,000 years ago and has been read again only within the last sixty years. This introduction explores some of the questions that Sumerian literature provokes—what is meant by 'literature' in such an ancient context? What is Sumerian: a language, a culture, or a people? What are the sources and evidence on which these translations are based? At the end are some suggestions for further reading on some of the topics covered.

THE LITERATURE OF ANCIENT SUMER

What does it mean to label as 'literature' writings that are four thousand years old? It is difficult to imagine anything further removed in time, space, and experience from us. Do modern notions of 'literature' even apply? And how do we know that 'literature' was a meaningful idea in ancient Sumer? Let's start by comparing a modern instance of 'literature' with an ancient Sumerian one.

> *London Airport*
> Last night at London Airport
> I saw a wooden bin
> labelled UNWANTED LITERATURE
> IS TO BE PLACED HEREIN.
> So I wrote a poem
> and popped it in.[1]

Nibruta-lu, the son of the merchant Lugal-šuba, has had this tin axe made for Nergal. Its wooden part is of *arganum* tree of the mountains, a wood which is superior even to the *alal* stone; its stone part is of *antasura*, a stone which has no equal. The arm of the man who strikes with it will never get tired.

Should it break, I will repair it for Nergal. Should it disappear, I will replace it for him.

May Nergal look after me during my life, and may he provide me with clean water in the Underworld after my death.

[1] From Christopher Logue, *Ode to the Dodo: Poems, 1953–1978* (Jonathan Cape: London, 1981).

It's not difficult to spot which is which. The first one is clearly a modern poem: it rhymes, it scans, and it is laid out very particularly on the page, with a title and line-breaks. (And of course there is the give-away reference to the airport.) The second, though, doesn't look much like literature at all: it isn't obviously a poem, it elicits very little emotional response (except perhaps bemusement), and there isn't much by way of character or plot. In fact, it seems very functional, perhaps a dedicatory inscription on a votive offering to a deity. To add to its peculiarity, it uses words and names which are unfamiliar and unpronounceable.

As we shall see though, *London Airport*, written in 1974 by the British poet Christopher Logue, and the Sumerian example, which is now called *The dedication of an axe to Nergal* (or just *Axe* for short), have more in common than might be expected—and some illuminating differences too.

Literariness

London Airport very deliberately plays with conflicting modern notions of 'literature'. The label over the bin, we assume, is soliciting airport maps, promotional leaflets, and flight schedules, not unloved poems or novels. One meaning of 'literature', then, is certainly the disposable, the ephemeral, the forgettable written detritus of everyday life. But it can mean just the opposite: literature as high art, culture, that which society values (and which people aren't likely, therefore, to throw away in an airport bin).

Either of those definitions could be applied to Sumerian writings too; but for our purposes we shall choose the second one, discarding at first cut the tens of thousands of administrative and legal records from ancient Sumer. They are fascinating and important sources of information on the history, language, people, and society of the time and place we are concerned with, and their evidence will often be useful; but they do not constitute the raw materials for the translations in this book.

Literary language

Literature as the literary, then—but how do we detect it? After all, *Axe* does not seem very literary at first reading. But nor might *London Airport* if it were rearranged on the page:

Last night at London Airport I saw a wooden bin labelled UNWANTED LITERATURE IS TO BE PLACED HEREIN. So I wrote a poem and popped it in.

Reading it like this, one has to work quite hard to make out its poetic qualities: the visual cues have disappeared, making it difficult to distinguish the rhymes and scansion unless it is read aloud. But the quality of the language remains—and once again we can see the poet playing, this time with the notion of literary language. The label uses difficult syntax and archaic vocabulary—the passive voice, 'herein'—whereas the poem itself uses relaxed, everyday words and constructions: 'So I wrote a poem and popped it in.' This confounds our expectations: we expect poems to be difficult to understand, convoluted to follow. On the other hand, we expect airport bins, if they are labelled at all, simply to say 'Rubbish' or 'Paper only'. Yet the poem remains resolutely literary in its structure: it has six lines (if it is laid out properly), every other one of which ends with the sound 'in'. The first four lines have three stresses each, and the last two only two stresses—a rhythmic change which emphasizes the difference between the 'literary' language of the label and the 'unliterary' language of the poem. Logue has also closely tied rhythm to alliteration—the repetition of similar consonant sounds. In the first and third lines the sound 'l' (for 'literature') is prominent, while the last two feature 'p' (for 'poem').

Literary language is also distinguishable in the writings of ancient Sumer. Because Sumerian is long dead as a spoken language it is very difficult to detect aural qualities such as rhythm or metre, rhyme, alliteration, and assonance—the repetition of similar vowel sounds. Nevertheless, Sumerian literature is quite clearly laid out in lines—although the great differences in Sumerian and English syntax, or word order, make it impossible to follow those line divisions in translation. We shall discuss the Sumerian language, and how we make sense of it, later. Just for fun, though, here is a transcription, or representation in modern alphabetic characters, of *Axe*, following the original line patterns. Bearing in mind that nothing very precise is known about the qualities of Sumerian vowels and consonants, or where the stress might have fallen, you might like to experiment with reading this out and looking for aural qualities within it. The sign ḫ represents a sound like *ch* in 'loch'; g̃ represents *ng*, as in 'sing', while *g* is always hard, as in 'go'; and *š* represents the *sh* of 'ship'.

nibrutalu
dumu lugalšuba damg̃arake
nergalra
ḫazin nagga munanindim
g̃išbi arganum ḫursag̃a
alale dirigam
nabi antasuram
gabari nutukuam

ḫesige ani nankušu
ḫebtatare
gamunabsilim
ugu ḫenibde
kibi gamunabgi
ud tilaga igi ḫumundu
ud baugen kura
a siga ḫumunana

Perhaps you have detected the three consecutive lines ending in 'am' or the predominance of the vowel 'u' in the last part of the composition. Lines, then, are a distinguishing feature of Sumerian literature. Even if we don't always know what they sounded like, patterns can often be detected in them: lines are commonly grouped by meaning or structure as well as sound. Such parallel pairs of line groups are found throughout *Axe*:

> Its wooden part is of *arganum* tree of the mountains, a wood which is superior even to the *alal* stone;
> its stone part is of *antasura*, a stone which has no equal.

> Should it break, I will repair it for Nergal.
> Should it disappear, I will replace it for him.

> May Nergal look after me during my life,
> and may he provide me with clean water in the Underworld after my death.

The first pair also exhibits two further features of Sumerian literary language: imagery and poetic vocabulary. We have already seen how 'herein' stands out in *London Airport* as a literary word incongruously placed. In our translation of *Axe* too, there are three words which stand out from the print on the page: *arganum*, *alal*, and *antasura*. Now, they stand out because they are in italic type and obviously not English; but the fact that they have not been translated suggests that they might be rare or difficult words for which no English equivalent exists, or is known. The fact that they all begin with *a* may be poetically meaningful too. In fact *antasura* was indeed a rare and difficult word in the eighteenth century BCE, the period from which the surviving copies of *Axe* date. On the other hand, it is found frequently in Sumerian royal inscriptions from six centuries or more before. So *antasura* is just as old-fashioned as 'herein': it is not part of everyday language and is thus marked as 'poetic' or 'literary'.

Figurative imagery often clusters densely within Sumerian literary works—although not every composition uses it to the same degree, if at all. *Axe* is rather light on imagery (as indeed is *London Airport*) but we can detect

comparatives and superlatives in the description of the raw materials—
'superior even to the *alal* stone', 'a stone which has no equal'. Then comes
hyperbole or exaggeration for emotive effect: 'The arm of the man who strikes
with it will never get tired.' We know from our own experience that there can
be no such axe: however strong we are, and however well made the axe, we
will exhaust ourselves sooner or later through repeated striking. The
Sumerian literary corpus as a whole uses a wide range of figures of speech. It
would be tedious to list examples here, but do look out for different kinds of
figurative language as you read through the translations. We will make do
with an image-dense passage from a hymn to Nergal, divine recipient of the
offering in *Axe.*

Nergal, great battle-net for malefactors, covering all enemies! Warrior, you are a great
and furious storm upon the land which disobeys your father! Nergal, you terrify the
walled cities and the settlements as you stand in your path like a wild bull, smiting them
with your great horns! Nergal, you have consumed their brickwork as if it were chaff in
the air.   (*An* adab *to Nergal for Šu-ilišu*, Group E)

Here both Nergal and his enemies are compared to, or identified with,
other things. Nergal is a 'great battle-net' thrown over evil-doers to stop
them in their tracks. He is a destructive 'furious storm'; he is like a terrifying
'wild bull' with 'great horns'. The 'walled cities and settlements' stand for the
people who inhabit them; they thus have 'brickwork' which Nergal has 'consumed' (that is, destroyed), like insubstantial 'chaff'.

Sumerian word order too can be as complex as modern instances: for
example, the second sentence of *The lament for Sumer and Urim* (Group D)
takes 55 lines to resolve itself. Further discussion of Sumerian syntax is left
until later.

Genre

So if all Sumerian literary works have poetic lines and heightened language,
does that make them all poetry? In a sense, yes, but there are further distinc-
tions that can be made, based both on our own criteria and those found in
the literature itself.

Nowadays, we think of literature as comprising poems, novels, and plays.
Something resembling all three can be found within Sumerian literature,
often within the same composition. A hymn of praise may preface a mythological account, as in *Inana and Ebiḫ* (Group J); or a work may consist
entirely of dialogue—as, for instance, *A balbale to Inana and Dumuzid*
(Group F). More generally, the Sumerian literary corpus can be described as

including within it a whole variety of genres, including myth, epic, praise poetry, hymns, laments, prayers, songs, fables, didactic poems, debates, and proverbs. But these are all labels that we impose upon the corpus, and there are many instances of compositions which cannot be neatly categorized. *The heron and the turtle* (Group G), for instance, is both fable (a narrative about two anthropomorphized animals) and debate (a typically Sumerian contest dialogue). The problem arises partly because these labels all post-date the works we are classifying by many centuries, if not millennia; and partly because it is a feature of all creative works that they bend and break the rules and conventions of genre.

But, as the very title *A balbale to Inana and Dumuzid* hints, about a fifth of known Sumerian literary compositions have native genre designations, invariably given at the end of the composition. Some are types of song— *šir-gida*, literally 'long song', for instance—and others are named after musical instruments, such as the *tigi* drum. This suggests that these labels are derived from particular types of *performance* genre rather than literary, or compositional genre; some *šir-gidas*, for instance, look to us like mythical narratives, while others we might label as hymns. Neither do they have to be particularly lengthy: *A šir-gida to Ninisina* (Group H) is only 136 lines long. There are other generic labels, such as *balbale*, whose meaning can now only be guessed at.

Unlike most modern poems (such as *London Airport*) Sumerian literary works had no titles. Rather, they were known and recalled by their first lines, or incipits—as indeed are some poems nowadays. So what we have called *Axe*, for instance, should more properly be called *Nibruta-lu, the son of the merchant*, according to Sumerian convention. Ancient catalogues survive which list works by their incipits (see *Literary catalogue from Nibru*, Group J). Sometimes it is difficult to distinguish which composition is meant, as there were some favoured openings, equivalent to our 'once upon a time'. However, sometimes the catalogues do list or summarize by genres that we can recognize: 11 *lugal* 'royal (hymns)', for instance, or 3 *dumu eduba* 'school-boy (stories)'. We also find the word *adamin* 'debate'.

Some compositions are formally divided into sections, either by horizontal rulings or through labels which are even more difficult to translate and comprehend than generic labels. The two are not always closely tied: works may use either, or both or none of them. This topic is discussed further in the introduction to Group H.

Fictionality

Another way of looking at literature is through fictionality: the fact that it is
not literally true. When we read, 'Last night at London Airport I saw a
wooden bin', we do not know whether this actually happened: was Logue
really at London Airport, and did the bin really exist, and was the label
worded exactly as he describes? Did he really do what he claims, or did the
idea only come to him later? We don't even know if the 'I' of the poem is
meant to be Logue himself, or some other poet, or even a business traveller
moved to a creative act by the challenge of the label. But he uses particulariz-
ing details to make us believe in its veracity and to visualize the event it
describes: this happened 'last night', at 'London Airport' (not Heathrow,
Gatwick, or Stansted), and the bin was 'wooden'. Yet when we remember all
the alliterating 'l's in the first four lines of the poem we might wonder
whether 'London' hasn't been chosen for its sound alone—and the fact that
it fits the metre. 'Yesterday at JFK' would not have produced the particular
poetic effect he was aiming for.

Similarly, *Axe* gives all sorts of circumstantial details: 'Nibruta-lu, the son
of the merchant Lugal-šuba, has had this tin axe made for Nergal.' Not only
Nibruta-lu's name is known, but also his father's and his father's profession.
We are also given all sorts of information about the materials the axe is made
of (just like the 'wooden bin'). Even though the words we read are only ink
on paper (or wedges on clay) we can visualize the axe as clearly as we can
visualize the labelled bin. But (just like the name 'London Airport') there
are clues within these very words that this isn't an inscription on a real
axe. We have already seen on page xxii that the materials it is made of are
all assonant—they each begin with 'a'. And 'Nibruta-lu', when translated
literally, means 'Man from the city of Nibru'. He's the man on the street, Joe
Bloggs, everyman.

In other instances, Sumerian literary works are more obviously fictive:
their main protagonists are gods, or talking animals, or even supposedly
inanimate objects. But in each case the composition works hard to convince
you of its plausibility, whether through setting, circumstantial detail, dialogue, or plot.

Narrative and character

Plot: we expect literary works to have a beginning that draws us in, a middle
in which something happens, and an end that satisfies us. In *London Airport*
there is a wooden bin—so what? There are bins in airports (except at times of

heightened security). But the bin carries an intriguing notice. The poet responds to the notice literally, thus satisfying the bin, himself (we assume), and us (by making us laugh or smile). The end. What more is there to know? We might want to know what the poem said, whether the poem was found, and what the finder made of it—but arguably they are matters for other stories (or poems). The narrative as presented is entire in itself.

Axe works in a similar way. Nibruta-lu dedicates the axe to Nergal. He promises to look after it. In exchange he requests that Nergal looks after *him* for evermore. Nibruta-lu is satisfied, and so are we: the deal is done and our hero lives (and dies) happily ever after. It doesn't seem like much of a plot, but if we compare *Axe* to a contemporary dedicatory inscription on a real mace-head, we can see the difference:

To Nergal, his master—for the life of Abisarē, mighty man, king of Urim, king of Larsa, and for his own life—Arad-Utu the seal-cutter, the son of Lu-Enki, has dedicated this.[2]

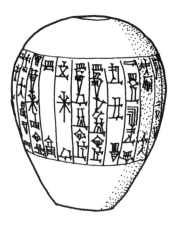

FIG. 3. 'To Nergal, his master'—
stone mace-head dedicated in the reign of Abisarē

Although *Axe* and the inscription are on basically the same theme—man dedicates weapon to god—their structure is very different. The inscription prioritizes first the god Nergal and then king Abisarē (who ruled the southern Mesopotamian kingdom of Larsa in 1905–1895 BCE). Only then is the donor Arad-Utu mentioned—with familial details of the sort that give verisimilitude to *Axe*. But we discover little about his motivation except that

---

[2] After D. Frayne, *Royal Inscriptions of Mesopotamia*, 4: *Old Babylonian Period (2003–1595 BC)* (University of Toronto Press: Toronto, 1990), no. E4.2.6.2001.

the dedication is 'for his life' and his king's. In *Axe*, on the other hand, our everyman hero Nibruta-lu comes first, literally and figuratively. We read about how beautiful his gift is, what he promises, what he wants in return: we get inside his head, we understand his motivation, we can relate to him. Arad-Utu is just a name to us whereas Nibruta-lu is a character.

Not all Sumerian literary works are as straightforwardly narrative and character-driven as *Axe*, though, and this makes it difficult for a modern reader to follow them. Some may appear to be endless, undifferentiated paeans of praise, although on closer reading it is always possible to pick out development and structure. (The introductions to each translation aim to help you do just that.) Sometimes, of course, our need for a satisfying ending is thwarted simply because the end does not survive; this is discussed more in the section on sources below.

Affect

So narrative provokes satisfaction in us at a well-turned ending. But literature is often designed to do more than that: it can make us laugh or cry, feel fear, suspense, anger, relief. We cannot fail to be moved by the wholesale destruction of cities, as in *The cursing of Agade* (Group C), or feel disturbed by the disjuncture between experienced and idealized prison life in *A hymn to Nungal* (Group J). Will Inana make it out of the Underworld? Can Dumuzid escape the demons? What possessed Enkidu to kill Ḫuwawa? See *Inana's descent to the Underworld*, *Dumuzid's dream* (both Group B), and *Gilgameš and Ḫuwawa* (Group J) to find out.

Suspense is easy to detect and respond to, but Sumerian humour is more difficult to see and understand. Sometimes it works through suspense too: *Lu-digira's message to his mother* (Group F) is a marvellous example of humorous anticlimax. More often we find it as slapstick and insult, as in *The debate between Bird and Fish* (Group G). The scribe takes his pompous supervisor down a peg or two (*A supervisor's advice to a young scribe*, Group I); Gilgameš offers Ḫuwawa ridiculous presents (*Gilgameš and Ḫuwawa*, Group J).

But just as *London Airport* is designed to provoke the reader into thinking about the meaning of literature, so too many Sumerian literary works prompt reflection and consideration. Are prisons punitive or rehabilitative, asks *A hymn to Nungal* (Group J). Are unnecessary heroic adventures that involve the loss of another's life really an appropriate response to the fear of mortality? *Gilgameš and Ḫuwawa* (Group J) suggests not. And then there are the debates, which pit one essential feature of Sumerian life against another.

Is agriculture more important than animal husbandry? Are birds more useful to human society than fish? Decisions are made on the weight of evidence—but we as readers may choose to disagree. (See *The debate between Sheep and Grain* and *The debate between Bird and Fish*, both Group G.)

Intertextuality

What sort of a god is Nergal? From our reading of *Axe* we have already deduced that he must be a god and not a human or a dog, say, because an offering is made to him and because there is the expectation that he can provide everlasting protection, even after death. It may be significant that he has power in the Underworld—not every god might. We notice too that it is a weapon he receives and not, say, a bowl or a bunch of flowers. Reading through other Sumerian literary works we come across other references to Nergal, in both myths and royal hymns. Recall the image-dense passage from *An* adab *to Nergal for Šu-ilišu* (Group E, and above, page xxiii) which presents him as a terrifyingly destructive warrior. In *Gilgameš, Enkidu, and the Underworld* (Group A), Enkidu avoids capture at his demon's hands:

The *udug* demon of Nergal, who spares nobody, did not seize him, but the Underworld has seized him.

The dead king Ur-Namma makes an offering to Nergal when he reaches the Underworld (*The death of Ur-Namma*, Group A):

To Nergal, the Enlil of the Underworld, in his palace, the shepherd (king) Ur-Namma offered a mace, a large bow with quiver and arrows, an artfully made . . . dagger, and a multicoloured leather bag for wearing at the hip.

FIG. 4. Nergal with dagger and mace, on a terracotta plaque of the early second millennium BCE

These glimpses of Nergal present a coherent portrait then, confirming our deductions made from *Axe*: he is a warrior god, associated with the Underworld (perhaps because death is a likely outcome of battle, it might be inferred), to whom it is appropriate to offer weapons. We also learn that his divine parents are considered to be Enlil and Ninlil, and that he sometimes goes by the name Mešlamta-eda (*Enlil and Ninlil*, Group C):

At this one intercourse, at this one kissing he poured the seed of Nergal-Mešlamta-eda into her womb.

The character of Nergal coheres across different works of Sumerian literature. Gilgameš and Enkidu maintain the same basic relationship from narrative to narrative; the fortunes and misfortunes of Inana and Dumuzid can be traced through many myths and hymns. That is one kind of intertextuality. Another is the deliberate use of characters or passages from one work in another. When Gilgameš offers En-me-barage-si to be Ḫuwawa's wife, poor Ḫuwawa does not know that En-me-barage-si is the father of Aga, Gilgameš's enemy and king of Kiš. Gilgameš and the Sumerian-literate reader have a laugh at Ḫuwawa's expense (see *Gilgameš and Ḫuwawa*, Group J).³ Particular phrases or passages may crop up time and again, whether they are of the 'once upon a time' variety or more particular. The wish at the end of *Axe*, for instance, reappears almost word for word in a similar fictive dedication of a dog to the goddess of healing Nintinuga:

May she look after me during my life, and when I die may she provide me with clean water in the Underworld.⁴

Then too there is a literary work's relationship to other writings. *London Airport* asks us to ponder the relationship between poetry and non-literary 'literature'. We gain appreciation of *Axe* by reading it in the light of non-fictive dedicatory inscriptions. *Lu-diĝira's message to his mother* (Group F) requires us to understand the norms of letter-writing in order for us to find it funny. *The home of the fish* (Group G) wants us to believe it is a fishing song; but in fact it is much more closely related to a standard school vocabulary of Sumerian fish and bird names. And we can also read—we cannot help but read—Sumerian literary works in the light of all the other literature we have

---

³ See too *Gilgameš and Aga* (ETCSL 1.8.1.1) and *The Sumerian king list* (ETCSL 2.1.1). In fact the implications of the name may be even more complex, as it could be understood as a parody of a high priestess's name too. See P. Michalowski, 'A man called Enmebaragesi', in W. Sallaberger, K. Volk, and A. Zgoll (eds.), *Literatur, Politik und Recht in Mesopotamien: Festschrift für Claus Wilcke* (Harrassowitz: Wiesbaden, 2003), pp. 195–208.

⁴ *Nintinuga's dog* (ETCSL 5.7.2).

read, whether through deliberate comparison (as here with *Axe* and *London Airport*) or through freer associations conjured up in the course of our reading and reflection on it.

THE TABLETS OF ANCIENT SUMER

So far we have discussed the literary qualities of Sumerian literature as if it were just *text*: we have played down the fact that it is actually *in the Sumerian language* and written not on paper but on clay. So what do the sources for Sumerian literature look like, how do they work, and what relationship do they bear to the translations that you read in this book? Let's take *Axe* as an example.

Cuneiform tablets

Fig. 5 shows an ancient clay tablet (front, right edge, and back), carrying the whole 16 lines of *The dedication of an axe to Nergal.* It is made of river mud that has been levigated—that is, all gravel, plant matter, and other foreign objects have been removed—and shaped by hand into a smooth block 6 by 9.5 by 3 centimetres, a little larger than a mobile phone. Tablets can be as small as a minidisc or as big as a laptop, but most are of a size and weight to sit comfortably in one hand. If you picked up this tablet you would feel in the gentle curvature of its sides the hand of the scribe who made it. This particular tablet was excavated from the ancient city of Nibru in southern Iraq in 1951. We will return to this excavation later, but for the moment we shall simply note that the tablet was given the excavation number 3N-T 436 signifying that it was the 436th tablet (T) to be catalogued in the 3rd season of excavations at Nibru (N). It came out of the ground as unbaked clay but

FIG. 5. UM 55-21-327 = 3N-T 436, University of Pennsylvania Museum (9.5 × 6 × 3 cm)

was baked on site in a kiln to conserve it. When the excavation season was over it was allotted to the University Museum of Archaeology and Anthropology at the University of Pennsylvania in Philadelphia, where it was assigned a museum number in 1955: UM 55-21-327. This is how it is referred to today.

It is rather damaged, as are many cuneiform tablets. The front, or obverse, has cracks in it, and three of its corners are missing. But considering it is nearly four thousand years old it is in pretty good shape for its age. Many tablets survive only in tiny fragments which have to be joined together again—an extraordinarily painstaking, laborious yet rewarding task. On the obverse sixteen lines of writing can be made out, interspersed with a few horizontal rulings. On the back, or reverse, the traces of two further lines are just visible followed by a double line and a lot of blank surface.

If you look closely you can see that the writing is made up of lots of wedge or nail-shaped impressions on the surface of the clay; this is the reason the Latinate term *cuneiform* ('wedge-shaped') is used to describe the script. Cuneiform script was used to write many different languages in the ancient Middle East, many of them unrelated, just as today the Latin alphabet is used to write English or Basque, Finnish or French. Cuneiform has no punctuation marks and no word separators. But it has far more characters than our alphabet: there are 52 *different* cuneiform signs amongst the 82 signs surviving on this tablet alone; only a third of them, 18, have been used more than once. Cuneiform, then, is not an alphabet but a mixed system: mostly syllables, but with other types of signs called determinatives and logograms, as we shall see. The same sign can function in different ways depending on the immediate context in which it is used.

When we looked briefly at the aural qualities of *Axe* we used a *transcription* or representation of Sumerian in alphabetic script, to approximate how it might have sounded. Let's now look at a *transliteration*, a representation showing how each word was written in cuneiform signs, which links with hyphens the signs which make up each word. Here, for instance, are a transliteration, transcription, and translation of one sentence from *Axe*:

ǵiš-bi ^{ǵiš}ar-ga-nu-um ḫur-saǵ-ǵa$_2$ a-lal$_3$-e dirig-ga-am$_3$

ǵišbi arganum ḫursaǵa alale dirigam

Its wooden part is of *arganum* tree of the mountains, a wood which is superior even to the *alal* stone.

Two things strike us immediately as odd in the transliteration: there are some characters in superscript, and some numbers in subscript. What are they for? Modern scholars use superscript characters to show when a cuneiform sign is being used as a *determinative*: that is, as a reading aid which signifies the class of word that follows or precedes it but which is not part of the word itself. In this case, the sign ĝiš occurs twice, the first time as the logogram with the meaning 'wood', the second time two signs later as a determinative before *arganum*: '*arganum* wood' or '*arganum* tree'. The determinative ĝiš does not appear in the transcription because it had no counterpart in spoken Sumerian.

The subscript numerals, on the other hand, are to enable us to distinguish between visually different signs that represent the same sequence of sounds (just as 'I' and 'eye' sound the same in English, but look different on the page and have completely different functions). So the final sign, am₃, looks like this: 𒄠 and means 'is'. am (or am₁), looks like this: 𒄠 and means 'wild bull' (as a *logogram*, or representation of a whole word) or represents the syllable *am* with no particular fixed meaning.

Literary Sumerian

While most languages are related to others (as English belongs to the Indo-European language family, for instance), Sumerian is an *isolate*: it is related to no other surviving language, because any linguistic relatives it had died out without ever being written down. We can distinguish four vowels—a, e, i, u—and fifteen consonants—b, d, g, ĝ (*ng*), ḫ (*ch*), k, l, m, n, p, r, s, š (*sh*), t, z—though we cannot be very precise about what they sounded like. The length of the vowels, the quality of the consonants, the intonation and rhythms of speech are all lost to us.

The vocabulary of Sumerian is by and large unrelated to neighbouring languages, although there are many loan-words, especially nouns, both to and from the Semitic language Akkadian. Akkadian was always in close contact with Sumerian: they were the two most important written languages of ancient Iraq and both used the same cuneiform script and clay tablet technology. In this case *arganum* is a loan from Akkadian *argānum,* a sort of coniferous tree: we can tell this because it has the Akkadian nominative ending *-um. ḫursaĝ,* 'mountains', on the other hand, was loaned into Akkadian as *ḫuršānu.*

In fact, Akkadian is our primary means of access to the sounds and meanings of the Sumerian language. As a Semitic language related to Hebrew and Arabic, Akkadian (as we shall see) was deciphered much earlier than Sumerian and even today is much better understood. So ancient Akkadian translations of Sumerian literary works—often line by line on the same tablet—and thematic 'dictionaries' of Sumerian words and phrases with their Akkadian counterparts have provided invaluable aids to modern under-standing. But they have drawbacks too: sometimes the scribes misunder-stood the Sumerian, or listed a whole barrage of equivalent Akkadian words if there was no straightforward translation.

Perhaps you have noticed too that the Sumerian sentence we are looking at has five words and its English translation has twenty. Is English really four times as inefficient as Sumerian in conveying meaning? Yes and no. Sumerian is an agglutinative language: that is, its grammatical parts (case, person, tense, aspect) are attached to the lexical bases (as in 'like', 'likes', 'liked', 'liking', 'liken', 'unlikely', 'dislike'), whereas in English they are as often carried in separate words (e.g. 'she likes', 'we like', 'don't like'). The following sketch will give only a taste of how Sumerian grammar works. To start with, the words of the Sumerian sentence can be split into their lexical and grammatical parts:

ĝiš.bi arganum ḫursaĝ.ak alal.e dirig.am

wood.its *arganum* mountains.of alal.than superior.is

Whereas English word order is normally Subject—Verb—Object ('I like you'), Sumerian word order is normally Subject—Object—Verb ('I you like'): a Sumerian sentence almost always ends with a verb. The sentence can be analysed word by word, starting with the subject, 'wood'. Sumerian distinguishes gender not as masculine, feminine, and neuter, but as 'human' (people and gods) and 'non-human' (all other things). *ĝišbi* 'its wood' is thus distinguished from *ĝišani* 'his or her wood': we know then that the wood in this sentence belongs to the non-human axe, not to the man Nibruta-lu or the god Nergal. Next there is the Akkadian loan-word *arganum*, which is described as 'of the mountains' by means of the genitive suffix *ak* 'of' attached to *ḫursaĝ*. (*ak* is usually written without the final *k*. English more often has the opposite phenomenon, where a letter is written but not pronounced: think of the silent 't' in 'often'.)

In English, some verbs are transitive; that is, they have to have an object (you have to 'like' something; you cannot just 'like'). Others are intransitive ('I fall', for instance, involves only me; if I want to make something else fall I have to 'fell' it, like a tree). Many are both ('Mary walks'; 'Mary walks the dog'). But Sumerian uses the ergative marker *-e* to mark the subject of a transitive verb ('Mary-*e* dog walks'). If Mary were walking alone, though, she would not need the ergative to mark her as the subject of an intransitive verb

('Mary walks'). Here 'its wood' has no ergative marker, so the verb will be intransitive.

Then, in the sentence above *alal* carries the so-called locative-terminative marker (confusingly also written -*e*). The last word has the base *dirig*, which can be either an adjective 'extra, excessive', or a verb 'to be better/bigger/more'. The morphology of the Sumerian verb is often rather complex, with successions of markers indicating person, tense, aspect, and the verb's relationship to the nouns in the sentence. But here there is only the suffixed copula *am* 'is', so *dirigam* should be understood as 'is better'. This prompts the question 'than what?' and the context suggests that the answer should not be *arganum*, the wood from which the axe is in fact made. The case marker -*e* on the word *alal* here has the sense 'than'. Putting the translation together in its simplest form, it reads:

> Its wood is mountain *arganum*, which is better than *alal*.

Now this is fine as a literal translation of the Sumerian, but it is a little too terse and stiff. The English catches none of the nuances of the original. We might guess from the context that *arganum* is a type of wood; but we might, wrongly, also think that *alal* is. But because the translation sounds so flat we would probably never guess that Nibruta-lu was speaking to the fearsome warrior god Nergal about a fantastic gift. So the extra words of the English translation on page xxxii serve to help us get closer to the original intent (or at least what the translator judges it to have been): not just the literal meaning of the words, but the emotional affect of the literary work they comprise. Just how the transition is made from tablet to translation is what we shall look at next.

From tablet to translation

We have seen that there are cuneiform signs missing from our tablet UM 55-21-327, yet the translation of *Axe* is complete: there are no missing words. How can this be? And when we count the lines of the transcription we can see that there are 16; but 18 on the tablet. What is going on?

In fact, UM 55-21-327 is just one of eight cuneiform sources for *Axe*, all of them different. Three are a similar size and shape to UM 55-21-327 but one is a large four-sided tablet (known as a 'prism') which originally had nine or more other compositions inscribed on it too; another is a tiny flake from the surface of a tablet which is otherwise completely lost. Four of them are in the University Museum, Philadelphia, one in the Museum of the Ancient

Siglum	Museum number	Collection	Type of tablet	Excavation number	Date of handcopy	Lines of *Axe*
H	CBS 2231	Philadelphia	Collective	—	1914	14–16
G	Ni 3023	Istanbul	Collective	—	1944	9–16
F	CBS 14049 + N 864	Philadelphia	Collective	—	1964	3–16
A	HS 1511	Jena	Single	—	1967	1–16
D	CBS 7848 + CBS 7849 + CBS 7856 (+) Ni 4574	Philadelphia and Istanbul	Collective prism	—	1922, 1964, 1969	1–12
E	—	Philadelphia	Single	3N-T 916, 339	1979	2–16
C	UM 55-21-327	Philadelphia	Single	3N-T 436	1989	1–16
B	IM 58417	Baghdad	Single	3N-T 310	(1989)	1–16

Orient, Istanbul, one in the collection of the University of Jena, Germany, and one in the Iraq Museum, Baghdad. The prism is broken into pieces, three of which ended up in Philadelphia, another in Istanbul. We shall discover how they got there later; for now we shall discuss how this is known, and how they come together for editing.

Many cuneiform tablet collections are huge and only partially catalogued. Fortunately, though, many curators have encouraged the systematic publication of Sumerian literary tablets in their collections by means of stylized drawings, or *handcopies.* It is often difficult to read the curved and abraded surfaces of cuneiform tablets from all but the very best photographs; and until the recent advent of digital photography, good photos have been prohibitively expensive to produce and publish. In Fig. 6, for instance, is the handcopy of UM 55-21-327.[5] You can see that the cuneiform script is much clearer than on the photo because the copyist (Hermann Behrens of the University of Pennsylvania) did not attempt to reproduce all the discoloration of the tablet, or the wear and tear on the surface except where it interferes with the legibility of the script. He tried to place the signs as accurately

5 H. Behrens, 'Ein Axt für Nergal', in M. de J. Ellis, P. Gerardi, and E. Leichty (eds.), *A Scientific Humanist: Studies in Memory of Abraham Sachs* (The University Museum: Philadelphia, 1988), pp. 27–32.

as possible, showing where they touch and overlap, and where there are gaps between them.

The first modern 'edition' of *Axe* came out just after the first complete tablet was published in handcopy (see table above). The German Sumerologist Claus Wilcke in 1969 used the four tablet manuscripts labelled here as H, G, F, and A, including two from the Philadelphia collection (one of which consisted of two joined fragments).[6] Unexpectedly, perhaps, his edition appeared as a footnote in his edition of a much longer Sumerian literary work, *Lugalbanda and the Anzud bird* (Group A). Why? Intertextuality again: in line 110, the hero Lugalbanda is given 'an axe whose metal is tin, imported from the Zubi mountains', which crops up again twice later in the narrative (lines 353, 363). Wilcke used *Axe* to shed light on the meaning of *Lugalbanda*.

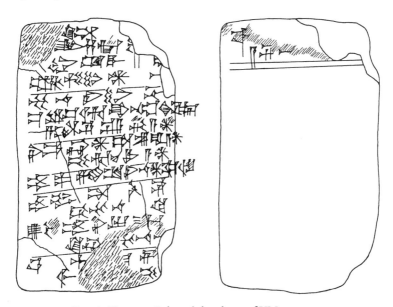

FIG. 6. Hermann Behrens's handcopy of UM 55-21-327

Behrens re-edited *Axe* twenty years later, using two further exemplars since published as handcopies as well as a plaster cast in the Philadelphia collection of a tablet held in Baghdad and his own copy of UM 55–21–327. The letters, or *sigla*, he used to refer to the sources are the ones used in the table above.

---

6 C. Wilcke, *Das Lugalbandaepos* (Harrassowitz: Wiesbaden, 1969) p. 58 n. 210.

How are the various sources combined into an edition? There are two ways of doing it. You can choose the best preserved of your manuscripts and take that as your primary source, noting variants in the other sources as you go. Wilcke chose that method. For the lines we have just been looking at, such a *copy-text edition*, using A as the primary source, would look like this:

5 ĝiš-bi ar-ga-nu-um ḫur-saĝ-ĝa₂
6 a-lal₃-e dirig-ga-am₃

line 5: B, C ᵍⁱˢar-ga-nu-um; C ĝiš-RU; D] ꜓ᵍⁱˢ꜓ar-꜓ga꜓-[; F ꜓ĝiš꜓-[bi] ar-ga-꜓nu꜓-[; E, G, H missing line 6: B e-lal₃-la; D aꜞ-lal₃ꜞ-e-꜓a꜓; E ꜓x꜓-lal₃-e [; F ꜓a꜓-lal₃-e ꜓dirig꜓-[; G, H missing

This style of edition assumes that one source is somehow best—most reliable, most authoritative, most complete—and that the others are only (slightly) interesting when they give variants from 'the' text. It takes some study to notice that source C is identical to source A in line 6, for instance, and it is hard to get a sense of the completeness or accuracy (with respect to source A) of the subordinated sources. (You also need to know that the symbols [and] mark the start and end of missing passages on the tablet, ꜓ and ꜓ indicate stretches of damaged text, ꞈ indicates badly written signs, and signs in capital letters, such as RU, cannot be assigned a meaningful interpretation in the context.) In any event, this style of edition is *very* difficult to read. However, it does work well if all the sources are substantially the same, or one is much better preserved than the others (perhaps one whole tablet and a handful of small fragments).

Another method, which Behrens used and is now preferred by most Sumerologists, is known as a *lineated* or *(musical) score edition*. It gives equal value to all sources by comparing them line by line, enabling similarities and differences to be seen at a glance and the character of individual sources to be observed. Here is our sentence again, presented in lineated transliteration:

A ĝiš-bi ar-ga-nu-um ḫur-saĝ-ĝa₂
B ĝiš-bi ᵍⁱˢar-ga-nu-um ḫur-saĝ-ĝa₂
C ĝiš-RU ᵍⁱˢar-ga-nu-um ḫur-saĝ-ĝa₂
D [   ] ꜓ᵍⁱˢ꜓ar-꜓ga꜓-[   ]
F ꜓ĝiš꜓-[bi] ar-ga-꜓nu꜓-[   ]

A a-lal₃-e dirig-ga-am₃
B e-lal₃-la dirig-ga-am₃
C a-lal₃-e dirig-ga-am₃
D aꜞ-lal₃ꜞ-e-꜓a꜓ dirig-ga-am₃

E   ⸢x⸣-lal₃-e [   ]
F   ⸢a⸣-lal₃-e ⸢dirig⸣-[   ]

It is immediately clear that no one source matches another exactly: in the first line A and F omit the determinative ᵍⁱˢ, while C mistakenly has the sign *ru* instead of *bi*—which is meaningless in this context. In the next line B has *elalla* instead of *alal*, and the same word is written very badly in D (hence the exclamation marks in the edition). Only sources A–C preserve the lines completely. Nevertheless, the sources have enough in common between them to allow us to generate a one-line *composite text*, representing what we think the 'correct' text should be:

ĝiš-bi ᵍⁱˢar-ga-nu-um ḫur-saĝ-ĝa₂
a-lal₃-e dirig-ga-am₃

But this composite text matches none of the individual transliterations exactly: it is a *modern text*, not an ancient one. We cannot prove that it existed in ancient Sumer; it is just our best guess (or perhaps educated deduction) at how this line of the composition *might have been*.

So translations from lineated editions and composite texts (such as those in this book) are, in a way, based on a sleight of hand: we are not translating directly from the ancient sources but from modern interpretations, adaptations, and 'improvements' based on our understanding of the literary corpus as a whole—often, even, when we only have one cuneiform source for a particular composition. Is that cheating? We think not: all of the ancient sources have been taken equally into account, without going to the extreme of providing eight different translations—which would all be the same, except for some annoying gaps marked . . . where a tablet was broken or illegible. Sometimes tablets have substantive differences, or *variants*, which do need to be translated differently and in those cases we have put them in the notes at the end of each composition.

As you have already seen, translation is not a mechanical process. Word-for-word cribs can be made but they are unsatisfactory, not least because the words of Sumerian often have a very different semantic range from their (approximate) equivalents in English. An axe is an axe, more or less, and (Akkadian) *argānum* is some sort of coniferous tree; but what about *dirig*? Here it must mean 'is better than', 'is superior to'; but in line 75 of *Enki's journey to Nibru* (Group J) Enki uses *dirig* to describe his temple:

ḫur-saĝ galam kad₅-am a-e ba-dirig
mountain artful build.(is) water.(loc.-term.) (non-human).float
It is an artfully built mountain which floats on the water.

We *could* look for common ground and then choose to translate all instances of *dirig* as 'to be over', say, but that would not work either, even if we were content to produce flat and lifeless translations. The English word has overtones of recovery ('I'm over the flu now'), ending ('they think it's all over; it is now'), or being on the other side ('over the water') which are not present in Sumerian *dirig*. We must choose our translations carefully, taking into account both individual words and their immediate context, as well as what they do in the corpus as a whole, *and* the flavour and texture of the passage we are translating.

However, because we cannot be fully confident of the poetics of Sumerian literature we have chosen to ignore the lineation and any aural qualities of the original. We have preferred to focus on the emotive affect of the works, and to represent them in English as naturally and readably as possible.

THE SCRIBES OF ANCIENT SUMER

Who wrote those eight different tablets which are the sources for *Axe*? Why are they different and how are they related? What did *Axe* and other literary works mean to those who wrote, copied, read, heard, and thought about literature in ancient Sumer?

Readership and literacy

Today it is virtually impossible to escape from the written word. Even when we are far from 'civilization' we carry it with us: on the manufacturers' washing instructions on the labels of our clothes; on the identity cards, driving licences, and till receipts in our wallets; on the number plates of our cars and serial numbers on our bicycle tyres. The young child learns to read and write through everyday environmental exposure to words in print as much as through planned and structured lessons with parents or teachers. Those who fail to read and write competently are effectively excluded from many activities that modern society takes for granted. Without functional literacy it becomes difficult to email, shop, vote.

Imagine, instead, a world in which the literate were in the minority; in which only large public institutions and particularly wealthy families *needed* writing. Knowledge of writing was as restricted in ancient Sumer as the ability to understand the intricacies of the stock market is today; it was a tool for managing wealth, for proving ownership. There were different degrees of literacy, painstakingly acquired over many years. The stock-taker of a temple warehouse would have had a different level or quality of literacy from a notary specializing in family legal documents; even the members of the ruling elite might have only the shakiest grasp of reading and writing. There was, in short, an economic and a social value to every cuneiform sign recorded. Writing was not therefore something to be scattered around freely but a hard-won professional skill to be dispensed judiciously and sparingly—and usually for a fee.

Seen in this light the existence of written literature in Sumerian society is absolutely extraordinary. It had no obviously economic value or function; there was no market for leisure reading. But it must have served some purpose. What was Sumerian literature *for*? Who were its producers and consumers (to continue the economic theme)?

Of course, it would be naive to expect just one single context and function for Sumerian literature as a whole, or even for a single Sumerian literary work. It is instructive to look at *London Airport*'s long and varied publication history. It first appeared in 1974 in Christopher Logue's pamphlet *Mixed Rushes* and was then published in a collection of his works called *Ode to the Dodo: Poems 1953–1978*, which came out in 1981. In the early 1990s it appeared on posters on London tube trains as part of a scheme called *Poems on the Underground*. Since then it has been anthologized many times and now can be found in school textbooks, on the web—and even in the introductions to books on Sumerian literature! It also travels in people's memories and is passed on, as are many poems, through recitation and repetition. Despite its wry suggestion that literature is only fit for the rubbish bin, the poem has found a wide variety of homes: scholarly, public, scholastic, private, institutional. Sumerian literature was disseminated in all these sorts of contexts too, and in each we can detect a reason for it being there.

An urban scribal school

Although, as in the case of *Axe*, Sumerian literary tablets are often published and studied as textual sources for Sumerian literary works (as might be expected), they are also archaeological artefacts. If we look at them as objects, like a bin or an axe, we can learn something about what they meant to the society and the individual people who made, used, and disposed of them.

We have already mentioned that UM 55-21-327, our source C for *Axe*, was excavated from the ancient city of Nibru in 1951. That means that there is an archaeological context for it, which can shed light on the circumstances of its production, use, and disposal. You may also have noticed that two of the others, sources B and E, have excavation numbers like that of source C, beginning with the sequence 3N-T. So they too were excavated in the same place and year, though one of them, source B (IM 58417), remained in the Iraq Museum in Baghdad. The other has not been assigned a museum number: although it has been in the University Museum in Philadelphia since the end of the dig, it is only on long-term loan and will be returned to Baghdad in due course.

Notes, plans, and catalogues made in the field during excavation show that all three tablets B, C, and E were found in a small mud-brick house in a densely populated area just a hundred metres or so south of the god Enlil's great temple complex E-kur, at the heart of Nibru. As sun-dried mud brick weathers easily, houses made of it need to be repaired or rebuilt about once a generation. This particular house, which the excavators named House F, had been built some time after 1843 BCE (the date on a tablet recording a loan of silver, which was found in the foundations) and was remodelled three or four times, each time making a new floor above the old one and thus leaving traces of how the house had been before. It was finally abandoned after 1721 BCE (the latest date amongst the tablets left behind in the last occupation level). The house had four tiny rooms, including a kitchen, and two small court-yards. The entire living area was less than 50 square metres. It looked much like the neighbouring houses and contained much the same sorts of objects: the remains of domestic crockery, the ceramic plaques and figurines which decorated people's homes at this period, some family legal contracts (loans, sales, adoptions) and letters. The only peculiar thing about it was that in the penultimate occupation level, abandoned in or after 1739 BCE, the excavators found *seven hundred* pieces of Sumerian literary tablets and a similar number of tablets with elementary scribal exercises on them. There were also three waterproofed baked-brick recycling bins, where fresh clay and old used tablets were soaked and shaped into new tablets. At that point in its life House F must have been home to a small scribal school.

The study of this vast cache of sources for Sumerian literature was hampered by the fact that the season's finds were, following established prac-tice, shared out (while the tablets were still in pieces) between the Universi-ties of Chicago and Philadelphia, who had run the expedition, and the Iraq Museum for the host country. Joins between fragments have since reduced the total number of literary tablets to just under 600, but there are doubtless many more joins to be made. Over eighty different literary compositions are attested in House F—more than the works presented in this book. Fully three-quarters of them are narratives: myths, epics, city laments, epistolary works, debates, fables. Just twenty are hymns addressed to deities or kings—

the most recent of whom, Enlil-bāni, ruled about a century before House F was operating as a school.

Some twenty-four compositions were copied frequently—18 or 20 times—at House F. They can be divided into two different curricular sequences, as discussed in the introduction to Group J. The others survive in just single copies, or perhaps three or four, as does *Axe*. But *Axe* too belonged to a larger, somewhat fluid group, called by modern scholarship rather prosaically, and slightly misleadingly, Letter Collection B. These twenty or so short compositions, mostly fictive letters, cohere through their length (11–34 lines), the themes they address, their fictional senders and recipients, and other elements of intertextuality. (The group also includes *Nintinuga's dog*, the fictive dedication that shares the last three lines with *Axe*.) Collection B is recognizable through the existence of tablets from elsewhere in Nibru (such as Sources D, F, and H of *Axe*) which contain all or part of the collection—so-called *collective* sources. Nineteen members of Collection B were found in House F, all on single tablets of the same shape and size as UM 55-21-327, and all in one to three copies.

Tiny scribal schools like House F were undoubtedly training the next generation in Sumerian literacy. But to learn *literature* is to learn more than literacy. The students were being inculcated with the values of their society and the values of the profession in which they were to serve. As the compositions in Groups I and J show, Sumerian school literature demarcated the boundaries of appropriate professional behaviour and demeanour, and the values of the institutions (whether temples or palaces) that employed scribes. The works emphasized the differences between scribes and non-scribes, instilled a sense of pride and duty to their profession—and hinted at the shame and humiliation of those who did not come up to the mark.

A provincial scholar's house

The House F literary tablets are strikingly representative of the Sumerian literary corpus as a whole. That is partly because they have deeply influenced our notions of what that representative corpus *is*; and partly because they originate from Nibru, where nineteenth-century American digs had already uncovered the vast bulk of known Sumerian literature. (Frustratingly, this was in the days before stratigraphic excavation and systematic recording, so that we have no idea where exactly within Nibru those tablets come from; but their overall character is so like the finds from House F that the archaeologists must in fact have discovered three or four similar such schools, where the other sources for *Axe* were probably written.) Nibru was also at the intellectual heart of Sumer, as the home of Enlil, father of the gods, and geographically close to its core. If we compare House F with a contemporaneous house in a more provincial town, we can see that Sumerian literature was rather more diverse than the homogeneous picture we get through the preponderance of sources from Nibru.

Me-Turan was just such a small town in the back of beyond, far up the Diyala river to the north-east of flat Sumer, in the foothills of the Zagros mountains. It was excavated by an Iraqi team in the early 1980s prior to the area being flooded for a dam. One house in particular, abandoned at least twenty years before the House F school, no later than 1760 BCE, has become known as the 'scholar's house'. It was about twice the size of House F, and had eight living spaces (rooms or courtyards). The excavators found nearly forty tablets in the front courtyard or in doorways leading off it and a similar number in a back room, the furthest away from the public areas in the front of the house. A dozen or so tablets were scattered through the other rooms too. Significantly, the character of the tablets was different in each space.

The scattered tablets were all household documents and elementary school exercises. The private back room (a storeroom?) held more household records and school work but also magical incantations in Sumerian, a collection of mathematical problems in Akkadian, and two bilingual hemerologies, or calendars of omens. The public front courtyard, on the other hand, had no household records and just two school exercises. The other tablets there were all works of Sumerian literature, magical incantations and liturgical works in Sumerian. The Sumerian works were mostly preserved in two copies and included some well-known compositions such as *Gilgameš, Enkidu, and the Underworld* (Group A), *Gilgameš and Ḫuwawa*, and *Inana and Ebiḫ* (both Group J). But four of the compositions were previously unknown, or known only in fragments: they do not seem to have been mainstream literary works, in Nibru at least. Even the previously well-known works were often significantly different versions from those known from further south. And the fact that they were found with incantations and liturgical laments, also in multiple copies (and of which there was no sign in House F), raises questions about where the boundaries of Sumerian 'literature' really lie. Both incantations and liturgy (often in the difficult Emesal register of Sumerian, which is phonologically and lexically defined) are arguably professional 'literatures' associated with particular classes of priesthood—but so, perhaps, are some of the Sumerian hymns. It has been suggested that the owner of these tablets was an incantation priest or exorcist, Akkadian *wāšipum*, whose choices of Sumerian literature were closely tied to his professional interests. On the other hand, many of the literary works in the scholar's house are obviously curricular (or would be described as such if found in Nibru). One tablet in particular contains all four of the elementary Sumerian literary works now known as the Tetrad (see *A hymn to Nisaba*, Group I), and as we have seen there were other school tablets in the house too. Many questions remain to be answered about this 'scholar's house' and what it can tell us about the diversity of content, meaning, and function of Sumerian literature in ancient Iraq.

Patronage and performance

We have already seen that some of the ancient generic classifications discussed earlier should perhaps best be understood as indicating types of performance, while *šir-namgala*, for instance, literally means 'song of the *gala* priestly class' (see Group H). It would be perverse to argue that many of the hymns to deities or rulers did not start out in cultic or court settings, even if they were eventually adopted and adapted for scholastic purposes. Administrative records document the existence of various types of musicians, singers, and other performers attached to both temples and palaces. Officially commissioned art objects depict deities, royalty, and dignitaries being entertained in music and song. *A praise poem of Lipit-Eštar* (Group J) was even carved onto a large boulder, suggesting that it served as the text of a monument, perhaps in a temple or other public space.

The contents of some royal hymns can be closely related to particular events in courtly life. Hymns were commissioned for events as varied as 'sacred marriage' ceremonies, involving the king and the cult of the goddess Inana (see *Inana and Išme-Dagan*, Group B), the inauguration of new cultic furniture (see *Šulgi and Ninlil's barge*, Group C), and perhaps the renovation of temples (*Enki's journey to Nibru*, Group J). The naming of the new year could also be commemorated with a hymn of praise: the sixth year of king Šulgi's reign, for instance, was named 'The year the king put in order the road to Nibru', which closely relates to *A praise poem of Šulgi* (Group J) celebrating Šulgi's heroic run from his capital city Urim to Nibru and back in a single day—a distance of a few hundred kilometres!

The literary works themselves often mention cultic or courtly settings for the performance of songs with the same generic names that we find in the literary corpus. In a hymn commemorating king Ur-Namma's death (*The death of Ur-Namma*, Group A), the dead monarch is made to say:

My *tigi*, *adab*, flute and *zamzam* songs have been turned into laments because of me.

FIG. 7. A harpist on a terracotta plaque
of the early second millennium BCE

And *The Keš temple hymn* (Group J) provides a glimpse into performance in
a cultic setting:

The bull's horn is made to growl; the drumsticks (?) are made to thud. The singer cries
out to the *ala* drum; the grand sweet *tigi* drum is played for him. The house is built; its
nobility is good!

The literary compositions can even be self-referential. At the end of *Inana
and Šu-kale-tuda* (Group F) even as the goddess condemns Šu-kale-tuda to
death she says:

Your name, however, shall not be forgotten. Your name shall exist in songs and make
the songs sweet. A young singer shall perform them most pleasingly in the king's palace.
A shepherd shall sing them sweetly as he tumbles his butter-churn. A shepherd boy shall
carry your name to where he grazes the sheep.

And this, we are to believe, is one such song. However, the reference to the
'shepherd boy' should not necessarily lead us to imagine the widespread dis-
semination of such compositions amongst the illiterate peasant classes.
Rather, Inana may be humiliating Šu-kale-tuda one last time by reminding
him of the existence of her lover, the shepherd-god Dumuzid.

But Inana's words do capture here the importance of Sumerian literature for its royal patrons. A good literary work will survive, one hopes, long after the individual patron is dead. Thus immortality of a kind is achieved. Šulgi and Išme-Dagan's commissions lived on in House F and elsewhere for centuries after they had died, and long after their dynasties had collapsed— and we are remembering and celebrating the literature they patronized some four thousand years later.

Tradition and innovation

There was no hope of fame, however, for the anonymous authors of Sumerian literary works. With the exception of some 'occasional' works composed for named rulers for specific occasions, even the circumstances of composition have been lost to us. Even dating the tablets we have, which are most unlikely to be authors' originals, is difficult. Our understanding of the palaeography, or history of handwriting, of cuneiform is in its infancy—and will probably be hampered by the fact that many scribes of our sources were trainee scribes whose style had not yet cohered and who were often encouraged, it appears, to use old-fashioned hands. The tablets themselves are only rarely signed and dated: for instance, a manuscript of *The lament for Sumer and Urim* (Group D), itself from Urim, finishes with the colophon:

Sixty (lines), exercise tablet of Damqi-ilišu, month Ab-eda, day 12.

Year names, when we find them, are typically from the reigns of Rīm-Sîn of Larsa (1822–1763 BCE) and Samsu-iluna of Babylon (1749–1712 BCE). Like-wise, archaeologically recovered tablets are almost all from the eighteenth century BCE and later. (A dozen or so literary sources which appear to be from the twenty-first century were found reused as building rubble in a temple in Nibru which post-dated them by some two millennia!) Yet the majority of the royal praise poems at least, and historically rooted narratives where we can identify them, celebrate kings and commemorate events of the twenty-third to nineteenth centuries BCE. So the scholastic literary tradition appears to have been very conservative in the eighteenth century. But why do so few earlier copies of literary works survive?

As the recycling bins in House F hint, tablets were not meant to be kept unless there was a good economic need for them: to prove ownership or rights. The Mesopotamian library tradition, which is so clear in the later second millennium and later, had not yet developed. Well-run schools, households, and scribal institutions regularly cleared out their storage areas of outdated tablets and soaked them in bins for reuse. Thus we find large caches of tablets only when they were thrown away *en masse*, reused as building materials (as in House F), or abandoned suddenly along with the building they were stored in (the Me-Turan scholar's house). For the Sumerian literary tradition was, paradoxically, not exclusively a *literate* one. Examining the different sources for individual works shows us that compositions were passed on not through the copying of earlier manuscripts but through dictation, repetition, and memorization.

First, many of the variants appear to derive from *mishearing* rather than *misreading*. For instance, source B of *Axe* has e-lal$_3$-la where all the other manuscripts have a-lal$_3$-e, while sources A and F are both missing the determinative ^{ĝiš} (which was not pronounced). It is rare to find instances where signs or sign sequences have been misinterpreted visually and rendered as some other sign. (On the other hand, scribal students often forgot exactly how to write a sign, as in source D of *Axe*, where the signs are simply malformed and not readable as something else.)

Second, for longer literary works there are far more manuscript sources for the beginning of a composition than the end. From schools such as House F there are predominantly two different types of literary source: small tablets like UM 55-21-327, our source C of *Axe*, which contain 20–30 lines of a composition; and larger ones which may contain the whole composition (or a group of shorter works, like Collection B), or a half of it, or a third. Often these large tablets (and prisms, like source D of *Axe*) look very beautifully written but are full of errors and inaccuracies. It appears that the students learned Sumerian literary works in 20-30 line passages by writing them out, committing them to memory, and writing out again all the passages of that work learned so far. They thus had far more opportunities to write out the first 30 lines than the last. So, for instance, the long composition *The lament for Sumer and Urim* (Group D) has a mean of 5.9 sources for each of its first ten lines, 2.7 sources for lines 256–65 half-way through the work, and just 1.7 sources for the final lines 510–19. (And this explains why some of our translations are much more fragmentary towards the end than the beginning, and why some break off altogether before the conclusion of the work.)

Third, we also find examples of *misremembering* whole words or perhaps remembering differently: near-synonymous word substitutions, lines or line groups reordered, elaborated, or simplified. *Gilgameš and Huwawa* (Group J) was even known in two completely different versions. The one translated in this book—which itself has many variants—begins, 'Now the lord once decided to set off for the mountain where the man lives'. The other starts 'So come on now, you heroic bearer of a sceptre of wide-ranging power!' which is the 130th line of the first.[7] Both versions are listed in the *Literary catalogue from Nibru* (Group J) and so must have been known by the same people at the same time.

Other works were known in slightly variant versions in different cities or schools (though as the variants are often known from very fragmentary sources we have chosen not to include their translations here). We are very rarely able to trace change over long periods of time; and when we can we find no consistent patterns. *The Keš temple hymn* (Group J) apparently changed little between the mid-third millennium BCE (from which time we have four fragmentary sources) and the eighteenth and seventeenth centuries. In the intervening period it was formally divided into eight sections called 'houses' and a few lines were altered. But *The instructions of Šuruppag* (Group I) was radically transformed over the same period, having been considerably lengthened and reorganized: many lines and even whole blocks were moved, added, taken away. Other literary works from the same period, and later in the third millennium, did not survive into the second. Conversely, a few Sumerian literary works, such as *Lugalbanda and the Anzud bird* (Group A), *Enlil and Sud* (Group C), and indeed *The instructions of Šuruppag*, did live on into the later second and early first millennium, acquiring line-by-line translations into Akkadian (though we have chosen to include neither the very early versions nor the later ones here).

If the literary tradition was essentially an aural one within the community of scribes, then presumably it—or parts of it—was accessible to the vast illiterate majority too. We have already seen some evidence for courtly performances. On the other hand, many literary works, from collections of proverbs (Group I) to *The home of the fish* (Group G), give the impression (perhaps falsely) of being culled from some sort of 'folk tradition'. But in that case the survival of Sumerian literature must have been dependent on the continued understanding of Sumerian as a *spoken* language, and that is extremely difficult to track through the *written* record.

For centuries after the first appearance of writing in southern Iraq in the late fourth millennium BCE it served an exclusively administrative function. Cuneiform was a mnemonic device designed to aid accountants and bureaucrats, rather than a vehicle for high art. Nevertheless, there are clues within the writing system that the language of its users was indeed Sumerian—amongst others. Speakers of Akkadian, Hurrian, and later Amorite (West Semitic) were also Sumerian-literate and choices about which language to

----

7 *Gilgameš and Ḫuwawa, version B* (ETCSL 1.8.1.5.1).

write in were based only tangentially on the *spoken* language preferences of the writer. Like Latin in the European Middle Ages, written Sumerian carried a religious and often political cachet that was from time to time challenged by Akkadian but was never completely extinguished. By the eighteenth century BCE it appears that in schools like House F, Akkadian was actually the language of instruction although the vast majority of the curriculum was still in Sumerian; and in some places Sumerian remained the language of legal documentation until late in the eighteenth century. Many attempts have been made to pinpoint the death of Sumerian as a mother tongue, which have ranged from the middle of the third millennium BCE (when people started to record its grammatical elements more fully, at the same time that Akkadian first began to be written down) to the middle of the second (when literature was committed to clay as the act of comprehension and thus memorization became ever more difficult). In fact, we shall never be able to resolve that question, precisely because of the limited spread of literacy, and because in general languages tend to die out very, very gradually. But it does raise interesting issues about what should be understood by 'Sumer', 'Sumerian', and 'the Sumerians', to which we now turn.

THE STUDY OF ANCIENT SUMER

It is fairly straightforward to give a first approximation to the questions, 'What was Sumer?' and 'Who were the Sumerians?' Roughly speaking, Sumer is the name we give to the south of Iraq (roughly below the latitude of modern Najaf and Kut) in the late fourth to mid-second millennia BCE. Sumer was not a political entity—cities were the focus of political power— but rather a cultural assemblage. It was the area in which the majority (or a powerful minority) wrote (and presumably spoke) the Sumerian language, shared a common belief system, a set of social behaviours, and a self-identity. Sumerian literature itself refers more often to 'the Land' than it does to 'Sumer', and to its inhabitants simply as 'the black-headed people'. The Sumerian word for the Sumerian language, *emegir*, probably means 'normal language'. Our word 'Sumer' is in fact derived from the Akkadian word *šumerum* which was used for the Sumerian language or the land, not the people.

So perhaps it is easiest to start by saying that Sumer was simply the area in which Sumerian was prevalent as a written (and literary) language—more or less southern Iraq in the late fourth to mid-second millennium BCE—and the Sumerians the culturally homogeneous inhabitants of that area. But as we shall see, 'Sumer', 'Sumerian', and 'the Sumerians' have meant very different things to different scholars in the modern world.

A forgotten script

The last writers of Sumerian were among the last writers of cuneiform: an ever-dwindling community of scholars attached to the great temples at Babylon and Uruk in the last centuries BCE. Long laments in the Emesal register of Sumerian played an important role in their rituals. But after their demise the very existence of Sumerian was forgotten for nearly two thousand years. When in the early nineteenth century European adventurers, historians, and philologists became interested in the ancient Middle East, their focus was on Egypt, Persia, Assyria, and Babylon. Relying on biblical and Classical authors as their guides, it never crossed their minds that the remains of another civilization might lie undetected under the soil.

The Rosetta stone of cuneiform writing is the Bisutun, or Behistun, inscription, an enormous trilingual rock relief carved inaccessibly high up a mountainside in modern Iran near the border with Iraq. The first serious attempt to examine it was made in 1835 by a British diplomat, Henry Rawlinson, who was in Persia as military adviser to the governor of Kurdistan. He managed to climb the cliffs several times in order to make a papier-mâché copy of the then unintelligible cuneiform. Within two weeks, and with the help of work that the German scholar Georg Friedrich Grotefend had done on inscriptions from the Persian capital Persepolis, Rawlinson was able to establish that one of the three inscriptions used a 42-letter cuneiform alphabet and started with a description of the Persian king Darius which was almost identical to that given by the ancient Greek historian Herodotus in his *Histories*. Within three years, after a return to the monument and using his knowledge of Middle and Modern Persian, Rawlinson had deciphered 200 lines of the Old Persian alphabetic inscription—an account of Darius' rise to power—and presented his work to the Royal Asiatic Society in London and the Société Asiatique in Paris.

The translation caused a sensation, as it confirmed one of the most unbelievable and romantic stories told by Herodotus. However, there was still much to be done: the other two inscriptions remained undeciphered. In 1844 Rawlinson and three colleagues again climbed the cliffs at Bisutun, now making a complete papier-mâché mould. Using this copy, and working on the assumption that all three inscriptions told essentially the same story, Nils Westergaard and Edwin Norris managed to decipher the second. Its script used 131 characters and the language, Elamite, turned out to be an isolate, related to no other known. But the third version of the inscription, which was by far the most complex, remained a mystery. Further evidence was needed—and it wasn't long in coming.

In the early 1840s rival French and British teams, led by Emile Botta and Henry Layard, had started to dig at the ancient Assyrian capitals of Khorsabad (ancient Dur-Šarrukin), Nimrud (Kalḫu), and Nineveh in the north of Iraq. They were finding large numbers of stone inscriptions and clay tablets in the same script as the third Behistun inscription, which they naturally named Assyrian. Decipherment became an international enterprise to which many scholars contributed. It was recognized that Assyrian must be a Semitic language, somehow related to Hebrew and Arabic. Assyrian cuneiform was essentially composed of syllables, but logograms (signs representing whole words) could replace syllabic spellings in otherwise identical texts. But there was still much public scepticism about the success of decipherment, so in 1857 Henry Fox Talbot persuaded the Royal Asiatic Society to hold a competition in which he, Rawlinson, Edward Hincks, and Jules Oppert were each given a copy of the same Assyrian royal inscription to translate independently. When their translations were compared they were virtually identical, and the decipherment of Assyrian could officially be considered essentially complete.

This is where the standard stories of decipherment end; and indeed the continuing study of Akkadian (Assyrian together with its southern neighbour Babylonian) has been relatively unproblematic. But it was a different story for the Sumerian language, whose existence Rawlinson, Fox Talbot, and their contemporaries were only just beginning to discern.

A contested language

As early as 1850, Hincks had already deduced that the cuneiform script had not been invented expressly for Assyrian or Babylonian. It simply didn't fit the language very well; there was no unambiguous way of representing the Semitic consonants q, $ṣ$, or $ṭ$ for instance. But what should that original language be called? As his colleague Jules Oppert later recalled, Hincks

proposed the term Akkadian and based it on the following consideration: all the kings of Mesopotamia following their principal title used the subsidiary one of 'King of Sumer and Akkad'. It therefore seemed probable to him that one of the two people [Sumerian or Akkadian] was the inventor of the writing. He proposed Akkad because the name appeared in the Bible.[8]

[8] J. Oppert, 'Études sumériennes', *Journal Asiatique*, 5 (1875), 268. Translated from French by T. B. Jones, *The Sumerian Problem* (Wiley: New York, 1969), p. 23.

So Akkadian it was, on biblical authority. (Now, however, following ancient usage, we use 'Akkadian' for the Semitic language of which Assyrian was the northern dialect, and 'Sumerian' for what Hincks and Oppert had at first called Akkadian.)

Much became invested in the potential of the cuneiform textual record to provide independent evidence of the veracity of the Bible, at a time when it was coming under increasing attack from new scientifically based interpretations of the world. Charles Lyell had published his seminal and much-discussed work *The Principles of Geology* in the 1830s which seriously threatened the accepted biblically derived date for the creation of the world in 4004 BC. And then in the 1840s the existence and scientific significance of dinosaurs were just hitting the British public: perhaps the world had not been created in seven days after all. Charles Darwin's *On the Origin of Species by Means of Natural Selection* was to follow in 1859, arguing that all living beings had evolved in adaptation to their environments and could not therefore be the outcome of a single divine act of creation. Thus the evidence from the Assyrian palaces was crucial to upholding the authority of the Bible: independent corroboration at last that parts, at least, of the Old Testament were historically true.

Meanwhile, some scholars were not convinced by Hincks's arguments for the existence of an 'original language' for cuneiform. In 1873 Joseph Halévy wrote:

I have never disputed the decipherment itself of the so-called Akkadian [= Sumerian] texts; on the contrary, I shall use the results of decipherment to demonstrate that the texts in question . . . are Assyrian texts couched in a special ideographic system which because of its antiquity was considered to be more sacred than purely phonetic writing. That is why, in my opinion, the Assyrian-Babylonian priests preferred to employ ideographic characters in magic formulae and incantations which they thought gained in efficacy through the mystic virtue of the writing.[9]

It was, in other words, no more than a secret writing used by priests, which no one had ever really spoken. The debate raged for years. Halévy's belief was definitively disproven only in 1900 in a tightly argued article by the British cuneiformist Theophilus Pinches, who also established the correct name for Sumerian. Here are the most important points of his summary:

1. There are numerous tablets written in a non-Semitic dialect, with and without translation [into Assyrian] and in two cases at least these non-Semitic texts are expressly designated as Sumerian.

---

[9] J. Halévy, 'Observations critiques sur les prétendus Touraniens de la Babylonie', *Journal Asiatique*, 3 (1874), 465. Translated from French by T. B. Jones, *The Sumerian Problem* (Wiley: New York, 1969), p. 24.

2. That Sumerian (or Akkadian) was not an allography [alternative writing] is proved by the fact that it possessed a dialect showing clear laws of sound change. It is to be noted also that the grammar is entirely different from that of the Semitic idiom.

5. Not only hymns, psalms, incantations, charms, and similar literary products were written in the non-Semitic language to which I have referred, but also royal inscriptions, legal precepts, and law documents, the latter classes of texts being such as no sane person would write in any so-called 'allography'.[10]

In short, Sumerian could not have been a 'secret writing' for Assyrian because their linguistic and phonological structures are completely different; and anyway Sumerian was used for all sorts of mundane purposes for which 'secret writing' would have been inappropriate and unnecessary. Meanwhile, archaeological finds in the south of Iraq were proving the existence of a culture that long pre-dated the Assyrians in the north and whose writings were almost exclusively in Sumerian. Here was a major civilization that was mentioned neither in Classical nor in biblical sources, seriously undermining the authority of both.

A contested archaeology

These new excavations gave weight to Pinches's assessment. Already in the 1850s some puzzling finds had been made in the far south of Mesopotamia, at Warka (ancient Unug) and Ur (Urim), which suggested that these sites were far older than the Assyrian cities of the north. In 1877 the underemployed French consul Ernest de Sarzec began to dig at Tello, after a local antiquities dealer tipped him off about the fine quality of the statues to be found there. Over the course of the next three decades de Sarzec and his compatriots dug systematically over the ruin mounds in search of objects for the Louvre museum. As the 'Akkadian' (Sumerian) inscriptions on tablets and monuments were deciphered it became apparent that he had discovered ancient Lagaš, a major city-state of the late third millennium BCE and later an important regional city of the Third Dynasty of Urim.

But Lagaš attracted the attention of others too. British Museum agents, taking advantage of the fact that de Sarzec was digging without a permit from the Ottoman authorities, took a turn at the site while de Sarzec was in France, as did local men, spurred on by the large sums of money that the Louvre and British Museum were now paying for Mesopotamian antiquities. During the 1880s some 35,000–40,000 cuneiform tablets from Lagaš thus made their way to the antiquities dealers who were springing up all over Baghdad, and

---

[10] T. Pinches, 'Sumerian or Cryptography', *Journal of the Royal Asiatic Society*, 32 (1900), 95.

onwards to private and institutional collections all over the world. Identi-fying, publishing, and reconstructing the constituents of this shattered archive is still an ongoing project.

Until the late 1880s Mesopotamian exploration had been almost exclu-sively a by-product of British and French colonial interests in the Middle East designed to furnish their great national museums. But around this time a large-scale American expedition to Nippur (Nibru) was established, in order to bring the USA into the game. But whereas the French and British collectors all had long-standing interests and expertise in the area, only one of the American expedition members had even set foot in the Middle East before. In 1888 their first season went disastrously wrong within weeks as the local men they employed as labourers revolted. Undeterred, the Nippur expedition regrouped and went on to run until 1900, gradually bringing to light many tens of thousands of cuneiform tablets. Under new antiquities laws many were deposited at the Imperial Ottoman Museum in Istanbul, but some 30,000 went to the University Museum in Philadelphia, newly founded specially to accommodate the Nippur finds. A significant number were also given as a personal gift to the expedition's German 'scientific director' Hermann Hilprecht; they are now housed at the University of Jena. Amongst the vast mass of Nippur tablets are over two and a half thousand literary manuscripts, which remain our single most important body of sources for Sumerian literature.

Neither de Sarzec nor Hilprecht was an archaeologist as we would under-stand the term today. They and their contemporaries were out to furnish museum collections and to record large-scale architectural remains. It was not until the first years of the twentieth century that German excavators at Babylon and Assur developed methodical techniques of stratigraphic excavation and detailed recording systems of their finds; and even in the decades that followed their standards were not universally maintained by others in the field.

In the aftermath of the First World War, on the collapse of the Ottoman Empire, Iraq became a nation state, first under formal British mandate and then from 1932 as a nominally independent kingdom (though still under heavy British influence). Gertrude Bell, its first (British) director of antiqui-ties, oversaw a massive increase in the quantity and quality of archaeological excavation in Iraq: archaeology was no longer a hunt for objects but a scientific exploration of past lives. Of most importance for Sumerian litera-ture were Sir Leonard Woolley's enormous excavations at Ur (Urim) in the far south of Iraq, starting in 1922. Although some might now consider his motives misguided—he was looking for traces of 'Ur of the Chaldees', according to Genesis the patriarch Abraham's original home—his results were invaluable. In a move away from the traditional concerns with palace and temple architecture, he uncovered two large areas of domestic housing in the city centre which dated to the early second millennium BCE. He found some 450 Sumerian literary tablets in context, mostly in two eighteenth-century houses which he called '1 Broad Street' and '7 Quiet Street': an essential corrective to the overwhelming numbers of tablets from Hilprecht's expedition which provide our very Nibru-centric view of Sumerian literature.

A contested race

In the first half of the twentieth century, when western culture was much preoccupied with ideas of racial difference, research questions centred on the origins of the Sumerian people, the date of their apparent migration into Iraq, and their first contact with the Semitic Akkadians with whom, it was supposed, they had vied for political and cultural control of southern Iraq. All sorts of evidence for racial typing came into play, from cranial measurements to the fashions in clothes and hair on early Mesopotamian statues. Semites supposedly had long hair and beards; Sumerians wore their heads and faces shaved. (Interestingly, the attributes of *female* attire were not part of the debate, although images of women were known.) The Semites, it was generally agreed, had made their homeland in the area just south of modern-day Baghdad, the Sumerians nearer the Gulf coast around modern-day Nasiriya. Which racial group entered the region first and from what direction were hotly disputed. Did the prehistoric pottery show that Sumerians had been in Iraq from at least the early fifth millennium BCE or only from the very early third millennium? And were they more closely related to the Turkic peoples of central Asia or the inhabitants of the Harappan cities of the Indus Valley? Maybe there was also a third population group to consider, neither Semitic nor Sumerian, whose linguistic remains could be detected in the written record too. As the results of the staggeringly large-scale excavations of the inter-war years began to be published and assimilated, the question got more and more confusing. By 1939 Ephraim Speiser, one of the major protagonists in the debate, had to admit:

To identify the individual ethnic elements which cooperated in producing the civilization of preliterate Mesopotamia is a more hopeless task today than it ever appeared to be. It did not seem nearly as difficult before we found out that the culture of each period was a composite fabric. Furthermore, physical anthropology held out the hope that racial strains might be disentangled. But this promise has not been fulfilled. In fact, the available anthropometric evidence is less conclusive in this regard than the circumstantial evidence from material remains. The process of racial levelling is immeasurably older than that of cultural blending.[11]

In the same year—in fact, in the very same journal—Thorkild Jacobsen used third-millennium historical evidence to argue that the ancient inhabitants of southern Iraq did not view themselves along racial or ethnic lines, and that all recorded conflicts were between city-based political entities and not between different 'peoples' of the Land. Race, in other words, was neither part of the early Mesopotamian conceptual framework nor a fruitful subject for modern inquiry.

The debate eventually petered out as the notion of 'race' became discredited at the same time that archaeological theory began to recognize that developments in material culture did not necessarily imply population shifts too. By the mid-1960s the so-called 'Sumerian problem' was a dead issue for Georges Roux, author of the influential history book *Ancient Iraq* (1964):

From the point of view of the modern historian the line of demarcation between [the ethnic] components of the first historical population of Mesopotamia is neither political nor cultural but linguistic. All of them had the same institutions; all of them shared the same way of life, the techniques, the artistic traditions, the religious beliefs, in a word the civilization which had originated in the extreme south and is rightly attributed to the Sumerians . . . The appellation 'Sumerians' should be taken as meaning 'Sumerian-speaking people' and nothing else. . . . Another point should be made quite clear: there is no such thing as a Sumerian 'race' neither in the scientific nor in the ordinary sense of the term. . . . One is even tempted to wonder whether there is any problem at all. The Sumerians were, as we all are, a mixture of races and probably of peoples; their civilization, like ours, was a blend of foreign and indigenous elements . . . they may have 'always' been in Iraq, and this is all we can say.[12]

Modern textbooks rarely mention the topic at all.

A contested literature

If 'Who were the Sumerians?' was no longer a valid topic for debate in the post-war years, 'What is Sumerian literature?' most certainly was. Sumerology had come of age in the early twentieth century, with the start of the French publications of documents and inscriptions from Lagaš. But it was Hilprecht's finds at Nibru, now housed in Istanbul, Jena, and Philadelphia, that were to prove essential to the discovery and decipherment of Sumerian

---

[11]   E. Speiser, 'The Beginnings of Civilization in Mesopotamia', *Journal of the American Oriental Society*, 59 (1939), 17–31.

[12]   G. Roux, *Ancient Iraq* (1st edn., Penguin: Harmondsworth, 1964), p. 85.

literature. Hilprecht had resigned from the University of Pennsylvania in 1909 under long-running accusations of misrepresenting his finds and holding up the publication process. His former students and underlings were now free to follow their own research paths. Arno Poebel published an influential grammar of the Sumerian language in 1923. Edward Chiera led the way in cataloguing and copying hundreds of fragments of Sumerian literary tablets in the Istanbul and Philadelphia collections until his untimely death in the early 1930s. His unfinished work was entrusted for publication to another former Penn student, Samuel Noah Kramer, who like Poebel and Chiera had since become attached to the great Assyrian (Akkadian) Dictionary project at the University of Chicago. By the mid-1930s Kramer had amassed enough fragments of literary tablets to start to reconstruct whole compositions; he published a translation of *Inana's descent to the Underworld* (Group B) in 1937, followed over the next few years by several of the Gilgameš narratives.

Major uncertainties over the vocabulary and grammar of Sumerian still meant that literary translation and interpretation were extremely difficult and highly dependent on personal intuition. So in 1952, almost exactly a century after Fox Talbot's Assyrian challenge to the Royal Asiatic Society, Kramer (by then back at Penn) decided to test the field's progress in Sumerian literary studies by sending 48 Sumerian proverbs to twenty scholars for independent translation. As Kramer recalled in 1986,[13]

Eight scholars responded . . . Ten of the proverbs were translated by all eight participants; of the others, the number of translations varied from one to seven. There was considerable disagreement about practically all of the proverbs, and no agreement whatsoever in the case of some. Nevertheless, it was my feeling that the experiment was by no means a failure.

Undaunted, Kramer continued the painstaking work of tablet copying, as well as the editing and interpretation of Sumerian literary works, right up until his death in 1990.

But as his anecdote suggests, Kramer was not alone in his devotion to the Sumerian literary cause. Foremost amongst his contemporaries and colleagues was the Danish scholar Thorkild Jacobsen, whom we have already met debunking the 'Sumerian problem' in 1939. He had studied with Poebel and Chiera at the University of Chicago, and went on to teach there and at Harvard. In the late 1940s he was responsible for initiating new American excavations at Nibru, which in 1951 were to turn up House F and its literary

[13] S. N. Kramer, *In the World of Sumer: An Autobiography* (Wayne University Press: Detroit, 1986), p. 129.

tablets, giving further impetus to the post-war drive to publish and comprehend Sumerian literature. The two men often worked together, and Kramer dubbed their relationship one of 'friendly adversaries'. Jacobsen outlived Kramer by just three years.

Kramer and Jacobsen each published anthologies of Sumerian literary works, which remain in print and are still this book's only predecessors in English. It is difficult to imagine two more radically different approaches to the translation and interpretation of Sumerian literature. For Kramer the Sumerians were tangible and familiar, and literature a straightforward means of accessing them. In popularizing books, with titles such as *History begins at Sumer* (1956) and *The Sumerians: their history, culture, and character* (1970), he used translations of Sumerian literary works as unmediated reports of world 'firsts' in history. Thus *A praise poem of Šulgi* (Group J) became 'the first long-distance champion' and *The home of the fish* (Group G) 'the first aquarium'! Literary works were mined for historical evidence of Sumerian society, their fictional character left unproblematically to one side.

Jacobsen too was inclined to use literature in this way (such as for evidence of 'primitive democracy'), but was more concerned to use it to construct a history of Sumerian religion. He saw Sumerian literature as essentially alien, with a numinous, exotic aesthetic. His popularizing works carry titles like *The Harps that Once . . .* (1987; ellipsis included) and *Treasures of Darkness* (1976). It appealed to him as 'bearing witness to a strange, long-vanished world'.[14]

Their differing interpretative stances were reflected clearly in their translations. Here for instance are their renderings of the first four lines of the hymn *Enlil in the E-kur* (Group J):

Enlil—his orders august
   into the far yonder,
  his words holy,
his unalterable utterances
   decisive
  into the far future,
his lifting up the eyes
   taking in the mountains,
his raising of eyebeams
  scanning the highland's heart—[15]

---

[14] T. Jacobsen, *The Harps that Once . . . Sumerian Poetry in Translation* (Yale University Press: New Haven, 1987), p. xi.

[15] T. Jacobsen, *The Harps that Once*, pp. 101–2.

Enlil, whose command is far-reaching, whose word is holy,
The lord whose pronouncement is unchangeable, who forever decrees destinies,
Whose lifted eye scans the lands,
Whose lifted light searches the heart of all the lands[16]

The 'poetic' translation is of course Jacobsen's, the prosaic one Kramer's. You might also like to compare them with the one given in this book (Group J).

Jacobsen's and Kramer's approaches are two ends of a spectrum. Since their day many scholars in many countries have laboured to reconstruct and understand Sumerian literature. In recent years, the cumulative effect of primary publication, as well as the gradual creation of research tools, has allowed for a wide variety of nuanced interpretations which seek to understand it *as literature* and not as a historical source. Let's finally turn to the state of Sumerian literary studies as it stands in the early twenty-first century and our project's place within it.

A collaborative present; an uncertain future

By the mid-1990s it had become clear that a new approach was needed to the study of Sumerian literature. Despite a growing number of excellent new studies, many important compositions still had to be consulted in out-of-date editions, with translations that had become unusable because of progress in knowledge of the language. Some were available only as semi-published books that circulated among specialists; and many remained wholly unedited. There was still no complete dictionary, no suitable reference list of cuneiform signs, no agreed interpretation of the grammar. The slow progress of research, with little organized collaboration, meant that Sumerian literature remained inaccessible to most people who might wish to read or study it, and virtually unknown to a wider public.

Sumerology had so far relied on individual scholars pursing their own research interests, primarily text editions and the literary analysis of small groups of compositions. It was almost impossible to get a picture of the whole, and that picture tended to be impressionistic and intuitive. Some of us felt an urgent need for quantitative research, which could draw both on current developments in literary theory and on the extensive and growing discipline of corpus linguistics to aim at precise explanations rather than impressionistic answers. Rapid developments elsewhere in the humanities in electronic text production and management suggested that there were

---

[16] S. N. Kramer, *History Begins at Sumer* (Thames & Hudson: London, 1958), p. 147.

ways of producing statistical analyses of Sumerian literature through close quantitative study.

Quantitative analysis required an extensive corpus, consistently edited and publicly accessible. Thus was the Electronic Text Corpus of Sumerian Literature (ETCSL) born in 1997. It is based at the University of Oxford but works in close collaboration with the Sumerian dictionary project at the University of Pennsylvania and benefits immeasurably from the active co-operation of Sumerologists all over the world. Its first aim was to create a digital library comprising hundreds of reconstructed Sumerian compositions (presented in transliteration in alphabetic script)—composite texts editorially assembled from individual manuscripts, but including details of substantive textual variants—each with an English prose translation and bibliography. At the time of writing the project has been running for nearly seven years with as many staff members, and has published nearly four hundred Sumerian literary works on its website. The project is now mainly focused on the analysis rather than the publication of Sumerian literature—which in turn, we hope will feed back into improved editions and translations of these works.

An electronic corpus by no means supersedes the need for scholarly critical editions of literary works, but it does enable research on all sorts of levels. It has become raw material for the web-based Sumerian dictionary in Philadelphia; it has provided accessible teaching editions for Sumerological colleagues in universities all over the world, allowing greater access of students into Sumerology; and has disseminated an unprecedentedly large body of translations for students and scholars of neighbouring fields. The corpus is searchable, immeasurably speeding up the identification and publication of previously unpublished or unidentified sources. In short, it has enabled a larger number of people to grasp a bigger picture of Sumerian literature than perhaps at any time in the history of the world!

But the future is not unequivocally bright. We write this introduction just six months after the American-British invasion of Iraq and the subsequent looting of its museums, libraries, and archaeological sites. The future of the ancient Sumerian cities looks grim. Large-scale pillaging of places such as Isin and Umma, now in remote desert locations, began in May 2003 and has continued unabated over the summer months. Similar looting also took place in the aftermath of the 1991 Gulf War. Armed gangs often prove too much for site guards or even the occasional military patrol to deal with—and will in any case return once the coast is clear again. The fledgeling police force is too overstretched to deal with the informal antiquities markets that have sprung up on street corners. And there is effectively no judicial system yet by which to prosecute, try, and sentence looters and dealers if and when they are arrested.

Whereas the articulate pleas of the Iraq Museum's curators have attracted publicity, controversy, and practical assistance from all over the world, it is the looting of archaeological sites that is most distressing and difficult to deal with. Museum artefacts have for the most part been catalogued, documented, conserved and security-marked. They at least stand some chance of surviving outside the museum, and of being identified and returned. Objects taken from the ground are at much greater risk. Only the most complete, robust, and attractive artefacts make it from the looter's pick to the middleman's hands: somewhat less than 1 per cent of the assemblage a professional archaeologist might salvage. The other 99 per cent is destroyed in the process of excavation or discarded as unsaleably unattractive or unstable. Needless to say, all archaeological context is demolished in the looting process too, from the large-scale built environment (usually made of fragile mud-brick) to the microscopic food residues detectable on ancient floors and storage vessels.

As the example of House F shows, incomparably more data can be recovered from carefully recorded, archaeologically contextualized bodies of Sumerian literary tablets than is possible from single, unprovenanced fragments. We are still picking up the pieces, both literally and metaphorically, from the institutionalized looting of Sumerian sites a century or more ago. The Sumerological community, in Iraq and in the rest of the world, now faces the daunting prospect of having to do so all over again. The immediate future will bring many unforeseen challenges but we shall continue to work with our Iraqi colleagues in the recovery, study, and enjoyment of Iraq's rich, fascinating, and most ancient literature.

FURTHER READING

General reading and background

Black, Jeremy, and Green, Anthony, *Gods, Demons, and Symbols of Ancient Mesopotamia* (British Museum Press: London, 1992) is a useful reference work for many of the deities and images that feature in Sumerian literature.

Kuhrt, Amélie, *The Ancient Near East, c.3000–330 BC* (Routledge: London and New York, 1995), in two volumes, is a thorough political history of ancient Egypt and the Middle East; volume 1 deals with the periods we are concerned with here.

Van De Mieroop, Marc, *A History of the Ancient Near East, c.3000–323 BC* (Blackwell: Oxford, 2003) is shorter than Kuhrt's history but also addresses questions of historical interpretation.

Postgate, Nicholas, *Early Mesopotamia: Society and Economy at the Dawn of History* (Routledge: London, 1992) will give you a rounded overview of the setting of Sumerian literature.

Roaf, Michael, *Cultural Atlas of Mesopotamia and the Near East* (Facts on File: New York, 1990) is a highly illustrated account of ancient Iraq and its neighbours from prehistory to the Persians.

Sasson, Jack M. (ed.), *Civilisations of the Ancient Near East* (Charles Scribners' Sons: New York, 1995), in two volumes or four, includes a wealth of short, accessible articles on many aspects of Sumerian language, culture, and history (as well as many other topics) by authors who are experts in their field.

Dalley, Stephanie, *Myths from Mesopotamia* (Oxford University Press: Oxford, rev. edn. 2000) gives translations of some of the great works of Akkadian literature.

Foster, Benjamin, *Before the Muses* (CDL Press: Bethesda, Md., 3rd edn. 2005) has a wider scope than Dalley.

Introduction

Black, Jeremy, *Reading Sumerian Poetry* (Athlone: London, 1998) addresses theories and approaches to the study of Sumerian literature.

Walker, Christopher, *Cuneiform* (British Museum Press: London, 1987) explains very clearly how cuneiform script works and how decipherment came about.

Michalowski, Piotr, 'Sumerian', in R. D. Woodard (ed.), *Cambridge Encyclopedia of the World's Ancient Languages* (Cambridge University Press: Cambridge, 2004, pp. 19–59) is an up-to-date and accessible survey of the Sumerian language, with further bibliography.

Robson, Eleanor, 'The Tablet House: A Scribal School in Old Babylonian Nippur', *Revue d'Assyriologie*, 95 (2001), 39–67 is a preliminary presentation of the archaeology and tablets of House F for a specialist readership.

Cavigneaux, Antoine, 'A Scholar's Library in Meturan? With an Edition of the Tablet H 72 (Textes de Tell Haddad VII)', in T. Abusch and K. van der Toorn (eds.), *Mesopotamian Magic: Textual, Historical, and Interpretative Perspectives* (Styx: Groningen, 1999, pp. 253–73) does a similar job for the 'scholar's house' at Me-Turan.

Lloyd, Seton, *Foundations in the Dust: A History of Mesopotamian Exploration* (Penguin: Harmondsworth, 1955; Thames & Hudson: London, 2nd edn. 1980) is a sparkling and sympathetic account of nineteenth- and early twentieth-century archaeology in Iraq.

An extensive bibliography on Sumerian literature, including the print editions which have aided our translations, as well as many other excellent and influential works in French, German, and other languages, can be found at the ETCSL website, <http://etcsl.orinst.ox.ac.uk>.

A. HEROES AND KINGS

It is not clear that the legendary heroes whose exploits feature in several Sumerian literary narratives can be distinguished from gods. Usually their names are written with the same determinative sign used to write the names of deities, and it is known from documentary evidence that some received a cult and offerings. They were often considered to be the offspring of gods. Some, such as Lugalbanda, were envisaged as culture-heroes who had benefited mankind, while others, such as Gilgameš, were considered to have ruled well-known cities in ancient times. However, it is precisely this connection to identified terrestrial locations that characterizes the figures we can call heroes.

If this is so, then equally, but for different reasons, it is difficult to distinguish some undeniably historical kings from gods. This is because during most of the period from which the Sumerian literature translated here derives, rulers considered themselves as deified in their own lifetimes. Their names, equally, were written with the determinative sign for deities, and temples were built in their honour, where they received a cult. Not surprisingly these rulers are described in extravagant terms, and their belief was that they shared divine parentage with the gods, and thus in some sense could be, for instance, the husband of the goddess Inana, or son of the goddess Ninsumun and therefore the brother of Gilgameš. Such statements were part of the complex tissue of ritual with which rulers surrounded themselves; clearly, propaganda of this sort did not arrest the mortality of Mesopotamian kings when their time came, and a work such as *The death of Ur-Namma* comes to terms with exactly this problem.

None the less, it makes it difficult to draw a line where the legendary past ended and the historical past began. Several of the narratives have many of the characteristics of legends or folk-tales. In contrast to the Lugalbanda and Enmerkar narratives, which express in different forms the conflict between Unug and the legendary city of Aratta (*Enmerkar and En-suhgir-ana*, *Lugalbanda in the mountain cave*, and *Lugalbanda and the Anzud bird*), the five Sumerian poems about Gilgameš, also ruler of Unug and in one tradition the son of Lugalbanda, present different events in that hero's life. In three of these, Gilgameš defeats different types of opponent: Aga, the king of Kiš, the dominant city in the Semitic-speaking north (*Gilgameš and Aga*, ETCSL 1.8.1.1); monstrous Ḫuwawa, the divinely appointed guardian of the cedar forests (*Gilgameš and Ḫuwawa*, Group J); and the rampaging Bull of Heaven, the constellation Taurus brought to earth at the request of the goddess Inana (*Gilgameš and the Bull of Heaven*, ETCSL 1.8.1.2). In a fourth poem, his servant and comrade in these exploits, Enkidu, is himself defeated by the Underworld (*Gilgameš, Enkidu, and the Underworld*). And in a fifth (*The death of Gilgameš*, ETCSL 1.8.1.3), the two companions are reunited in the Underworld; the theme of the death of a ruler and his state burial is also developed in *The death of Ur-Namma*.

The more or less historical events that form the background to *Sargon and Ur-Zababa* are at least in agreement with other sources, and the historical context is confirmed by original inscriptions left by both Lugal-zage-si and Sargon. The building by Gudea, a historical ruler of Lagaš, of the temple of Ningirsu is presented as of cosmic import (see *The building of Ningirsu's temple*). Meanwhile *An adab to An for Lipit-Eštar*, a ruler of Isin, and *A prayer for Samsu-iluna*, king of Babylon and son of the famous Ḫammurabi, both allude to the divine status of their royal addressees.

FURTHER READING

Flückiger-Hawker, E., *Urnamma of Ur in Sumerian Literary Tradition* (University Press/Vandenhoeck & Ruprecht: Fribourg/Göttingen, 1999) studies all the extant praise poetry written for Ur-Namma.

George, A. E., *The Epic of Gilgamesh: The Babylonian Epic Poem and Other Texts in Akkadian and Sumerian* (Penguin: Harmondsworth, 1999) gives all the Gilgameš narratives in translation, with an extensive introduction.

Vanstiphout, H. L. J., *Epics of Sumerian Kings: The Matter of Aratta* (Society of Biblical Literature: Atlanta, GA, 2003) introduces and edits four legends of Lugalbanda.

Westenholz, J. G., *Legends of the Kings of Akkade* (Eisenbrauns: Winona Lake, Ind., 1999) explores the literary traditions about Sargon of Agade and his grandson Naram-Suen, in Akkadian.

OTHER COMPOSITIONS ON THIS THEME INCLUDE

Group B   A love song for Šu-Suen
                  Inana and Išme-Dagan

Enmerkar and En-suḫgir-ana

Enmerkar and En-suḫgir-ana gives narrative expression to the supremacy of Unug, the idealised Sumerian city, over its rival Aratta. The poem begins by praising Unug and its god-like ruler Enmerkar, before introducing the first in a series of three contests between him and En-suḫgir-ana, his adversary in Aratta.

The opening contest takes the form of claims conveyed by the rulers' messengers. The lord of Aratta dictates his message first, declaring that he is the favoured sexual partner of the goddess Inana. Tumbling across space in a sequence of vivid similes, a messenger races to Unug where he delivers his lord's challenge. Enmerkar, however, is unperturbed: he retorts that he was brought up by deities and that Unug is Inana's earthly home.

En-suḫgir-ana concedes that his message has been surpassed but vows that he will never submit to the lord of Unug. Help is at hand from a sorcerer named Ur-ĝirnuna whose opposition to Unug is conveyed to En-suḫgir-ana by his minister. The second contest now begins: a series of speeches tells how the sorcerer inverts the fertility of Sumer, focusing on the city of Ereš whose patron deity is Nisaba, the goddess of writing and thus of both literature and the bureaucracy essential to successful agricultural administration. The consequences of this inversion of the natural order are conveyed in desolate images of silent sheepfolds and empty milk-churns that occur in such other compositions as the *Lament for Sumer and Urim* (Group D). In *Enmerkar and En-suḫgir-ana*, however, the generalizing imagery is supplemented by references to the predicament of specific individuals.

The sorcerer Ur-g̃irnuna wins the second contest for Aratta. However, Sumer too can turn to an individual adept in magical skills, a wise woman known as Sag̃-buru. Alone by the banks of the Euphrates, the two rivals engage in a third contest, each using fish spawn to create a series of animals. The animals made by Sag̃-buru consistently surpass those created by Ur-g̃ir-nuna. Defeated, the sorcerer pleads for mercy, but his threat to the natural—and thus divine—order allows no forgiveness and he is killed by Sag̃-buru. En-suḫgir-ana responds with his final message to the lord of Unug, now praising Enmerkar as his superior.

The poem concludes with one line in praise of the goddess Nisaba, preceded by two lines whose implications are less certain. These refer to the composition as an *adamin*, 'debate'. More often, however, this term was applied to compositions, such as the *Debate between Bird and Fish* (Group G), in which the contest takes the form of verbal jousting between two anthropomorphized aspects of nature, and a deity decides which of the two has precedence.

Translation

1–5 Brickwork rising out from the pristine mountain°—Kulaba, city which reaches from heaven to earth; Unug, whose fame like the rainbow reaches up to the sky, a multicoloured sheen, as the new moon standing in the heavens.

6–13 Built in magnificence with all the great powers, lustrous mount founded on a favourable day, like moonlight coming up over the land, like bright sunlight radiating over the land, the rear cow and . . . cow coming forth in abundance: all this is Unug, the glory of which reaches the highland and its radiance, genuine refined silver, covers Aratta like a garment, is spread over it like linen.

14–24 At that time the day was lord, the night was sovereign, and Utu was king. Now the name of the lord of Aratta's minister was minister Ansiga-ria. The name of the minister of Enmerkar, the lord of Kulaba, was Namena-tuma. He with the . . . lord, he with the . . . prince; he with the . . . lord, he with the . . . prince; he with the . . . lord, he with the . . . prince; he with the man born to be a god; he

with a man manifest as a god, with the lord of Unug, the lord of
Kulaba—En-suḫgir-ana, the lord of Aratta, is to make a contest with
him, saying first to the messenger concerning Unug:

25–39 'Let him submit to me, let him bear my yoke. If he submits to me,
indeed submits to me, then as for him and me—he may dwell with
Inana within a walled enclosure (?), but I dwell with Inana in the
E-zagin of Aratta; he may lie with her on the splendid bed, but I lie
in sweet slumber with her on the adorned bed, he may see dreams
with Inana at night, but I converse with Inana awake. He may feed
the geese with barley, but I will definitely not feed the geese with
barley. I will . . . the geese's eggs in a basket and . . . their goslings. The
small ones into my pot, the large ones into my kettle, and the rulers
of the land who submitted will consume, together with me, what
remains from the geese.' This is what he said to Enmerkar.

40–51 The messenger runs like a wild ram and flies like a falcon. He leaves
in the morning and returns already at dusk, like small birds at dawn,
he . . . over the open country, like small birds at midnight, he hides
himself in the interior of the mountains. Like a throw-stick, he
stands at the side. Like a perfect donkey of Šakkan, he runs over° the
mountains, he dashes like a large, powerful donkey. A slim donkey,
eager to run, he rushes forth. A lion in the field at dawn, he lets out
roars; like a wolf which has seized a lamb, he runs quickly. The small
places he has reached, he fills with . . . for him; the large places he has
reached, he . . . boundary (?).

52 He entered the presence of the lord in his holy ǧipar shrine°.

53–69 'My king has sent me to you. The lord of Aratta, En-suḫgir-ana, has
sent me to you.° This is what my king says: "Let him submit to me,
let him bear my yoke. If he submits to me, indeed submits to me,
then as for him and me—he may dwell with Inana within a walled
enclosure (?), but I dwell with Inana in the E-zagin of Aratta; he may
lie with her on the splendid bed, but I lie in sweet slumber with her
on the adorned bed, he may see dreams with Inana at night, but I
converse with Inana awake. He may feed the geese with barley, but I
will definitely not feed the geese with barley. I will . . . the geese's eggs
in a basket and . . . their goslings. The small ones into my pot,
the large ones into my kettle, and the rulers of the land who submitted will consume, together with me, what remains from the
geese." '

70–6 The lord of Unug . . . he is their . . . , he is their rudder . . . . he is the neck-stock which clamps down upon them, . . . to the place of its foundation. He is their falcon which flies in the sky, he is their bird-net. The brickwork of the great temple of Aratta . . . . in Aratta . . . great . . . . bring (?) . . . .

77–113 He patted it like a lump of clay, he examined it like a clay tablet: 'He may dwell with Inana in the E-zagin of Aratta, but I dwell with her . . . as her earthly companion (?). He may lie with her in sweet slumber on the adorned bed, but I lie on Inana's splendid bed strewn with pure plants. Its back is an *ug* lion, its front is a *pirig̃* lion. The *ug* lion chases the *pirig̃* lion, the *pirig̃* lion chases the *ug* lion. As the *ug* lion chases the *pirig̃* lion and the *pirig̃* lion chases the *ug* lion, the day does not dawn, the night does not pass. I accompany Inana for a journey of 15 *danna*° and yet Utu the sun-god cannot see my holy crown, when she enters my holy *g̃ipar* shrine. Enlil has given (?) me the true crown and sceptre. Ninurta, the son of Enlil, held me on his lap as the frame holds the water-skin. Aruru, the sister of Enlil, extended her right breast to me, extended her left breast to me. When I go up to the great shrine, the Mistress screeches like an Anzud chick, and other times when I go there, even though she is not a duckling, she shrieks like one. She . . . from the city of her birth. No city was made to be so well-built as the city of Unug (?). It is Unug where Inana dwells and as regards Aratta, what does it have to do with this? It is brick-built Kulaba where she lives, and as regards the mount of the lustrous divine powers, what can it do about this? For five or ten years she will definitely not go to Aratta. Since the great holy lady of the E-ana took counsel with me (?) about whether to go also to Aratta, since she let me know° about this matter, I know that she will not go to Aratta. He who has nothing shall not feed the geese with barley, but I will feed the geese with barley. I will . . . the geese's eggs in a basket and . . . their goslings. The small ones into my pot, the old ones into my kettle, and the rulers of the Land° who sub-mitted will consume, together with me, what remains from the geese.'

114–19 The messenger of Enmerkar reached En-suhgir-ana, reached his holy *g̃ipar* shrine, his most holy place, the most holy place where he was sitting, its . . . . En-suhgir-ana asked for instructions, he searched for an answer. He summoned the purification priests, the *lumah* priests, the *gudug* priests, and *girsiga* attendants who dwell in the *g̃ipar* shrine, and took counsel with them.

120–7 'What shall I say to him? What shall I say to him? What shall I say to the lord of Unug, the lord of Kulaba? His bull stood up to fight my bull and the bull of Unug has defeated it. His man has been struggling with my man and the man of Unug has defeated him. His warrior (?) has been struggling with my warrior (?) and the warrior (?) of Unug . . . him.'

128–32 The convened assembly answered him straightforwardly: 'It was you who first sent a boastful (?) message to Unug for Enmerkar. You cannot hold back (?) Enmerkar, you have to hold back (?) yourself. Calm down; your heart will prompt you to achieve nothing, as far as can be known (?).'

133–4 'If my city becomes a ruin mound, then I will be a potsherd of it, but I will never submit to the lord of Unug, the lord of Kulaba.'

135–49 A sorcerer whose skill was that of a man of Ḫamazu, Ur-g̃irnuna, whose skill was that of a man of Ḫamazu, who came over to Aratta after Ḫamazu had been destroyed, practised (?) sorcery in the inner chamber at the *g̃ipar* shrine. He said to minister Ansiga-ria: 'My lord, why is it that the great fathers of the city, the founders in earlier times (?), do not . . . , do not give advice. I will make Unug dig canals. I will make Unug submit to the shrine of Aratta. After the word of Unug . . . , I will make the territories from below to above, from the sea to the cedar mountain, from above to the mountain of the aromatic cedars, submit to my great army. Let Unug bring its own goods by boat, let it tie up boats as a transport flotilla towards the E-zagin of Aratta.'

150–2 The minister Ansiga-ria rose up in his city, he . . . . Ansiga-ria . . . , if only . . . .

153–62 'My lord, why is it that the great fathers of the city, the founders in earlier times (?), do not . . . , do not give advice. I will make Unug dig canals. I will make Unug submit to the shrine of Aratta. After the word of Unug . . . , I will make the territories from below to above, from the sea to the cedar mountain, from above to the mountain of the aromatic cedars, submit to my great army. Let Unug bring its own goods by boat, let it tie up boats as a transport flotilla towards the E-zagin of Aratta.'

163–9 This made the lord extremely happy, so he gave five minas° of gold to him, he gave five minas of silver to him. He promised him that he would be allotted fine food to eat, he promised him that he would be allotted fine drink to drink. 'When their men are taken captive, your life . . . happiness (?) in your hand (?) prosperity (?)', he promised to him.

170–5 The sorcerer, farmer of the best seeds, directed his steps towards Ereš, the city of Nisaba, and reached the cattle-pen, the house where the cows live. The cow trembled with fear at him in the cattle-pen. He made the cow speak so that it conversed with him as if it were a human being: 'Cow, who will eat your butter? Who will drink your milk?'

176–82 'My butter will be eaten by Nisaba, my milk will be drunk by Nisaba. My cheese, skilfully produced bright crown, was made fitting for the great dining hall, the dining hall of Nisaba. Until my butter is delivered from the holy cattle-pen, until my milk is delivered from the holy sheepfold, the steadfast wild cow Nisaba, the first-born of Enlil, will not impose any levy on the people.'

183 'Cow, your butter to your shining horn; your milk to your back.'

184 So the cow's butter was . . . to its shining horn; its milk was . . . to its back . . . .

185–8 He reached the holy sheepfold, the sheepfold of Nisaba. The goat trembled with fear at him in the sheepfold. He made the goat speak so that it conversed with him as if it were a human being: 'Goat, who will eat your butter? Who will drink your milk?'

189–95 'My butter will be eaten by Nisaba, my milk will be drunk by Nisaba. My cheese, skilfully produced bright crown, was made fitting for the great dining hall, the dining hall of Nisaba. Until my butter is delivered from the holy cattle-pen, until my milk is delivered from the holy sheepfold, the steadfast wild cow Nisaba, the first-born of Enlil, will not impose any levy on the people.'

196 'Goat, your butter to your shining horn, your milk to your back.'

197 So the goat's butter was . . . to its shining horn; its milk was made to depart to its back.

198–205 On that day the cattle-pen and the sheepfold were turned into a house of silence; they were dealt a disaster. There was no milk in the udder of the cow, the day darkened for the calf, its young calf was hungry and wept bitterly. There was no milk in the udder of the goat; the day darkened for the kid. The kid and its goat lay starving, its life . . . . The cow spoke bitterly to its calf; the goat . . . to its kid. The holy churn was empty, . . . was hungry, . . . lay starving.

206–21 On that day the cattle-pen and the sheepfold were turned into a house of silence; they were dealt a disaster. The cowherd dropped his

staff from his hand: he was shocked. The shepherd hung the crook at
his side and wept bitterly. The shepherd boy did not enter (?) the
sheepfold and cattle-pen, but took another way; the milk carrier did
not sing loudly, but took another road. The cowherd and shepherd
of Nisaba, sons born of the same mother, were brought up in the
cattle-pen and sheepfold. The name of the first one was Maš-gula,
the name of the second one was Ur-edina. At the great gate, facing
sunrise, the place marvelled at by the land, both of them crouched in
the debris and appealed to Utu for help: 'The sorcerer from Aratta
entered the cattle-pen. He made the milk scarce, so the young calves
could not get any. In the cattle-pen and the sheepfold he caused
distress; he made the butter and milk scarce.° He threw its . . . , . . .
was dealt a disaster.'

222–7   . . . approached. . . . caused damage (?) . . . . turned toward Ereš.
. . . the Euphrates . . . the river of the gods. She made her way to the
city whose destiny was decreed by An and Enlil . . . . Wise Woman
Saĝ-buru . . . hand . . . for him.

228–31 Both of them threw fish spawn (?) into the river. The sorcerer made
a giant carp come out° from the water. Wise Woman Saĝ-buru, however, made an eagle come out° from the water. The eagle seized the
giant carp and fled to the mountains.°

232–5   A second time they threw fish spawn (?) into the river. The sorcerer
made a ewe and its lamb come out° from the water. Wise
Woman Saĝ-buru, however, made a wolf come out° from the water.
The wolf seized the ewe and its lamb and dragged them to the wide
desert.

236–9   A third time they threw fish spawn (?) into the river. The sorcerer
made a cow and its calf come out° from the water. Wise Woman Saĝ-
buru, however, made a lion come out° from the water. The lion
seized the cow and its calf and took° them to the reedbeds.

240–3   A fourth time they threw fish spawn (?) into the river. The sorcerer
made an ibex and a wild sheep come out° from the water. Wise
Woman Saĝ-buru, however, made a mountain leopard come out°
from the water. The leopard seized the ibex and the wild sheep and
took them to the mountains.

244–8   A fifth time they threw fish spawn (?) into the river. The sorcerer
made a gazelle kid come out from the water. Wise Woman Saĝ-buru,
however, made a tiger and a . . . lion come out from the water. The
tiger and the . . . lion seized the gazelle kid and took° them to the

forest. What happened made the face of the sorcerer darken, made
his mind confused.

249–54 Wise Woman Saḡ-buru said to him: 'Sorcerer, you do have magical
powers, but where is your sense? How on earth could you think of
going to do sorcery at Ereš, which is the city of Nisaba, a city whose
destiny was decreed by An and Enlil, the primeval city, the beloved
city of Ninlil?'

FIG. 8. 'The lion seized the cow and its calf'—animal combat scene
on a stone plaque from Early Dynastic Nibru

255–63 The sorcerer answered her: 'I went there without knowing all about
this. I acknowledge your superiority—please do not be bitter.' He
pleaded, he prayed to her: 'Set me free, my sister; set me free. Let me
go in peace to my city. Let me return safely to Aratta, the mount of
the lustrous divine powers. I will make known° your greatness in all
the lands. I will sing your praise in Aratta, the mount of the lustrous
divine powers.'

264–73 Wise Woman Saḡ-buru answered him: 'You have caused distress in
the cattle-pen and the sheepfold; you have made the butter and milk
scarce there. You have removed the lunch-table, the morning- and
evening-table. You have cut off butter and milk from the evening
meal of the great dining hall, . . . distress . . . . Your sin that butter and
milk . . . cannot be forgiven. Nanna the king . . . the sheepfold . . .
milk; . . . established that it was a capital offence and I am not
pardoning your life.' Wise Woman Saḡ-buru . . . her decision about
the sorcerer in the assembly (?). She threw her prisoner from the

bank of the Euphrates. She seized from him his life-force and then returned to her city, Ereš.

274–80 Having heard this matter, En-suḫgir-ana sent a man to Enmerkar: 'You are the beloved lord of Inana, you alone are exalted. Inana has truly chosen you for her holy lap, you are her beloved. From the west to the east, you are the great lord, and I am only second to you; from the moment of conception I was not your equal, you are the older brother. I cannot match you ever.'

281–3 In the contest between Enmerkar and En-suḫgir-ana, Enmerkar proved superior to En-suḫgir-ana. Praise be to Nisaba!

Notes

1–5 After 'from the pristine mountain' 1 MS adds: 'of the shining plain'.

40–51 Instead of 'runs over' 1 MS has: 'cuts through'.

52 Instead of 'his holy *ĝipar* shrine' 1 MS has: 'in his most holy place'; then 1 MS adds the line: 'He entered the presence of Enmerkar in his most holy place.'

53–69 After ' "has sent me to you." ' some MSS add the lines: ' "What does your king have to tell me, what does he have to add to me? What does En-suḫgir-ana have to tell me, what does he have to add to me?" "This is what my king said, what he added, this is what En-suḫgir-ana said, what he added." '

77–113 15 *danna* is equivalent to about 160 kilometres. Instead of 'let me know' 1 MS has: 'told me'; instead of 'of the Land' some MSS have: 'of Sumer'.

163–9 Five minas is equivalent to about 2½ kilograms.

206–21 Instead of 'In the cattle-pen and the sheepfold he caused distress; he made the butter and milk scarce.' 1 MS has: '. . . diminished . . . , . . . he made the milk of the goat scarce.'

228–31 Instead of 'come out' 1 MS has: 'arise'. Instead of 'The eagle seized the giant carp and fled to the mountains' 1 MS has: 'The eagle seized the giant carp out of the waves and went up to the sky'.

232–5 Instead of 'come out' 1 MS has: 'arise'.

236–9 Instead of 'come out' 1 MS has: 'arise'; instead of 'took' some MSS have: 'dragged'.

240–3 Instead of 'come out' 1 MS has: 'arise'.

244–8 Instead of 'took' 1 MS has: 'dragged'.

255–63 Instead of 'make known' 1 MS has: 'declare'.

Lugalbanda in the mountain cave

This first Lugalbanda narrative divides into two sections, focusing initially on a military campaign being led against the legendary and remote city of

Aratta by Enmerkar, the king of Unug. It soon shifts mood to concentrate on an illness suffered by one of his commanders, Lugalbanda, whose holiness and purity are emphasized as distinctive throughout the poem.

However, before either protagonist makes his appearance, the poem places the events about to be narrated in an imagined time when the world was first created and Unug was the dominant city in Sumer. In those days, continues the poem, Enmerkar set off at the head of his troops to wage war on Aratta. Half-way there, however, and in the middle of the mountains, illness overcomes Lugalbanda and, in the words of the poem, 'his mouth bit the dust, like a gazelle caught in a snare'. Left alone in a cave by his companions, Lugalbanda waits in this mountainous wilderness, now envisaged as outside the natural constraints of place and time, to see whether the deities will bring him recovery or death.

A trilogy of prayers—first to the sun-god Utu as he is setting, next to the goddess Inana as manifested in the evening star, and finally to the moon-god Suen—brings Lugalbanda life rather than death and in gratitude he praises the rising sun. Restored to life, he remains alone and has to fend for himself, discovering skills in fire-making, cooking, and trapping animals. A dream comes to him during the next night, advising him to sacrifice the animals, and the next day the principal deities of the Sumerian pantheon enjoy the banquet that he has prepared for them. The events of the following night remain poorly understood but have been interpreted as representing some form of cosmic conflict, resolved by the fresh appearance of the sun-god on the next day. The conclusion of the narrative has so far not been recovered.

Translation

1–19 When in ancient days heaven was separated from earth, when in ancient days that which was fitting . . . , when after the ancient harvests . . . barley was eaten (?), when boundaries were laid out and borders were fixed, when boundary-stones were placed and inscribed with names, when dykes and canals were purified, when . . . wells were dug straight down; when the bed of the Euphrates, the plenteous river of Unug, was opened up, when . . . , when . . . , when holy An removed . . . , when the *en* priesthood and kingship were famously exercised at Unug, when the sceptre and staff of Kulaba were held high in battle—in battle, Inana's game; when the black-headed were blessed with long life, in their settled ways and in their . . . , when they presented the mountain goats with pounding hooves and the mountain stags beautiful with their antlers to Enmerkar son of Utu—

20–34 now at that time the king set his mace towards the city, Enmerkar the son of Utu prepared an . . . expedition against Aratta, the mountain of the holy divine powers. He was going to set off to destroy the rebel land; the lord began a mobilization of his city. The herald made the horn signal sound in all the lands. Now levied Unug took the field with the wise king, indeed levied Kulaba followed Enmerkar. Unug's levy was a flood, Kulaba's levy was a clouded sky. As they covered the ground like heavy fog, the dense dust whirled up by them reached up to heaven. As if to rooks on the best seed, rising up, he called to the people. Each one gave his fellow the sign.

35–46 Their king went at their head, to go at the . . . of the army. Enmerkar went at their head, to go at the . . . of the army. (2 *lines unclear*) . . . *gu-nida* emmer wheat to grow abundantly. When the righteous one who takes counsel with Enlil° took away the whole of Kulaba, like sheep they bent over at the slope of the mountains, . . . at the edge of the hills they ran forward like wild bulls. He sought . . . at the side— they recognized the way. He sought . . . .

47–58 Five days passed. On the sixth day they bathed. . . . on the seventh day they entered the mountains. When they had crossed over on the paths—an enormous flood billowing upstream into a lagoon . . . Their ruler°, riding on a storm, Utu's son, the good bright metal, stepped down from heaven to the great earth. His head shines with brilliance, the barbed arrows flash past him like lightning; the . . . of the bronze pointed axe of his emblem shines for him, it protrudes from the pointed axe for him prominently, like a dog eating a corpse.

59–70 At that time there were seven, there were seven—the young ones, born in Kulaba, were seven. The goddess Uraš had borne these seven, the Wild Cow had nourished them with milk. They were heroes, living in Sumer, they were princely in their prime. They had been brought up eating at the god An's table. These seven were the overseers for those that are subordinate to overseers, were the captains for those that are subordinate to captains, were the generals for those that are subordinate to generals. They were overseers of 300 men, 300 men each; they were captains of 600 men, 600 men each; they were generals of 25,200 soldiers, 25,200 soldiers each. They stood at the service of the lord as his elite troops.

71–86 Lugalbanda, the eighth of them, . . . was washed in water. In awed

silence he went forward, . . . he marched with the troops. When they
had covered half the way, covered half the way, a sickness befell him
there, 'head sickness' befell him. He jerked like a snake dragged by its
head with a reed; his mouth bit the dust, like a gazelle caught in a
snare. No longer could his hands return the hand grip, no longer
could he lift his feet high. Neither king nor contingents could help
him. In the great mountains, crowded together like a dustcloud over
the ground, they said: 'Let them bring him to Unug.' But they did
not know how they could bring him. 'Let them bring him to
Kulaba.' But they did not know how they could bring him. As his
teeth chattered (?) in the cold places of the mountains, they brought
him to a warm place there.

87–122   . . . a storehouse, they made him an arbour like a bird's nest. . . . dates,
figs and various sorts of cheese; they put sweetmeats suitable for the
sick to eat, in baskets of dates, and they made him a home. They set
out for him the various fats of the cattle-pen, the sheepfold's fresh
cheese, oil with cold eggs, cold hard-boiled eggs, as if laying a table
for the holy place, the valued place°. Directly in front of the table
they arranged for him beer for drinking, mixed with date syrup and
rolls . . . with butter. Provisions poured into leather buckets, provisions all put into leather bags—his brothers and friends, like a boat
unloading from the harvest-place, placed stores by his head in the
mountain cave. They . . . water in their leather waterskins. Dark
beer, alcoholic drink, light emmer beer, wine for drinking which is
pleasant to the taste, they distributed by his head in the mountain
cave as on a stand for waterskins. They prepared for him incense
resin, . . . resin, aromatic resin, *ligidba* resin and first-class resin on
pot-stands in the deep hole; they suspended them by his head in the
mountain cave. They pushed into place at his head his axe whose
metal was tin, imported from the Zubi mountains. They wrapped
up by his chest his dagger of iron imported from the Black
Mountains. His eyes—irrigation ditches, because they are flooding
with water—holy Lugalbanda kept open, directed towards this. The
outer door of his lips—overflowing like holy Utu—he did not
open to his brothers. When they lifted his neck, there was no breath
there any longer. His brothers, his friends took counsel with one
another:

123–7   'If our brother rises like Utu from bed, then the god who has smitten
him will step aside and, when he eats this food, when he drinks (?)

this, will make his feet stable. May he bring him over the high places of the mountains to brick-built Kulaba.

128–32 'But if Utu calls our brother to the holy place, the valued place°, the health of his limbs will leave (?) him. Then it will be up to us, when we come back from Aratta, to bring our brother's body to brick-built Kulaba.'

133–40 Like the dispersed holy cows of Nanna, as with a breeding bull when, in his old age, they have left him behind in the cattle-pen, his brothers and friends abandoned holy Lugalbanda in the mountain cave; and with repeated tears and moaning, with tears, with lamentation, with grief and weeping, Lugalbanda's older brothers set off into the mountains.

141–7 Then two days passed during which Lugalbanda was ill; to these two days, half a day was added. As Utu turned his glance towards his home, as the animals lifted their heads toward their lairs, at the day's end in the evening cool, his body was as if anointed with oil. But he was not yet free of his sickness.

148–50 When he lifted his eyes to heaven to Utu, he wept to him as if to his own father. In the mountain cave he raised to him his fair hands:

151–70 'Utu, I greet you! Let me be ill no longer! Hero, Ningal's son, I greet you! Let me be ill no longer! Utu, you have let me come up into the mountains in the company of my brothers. In the mountain cave, the most dreadful spot on earth, let me be ill no longer! Here where there is no mother, there is no father, there is no acquaintance, no one whom I value, my mother is not here to say "Alas, my child!" My brother is not here to say "Alas, my brother!" My mother's neighbour who enters our house is not here to weep over me. If the male and female protective deities were standing by, the deity of neighbourliness would say, "A man should not perish". A lost dog is bad; a lost man is terrible.° On the unknown way at the edge of the mountains, Utu, is a lost man, a man in an even more terrible situation. Don't make me flow away like water in a violent death! Don't make me eat saltpetre as if it were barley! Don't make me fall like a throwstick somewhere in the desert unknown to me! Afflicted with a name which excites my brothers' scorn, let me be ill no longer! Afflicted with the derision of my comrades, let me be ill no longer! Let me not come to an end in the mountains like a weakling!'

171–2 Utu accepted his tears. He sent down his divine encouragement to him in the mountain cave.

173–82 She who makes . . . for the poor, whose game° is sweet, the prostitute who goes out to the inn, who makes the bedchamber delightful, who is food to the poor man—Inana°, the daughter of Suen, arose before him like a bull in the Land. Her brilliance, like that of holy Šara, her stellar brightness illuminated for him the mountain cave. When he lifted his eyes upwards to Inana, he wept as if before his own father. In the mountain cave he raised to her his fair hands:

183–96 'Inana, if only this were my home, if only this were my city! If only this were Kulaba, the city in which my mother bore me . . . ! Even if it were to me as the waste land to a snake! If it were to me as a crack in the ground to a scorpion! My mighty people . . . ! My great ladies . . . ! . . . to E-ana! (2 lines unclear) The little stones of it, the shining stones in their glory, saĝkal stones above, . . . below, from its crying out in the mountain land Zabu, from its voice . . . open—may my limbs not perish in the mountains of the cypresses!'

197–200 Inana accepted his tears. With power of life she let him go to sleep just like the sleeping Utu. Inana enveloped him with heart's joy as if with a woollen garment. Then, just as if . . . , she went to brick-built Kulaba.

201–14 The bull that eats up the black soup, the astral holy bull-calf°, came to watch over him. He shines (?) in the heavens like the morning star, he spreads bright light in the night. Suen, who is greeted as the new moon, Father Nanna, gives the direction for the rising Utu. The glorious lord whom the crown befits, Suen, the beloved son of Enlil, the god° reached the zenith splendidly. His brilliance like holy Šara°, his starry radiance illuminated for him the mountain cave. When Lugalbanda raised his eyes to heaven to Suen, he wept to him as if to his own father. In the mountain cave he raised to him his fair hands:

215–25 'King whom one cannot reach in the distant sky! Suen, whom one cannot reach in the distant sky! King who loves justice, who hates evil! Suen, who loves justice, who hates evil! Justice brings joy justly to your heart. A poplar, a great staff, forms a sceptre for you, you who loosen the bonds of justice, who do not loosen the bonds of evil. If you encounter evil before you, it is dragged away behind . . . . When your heart becomes angry, you spit your venom at evil like a snake which drools poison.'

226–7 Suen accepted his tears and gave him life. He conferred on his feet the power to stand.

228–39 A second time°, as the bright bull rising up from the horizon, the bull resting among the cypresses, a shield standing on the ground, watched by the assembly, a shield coming out from the treasury, watched by the young men—the youth Utu extended his holy, shining rays down from heaven°, he bestowed them on holy Lugalbanda in the mountain cave. His good protective god hovered ahead of him, his good protective goddess walked behind him. The god which had smitten him stepped aside°. When he raised his eyes heavenward to Utu, he wept to him as to his own father. In the mountain cave he raised to him his fair hands:

240–63 'Utu, shepherd of the land, father of the black-headed, when you go to sleep, the people go to sleep with you; youth Utu, when you rise, the people rise with you. Utu, without you no net is stretched out for a bird, no slave is taken away captive. To him who walks alone, you are his brotherly companion; Utu, you are the third of them who travel in pairs. You are the blinkers for him who wears the neck-ring. Like a holy *zulumhi* garment, your sunshine clothes the poor man and the scoundrel as well as him who has no clothes; as a garment of white wool it covers the bodies even of debt slaves. Like rich old men, the old women praise your sunshine sweetly, until their oldest days.° Your sunshine is as mighty as oil. Great wild bulls run forward, (*1 line unclear*) Hero, son of Ningal, . . . to you. (*2 lines unclear*) Brother . . . his brother. He causes his plough to stand in the . . . . Praise to you is so very sweet, it reaches up to heaven. Hero, son of Ningal, they laud you as you deserve.'

264–75 Holy Lugalbanda came out from the mountain cave. Then the righteous one who takes counsel with Enlil° caused life-saving plants to be born. The rolling rivers, mothers of the hills, brought lifesaving water. He bit on the life-saving plants, he sipped from the lifesaving water. After biting on the life-saving plants, after sipping from the life-saving water, here on his own he set a trap (?) in the ground, and from that spot he sped away like a horse of the mountains. Like a lone wild ass of Šakkan he darted over the mountains. Like a large powerful donkey he raced; a slim donkey, eager to run, he bounded along.

276–99 That night, in the evening, he set off, hurrying through the mountains, a waste land in the moonlight. He was alone and, even to his sharp eyes, there was not a single person to be seen. With the provisions stocked in leather pails, provisions put in leather bags, his brothers and his friends had been able to bake bread on the ground, with some cold water. Holy Lugalbanda had carried the things from the mountain cave. He set them beside the embers. He filled a bucket . . . with water. In front of him he split what he had placed. He took hold of the . . . stones. Repeatedly he struck them together. He laid the glowing (?) coals on the open ground. The fine flintstone caused a spark. Its fire shone out for him over the waste land like the sun. Not knowing how to bake bread or a cake, not knowing an oven, with just seven coals he baked *giziešta* dough. While the bread was baking by itself, he pulled up *šulḫi* reeds of the mountains, roots and all, and stripped their branches. He packed up all the cakes as a day's ration. Not knowing how to bake bread or a cake, not knowing an oven, with just seven coals he had baked *giziešta* dough. He garnished it with sweet date syrup.

300–13 A brown wild bull, a fine-looking wild bull, a wild bull tossing its horns, a wild bull in hunger (?), resting, seeking with its voice the brown wild bulls of the hills, the pure place—in this way it was chewing aromatic *šimgig* as if it were barley, it was grinding up the wood of the cypress as if it were esparto grass, it was sniffing with its nose at the foliage of the *šenu* shrub as if it were grass. It was drinking the water of the rolling rivers, it was belching from *ilinnuš*, the pure plant of the mountains. While the brown wild bulls, the wild bulls of the mountains, were browsing about among the plants, Lugalbanda captured this one in his ambush (?). He uprooted a juniper tree of the mountains and stripped its branches. With a knife holy Lugalbanda trimmed its roots, which were like the long rushes of the field. He tethered the brown wild bull, the wild bull of the mountains, to it with a halter.

314–25 A brown goat and a nanny-goat—flea-bitten goats, lousy goats, goats covered in sores—in this way they were chewing aromatic *šimgig* as if it were barley, they were grinding up the wood of the cypress as if it were esparto grass, they were sniffing with their noses at the foliage of the *šenu* shrub as if it were grass. They were drinking the water of the rolling rivers, they were belching from *ilinnuš*, the pure plant of the mountains. While the brown goats and the nanny-goats were browsing about among the plants, Lugalbanda captured these two in his ambush (?). He uprooted a juniper tree of the mountains and stripped its branches. With a knife holy Lugalbanda cut off its roots, which were like the long rushes of the field. With chains he fettered the brown goat and the nanny-goat, both the goats.°

326–50 He was alone and, even to his sharp eyes, there was not a single person to be seen. Sleep overcame the king°—sleep, the country of oppression; it is like a towering flood, a hand like a brick wall knocked over, whose hand is elevated, whose foot is elevated; covering like syrup that which is in front of it, overflowing like syrup onto that which is in front of it; it knows no overseer, knows no captain, yet it is overpowering for the hero. And by means of Ninkasi's wooden cask°, sleep finally overcame Lugalbanda. He laid down *ilinnuš*, pure herb of the mountains, as a couch, he spread out a *zulumḫi* garment, he unfolded there a white linen sheet. There being no . . . room for bathing, he made do with that place. The king lay down not to sleep, he lay down to dream—not turning back at the door of the dream, not turning back at the door-pivot. To the liar it talks in lies, to the truthful it speaks truth. It can make one man happy, it can make another man sing, but it is the closed tablet-basket of the gods. It is the beautiful bedchamber of Ninlil, it is the counsellor of Inana. The multiplier of mankind, the voice of one not alive—Zangara, the god of dreams, himself like a bull, bellowed at Lugalbanda. Like the calf of a cow he lowed:

351–60 'Who will slaughter (?) a brown wild bull for me? Who will make its fat melt for me? He shall take my axe whose metal is tin, he shall wield my dagger which is of iron. Like an athlete I shall let him bring away the brown wild bull, the wild bull of the mountains, I shall let him like a wrestler make it submit. Its strength will leave it. When he offers it before the rising sun, let him heap up like barleycorns the heads of the brown goat and the nanny-goat, both the goats; when he has poured out their blood in the pit—let their smell waft out in the desert so that the alert snakes of the mountains will sniff it.'

361–70 Lugalbanda awoke—it was a dream. He shivered—it was sleep. He rubbed his eyes, he was overawed. He took his axe whose metal was tin, he wielded his dagger which was of iron. Like an athlete he brought away the brown wild bull, the wild bull of the mountains, like a wrestler he made it submit. Its strength left it. He offered it before the rising sun. He heaped up like barleycorns the heads of the brown goat and the nanny-goat, both of the goats. He poured out their blood in the pit so that their smell wafted out in the desert. The alert snakes of the mountains sniffed it.

371–93 As the sun was rising . . . , Lugalbanda, invoking the name of Enlil, made An, Enlil, Enki, and Ninḫursaĝa sit down to a banquet at the pit, at the place in the mountains which he had prepared. The banquet was set, the libations were poured—dark beer, alcoholic drink, light emmer beer, wine for drinking which is pleasant to the taste. Over the plain he poured cool water as a libation. He put the knife to the flesh of the brown goats, and he roasted the dark livers there. He let their smoke rise there, like incense put on the fire. As if Dumuzid had brought in the good savours of the cattle-pen, so An, Enlil, Enki, and Ninḫursaĝa consumed the best part of the food prepared by Lugalbanda. Like the shining place of pure strength, the holy altar of Suen, ... On top of the altar of Utu and the altar of Suen . . . , he decorated the two altars with the lapis lazuli . . . of Inana. Suen . . . . He bathed the *ankar* weapon. When he had bathed the . . . , he set out all the cakes properly.

394–432 They° make . . . Enki, father of the gods; they are . . . , they . . . ; like a string of figs dripping with lusciousness, they hang their arms. They are gazelles of Suen running in flight, they are the fine smooth cloths of Ninlil, they are the helpers of Iškur; they pile up flax, they pile up barley; they are wild animals on the rampage, they descend like a storm on a rebel land hated by Suen, indeed they descend like a storm. They lie up during all the long day, and during the short night they enter . . . houses (?); during the long day, during the short night they lie in beds . . . , they give . . . . At dead of night they sing out . . . , in the breeze . . . swallows of Utu; they enter into house after house, they peer into street after street, they are talkers, they are repliers to talkers, seeking words with a mother, replying to a great lady; they nestle at the bedside, they smite . . . , when the black . . . are stolen, they leave . . . the doors and tables of humans, they change . . . , they tie the door-pivots together. The hero who . . . , Utu who . . . , the heroic youth Utu of the good word (*2 lines unclear*) the incantation . . . of the youth Utu, which the Anuna, the great gods, do not know, from that time . . . , (*3 lines unclear*)

433–61 The wise elders of the city . . . (*1 line unclear*) the incantation . . . of the youth Utu, which the Anuna, the great gods, do not know, (*5 lines unclear*) they are able to enter the presence of Utu, of Enlil, god of the . . . , the bearded son of Ningal . . . ; they give to Suen . . . , they confirm with their power the fate of the foreign lands. At dead of night they know the black wild boar, at midday to Utu . . . he can . . . his incantation, (*3 lines unclear*). They enter before An, Enlil, . . . , Inana, the gods; they know . . . , they watch . . . , they . . . at the

window; the door . . . , the pot-stand . . . ; (*4 lines unclear*) they stand
. . . (*1 line unclear*)

462–84 They pursue . . . Inana . . . , who are favoured by Inana's heart, who
stand in the battle, they are the fourteen torches of battle . . . , at midnight they . . . , at dead of night they pursue like wildfire, in a band
they flash together like lightning, in the urgent storm of battle,
which roars loudly like a great flood rising up; they who are favoured
in Inana's heart, who stand in the battle, they are the seven torches of
battle . . . ; they stand joyfully as she wears the crown under a clear
sky, with their foreheads and eyes they are a clear evening. Their ears
. . . a boat, with their mouths they are wild boars resting in a reed
thicket; they stand in the thick of battle, with their life-force they
. . . , (*1 line unclear*) who are favoured in Inana's heart, who stand in
the battle, by Nintud of heaven they are numerous, by the life of
heaven they hold . . . ; the holy shining battle-mace reaches to the
edge of heaven and earth, . . . reaches. (*1 line unclear*)

485–99 As Utu comes forth from his chamber, the holy battle-mace of An
. . . , the just god who lies alongside a man; they are wicked gods with
evil hearts, they are . . . gods. It is they, like Nanna, like Utu, like
Inana of the fifty divine powers, . . . in heaven and earth . . . ; they are
the interpreters of spoken evil, the spies of righteousness, (*2 lines
unclear*) . . . a clear sky and numerous stars, (*1 line unclear*) . . . fresh
cedars in the mountains of the cypress, . . . a battle-net from the
horizon to the zenith, (*unknown number of lines missing*)

Notes

35–46 'the righteous one who takes counsel with Enlil' refers to Enmerkar.

47–58 'Their ruler' refers to Enmerkar.

87–122 'as if laying a table for the holy place, the valued place': that is, as if for a
funerary offering.

128–32 'the holy place, the valued place' refers to the hereafter.

151–70 'A lost dog is bad; a lost man is terrible.': see *The instructions of Šuruppag*
(Group I), lines 266–71.

173–82 'game': that is, battle; 'Inana': here as Venus, the evening star.

201–14 'the astral holy bull-calf' refers to the moon; instead of 'the god' 1 MS has: 'the
lord'; instead of 'holy Šara' 1 MS has: 'holy Utu' and 1 MS has: 'lapis lazuli'.

228–39 'A second time': that is, at the following sunrise. After 'down from heaven'
1 MS from Urim adds: '. . . holy, his brilliance illuminated for him the
mountain cave'. Instead of 'stepped aside' 1 MS has: 'went out from him' and
1 MS has: 'went up and away from him'.

240–63 'Like rich old men, the old women praise your sunshine sweetly, until their oldest days.' alludes to a proverb.

264–75 'Then the righteous one who takes counsel with Enlil' may refer to Utu.

314–25 After 'both the goats.' 1 MS adds: '. . . , he piled up . . . .'

326–50 'the king' refers to Lugalbanda; 'by means of Ninkasi's wooden cask': that is, with the help of beer (see *A hymn to Ninkasi*, Group I).

394–432 Description of the demons.

Lugalbanda and the Anzud bird

This second Lugalbanda narrative reverses the structure of the first, beginning with its hero still stranded in the mountains and ending with him reunited first with his king, Enmerkar, and then with his city, Unug. In addition, it introduces another actor to the drama, the monstrous and terrifying Anzud bird, the divinely appointed guardian of this mountainous region who plays the role of helper to Lugalbanda, providing him with the gift of speed that is essential to the second part of the narrative.

Alone in the mountains, Lugalbanda resolves to befriend Anzud by lavishing attention on his fledgeling and turning his nest into a palatial residence. Lugalbanda's plan is successful and in return Anzud offers him various kinds of worldly success. What he requests instead as his destiny is miraculous speed. His wish granted, the bird in the sky and the hero below set off to find Enmerkar's troops, and in doing so leave behind the liminal landscape of the mountains. Advising Lugalbanda not to reveal his newly granted power, Anzud departs and Lugalbanda rejoins the troops with startling suddenness, offering less than full answers to the questions with which he is greeted.

The military narrative now resumes, describing the siege of Aratta as unsuccessful and Enmerkar as despondent. The king needs a messenger to return to Unug and seek support from its patron deity Inana whom he fears is abandoning him. Lugalbanda volunteers, provided that he is allowed to go alone and thus keep his mysterious power secret. After a miraculously swift journey he reaches Unug and delivers Enmerkar's passionate plea to Inana. Her reply promises Enmerkar victory but only if he can capture a certain fish which will serve to restore the strength of his army. But while it is Enmerkar who is promised success, and access to the wealth of Aratta, it is holy Lugalbanda who is praised in the final line of the poem.

Translation

1–27 Lugalbanda lies idle in the mountains, in the faraway places; he has ventured into the Zabu mountains. No mother is with him to offer advice, no father is with him to talk to him. No one is with him whom he knows, whom he values, no confidant is there to talk to him. In his heart he speaks to himself: 'I shall treat the bird as befits him, I shall treat Anzud as befits him. I shall greet his wife affectionately. I shall seat Anzud's wife and Anzud's child at a banquet. An will fetch Ninguenaka for me from her mountain home—the expert woman, who redounds to her mother's credit, Ninkasi the expert, who redounds to her mother's credit: her fermenting-vat is of green lapis lazuli, her beer cask is of refined silver and of gold; if she stands by the beer, there is joy, if she sits by the beer, there is gladness; as cupbearer she mixes the beer, never wearying as she walks back and forth, Ninkasi, the keg at her side, on her hips; may she make my beer-serving perfect. When the bird has drunk the beer and is happy, when Anzud has drunk the beer and is happy, he can help me find the place to which the troops of Unug are going, Anzud can put me on the track of my brothers.'

28–49 Now the splendid 'eagle'-tree of Enki on the summit of Inana's mountain of multicoloured cornelian stood fast on the earth like a tower, all shaggy like an *aru*. With its shade it covered the highest eminences of the mountains like a cloak, was spread out over them like a tunic. Its roots rested like *saĝkal* snakes in Utu's river of the seven mouths. Near by, in the mountains where no cypresses grow, where no snake slithers, where no scorpion scurries, in the midst of the mountains the *buru-az* bird had put its nest and laid its eggs inside; near by the Anzud bird had set his nest and settled his young inside. It was made with wood from the juniper and the box trees. The bird had made the bright twigs into a bower. When at daybreak the bird stretches himself, when at sunrise Anzud cries out, at his cry the ground quakes in the Lulubi mountains. He has a shark's teeth and an eagle's claws. In terror of him wild bulls run away into the foothills, stags run away into their mountains.

50–89 Lugalbanda is wise and he achieves mighty exploits. In preparation of the sweet celestial cakes he added carefulness to carefulness. He kneaded the dough with honey, he added more honey to it. He set them before the young nestling, before the Anzud chick, gave the baby salt meat to eat. He fed it sheep's fat. He popped the cakes into its beak. He settled the Anzud chick in its nest, painted its eyes with kohl, dabbed white cedar scent onto its head, put up a twisted roll of salt meat. He withdrew from Anzud's nest, awaited him in the mountains where no cypresses grow. At that time the bird was herding together wild bulls of the mountains, Anzud was herding together wild bulls of the mountains. He held a live bull in his talons, he carried a dead bull across his shoulders. He poured forth his bile like ten *gur*° of water. The bird flew around once, Anzud flew around once. When the bird called back to his nest, when Anzud called back to his nest, his fledgeling did not answer him from its nest. When the bird called a second time to his nest, his fledgeling did not answer from its nest. Before, if the bird called back to his nest, his fledgeling would answer from its nest; but now when the bird called back to his nest, his fledgeling did not answer him from its nest. The bird uttered a cry of grief that reached up to heaven, his wife cried out 'Woe!' Her cry reached the Abzu. The bird with this cry of 'Woe!' and his wife with this cry of grief made the Anuna, gods of the mountains, actually crawl into crevices like ants. The bird says to his wife, Anzud says to his wife: 'Foreboding weighs upon my nest, as over the great cattle-pen of Nanna. Terror lies upon it, as when wild bulls start butting each other. Who has taken my child from its nest? Who has taken the Anzud chick from its nest?'

90–110   But it seemed to the bird, when he approached his nest, it seemed to Anzud, when he approached his nest, that it had been made like a god's dwelling-place. It was brilliantly festooned. His chick was settled in its nest, its eyes were painted with kohl, sprigs of white cedar were fixed on its head. A twisted piece of salt meat was hung up high. The bird is exultant, Anzud is exultant: 'I am the prince who decides the destiny of rolling rivers. I keep on the straight and narrow path the righteous who follow Enlil's counsel. My father Enlil brought me here. He let me bar the entrance to the mountains as if with a great door. If I fix a fate, who shall alter it? If I but say the word, who shall change it? Whoever has done this to my nest, if you are a god, I will speak with you, indeed I will befriend you. If you are a man, I will fix your fate. I shall not let you have any opponents in the mountains. You shall be "Hero-fortified-by-Anzud".'

FIG. 9. 'Bird with sparkling eyes'—Anzud depicted
on an Early Dynastic mace-head

111–31 Lugalbanda, partly from fright, partly from delight, partly from
fright, partly from deep delight, flatters the bird, flatters Anzud:
'Bird with sparkling eyes, born in this district, Anzud with sparkling
eyes, born in this district, you frolic as you bathe in a pool. Your
grandfather, the prince of all patrimonies, placed heaven in your
hand, set earth at your feet. Your wingspan extended is like a bird-net
stretched out across the sky! . . . on the ground your talons are like a
trap laid for the wild bulls and wild cows of the mountains! Your
spine is as straight as a scribe's! Your breast as you fly is like Niraḫ
parting the waters! As for your back, you are a verdant palm garden,
breathtaking to look upon. Yesterday I escaped safely to you, since
then I have entrusted myself to your protection. Your wife shall be
my mother. You shall be my father. I shall treat your little ones as my
brothers. Since yesterday I have been waiting for you in the mountains where no cypresses grow. Let your wife stand beside you to
greet me. I offer my greeting and leave you to decide my destiny.'

132–41 The bird presents himself before him, rejoices over him, Anzud
presents himself before him, rejoices over him. Anzud says to holy
Lugalbanda: 'Come now, my Lugalbanda. Go like a boat full of
precious metals, like a grain barge, like a boat going to deliver apples,
like a boat piled up high with a cargo of cucumbers, casting a shade,
like a boat loaded lavishly at the place of harvest, go back to brick-
built Kulaba with head held high!'—Lugalbanda who loves the seed
will not accept this.

142–8 'Like Šara, Inana's beloved son, shoot forth with your barbed arrows
like a sunbeam, shoot forth with reed arrows like moonlight! May

the barbed arrows be a horned viper to those they hit! Like a fish killed with the cleaver, may they be magic-cut! May you bundle them up like logs hewn with the axe!'—Lugalbanda who loves the seed will not accept this.

149–54 'May Ninurta, Enlil's son, set the helmet Lion of Battle on your head, may the breastplate (?) that in the great mountains does not permit retreat be laid on your breast! May you . . . the battle-net against the enemy! When you go to the city, . . . !'—Lugalbanda who loves the seed will not accept this.

155–9 'The plenty of Dumuzid's holy butter churn, whose fat is the fat of all the world, shall be granted (?) to you. Its milk is the milk of all the world. It shall be granted (?) to you.'—Lugalbanda who loves the seed will not accept this. As a *kib* bird, a freshwater *kib*, as it flies along a lagoon, he answered him in words.

160–6 The bird listened to him. Anzud said to holy Lugalbanda: 'Now look, my Lugalbanda, just think again. It's like this: a wilful plough-ox should be put back in the track, a balking ass should be made to take the straight path. Still, I shall grant you what you put to me. I shall assign you a destiny according to your wishes.'

167–83 Holy Lugalbanda answers him: 'Let the power of running be in my thighs, let me not grow tired! Let there be strength in my arms, let me stretch my arms wide, let my arms not become weak! Moving like the sunlight, like Inana, like the seven storms, those of Iškur, let me leap like a flame, blaze like lightning! Let me go wherever I look to, set foot wherever I cast my glance, reach wherever my heart desires and let me loosen my shoes in whatever place my heart has named to me! When Utu lets me reach Kulaba my city, let him who curses me have no joy in it; let him who wishes to strive with me not say "Just let him come!" I shall have the woodcarvers fashion statues of you, and you will be breathtaking to look upon. Your name will be made famous in Sumer and will redound to the credit of the temples of the great gods.'

184–202 So Anzud says to holy Lugalbanda: 'The power of running shall be in your thighs! You shall not grow tired! Strength shall be in your arms! Stretch your arms wide, may your arms not become weak! Moving like the sun, like Inana, like the seven storms of Iškur, leap like a flame, blaze like lightning! Go wherever you look to, set foot wherever you cast your glance, reach wherever your heart desires, loosen your shoes in whatever place your heart has named to you!

When Utu lets you reach Kulaba your city, he who curses you shall
have no joy in it; he who wishes to strive with you shall not say "Just
let him come!" When you have had the woodcarvers fashion statues
of me, I shall be breathtaking to look upon. My name will be made
famous in Sumer and will redound to the credit of the temples of the
great gods. May . . . shake for you . . . like a sandal. . . . the Euphrates
. . . your feet . . . .'

203–19 He took in his hand such of his provisions as he had not eaten, and
his weapons one by one. Anzud flew on high, Lugalbanda walked on
the ground. The bird, looking from above, spies the troops. Lugalbanda, looking from below, spies the dust that the troops have
stirred up. The bird says to Lugalbanda: 'Come now, my Lugalbanda. I shall give you some advice: may my advice be heeded. I shall
say words to you: bear them in mind. What I have told you, the fate
I have fixed for you, do not tell it to your comrades, do not explain it
to your brothers. Fair fortune may conceal foul: it is indeed so. Leave
me to my nest: you keep to your troops.' The bird hurried to his nest.
Lugalbanda set out for the place where his brothers were.

220–32 Like a pelican emerging from the sacred reed-bed, like *laḫama* deities
going up from the Abzu, like one who is stepping from heaven to
earth, Lugalbanda stepped into the midst of his brothers' picked
troops. His brothers chattered away, the troops chattered away. His
brothers, his friends weary him with questions: 'Come now, my
Lugalbanda, here you are again! The troops had abandoned you as
one killed in battle. Certainly, you were not eating the good fat of the
herd! Certainly, you were not eating the sheepfold's fresh cheese.
How is it that you have come back from the great mountains, where
no one goes alone, from where no one returns to mankind?'

233–7 Again his brothers, his friends weary him with questions: 'The banks
of the mountain rivers, mothers of plenty, are widely separated. How
did you cross their waters?—as if you were drinking them?'

238–43 Holy Lugalbanda replies to them: 'The banks of the mountain rivers,
mothers of plenty, are widely separated. With my legs I stepped over
them, I drank them like water from a waterskin; and then I snarled
like a wolf, I grazed the water-meadows, I pecked at the ground like
a wild pigeon, I ate the mountain acorns.'

244–50 Lugalbanda's brothers and friends consider the words that he has
said to them. Exactly as if they were small birds flocking together all
day long they embrace him and kiss him. As if he were a *gamgam*

chick sitting in its nest, they feed him and give him drink. They drive away sickness from holy Lugalbanda.

251–83 Then the men of Unug followed them as one man; they wound their way through the hills like a snake over a grain-pile. When the city was only a *danna*° distant, the armies of Unug and Kulaba encamped by the posts and ditches that surrounded Aratta. From the city it rained down javelins as if from the clouds, slingstones numerous as the raindrops falling in a whole year whizzed down loudly from Aratta's walls. The days passed, the months became long, the year turned full circle. A yellow harvest grew beneath the sky. They looked askance at the fields. Unease came over them. Slingstones numerous as the raindrops falling in a whole year landed on the road. They were hemmed in by the barrier of mountain thornbushes thronged with dragons. No one knew how to go back to the city, no one was rushing to go back to Kulaba. In their midst Enmerkar son of Utu was afraid, was troubled, was disturbed by this upset. He sought someone whom he could send back to the city, he sought someone whom he could send back to Kulaba. No one said to him 'I will go to the city'. No one said to him 'I will go to Kulaba'. He went out to the foreign legion. No one said to him 'I will go to the city'. No one said to him 'I will go to Kulaba'. He stood before the elite troops. No one said to him 'I will go to the city'. No one said to him 'I will go to Kulaba'. A second time he went out to the foreign legion. No one said to him 'I will go to the city'. No one said to him 'I will go to Kulaba'. He stepped out before the elite troops.

284–6 Lugalbanda alone arose from the people and said to him: 'My king, I will go to the city, but no one shall go with me. I will go alone to Kulaba. No one shall go with me.'

287–9 'If you go to the city, no one shall go with you. You shall go alone to Kulaba, no one shall go with you.' He swore by heaven and by earth: 'Swear that you will not let go from your hands the great emblems of Kulaba.'

290–321 After he had stood before the summoned assembly, within the palace that rests on earth like a great mountain Enmerkar son of Utu berated Inana: 'Once upon a time my princely sister holy Inana summoned me in her holy heart from the bright mountains, had me enter brick-built Kulaba. Where there was a marsh then in Unug, it was full of water. Where there was any dry land, Euphrates poplars grew there. Where there were reed-thickets, old reeds and young reeds grew there. Divine Enki who is king in Eridug tore up for me the old reeds, drained off the water completely. For fifty years I built, for fifty years I gave judgments. Then the Mardu peoples, who know no agriculture, arose in all Sumer and Akkad. But the wall of Unug extended out across the desert like a bird-net. Yet now, here in this place, my attractiveness to her has dwindled. My troops are bound to me as a cow is bound to its calf; but like a son who, hating his mother, leaves his city, my princely sister holy Inana has run away from me back to brick-built Kulaba. If she loves her city and hates me, why does she bind the city to me? If she hates the city and yet loves me, why does she bind me to the city? If the mistress removes herself from me to her holy chamber, and abandons me like an Anzud chick, then may she at least bring me home to brick-built Kulaba: on that day my spear shall be laid aside. On that day she may shatter my shield. Speak this to my princely sister, holy Inana.'

322–6 Then holy Lugalbanda came forth from the palace. Although his brothers and his comrades barked at him as at a foreign dog trying to join a pack of dogs, he stepped proudly forward like a foreign wild ass trying to join a herd of wild asses. 'Send someone else to Unug for the lord.'

327–8 'For Enmerkar son of Utu I shall go alone to Kulaba. No one shall go with me.' How he spoke to them!

329–36 'Why will you go alone and keep company with no one on the journey? If our beneficent spirit does not stand by you there, if our good protective deity does not go with you there, you will never again stand with us where we stand, you will never again dwell with us where we dwell, you will never again set your feet on the ground where our feet are. You will not come back from the great mountains, where no one goes alone, whence no one returns to mankind!'

337 'Time is passing, I know. None of you is going with me over the great earth.'

338–44 While the hearts of his brothers beat loudly, while the hearts of his comrades sank, Lugalbanda took in his hand such of his provisions as he had not eaten, and each of his weapons one by one. From the foot of the mountains, through the high mountains, into the flat land, from the edge of Anšan to the top of Anšan, he crossed five, six, seven mountains.

345–56 By midnight, but before they had brought the offering-table to holy Inana, he set foot joyfully in brick-built Kulaba. His lady, holy

Inana, sat there on her cushion. He bowed and prostrated himself on the ground. With° eyes Inana looked at holy Lugalbanda as she would look at the shepherd Ama-ušumgal-ana. In a° voice, Inana spoke to holy Lugalbanda as she would speak to her son Lord Šara: 'Come now, my Lugalbanda, why do you bring news from the city? How have you come here alone from Aratta?'

357–87   Holy Lugalbanda answered her: 'What Enmerkar son of Utu declares and what he says, what your brother declares and what he says, is: "Once upon a time my princely sister holy Inana summoned me in her holy heart from the mountains, had me enter brick-built Kulaba. Where there was a marsh then in Unug, it was full of water. Where there was any dry land, Euphrates poplars grew there. Where there were reed-thickets, old reeds and young reeds grew there. Divine Enki who is king in Eridug tore up for me the old reeds, drained off the water completely. For fifty years I built, for fifty years I gave judgments. Then the Mardu peoples, who know no agriculture, arose in all Sumer and Akkad. But the wall of Unug extended out across the desert like a bird-net. Yet now, here in this place, my attractiveness to her has dwindled. My troops are bound to me as a cow is bound to its calf; but like a son who, hating his mother, leaves his city, my princely sister holy Inana has run away from me back to brick-built Kulaba. If she loves her city and hates me, why does she bind the city to me? If she hates the city and yet loves me, why does she bind me to the city? If the mistress removes herself from me to her holy chamber and abandons me like an Anzud chick, then may she at least bring me home to brick-built Kulaba: on that day my spear shall be laid aside. On that day she may shatter my shield. Speak this to my princely sister, holy Inana."'

388–98   Holy Inana uttered this response: 'Now, at the end, on the banks, in the water-meadows, of a clear river, of a river of clear water, of the river which is Inana's gleaming waterskin, the *suḫurmaš* carp eats the honey-herb; the *kigtur* fish eats the mountain acorns; and the . . . fish, which is a god of the *suḫurmaš* carp, plays happily there and darts about. With his scaly tail he touches the old reeds in that holy place. The tamarisks of the place, as many as there are, drink water from that pool.

399–409   'It stands alone, it stands alone! One tamarisk stands alone at the side! When Enmerkar son of Utu has cut that tamarisk and has fashioned it into a bucket, he must tear up the old reeds in that holy place roots and all, and collect them in his hands. When he has chased out from it the . . . fish, which is a god of the *suḫurmaš* carp, caught that fish, cooked it, garnished it and brought it as a sacrifice to the *ankar* weapon, Inana's battle-strength, then his troops will have success for him; then he will have brought to an end that which in the subterranean waters provides the life-strength of Aratta.

410–12 'If he carries off from the city its worked metal and smiths, if he carries off its worked stones and its stonemasons, if he renews the city and settles it, all the moulds of Aratta will be his.'

413–16 Now Aratta's battlements are of green lapis lazuli, its walls and its towering brickwork are bright red, their brick clay is made of tin-stone dug out in the mountains where the cypress grows.

417 Praise be to holy Lugalbanda!

Notes

50–89 Ten *gur* is equivalent to about 3,000 litres.

251–83 A *danna* is equivalent to about 11 kilometres.

345–56 After 'With' 1 MS adds: 'joyful'; after 'In a' 1 MS adds: 'joyful'.

Gilgameš, Enkidu, and the Underworld

The narrative drive of *Gilgameš, Enkidu, and the Underworld* leads from the creation of the world to a meditation on the nature of existence in the afterlife. It begins by describing how, in far-distant days, the universe was formed and its parts divided among the deities. Enki, the god of the subterranean freshwater ocean, was sailing towards his allotted domain when a severe storm blew up. The same storm uprooted a tree growing on the banks of the Euphrates. The goddess Inana took the tree to her earthly home in Unug where she replanted it, hoping that it would provide timber for furniture. However, malignant creatures infested the growing tree, thwarting her hopes.

In despair, she turns for help first to the sun-god Utu, recounting to him the story so far. He provides no assistance and so she repeats her story to Gilgameš, who takes up his weapons, defeats the infesting creatures, and turns the tree into timber. With some of the wood, he makes two playthings, an *ellag* and an *ekidma*, whose identities remain uncertain (and similarly the pronunciation of the latter word). Putting the two into action, Gilgameš

exhausts the men of Unug in a game, and the women of Unug with providing refreshments for their men. The next morning, as the game restarts,
the women complain and the two playthings fall down into the Underworld.

Now it is Gilgameš's turn to despair, but Enkidu vows to retrieve the playthings for him. Gilgameš warns Enkidu not to draw attention to himself
when he goes down to the Underworld, the domain of the goddess Ereškigala
who spends her time mourning for her son Ninazu. Enkidu, however,
behaves in exactly the opposite way and the Underworld claims him.
Gilgameš appeals unsuccessfully to the god Enlil in Nibru for help, and then
to the god Enki in Eridug, this time successfully: Enki instructs the sun-god
Utu to bring up Enkidu's ghost from the Underworld.

Reunited, Enkidu and Gilgameš embrace, but a dialogue on the nature of
existence in the Underworld soon darkens the joy of their reunion. As
Enkidu's initial answers to Gilgameš's questions reveal, the more sons a dead
man has, the more offerings he receives in the afterlife, and the better is his
existence there. In contrast, those with no heir have a joyless existence in the
Underworld. Further questions and answers reveal further disparate fates:
those who have died from a disfiguring disease twitch like an ox as the worms
eat at them, but stillborn children have a compensating afterlife of luxury.
The composition ends by describing the dreadful fate of those who have
burned to death: having been turned to smoke, they have no existence in the
Underworld.

A slightly different version of the second half of this composition, from
the loss of the playthings to the dialogue on the afterlife, exists in Akkadian,
appended to the Babylonian *Epic of Gilgameš*.

Translation

1–26   In those days, in those distant days, in those nights, in those remote
nights, in those years, in those distant years; in days of yore, when the
necessary things had been brought into manifest existence, in days of
yore, when the necessary things had been for the first time properly
cared for, when bread had been tasted for the first time in the shrines
of the Land, when the ovens of the Land had been made to work,
when the heavens had been separated from the earth, when the earth
had been delimited from the heavens, when the fame of mankind
had been established, when An had taken the heavens for himself,
when Enlil had taken the earth for himself, when the Underworld
had been given to Ereškigala as a gift; when he set sail, when he set
sail, when the Father set sail for the Underworld, when Enki set sail

for the Underworld—against the king a storm of small hailstones arose, against Enki a storm of large hailstones arose. The small ones were light hammers, the large ones were like stones from catapults (?). The keel of Enki's little boat was trembling as if it were being butted by turtles, the waves at the bow of the boat rose to devour the king like wolves, and the waves at the stern of the boat were attacking Enki like a lion.

27–35   At that time, there was a single tree, a single *ḫalub* tree, a single tree, growing on the bank of the pure Euphrates, being watered by the Euphrates. The force of the south wind uprooted it and stripped its branches, and the Euphrates picked it up and carried it away. A woman, respectful of An's words, was walking along; a woman, respectful of Enlil's words, was walking along, and took the tree and brought it into Unug, into Inana's luxuriant garden.

36–9   The woman planted the tree with her feet, but not with her hands. The woman watered it using her feet but not her hands. She said: 'When will this be a luxuriant chair on which I can take a seat?' She said: 'When this will be a luxuriant bed on which I can lie down?'

40–6   Five years, ten years went by, the tree grew massive; its bark, however, did not split. At its roots, a snake immune to incantations made itself a nest. In its branches, the Anzud bird settled its young. In its trunk, the phantom maid built herself a dwelling, the maid who laughs with a joyful heart. But holy Inana cried!

47–69   When dawn was breaking, when the horizon became bright, when the little birds, at the break of dawn, began to clamour, when Utu had left his bedchamber, his sister holy Inana said to the young warrior Utu: 'My brother, in those days when destiny was determined, when abundance overflowed in the Land, when An had taken the heavens for himself, when Enlil had taken the earth for himself, when the Underworld had been given to Ereškigala as a gift; when he set sail, when he set sail, when the Father set sail for the Underworld, when Enki set sail for the Underworld—against the lord a storm of small hailstones arose, against Enki a storm of large hailstones arose. The small ones were light hammers, the large ones were like stones from catapults (?). The keel of Enki's little boat was trembling as if it were being butted by turtles, the waves at the bow of the boat rose to devour the lord like wolves and the waves at the stern of the boat were attacking Enki like a lion.

70–8   'At that time, there was a single tree, a single *ḫalub* tree, a single tree

(?), growing on the bank of the pure Euphrates, being watered by the Euphrates. The force of the south wind uprooted it and stripped its branches, and the Euphrates picked it up and carried it away. I, a woman, respectful of An's words, was walking along; I, a woman, respectful of Enlil's words, was walking along, and took the tree and brought it into Unug, into holy Inana's luxuriant garden.

79–89   'I, the woman, planted the tree with my feet, but not with my hands. I, Inana°, watered it using my feet but not my hands. I said, "When will this be a luxuriant chair on which I can take a seat?" I said, "When will this be a luxuriant bed on which I can lie down?" Five years, ten years had gone by, the tree had grown massive; its bark, however, did not split. At its roots, a snake immune to incantations made itself a nest. In its branches, the Anzud bird settled its young. In its trunk, the phantom maid built herself a dwelling, the maid who laughs with a joyful heart. But holy Inana cried!'

90   Her brother, the young warrior Utu, however, did not stand by her in the matter.

91–113   When dawn was breaking, when the horizon became bright, when the little birds, at the break of dawn, began to clamour, when Utu had left his bedchamber, his sister holy Inana said to the warrior Gilgameš: 'My brother, in those days when destiny was determined, when abundance overflowed in the Land, when An had taken the heavens for himself, when Enlil had taken the earth for himself, when the Underworld had been given to Ereškigala as a gift; when he set sail, when he set sail, when the Father set sail for the Underworld, when Enki set sail for the Underworld—against the lord a storm of small hailstones arose, against Enki a storm of large hailstones arose. The small ones were light hammers, the large ones were like stones from catapults (?). The keel of Enki's little boat was trembling as if it were being butted by turtles, the waves at the bow of the boat rose to devour the lord like wolves and the waves at the stern of the boat were attacking Enki like a lion.

114–22   'At that time, there was a single tree, a single ḫalub tree, a single tree (?), growing on the bank of the pure Euphrates, being watered by the Euphrates. The force of the south wind uprooted it and stripped its branches, and the Euphrates picked it up and carried it away. I, a woman, respectful of An's words, was walking along; I, a woman, respectful of Enlil's words, was walking along, and took the tree and brought it into Unug, into Inana's luxuriant garden.

123–33 'The woman planted the tree with her feet, but not with her hands. Inana watered it using her feet but not her hands. She said, "When will this be a luxuriant chair on which I can take a seat?" She said, "When will this be a luxuriant bed on which I can lie down?" Five years, ten years had gone by, the tree had grown massive; its bark, however, did not split. At its roots, a snake immune to incantations made itself a nest. In its branches, the Anzud bird settled its young. In its trunk, the phantom maid built herself a dwelling, the maid who laughs with a joyful heart. But holy Inana° cried!'

134–5 In the matter which his sister had told him about, her brother, the warrior Gilgameš, stood by her.

136–50 He strapped his . . . belt of 50 minas weight to his waist—50 minas were to him as 30 shekels°. He took his bronze axe used for expeditions, which weighs seven talents and seven minas°, in his hand. He killed the snake immune to incantations living at its roots. The Anzud bird living in its branches took up its young and went into the mountains. The phantom maid living in its trunk left (?) her dwelling and sought refuge in the wilderness. As for the tree, he uprooted it and stripped its branches, and the sons of his city, who went with him, cut up its branches and bundled them°. He gave it to his sister holy Inana for her chair. He gave it to her for her bed. As for himself, from its roots, he manufactured his *ellag* and, from its branches, he manufactured his *ekidma*.

151–65 He played *ellag* in the broad square, never wanting to stop playing it, and he praised himself in the broad square, never wanting to stop praising himself.° For (?) him who made the team of the widows' children . . . , they lamented: 'O my neck! O my hips!' For those who had a mother, the mother brought bread for her son; for those who had a sister, the sister poured water for her brother. As the evening came, he marked the spot where the *ellag* had been placed, and he picked up his *ellag* from in front of him and took it home. But early in the morning as he . . . the place marked, the widows' accusation and the young girls' complaint caused his *ellag* and his *ekidma* to fall down to the bottom of the Underworld.° He tried with his hand but could not reach° them, tried with his foot but could not reach° them.

166–75 At the gate of Ganzer, in front of the Underworld, he sat down. Gilgameš wept, crying bitterly: 'O my *ellag*! O my *ekidma*! O my *ellag*, I am still not sated with its charms, the game with it has not yet palled for me! If only my *ellag* waited still in the carpenter's house for me! I would treat the carpenter's wife like my own mother—if only it waited still there for me! I would treat the carpenter's child like my little sister—if only it waited still there for me! My *ellag* has fallen down to the Underworld—who will retrieve it for me? My *ekidma* has fallen down to Ganzer—who will retrieve it for me?°'

176–9   His servant Enkidu answered° him°: 'My king, you weep; why does your heart worry? Today I shall retrieve your *ellag* from the Underworld, I shall retrieve your *ekidma* from Ganzer.'

180–3   Gilgameš answered Enkidu: 'If today° you are going to go down to the Underworld, let me advise you! My instructions should be followed. Let me talk to you! Pay attention to my words°!

184–98   'You should not put on your clean garments: they would recognize immediately that you are alien. You should not anoint yourself with fine oil from a bowl: they would surround you at its° scent. You should not hurl throw-sticks in the Underworld: those struck down by the throw-sticks would surround you. You should not hold a cornel-wood stick in your hand: the spirits would feel insulted by you. You should not put sandals on your feet. You should not shout in the Underworld. You should not kiss your beloved wife. You should not hit your wife even if you are annoyed with her. You should not kiss your beloved child. You should not hit your son even if you are annoyed with him. The outcry aroused would detain you in the Underworld.

199–204   'She who lies there, she who lies there, Ninazu's mother who lies there—her pure shoulders are not covered with a garment, and no linen is spread over her pure breast. She has fingers like a pickaxe, she plucks her hair out like leeks.'

205–20   Enkidu, however, did not heed his master's words. He put on his clean garments and they recognized that he was alien. He anointed himself with fine oil from a bowl and they surrounded him at its scent. He hurled throw-sticks in the Underworld and those struck down by the throw-sticks surrounded him. He held a cornel-wood stick in his hand and the spirits felt insulted by him. He put sandals on his feet. He caused irritation in the Underworld. He kissed his beloved wife and hit his wife when he was annoyed with her. He kissed his beloved child and hit his son when he was annoyed with him. He aroused an outcry and was detained in the Underworld.

221–8   The warrior Gilgameš, son of Ninsumun, directed his steps on his own to E-kur, the temple of Enlil. He cried before Enlil: 'Father Enlil, my *ellag* fell down into the Underworld, my *ekidma* fell down into Ganzer. Enkidu went down to retrieve them but the Underworld has seized him. Namtar did not seize him, the Asag did not seize him; but the Underworld has seized him. The *udug* demon of Nergal, who spares nobody, did not seize him, but the Underworld has seized him. He did not fall in battle on the field of manhood, but the Underworld has seized him.'

229 Father Enlil did not stand by him in the matter, so he went to Eridug.

230–6 In Eridug he directed his steps on his own to the temple of Enki. He cried before Enki: 'Father Enki, my *ellag* fell down into the Underworld, my *ekidma* fell down into Ganzer. Enkidu went down to retrieve them but the Underworld has seized him. Namtar did not seize him, the Asag did not seize him; but the Underworld has seized him. The *udug* demon of Nergal, who spares nobody, did not seize him, but the Underworld has seized him. He did not fall in battle on the field of manhood, but the Underworld has seized him.'

237 Father Enki stood by him in this matter.

238–42 He said to the young warrior Utu, the son born of Ningal: 'Open a hole in the Underworld immediately, and then bring up his servant from the Underworld!' He opened a hole in the Underworld and brought up his servant with his breeze (?) from the Underworld.

243–6 They hugged and kissed. They wearied each other with questions: 'Did you see the order of the Underworld? If only you would tell me, my friend, if only you would tell me!'

247–52 'If I tell you the order of the Underworld, sit down and weep! I shall sit down and weep! . . . , which your heart rejoiced to touch, is . . . , worms infest it like an old garment (?); like . . . of (?) a crevice, it is full of dust.'

253 'Alas!' he said and sat down in the dust.

254 'Did you see him who had one son?'
'I saw him.'
'How does he fare?'

255 'He weeps bitterly at the wooden peg which was driven into his wall.'

256 'Did you see him who had two sons?'
'I saw him.'
'How does he fare?'

257 'He sits on a couple of bricks, eating bread.'

258 'Did you see him who had three sons?'

'I saw him.'

'How does he fare?'

259 'He drinks water from a saddle waterskin.'

260 'Did you see him who had four sons?'

'I saw him.'

'How does he fare?'

261 'His heart rejoices like a man who has four asses to yoke.'

262 'Did you see him who had five sons?'

'I saw him.'

'How does he fare?'

263 'Like a good scribe he is indefatigable, he enters the palace easily.'

264 'Did you see him who had six sons?'

'I saw him.'

'How does he fare?'

265 'He is as cheerful as a ploughman.'

266 'Did you see him who had seven sons?'

'I saw him.'

'How does he fare?'

267 'As a companion of the gods, he sits on a throne and listens to judgments.'

268 'Did you see the palace eunuch?'

'I saw him.'

'How does he fare?'

269 'Like a useless *alala* stick he is propped in a corner.'

270 'Did you see the woman who never gave birth?'

'I saw her.'

'How does she fare?'

271 'Like a . . . pot, she is thrown away violently, she gives no man joy.'

272 'Did you see the young man who never undressed his wife?'

'I saw him.'

'How does he fare?'

273 'You finish a rope, and he weeps over the rope.'

274 'Did you see the young woman who never undressed her husband?'

'I saw her.'

'How does she fare?'

275 'You finish a reed mat, and she weeps over the reed mat.'

276 'Did you see him who had no heir?'

'I saw him.'

'How does he fare?'

277 'Like him who . . . bricks (?), he eats bread.'
278 '. . . ?'
  'I saw him.'
  'How does he fare?' (*7 lines fragmentary or missing*)
286 'Did you see . . . ?'
287 'His food is set apart, his water is set apart, he eats the food offered (?) to him, he drinks the water offered (?) to him.'°
288 'Did you see the leprous man?'
289 'He twitches like an ox as the worms eat at him.'
290 'Did you see him who fell in battle?'
  'I saw him.'
  'How does he fare?'
291 'His father and mother are not there to hold his head, and his wife weeps.'
292 'Did you see the spirit of him who has no funerary offerings?'
  'I saw him.'
  'How does he fare?'
293 'He eats the scraps and the crumbs . . . tossed out in the street.'
294 'Did you see him hit by a ship's board°? How does he fare?'
295–7 ' "Alas, my mother!" the man cries to her, as he pulls out the ship's board . . . , he . . . cross beam . . . crumbs.'
298 'Did you see my little stillborn children who never knew existence?'
  'I saw them.'
  'How do they fare?'
299 'They play at a table of gold and silver, laden with honey and ghee.'
300 'Did you see him who died . . . ?'
  'I saw him.'
  'How does he fare?'
301 'He lies on a bed of the gods.'
302 'Did you see him who was set on fire?'
303 'I did not see him. His spirit is not about. His smoke went up to the sky.'

Notes

79–89 Instead of 'Inana' 1 MS has: 'the woman'.
123–33 Instead of 'holy Inana' 1 MS has: 'I, holy Inana,'.
136–50 50 minas is equivalent to about 25 kilograms; 30 shekels is equivalent to about

250 grams; 7 talents and 7 minas is equivalent to just over 210 kilograms. Instead of 'bundled them' 1 MS has: 'piled them up'.

151–65   After 'praising himself.' MSS from Urim add: 'The young men of his city were playing *ellag*'. After 'the Underworld.' 1 MS adds: 'He could not reach them by . . . .'. Instead of 'reach' 1 MS has: 'touch'.

166–75   Instead of 'My *ellag* has fallen down to the Underworld—who will retrieve it for me?' 1 MS has: 'Who will retrieve my *ellag* from the Underworld?' Instead of 'My *ekidma* has fallen down to Ganzer—who will retrieve it for me?' 1 MS has: 'Who will retrieve my *ekidma* from Ganzer?'

176–9   Instead of 'answered' 1 MS has: 'said to'; instead of 'him' 1 MS has: 'Gilgameš'.

180–3   Instead of 'If today' 1 MS has: 'If'. Instead of 'Pay attention to my words' 1 MS has: 'My words should be followed'.

184–98   Instead of 'its' 1 MS has: 'your'.

287   After 'water offered (?) to him.' 1 MS adds: ' "Did you see him who was eaten by a lion?" "He cries bitterly 'O my hands! O my legs!'" "Did you see him who fell down from the roof?" They cannot . . . his bones." '

294   After 'ship's board' 1 MS adds: 'when diving (?)'.

Sargon and Ur-Zababa

The rulers of Agade, in particular the founder of the imperial line, Sargon, and his grandson and third successor, Naram-Suen, have an impressive literary legacy, primarily recounting their heroic deeds but also reflecting on the dynasty's catastrophic end. Much of this literature is in Akkadian. Two compositions, however, are in Sumerian: *Sargon and Ur-Zababa*, which recounts the founder's rise to power, and *The cursing of Agade* (Group C), which is concerned instead with the dynasty's downfall.

Little is known about Sargon's origins. According to a much later Akkadian legend, he was the illicit child of a priestess who, much in the manner of Moses in the Bible, was placed in a wicker basket and cast adrift upon the water, to be rescued and raised by a gardener. Such folk-tale motifs were also incorporated into Sumerian literature, including, in *Sargon and Ur-Zababa*, instances of dreams which foretell the future. This folk-tale motif is embedded within a narrative which has theological concerns, dreams being regarded as messages predicting a divinely ordained future which man alone cannot resist. Given the social status of the dreamers, political as well as theological significance also attaches to the dreams.

Sargon and Ur-Zababa has been tentatively reconstructed from two manuscripts, a fragment from Unug (Segments A and C) and a more complete tablet from Nibru (Segment B). While the events that concern the poem occur primarily in the north of Babylonia, the tablets on which it is recorded thus come from the south.

Segment A describes how Kiš has been restored to splendour under its king Ur-Zababa, but how the two chief deities, An and Enlil, have decided to bring its splendour to an end; then Sargon himself is mentioned in a fragmentary context. These lines belong to the tradition in Sumerian literature which interprets political events in terms of divine intervention, more specifically in this case in terms of intervention that brings royal dynasties to an end, a fate that also befalls Agade itself in *The cursing of Agade* (Group C) and the Third Dynasty of Urim in *The lament for Sumer and Urim* (Group D).

Segment B develops the relationship between Ur-Zababa, who has an ill-omened dream which he refuses to discuss, and Sargon, who is appointed to be his cupbearer, an important post in the royal household. Some days later, Ur-Zababa has a trembling reaction to his dream: 'Like a lion he urinated, sprinkling his legs.' A further dream then comes to Sargon which, to his horror, confirms that Ur-Zababa has reason to tremble. As Sargon recounts to the king, in his dream the goddess Inana, the patron deity of Kiš, drowned Ur-Zababa in 'a river of blood'.

Ur-Zababa distorts the contents of Sargon's dream, claiming that it is Sargon instead who is doomed, and instructs his chief smith to fulfil the distorted dream in melodramatic fashion, by disposing of the cupbearer in the type of mould used for casting statues. However, Inana, whose support lies with Sargon rather than Ur-Zababa, saves the cupbearer by advising him not to enter the fated temple because he is polluted with blood, presumably as a consequence of his own dream.

Sargon's survival fills Ur-Zababa with further foreboding and he devises another plot against the cupbearer: to send him to the ruler of Unug, Lugal-zage-si, with a message instructing that its bearer be killed. Thus an additional folklore motif is incorporated within the ideological narrative, another bearer of such a message being the ancient Greek hero Bellerophon in the *Iliad*.

The contents of Segment C, set not in Kiš but in Unug, whose patron deity was also Inana, remain unclear. They do, however, indicate the continued survival of Sargon. The historical evidence also supports his survival: he became king of Kiš, giving him control of the north of the Land; defeated Lugal-zage-si, giving him control of much of the south; and founded his own capital city, Agade, whose patron deity was again Inana.

Translation

A1–9 To ... the sanctuary like a cargo-ship; to ... its great furnaces; to see
that its canals ... waters of joy, to see that the hoes till the arable tracts
and that ... the fields; to turn the house of Kiš, which was like a
haunted town, into a living settlement again—its king, shepherd Ur-
Zababa, rose like Utu over the house of Kiš. An and Enlil, however,
authoritatively (?) decided (?) by their holy command to alter his
term of reigning and to remove the prosperity of the palace.

A10–13 Then Sargon—his city was the city of ... , his father was Lā'ibum,
his mother ... , Sargon ... with happy heart. Since he was born
.... (*unknown number of lines missing*)

FIG. 10. 'Ur-Zababa appointed him cupbearer'—a royal
banquet depicted on a stone plaque from Early Dynastic Nibru

B1–7 One day, after the evening had arrived and Sargon had brought the
regular deliveries to the palace, Ur-Zababa was sleeping (*and dream-
ing*) in the holy bedchamber, his holy residence. He realized what the
dream was about, but did not put it into words, did not discuss it
with anyone. After Sargon had received the regular deliveries for the
palace, Ur-Zababa appointed him cupbearer, putting him in charge
of the drinks cupboard. Holy Inana did not cease to stand by him.

B8–11 After five or ten days had passed, king Ur-Zababa . . . and became frightened in his residence. Like a lion he urinated, sprinkling his legs, and the urine contained blood and pus. He was troubled, he was afraid like a fish floundering in brackish water.

B12–19 It was then that the cupbearer of Ezina's wine-house, Sargon, lay down not to sleep, but lay down to dream. In the dream, holy Inana drowned Ur-Zababa in a river of blood. The sleeping Sargon groaned and gnawed the ground. When king Ur-Zababa heard about this groaning, he was brought into the king's holy presence, Sargon was brought into the presence of Ur-Zababa (*who said:*) 'Cupbearer, was a dream revealed to you in the night?'

B20–4 Sargon answered his king: 'My king, this is my dream, which I will tell you about: There was a young woman, who was as high as the heavens and as broad as the earth. She was firmly set as the base of a wall. For me, she drowned you in a great river, a river of blood.'

B25–34 Ur-Zababa chewed his lips, he became seriously afraid. He spoke to . . . , his chancellor: 'My royal sister, holy Inana, is going to change (?) my finger into a . . . of blood; she will drown Sargon, the cupbearer, in the great river. Bēliš-tikal, chief smith, man of my choosing, who can write tablets, I will give you orders, let my orders be carried out! Let my advice be followed! Now then, when the cupbearer has delivered my bronze hand-mirror (?) to you, in the E-sikil, the fated house, throw them (*the mirror and Sargon*) into the mould like statues.'

B35–8 Bēliš-tikal heeded his king's words and prepared the moulds in the E-sikil, the fated house. The king spoke to Sargon: 'Go and deliver my bronze hand-mirror (?) to the chief smith!'

B38a–42 Sargon left the palace of Ur-Zababa. Holy Inana, however, did not cease to stand at his right-hand side, and before he had come within five or ten *nindan*° of the E-sikil, the fated house, holy Inana turned around toward him and blocked his way, (*saying:*) 'The E-sikil is a holy house! No one polluted with blood should enter it!'

B43–5 Thus he met the chief smith of the king only at the gate of the fated house. After he delivered the king's bronze hand-mirror (?) to the chief smith, Bēliš-tikal, the chief smith, . . . and threw it into the mould like statues.

B46–52 After five or ten days had passed, Sargon came into the presence of Ur-Zababa, his king; he came into the palace, firmly founded like a great mountain. King Ur-Zababa . . . and became frightened in his residence. He realized what it was about, but did not put it into words, did not discuss it with anyone. Ur-Zababa became frightened in the bedchamber, his holy residence. He realized what it was about, but did not put it into words, did not discuss it with anyone.

B53–6 In those days, although writing words on tablets existed, putting tablets into envelopes did not yet exist. King Ur-Zababa dispatched Sargon, the creature of the gods, to Lugal-zage-si in Unug with a message written on clay, which was about murdering Sargon. (*unknown number of lines missing*)

C1–7 With the wife of Lugal-zage-si . . . She (?) . . . her feminity as a shelter. Lugal-zage-si did not . . . the envoy. 'Come! He directed his steps to brick-built E-ana!' Lugal-zage-si did not grasp it, he did not talk to the envoy. But as soon as he did talk to the envoy . . . The lord said 'Alas!' and sat in the dust.

C8–12 Lugal-zage-si replied to the envoy: 'Envoy, Sargon does not yield. After he has submitted, Sargon . . . Lugal-zage-si . . . Sargon . . . Lugal-zage-si . . . Why . . . Sargon . . . ?'

Note

B38a–42 A *nindan* is equivalent to about 6 metres. The line B38a is on the tablet's edge.

The building of Ninǵirsu's temple (extract)

The building of Ninǵirsu's temple is the longest account of temple-building known in Sumerian, and also the longest literary composition in the language. It is inscribed on two large clay cylinders and relates how Gudea, the ruler of the state of Lagaš, extended and rebuilt the temple E-ninnu as the magnificent principal earthly residence of the god Ninǵirsu. The temple complex was in Ǵirsu, the capital of Lagaš, a large and flourishing city in the third millennium BCE whose patron deity was the god who bore the city's name, Ninǵirsu (literally, 'Lord of Ǵirsu'). Two smaller cities in the same state also play a role in the narrative, Niǵin and Lagaš, the latter being the city after which the state was named.

Given the impressive appearance of the cylinders, it is possible that they were displayed within the rebuilt temple, commemorating the building work of which they give a dramatized account. However, the cylinders were excavated from a less glorious spot, a drain close to the temple's walls. They may have ended up in this ignominious position when the city was sacked, an event to which the many decapitated statues of Gudea bear witness.

The composition divides into two parts. One, the first cylinder, concludes with two lines marking the middle of the hymn. The other, the second cylinder, concludes with another two lines marking the end of the hymn. These lines refer to the composition as 'The building of Ninĝirsu's house' (more literally, 'Ninĝirsu's house having been built'); each pair is preceded by a line in praise of Ninĝirsu. The first part of the composition is primarily concerned with the construction of the temple, and the second primarily with its inauguration.

The first part begins by giving the building work divine approval: the senior deity in the pantheon, Enlil, the father of Ninĝirsu, blesses the project. Ninĝirsu then indicates his intentions to Gudea in a dream. For clarification and verification of the dream Gudea resolves to visit the goddess Nanše, the sister of Ninĝirsu whose skills include dream interpretation and whose principal earthly residence is in Niĝin. First, however, he visits the temple Bagara in the city of Lagaš, praying there in turn to Ninĝirsu and the birth-goddess Ĝatumdug.

Having received their blessings, Gudea goes to Niĝin, where he relates the contents of his dream to Nanše. She analyses the dream, interpreting its images one by one, and advises him to construct a fabulous chariot for Ninĝirsu to ensure his continuing approval.

Gudea returns to Ĝirsu and puts this advice into action. What he needs now, however, are more detailed instructions on how to proceed. To obtain these, he offers animals and incense to Ninĝirsu at Šu-galam, one of the gates to the E-ninnu, and then petitions him in the Ub-šu-unkena, another part of the temple complex. Ninĝirsu replies with a further dream, this time verified by a different type of divination, the performance of extispicy on a white kid. The extract given here ends at this point.

Translation

1–4 On the day when in heaven and earth the fates had been decided, Lagaš raised its head high in full grandeur, and Enlil looked at lord Ninĝirsu with approval. In our city there was perfection.

5–9 The heart overflowed with joy, Enlil's heart, a river in flood, overflowed with joy. The heart overflowed with joy, and just as the Tigris brings sweet water, so Enlil, whose will is an enormous flood, sparkling and awe-inspiring, came to a sweet decision:

10–16 'The lord called for his house and I intend to make the grandeur of

E-ninnu known everywhere. Using his wisdom, the ruler will achieve great things. He will direct faultless cattle and kids for offering. It is for him the fated brick is waiting. It is by him that the building of the holy house is to be done.'°

17–23 On that day, in a nocturnal vision Gudea saw his master, lord Ninĝirsu. Ninĝirsu spoke to him of his house, of its building. He showed him an E-ninnu with full grandeur. Outstanding though his mind was, the message remained to be understood for him.

24–32 'Well, I have to tell her about this! Well, I have to tell her about this! I will ask her to stand by me in this matter. Profound things (?) came suddenly to me, the shepherd, but I do not understand the meaning of what the nocturnal vision brought to me. So I will take my dream to my mother and I will ask my dream-interpreter, an expert on her own, my divine sister from Sirara, Nanše, to reveal its meaning to me.'

33–8 He stepped aboard his boat, directed it on the canal Niĝin-dua towards her city Niĝin, and merrily cut through the waves of the river. After he had reached Bagara, the house extending as far as the river, he offered bread, poured cold water, and went to the master of Bagara to pray to him.

39–51 'Warrior, rampant lion, who has no opponent! Ninĝirsu, important in the Abzu, respected in Nibru! Warrior, I want to carry out faithfully what you have commanded me; Ninĝirsu, I want to build up your house for you, I want to make it perfect for you, so I will ask your sister, the child born of Eridug, an authority on her own, the lady, the dream-interpreter among the gods, my divine sister from Sirara, Nanše, to show me the way.' His call was heard; his master, lord Ninĝirsu, accepted from Gudea his prayer and supplication.

52–63 Gudea celebrated the ešeš festival in the house of Bagara. The ruler set up his bed near to Ĝatumdug. He offered bread and poured cold water and went to holy Ĝatumdug to pray to her: 'My lady, child begotten by holy An, an authority on her own, proud goddess, living in the Land, . . . of her city! Lady, mother, you who founded Lagaš, if you but look upon your people, it brings abundance; the worthy young man on whom you look will enjoy a long life.

64–7 'For me, who has no mother, you are my mother; for me, who has no father, you are my father. You implanted my semen in the womb, gave birth to me in the sanctuary, Ĝatumdug, sweet is your holy name!

68–79 'Tonight I shall lie down here (?). You are my great dagger (?), being attached to my side; you are a . . . planted in great waters, providing me with life; you are a broad sunshade; let me cool off in your shade. May the favourable, right-hand palm of your lofty hands, my lady Ĝatumdug, lend me protection! I am going to the city, may my sign be favourable! May your friendly guardian go before me, and may your friendly protecting genius walk with me on the way towards Niĝin, the mountain rising from the water.

80–6 'Well, I have to tell her about this! Well, I have to tell her about this! I will ask her to stand by me in this matter. I will take my dream to my mother and I will ask my dream-interpreter, an expert on her own, my divine sister from Sirara, Nanše, to reveal its meaning to me.'

87–9 His call was heard; his lady, holy Ĝatumdug, accepted from Gudea his prayer and supplication.

90–100 He stepped aboard his boat, directed it towards her city Niĝin, mooring it at the quay of Niĝin. The ruler raised his head high in the courtyard of the goddess from Sirara. He offered bread, poured cold water, and went to Nanše to pray to her: 'Nanše, mighty lady, lady of most precious (?) powers, lady who like Enlil determines fates, my Nanše, what you say is trustworthy and takes precedence. You are the interpreter of dreams among the gods, you are the lady of all the lands. Mother, my matter today is a dream:

101–9 'In the dream there was someone who was as enormous as the heavens, who was as enormous as the earth. His head was like that of a god, his wings were like those of the Anzud bird, his lower body was like a flood storm. Lions were lying at his right and his left. He spoke to me about building his house, but I could not understand what he exactly meant, then daylight rose for me on the horizon.

110–14 'Then there was a woman—whoever she was. She . . . sheaves. She held a stylus of refined silver in her hand, and placed it on a tablet with propitious stars, and was consulting it.

115–23 'There was, furthermore, a warrior. His arm was bent, holding a lapis lazuli tablet in his hand, and he was setting down the plan of the house. The holy basket stood in front of me, the holy brick mould was ready and the fated brick was placed in the mould for me. In a fine *ildag* tree standing before me *tigidlu* birds were spending the day twittering. My master's right-side donkey stallion was pawing the ground for me.'

124–31   His mother Nanše answered the ruler: 'My shepherd, I will explain
your dream for you in every detail. The person who, as you said, was
as enormous as the heavens, who was as enormous as the earth,
whose head was like that of a god, whose wings, as you said, were like
those of the Anzud bird, and whose lower body was, as you said, like
a flood storm, at whose right and left lions were lying, was in fact my
brother Ningirsu. He spoke to you about the building of his shrine,
the E-ninnu.

132–3   'The daylight that had risen for you on the horizon is your personal
god Ningišzida, who will rise for you as the daylight on the horizon.

134–40   'The young woman . . . sheaves, who held a stylus of refined silver in
her hand, who had placed it on a tablet with propitious stars and was
consulting it, was in fact my sister Nisaba. She announced to you the
holy stars auguring the building of the house.

141–3   'The second one, who was a warrior and whose arm was bent, holding a lapis lazuli tablet in his hand, was Nindub, putting the plan of
the house on the tablet.

144–6   'As regards the holy basket standing in front of you, the holy brick
mould which was ready and the fated brick placed in the mould, this
part of the dream concerns the good brick of the E-ninnu.

147–9   'As regards the fine *ildag* tree standing before you, in which, as you
said, *tigidlu* birds were spending the day twittering, this means that
the building of the house will not let sweet sleep come into your eyes.

150–1   'As regards that part when the right-side donkey stallion of your
master, as you said, pawed the ground for you; this refers to you, who
will paw the ground for the E-ninnu like a choice steed.

152–72   'Let me advise you and may my advice be taken. Direct your steps to
Girsu, the foremost house of the land of Lagaš, open your storehouse
up and take out wood from it; build (?) a chariot for your master and
harness a donkey stallion to it; decorate this chariot with refined
silver and lapis lazuli and equip it with arrows that will fly out from
the quiver like sunbeams, and with the *ankar* weapon, the strength
of heroism; fashion for him his beloved standard and write your
name on it, and then enter before the warrior who loves gifts, before
your master lord Ningirsu in E-ninnu-the-white-Anzud-bird,
together with his beloved *balag* drum Ušumgal-kalama, his famous
instrument to which he keeps listening. Your requests will then be
taken as if they were commands; and the drum will make the inclination of the lord—which is as inconceivable as the heavens—will

make the inclination of Ninĝirsu, the son of Enlil, favourable for you so that he will reveal the design of his house to you in every detail. With his powers, which are the greatest, the warrior will make the house thrive (?) for you.'

173–95   The true shepherd Gudea is wise, and able too to realize things. Accepting what Nanše had told him, he opened his storehouse up and took out wood from it. Gudea checked (?) the wood piece by piece, taking great care of the wood. He smoothed *mes* wood, split *ḫalub* wood with an axe, and built (?) a blue chariot from them for him. He harnessed to it the stallion Piriĝ-kaše-pada. He fashioned for him his beloved standard, wrote his name on it, and then entered before the warrior who loves gifts, before his master lord Ninĝirsu in E-ninnu-the-white-Anzud-bird, together with his beloved *balaĝ* drum, Ušumgal-kalama, his famous instrument to which he keeps listening. He joyfully brought the drum to him in the temple. Gudea came out of the shrine E-ninnu with a radiant face.

196–206 Thereafter the house was the concern of all the days and all the nights that he made pass by. He levelled what was high, rejected chance utterances (?), he removed the sorcerers' spittle (?) from the roads. Facing Šu-galam, the fearful place, the place of making judgments, from where Ninĝirsu keeps an eye on all lands, the ruler had a fattened sheep, a fat-tail sheep, and a grain-fed kid rest on hides of a virgin kid. He put juniper, the mountains' pure plant, onto the fire, and raised smoke with cedar resin, the scent of gods.

207–16   He rose to his master in public and prayed to him; he went to him in the Ub-šu-unkena and saluted him: 'My master Ninĝirsu, lord who has turned back the fierce waters, true lord, semen ejaculated by the Great Mountain, noble young hero who has no opponent! Ninĝirsu, I am going to build your house for you, but I lack an ominous sign. Warrior, you asked for perfection, but, son of Enlil, lord Ninĝirsu, you did not let me know your will as to how to achieve it.

217–25   'Your will, ever-rising as the sea, crashing down as a destructive flood, roaring like gushing waters, destroying cities (?) like a flood-wave, battering against the rebel lands like a storm; my master, your will, gushing water that no one can stem; warrior, your will inconceivable as the heavens—can I learn anything about it from you, son of Enlil, lord Ninĝirsu?'

226–31   Afterwards, Ninĝirsu stepped up to the head of the sleeper, briefly touching him: 'You who are going to build it for me, you who are going to build it for me, ruler, you who are going to build my house for me, Gudea, let me tell you the ominous sign for building my house, let me tell you the pure stars of heaven indicating my regulations (?).

232–40   'As if at the roaring of the Anzud bird, the heavens tremble at my house, the E-ninnu founded by An, the powers of which are the greatest, surpassing all other powers, at the house whose owner looks out over a great distance. Its fierce halo reaches up to heaven, the great fearsomeness of my house settles upon all the lands. In response to its fame all lands will gather from as far as heaven's borders, even Magan and Meluḫa will come down from their mountains.

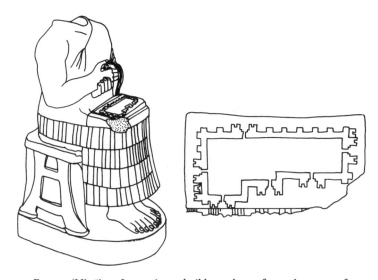

FIG. 11.   'Ninĝirsu, I am going to build your house for you'—statue of Gudea with a plan of the E-ninnu on his lap, from Ĝirsu

241–7   'I am Ninĝirsu who has turned back the fierce waters, the great warrior of Enlil's realm, a lord without opponent. My house the E-ninnu, a crown, is bigger than the mountains; my weapon the Šar-ur subdues all the lands. No country can bear my fierce stare, nobody escapes my outstretched arms.

248–53   'Because of his great love, my father who begot me called me "King, Enlil's flood, whose fierce stare is never lifted from the mountains, Ninĝirsu, warrior of Enlil", and endowed me with fifty powers.

254–61   'I lay the ritual table and perform correctly the hand-washing rites.

My outstretched hands wake holy An from sleep. My father who begot me receives the very best food from my hands. An, king of the gods, called me therefore "Ninḡirsu, king, lustration priest of An".

262–5 'I founded the Tiraš shrine with as much majesty as the Abzu. Each month at the new moon the great rites (?), my "Festival of An", are performed for me perfectly in it.

266–70 'Like a fierce snake, I built E-ḫuš, my fierce place, in a dread location. When my heart gets angry at a land that rebels against me—unutterable idea (?)—it will produce venom for me like a snake that dribbles poison.

271–276 'In the E-babbar, where I issue orders, where I shine like Utu, there I justly decide the lawsuits of my city like Ištaran. In the house Bagara, my dining place, the great gods of Lagaš gather around me.

277–85 'When you, true shepherd Gudea, really set to work for me on my house, the foremost house of all lands, the right arm of Lagaš, the Anzud bird roaring on the horizon, the E-ninnu, my royal house, I will call up to heaven for humid winds so that plenty comes down to you from heaven and the land will thrive under your reign in abundance.

286–93 'Laying the foundations of my temple will bring immediate abundance: the great fields will grow rich for you, the levees and ditches will be full to the brim for you, the water will rise for you to heights never reached by the water before. Under you more oil than ever will be poured and more wool than ever will be weighed in Sumer.

294–305 'When you drive in my foundation pegs for me, when you really set to work for me on my house, I shall direct my steps to the mountains where the north wind dwells and make the man with enormous wings, the north wind, bring you wind from the mountains, the pure place, so that this will give vigour to the Land, and thus one man will be able to do as much work as two. At night the moonlight, at noon the sun will send plentiful light for you so the day will build the house for you and the night will make it rise for you.

306–14 'I will bring *ḫalub* and *neḫan* trees up from the south, and cedar, cypress, and *zabalum* wood together will be brought for you from the uplands. From the ebony mountains I will have ebony trees brought for you, in the mountains of stones I will have the great stones of the mountain ranges cut in slabs for you. On that day I will touch your arm with fire and you will know my sign.'

315–22 Gudea rose—it was sleep; he shuddered—it was a dream. Accepting

Ninĝirsu's words, he went to perform extispicy on a white kid. He performed it on the kid and his omen was favourable. Ninĝirsu's intention became as clear as daylight to Gudea.

Note

10–16 'the lord': Ninĝirsu; 'the ruler': Gudea.

An *adab* to An for Lipit-Eštar

This hymn is one of many addressed to a deity on behalf of a king, in this instance to An, the sky-god and supreme, albeit somewhat remote, deity in the pantheon, for Lipit-Eštar, a ruler of the city of Isin. Some of these hymns were divided into various genres, this example being referred to as an *adab*, perhaps indicating that it was accompanied by the musical instrument of the same name (see *An* adab *to Bau for Išme-Dagan*, Group H). The hymn consists of nine sections of varying lengths. Two *šagbatuku* sections are framed by two-line *barsud* sections, which are contained in a *sa-gida*. They are followed by a brief *ĝišĝiĝal* and a *sa-ĝara* with a further brief *ĝišĝiĝal*. The final section of the hymn is a three-line *uru*. The significance of many of these terms remains uncertain.

In the opening *barsud*, An is referred to indirectly by a series of epithets, praising him, for example, as the 'almighty grandfather of all the lords'. Such epithets continue in the following *šagbatuku*, culminating in a direct reference to the god only in the final line of the section. The second *šagbatuku* describes how he has blessed Lipit-Eštar while the following *barsud* again stresses his pre-eminence in relation to the other deities.

An's status and his blessing of Lipit-Eštar, now referred to as the son of the god Enlil, are also the subject of the paired *sa-gida* and *ĝišĝiĝal*. The following *sa-ĝara*, the longest section in the hymn, develops these themes but in terms of a speech An addresses to Lipit-Eštar. The god proclaims his endorsement of the king, and extends this support to include the other senior deities, Enlil, Enki, Inana, and the moon-god Suen, thus incorporating within Lipit-Eštar's dominion the cities of which those deities were the patrons. The *ĝišĝiĝal* to the *sa-ĝara* repeats the blessing upon the king, while the concluding *uru* reaffirms An's status.

Translation

1-2 The august lord, pre-eminent, with the most complex divine powers, almighty grandfather of all the lords—

3 *Barsud.*

4-9 —head high, surpassing everyone, breed-bull, who makes the seeds sprout, whose name is respected, spreading great terror, whose august commands cannot be countermanded, who is imbued with awesomeness on the mountain of pure divine powers, who has taken his seat on the great throne-dais, An, the king of the gods—

10 *Šagbatuku.*

11-18 —has looked at him with long-lasting favour, has looked at prince Lipit-Eštar with favour. He has bestowed on him a long life, he has bestowed on prince Lipit-Eštar a long life. The words of what An says are firmly established; no god would oppose them. At the place where the destinies are to be decided, all the Anuna gods gather around him.

19 *Šagbatuku.*

20-1 He has made all the great divine powers manifest; the gods of heaven stand around him.

22 2nd *barsud.*

23-8 He has implemented their divine plans properly; the gods of the earth submit themselves to him°. With august and foremost (?) divine powers, great An has bestowed on Lipit-Eštar, son of Enlil, a kingship which is very precious.

29 *Sa-gida.*

30-1 An, the great, the great god shining forth, An, the almighty°, is indeed the support of king Lipit-Eštar.

32 Its *ĝišĝiĝal*°.

33-52 In the overflowing of his heart, An has chosen him as king and blessed the royal descendant: 'Lipit-Eštar, on whom I bestowed power, may you lift your head high! May you spread fearsome radiance as if you were the front of a rising tempest! May your storm cover the enemy territories, the disobedient countries! You have established justice in Sumer and Akkad, and made the Land feel content. Lipit-Eštar, son of Enlil, may you shine as brilliantly as the sunlight! May concord be created under you in the established cities, settlements and dwellings! May the black-headed people, numerous as flocks, follow the right path under you! Lipit-Eštar, even in far-

away foreign countries, you will be the king! Enlil has faithfully
bestowed on you the princely august throne, the eternal ornament of
kingship; he has made it firm for you. May you never cease to wear
the crown that Suen has placed firmly on your head! Enki has
adorned you with princely divine powers. Inana escorts (?) you with
the garment of princeship. The friendly guardians and the protecting genii of the E-kur stand by you. May the food offerings, wine,
and milk that you bring . . . ! Son and creature of Enlil, may everything be pleasant for you! (*2 lines missing*)'

53 *Sa-ĝara.*

54 May you, son of Enlil, chosen in his heart by the god imbued with
awesomeness, be provided abundantly with everything!

55 Its *ĝišgiĝal.*

56–8 What An says decides a good destiny; what the great An says decides
a good destiny. . . . for Lipit-Eštar, son of Enlil.

59 Its *uru.*

60 An *adab* of An.

Notes

23–8 Instead of 'submit themselves to him' 1 MS has: 'sit around him'.

30–1 Instead of 'the almighty' 1 MS has: 'eminent'.

32 Instead of 'Its *ĝišgiĝal*' 1 MS has: 'Its *ĝišgiĝal* of the *sa-gida*'.

A prayer for Samsu-iluna

Samsu-iluna was a ruler of Babylon, son of the more famous Ḫammurabi.
This composition begins by praising him as a king selected and supported by
a series of deities, followed by a request that he be granted a long life. This
opening statement is then repeated in a more elaborated form. Five deities
are praised for their respective divine roles, each being requested to provide
blessings for the king that correspond to those roles. An, the father of the
deities, is the first to be invoked, followed by Enlil, his wife Ninlil, their
warrior son Ninurta, and Nuska, the ministerial intermediary between the
king and the divine couple. Finally, the poem returns to the subject of the
king's life, this time requesting that it have the natural powers of growth
exhibited by fresh fruit.

Translation

1–12 My . . . of eternal fame, head lifted high in princely worth, . . . who loves righteousness and truth, . . . named with an august name, for whom Enlil . . . has determined a great destiny, and Ninlil . . . ! The valiant Ninurta is your helper. In the E-kur, Nuska the august minister of Enlil, the assembly leader of all lands, is your foremost palace superintendent. Throughout your life, may you carry your neck high; in princely manner may you lift your head high!— Prolong the days of his life for Samsu-iluna, of princely worth!

13–29 May An, king of the gods, look upon you favourably; the great and august An, the father of the gods, he with the splendid crown, full of great and august radiance, . . . your royal throne whose branches and sprouts . . . as wide as the sky. May he bestow upon you, during the days of your long life, the power to make decisions . . . , to direct . . . , to serve as the provider of the black-headed creatures in all their multitude! May Enlil, . . . , the king of all countries, protect you . . . command. May he . . . for you the city of your country. May he make firm for you the foundation of your country. May Ninlil, the queen of deities, joyfully . . . for you, and may she look upon you with shining face; may she who takes counsel . . . with Enlil, and who cares for . . . , . . . her favourable word.

30–46 May Ninurta, the strong warrior of Enlil, the lord of decisions, whose august commands are as weighty as those of An and Enlil, he of lordly character, terrifying splendour and heroism, who resists the forceful, the strong shepherd (?) who crushes the evil and wicked— may he spread out in heaps for you the inhabitants of the cities which you hate, and may he deliver your enemies into your hands! May Nuska, the august minister of Enlil, let you enter brick-built E-kur joyfully with your offerings, and escort you before the shining faces of Enlil and Ninlil; in Babylon, the city of heroes, may he make firm for you the foundation of your kingship. The august command . . . Enlil . . . . , may . . . be their king! . . . , may he . . . a place for you! . . . , like the light born monthly in the pure sky. . . . , and may you too grow throughout your life like a fresh fruit, O Samsu-iluna, my king!

The death of Ur-Namma

The death of Ur-Namma is a rare instance of a composition that honours a king in relation to what happens after his death rather than for great deeds performed in his life. Consequently it is more a lament than a hymn of praise to the founder of the Third Dynasty of Urim. It can be divided into four sections. The first is an account of Ur-Namma's death and burial (1–75). In the second section, subsequent events in the Underworld are described, climaxing in the king's lament for the life he has left behind (76–197). In the third section, the king's fate continues to be discussed by the deities (198–233). The brief, concluding section is a summation of what has come before (234–42). This composition is known in a version from Nibru, presented here, as well as a shorter, more fragmentary version from Susa.

While the second and third sections have a linear narrative development, the first is less sequential, expressing grief more through its unfocused narrative than the direct speech used later in the composition. It begins with a brief account of the cataclysmic events surrounding the death of the king, before describing in greater detail the impact of his dying on the withdrawn deities, his weeping divine mother, his mourning people, and his devastated land. Much of this imagery of desolation is also used to describe destroyed cities in such compositions as the *Lament for Sumer and Urim* (Group D). The dying king is brought to his palace in Urim where his offerings to the deities are insufficient to obtain his recovery and he dies. On the divine plane his death thus represents a decision made by the deities. The agency they use to enact their will on the human plane is less clear: references to, for example, the king being uprooted in his palace may be metaphors for enemy action, but equally for the general upheaval concomitant with his dying. Following his death, he is buried in grandeur and makes his way to the Underworld, referred to as Arali.

On arriving at the Underworld's gates manned by their seven porters, he is given a tumultuous welcome and a banquet is held. Observing the correct behaviour that is required of him as a great ruler, he provides individual offerings to various Underworld deities, receiving in return his own dwelling place and appointment as Underworld judge alongside Gilgameš. However, his regret for what he has lost remains unstaunched and is expressed in a long lament in which he bewails both his fate and the fate of those dependent upon him.

One deity in particular, the goddess Inana, his divine partner, was absent when his fate was decided. She now approaches the senior deity Enlil and is informed of the earlier—and unalterable—decision. She expresses her anger at this, and her grief that her lover has been banished from her. The text is somewhat fragmentary at this point but, possibly as a result of Inana's reaction, another deity, perhaps Ninĝišzida, pronounces a blessing for the king, guaranteeing him posthumous fame in the land that he has left behind.

The brief, final section represents a summary of what has come before, ending with two lines referring to tears and laments which reinforce the tenor of the composition.

Translation

1–7 . . . entire land . . . , . . . struck, the palace was devastated. . . . panic spread rapidly among the dwellings of the black-headed people. . . . abandoned places . . . in Sumer. . . . the cities were destroyed in their entirety; the people were seized with panic. Evil came upon Urim and made the trustworthy shepherd pass away. It made Ur-Namma, the trustworthy shepherd, pass away; it made the trustworthy shepherd pass away.

8–14 Because An had altered his holy words completely, . . . became empty, and because, deceitfully, Enlil had completely changed the fate he decreed, Ninmaḫ began a lament in her . . . . Enki shut (?) the great door of Eridug. Nudimmud withdrew into his bedchamber and lay down fasting. At his zenith, Nanna frowned at the . . . words of An. Utu did not come forth in the sky, and the day was full of sorrow.

15–21 The mother, miserable because of her son, the mother of the king, holy Ninsumun, was crying: 'Oh my heart!' Because of the fate decreed for Ur-Namma, because it made the trustworthy shepherd pass away, she was weeping bitterly in the broad square, which is otherwise a place of entertainment. Sweet sleep did not come to the people whose happiness . . . ; they passed their time in lamentation over the trustworthy shepherd who had been snatched away.

22–30 As the early flood was filling the canals, their canal-inspector was already silenced (?); the mottled barley grown on the arable lands, the life of the land, was inundated. To the farmer, the fertile fields planted (?) by him yielded little. Enkimdu, the lord of levees and ditches, took away the levees and ditches from Urim. (*1 line fragmentary*) As the intelligence and . . . of the Land were lost, fine food became scarce. The plains did not grow lush grass any more, they grew the grass of mourning. The cows . . . , their . . . cattle-pen has been destroyed. The calves . . . their cows mooed bitterly.

31–51 The wise shepherd . . . does not give orders any more. . . . in battle and combat. The king, the advocate of Sumer, the ornament of the assembly, Ur-Namma, the advocate of Sumer, the ornament of the assembly, the leader of Sumer, . . . lies sick. His hands which used to grasp cannot grasp any more, he lies sick. His feet . . . cannot step any more, he lies sick. (*1 line fragmentary*) The trustworthy shepherd, king, the sword of Sumer, Ur-Namma, the king of the Land, was taken to the . . . house. He was taken to Urim; the king of the Land was brought into the . . . house. The proud one lay in his palace. Ur-Namma, he who was beloved by the troops, could not raise his neck any more. The wise one . . . lay down; silence descended. As he, who was the vigour of the Land, had fallen, the Land became demolished like a mountain; like a cypress forest it was stripped, its appearance changed. As if he were a boxwood tree, they put axes against him in his joyous dwelling place. As if he were a sappy cedar tree, he was uprooted in the palace where he used to sleep (?). His spouse . . . resting place; . . . was covered by a storm; it embraced it like a wife her sweetheart (?). His appointed time had arrived, and he passed away in his prime.

52–75 His (?) pleasing sacrifices were no longer accepted; they were treated as dirty (?). The Anuna gods refused his gifts. An did not stand by an 'It is enough', and he could not complete his (?) days. Because of what Enlil ordered, there was no more rising up; his beloved men lost their wise one. Strangers turned into (?) . . . . How iniquitously Ur-Namma was abandoned, like a broken jar! His . . . with grandeur like (?) thick clouds (?). He does not . . . any more, and he does not reach out for . . . . '. . . Ur-Namma, alas, what is it to me?' Ur-Namma, the son of Ninsumun, was brought to Arali, the . . . of the Land, in his prime. The soldiers accompanying the king shed tears: their boat° was sunk in a land as foreign to them as Dilmun. . . . was cut. It was stripped of the oars, punting poles and rudder which it had. . . . ; its bolt was broken off. . . . was put aside; it stood (?) in saltpetre. His donkeys were to be found with the king; they were buried with him. His donkeys were to be found with Ur-Namma; they were buried with him. As he crossed over the . . . of the Land, the Land was deprived of its ornament. The journey to the Underworld is a desolate route. Because of the king, the chariots were covered over, the roads were thrown into disorder, no one could go up and down on them. Because of Ur-Namma, the chariots were covered over, the roads were thrown into disorder, no one could go up and down on them.

76–87 He presented gifts to the seven chief porters of the Underworld. As the famous kings who had died and the dead purification priests, *lumaḫ* priests, and *nindiĝir* priestesses, all chosen by extispicy, announced the king's coming to the people, a tumult arose in the Underworld. As they announced Ur-Namma's coming to the people, a tumult arose in the Underworld. The king slaughtered numerous bulls and sheep, Ur-Namma seated the people at a huge banquet. The food of the Underworld is bitter, the water of the Underworld is brackish. The trustworthy shepherd knew well the rites of the Underworld, so the king presented the offerings of the Underworld, Ur-Namma presented the offerings of the Underworld: as many faultless bulls, faultless kids, and fattened sheep as could be brought.

88–91 To Nergal, the Enlil of the Underworld, in his palace, the shepherd Ur-Namma offered a mace, a large bow with quiver and arrows, an artfully made . . . dagger, and a multicoloured leather bag for wearing at the hip.

92–6 To Gilgameš, the king of the Underworld, in his palace, the shepherd Ur-Namma offered a spear, a leather bag for a saddle-hook, a heavenly lion-headed *imitum* mace, a shield resting on the ground, a heroic weapon, and a battle-axe, an implement beloved of Ereškigala.

97–101 To Ereškigala, the mother of Ninazu, in her palace, the shepherd Ur-Namma offered a . . . which he filled with oil, a *šaĝan* bowl of perfect make, a heavy garment, a long-fleeced garment, a queenly *pala* robe, . . . the divine powers of the Underworld.

102–5 To Dumuzid, the beloved husband of Inana, in his palace, the shepherd Ur-Namma offered a . . . sheep, . . . , mountain . . . , a lordly golden sceptre, . . . a shining hand.°

106–9 To Namtar, who decrees all the fates, in his palace, the shepherd Ur-Namma offered perfectly wrought jewellery, a golden ring cast (?) as a . . . barge, pure cornelian stone fit to be worn on the breasts of the gods.

110–13 To Ḫušbisag, the wife of Namtar, in her palace, the shepherd Ur-Namma offered a chest (?) with a lapis lazuli handle, containing (?)

everything that is essential in the Underworld, a silver hair clasp adorned with lapis lazuli, and a comb of womanly fashion.

114–22 To the valiant warrior Niñgišzida, in his palace, the shepherd Ur-Namma offered a chariot with . . . wheels sparkling with gold, . . . donkeys, thoroughbreds, . . . donkeys with dappled thighs, . . . , followed . . . by a shepherd and a herdsman. To Dimpimekug°, who stands by his side, he gave a lapis lazuli seal hanging from a pin, and a gold and silver toggle-pin with a bison's head.

123–8 To his spouse, Ninazimua, the august scribe, denizen of Arali, in her palace, the shepherd Ur-Namma offered a headdress with the august ear-pieces (?) of a sage, made of alabaster, a . . . stylus, the hallmark of the scribe, a surveyor's gleaming line, and the measuring rod . . . .

129–31 To . . . , the great . . . of the Underworld, he gave (*2 lines fragmentary*).

132–44 After the king had presented properly the offerings of the Underworld, after Ur-Namma had presented properly the offerings of the Underworld, the . . . of the Underworld, the . . . , seated Ur-Namma on a great dais of the Underworld and set up a dwelling place for him in the Underworld. At the command of Ereškigala all the soldiers who had been killed by weapons and all the men who had been found guilty were given into the king's hands. Ur-Namma was . . . , so with Gilgameš, his beloved brother, he will issue the judgments of the Underworld and render the decisions of the Underworld.

145–54 After seven days, ten days had passed, lamenting for Sumer overwhelmed my king, lamenting for Sumer overwhelmed Ur-Namma. My king's heart was full of tears, he . . . bitterly that he could not complete the wall of Urim; that he could no longer enjoy the new palace he had built; that he, the shepherd, could no longer . . . his household (?); that he could no longer bring pleasure to his wife with his embrace; that he could not bring up his sons on his knees; that he would never see in their prime the beauty of their little sisters who had not yet grown up.

155–65 The trustworthy shepherd . . . a heart-rending lament for himself: 'I, who have been treated like this, served the gods well, set up chapels for them. I have created evident abundance for the Anuna gods. I have laid treasures on their beds strewn with fresh herbs. Yet no god stood by me and soothed my heart. Because of them, anything that could have been a favourable portent for me was as far away from me as the heavens, the . . . . What is my reward for my eagerness to serve during the days? My days have been finished for serving them sleeplessly during the night! Now, just as the rain pouring down from heaven cannot turn back, alas, nor can I turn back to brick-built Urim.

166–86 'Alas, my wife has become a widow (?)! She spends the days in tears and bitter laments. My strength has ebbed away . . . . The hand of fate . . . bitterly me, the hero. Like a wild bull . . . , I cannot . . . . Like a mighty bull, ... Like an offshoot . . . . Like an ass . . . , I died. . . . my . . . wife . . . . She spends the days in tears and bitter laments. Her kind protective god has left her; her kind protective goddess does not care for her any more. Ninsumun no longer rests her august arm firmly on her head. Nanna, lord Ašimbabbar, no longer leads (?) her by the hand. Enki, the lord of Eridug, does not . . . . Her . . . has been silenced (?), she can no longer answer. She is cast adrift like a boat in a raging storm; the mooring pole has not been strong enough for her. Like a wild ass lured (?) into a perilous pit she has been treated heavy-handedly. Like a lion fallen into a pitfall, a guard has been set up for her. Like a dog kept in a cage, she is silenced. Utu . . . does not pay heed to the cries "Oh, my king" overwhelming her.

187–97 'My *tigi*, *adab*, flute, and *zamzam* songs have been turned into laments because of me. The instruments of the house of music have been propped against the wall. Because I have been made to . . . on a heap of soil (?) instead of my throne whose beauty was endless; because I have been made to lie down in the open, desolate steppe instead of my bed, the sleeping place whose . . . was endless, alas, my wife and my children are in tears and wailing. My people whom I used to command (?) sing like lamentation and dirge singers because of her (?). While I was so treated, foremost Inana, the warlike lady, was not present at my verdict. Enlil had sent her as a messenger to all the foreign lands concerning very important matters.'

198–202 When she had turned her gaze away from there, Inana humbly entered the shining E-kur, she . . .° at Enlil's fierce brow. (*Then Enlil said:*) 'Great lady of the E-ana, once someone has bowed down, he cannot . . . any more; the trustworthy shepherd left E-ana, you cannot see him any more.'

203–15 My lady . . . among the people . . . . Then Inana, the fierce storm, the eldest child of Suen, . . . , made the heavens tremble, made the earth shake. Inana destroyed cattle-pens, devastated sheepfolds, saying: 'I want to hurl insults at An, the king of the gods: Who can change the matter, if Enlil elevates someone? Who can change the import of the august words uttered by An, the king? If there are divine ordinances imposed on the Land, but they are not observed, there will be no abundance at the gods' place of sunrise. My holy *g̃ipar* shrine, the shrine E-ana, has been barred up like (?) a mountain°. If only my shepherd could enter it before me in his prime—I will not enter it otherwise!° If only my strong one could grow for me like grass and herbs in the desert. If only he could hold steady for me like a river boat at its calm mooring.'

216   This is how Inana . . . a lament over him.°

217–33   Lord Ning̃išzida. . . . Ur-Namma, my . . . who was killed, (*1 line fragmentary*) Among tears and laments, . . . decreed a fate for Ur-Namma: 'Ur-Namma . . . , your august name will be called upon. From the south to the uplands, . . . the holy sceptre. Sumer . . . to your palace. The people will admire . . . the canals which you have dug, the . . . which you have . . . , the large and grand arable tracts which you have . . . , the reed-beds which you have drained, the wide barley fields which you . . . , and the fortresses and settlements which you have . . . . Ur-Namma, they will call upon . . . your name. Lord Nunamnir, surpassing . . . , will drive away the evil spirits . . . .'

234–42   After shepherd Ur-Namma . . . , Nanna, lord Ašimbabbar, . . . , Enki, the king of Eridug . . . . devastated sheepfolds . . .°. . . . holy . . . , lion born on high° . . . your city; renders just judgments. . . . , praise be to lord Ning̃išzida! My king . . . among tears and laments; . . . among tears and laments.

Notes

52–75   'their boat': that is, Ur-Namma.

102–5   After 'a shining hand.' 1 MS adds: 'He . . . a gold and silver . . . , a lapis lazuli . . . , and a . . . pin to Dimpikug . . . .'

114–22   Instead of 'Dimpimekug' 1 MS has: 'Dimpikug'.

198–202   Instead of '. . .' 1 MS has: 'like . . .'.

203–15   Instead of 'like (?) a mountain' some MSS have: 'like the heavens'. Instead of 'I will not enter it otherwise!' some MSS have: 'Why should I enter it otherwise?'

216   Instead of '. . . a lament over him.' 1 MS has: '. . . Ur-Namma . . . .'

234–42   Instead of '. . . devastated sheepfolds . . .' the other MS has: '. . . the foremost, the flood . . .'. Instead of '. . . holy . . . , lion born on high' the other MS has: '. . . basket (?) . . .'.

B. INANA AND DUMUZID

Inana was the most powerful and ambitious goddess in the Sumerian pantheon. Much of this power stemmed from her role as the goddess of sexual love and agricultural fertility, the relationship between the two conveyed in metaphors which equate making love with plant cultivation, and sexual satisfaction with fruitful livestock and crops. Her partner in these celebrations was the shepherd-god Dumuzid, although this male role was often taken by a king who thus established his pastoral responsibility for his (human) flock, proximity to the divine, and contribution to agriculture, the economic foundation on which urban civilization was based. In *Dumuzid and Enkimdu* the shepherd-god vies successfully with the farmer for the affections of Inana, with whom she was initially smitten. The relationship between Inana and her lover is celebrated joyously and lyrically in *Ploughing with the jewels* and *A love song for Šu-Suen*.

However, passion can have more than one object of desire, emotions take many forms, and, as the biblical Song of Songs reminds us, 'love is as strong as death'. Consequently Inana's fervour extends beyond the boundaries of sexual love and her power also exultantly manifests itself in rage and war, military success being a further essential to a Mesopotamian ruler. It is this terrifying aspect of the goddess which dominates *Inana and Išme-Dagan* and *A hymn to Inana*. In one case her wrath is harnessed for the king against his enemies; in the other it is turned against the priestess En-ḫedu-ana.

Sex and death are most closely intertwined in the narratives *Inana's descent to the Underworld* and *Dumuzid's dream*, which are interrelated yet not directly sequential. The first is concerned with Inana's attempt to extend her rule to the Underworld, recounting her confinement there and subsequent release from this land of no return on condition that she be replaced by another deity (in the end, Dumuzid and his sister Ĝeštin-ana in alternation). The second provides a different account of Dumuzid's capture by the demons of the Underworld. These works exploit parallels between, on the one hand, what happens to deities and, on the other, the fruitfulness and cycle of the seasons with which they were associated, the human world being depicted as an inextricable complement to the divine.

They also contrast, however, jealous and destructive sexual passions with other kinds of love. Although Ĝeštin-ana is selflessly devoted to her brother Dumuzid, just as Inana's entourage unequivocally miss and mourn her, Dumuzid and Inana quarrel as soon as they are reunited, with fatal consequences that they will regret for evermore. This is the flipside to the eroticism that is celebrated in the love songs of Inana and Dumuzid: an exploration of the ways in which emotional intensity can have the most terrible consequences when allowed to run out of control. (See also the Introduction to Group F.)

FURTHER READING

Abusch, T., 'Ishtar', K. van der Toorn, B. Becking, and P. W. van der Horst (eds.), *Dictionary of Deities and Demons in the Bible* (Brill: Leiden, 2nd edn. 1999, pp. 452–6) gives a stimulating discussion of Inana (whose Akkadian name was Ištar or Eštar), supplemented by an extensive bibliography.

Alster, B., 'Tammuz', in K. van der Toorn, B. Becking, and P. W. van der Horst (eds.), *Dictionary of Deities and Demons in the Bible* (Brill: Leiden, 2nd edn. 1999, pp. 828–34) performs the same service for Dumuzid (whose name in Hebrew was Tammuz).

Katz, D., *The Image of the Netherworld in the Sumerian Sources* (CDL Press: Potomac, 2003) surveys Sumerian literature on the Underworld.

Sefati, Y., *Love Songs in Sumerian Literature: Critical Edition of the Dumuzi-Inanna Songs* (Bar-Ilan University Press: Ramat-Gan, 1998) is an excellent edition of most of the relevant love songs.

OTHER COMPOSITIONS FEATURING INANA AND/OR DUMUZID INCLUDE

Group A   Lugalbanda in the mountain cave
Lugalbanda and the Anzud bird
Gilgameš, Enkidu, and the Underworld
Sargon and Ur-Zababa
The death of Ur-Namma
Group C   The cursing of Agade
Group F   Inana and Šu-kale-tuda
A love song for Išme-Dagan
A *balbale* to Inana and Dumuzid
Group G   Enki and the world order
The home of the fish
Group H   A *kunĝar* to Inana and Dumuzid
A *šir-namursaĝa* to Inana for Iddin-Dagan

Group J   The exaltation of Inana
           A praise poem of Lipit-Eštar
           Inana and Ebiḫ

Inana's descent to the Underworld

The brisk linear narrative of *Inana's descent to the Underworld* is made up of many repeated episodes and phrases, and creates thereby the atmosphere of a vividly told folk-tale. The end point of the story is to explain how it came about that the god Dumuzid and his sister, Ĝeštin-ana, spend alternating periods of six months in the Underworld, which was doubtless envisaged as an explanation for the seasonal cycle.

No explanation is offered why Inana should take it into her head to seek domination over the Underworld. The fierce, ambitious aspect of her character and her insatiable desire for power are reasons enough. She sets off for the Underworld, dressed up to the nines and taking various divine powers with her. She anticipates trouble, and leaves instructions with her minister Ninšubura in case she should not return. At the gates, she claims to have come to attend the funeral rites of her sister Ereškigala's husband. She is not prepared for being stripped of all her jewellery and clothes in order to gain admittance—but of course this is the only state in which one enters the Underworld. She ends up dead, a corpse hanging on a hook. Ninšubura eventually secures the assistance of the wise god Enki, who creates two assistants from the dirt under his fingernails. These were real enough: as classes of people, they were among the cultic personnel of Inana's temples. The *galatura* sang laments and the *kurĝara* sang and danced with swords. Both seem to have been slightly frightening.

The two nearly succeed in rescuing Inana from the Underworld. But as they are about to leave, the Underworld gods insist that she must provide a substitute to take her place, since no one leaves the Underworld unaccounted for. She is escorted by demons, functioning as the Underworld police, as they look for a suitable victim. Eventually they find Dumuzid, Inana's lover, who alone had made no effort to mourn her absence in the Underworld. Inana is incensed, and he is chosen as an acceptable substitute. Dumuzid nearly succeeds in escaping (a theme focused on in more detail in *Dumuzid's dream*) but is ultimately captured.

In an unexpected twist, Inana is overcome by a sense of loss and seems not to know where her husband is. A fly offers to show her, and in return is rewarded by being given perpetual access to the beer-house—where else are flies to be found?

Translation

1–5   From the great heaven she set her mind on the great below. From the great heaven the goddess set her mind on the great below. From the great heaven Inana set her mind on the great below. My mistress abandoned heaven, abandoned earth, and descended to the Underworld. Inana abandoned heaven, abandoned earth, and descended to the Underworld.

6–13   She abandoned the *en* priesthood, abandoned the *lagar* priesthood, and descended to the Underworld. She abandoned the E-ana in Unug, and descended to the Underworld. She abandoned the E-muš-kalama in Bad-tibira, and descended to the Underworld. She abandoned the Giguna in Zabalam, and descended to the Underworld. She abandoned the E-šara in Adab, and descended to the Underworld. She abandoned the Barag-dur-ĝara in Nibru, and descended to the Underworld. She abandoned the Ḫursaĝ-kalama in Kiš, and descended to the Underworld. She abandoned the E-Ulmaš in Agade, and descended to the Underworld.°

14–19   She took the seven divine powers. She collected the divine powers and grasped them in her hand. With the good divine powers, she went on her way. She put a turban, headgear for the open country, on her head. She took a wig for her forehead. She hung small lapis lazuli beads around her neck.

20–5   She placed twin egg-shaped beads on her breast. She covered her body with a *pala* robe, the garment of ladyship. She placed mascara which is called 'Let a man come, let him come' on her eyes. She pulled the pectoral which is called 'Come, man, come' over her breast. She placed a golden ring on her hand. She held the lapis lazuli measuring rod and measuring line in her hand.

26–7   Inana travelled towards the Underworld. Her minister Ninšubura travelled behind her.

28–31   Holy Inana said to Ninšubura: 'Come my faithful minister of E-ana, my minister who speaks fair words, my escort who speaks trustworthy words°.

32–6   'On this day I will descend to the Underworld. When I have arrived in the Underworld, make a lament for me on the ruin mounds. Beat the drum for me in the sanctuary. Make the rounds of the houses of the gods for me.

37–40 'Lacerate your eyes for me, lacerate your nose for me.° In private, lacerate your buttocks for me. Like a pauper, clothe yourself in a single garment and all alone set your foot in the E-kur, the house of Enlil.

41–7 'When you have entered the E-kur, the house of Enlil, lament before Enlil: "Father Enlil, don't let anyone kill your daughter in the Underworld. Don't let your precious metal be alloyed there with the dirt of the Underworld. Don't let your precious lapis lazuli be split there with the mason's stone. Don't let your boxwood be chopped up there with the carpenter's wood. Don't let young lady Inana be killed in the Underworld."

48–56 'If Enlil does not help you in this matter, go to Urim. In the E-mud-kura at Urim, when you have entered the E-kiš-nugal, the house of Nanna, lament before Nanna: "Father Nanna, don't let anyone kill your daughter in the Underworld. Don't let your precious metal be alloyed there with the dirt of the Underworld. Don't let your precious lapis lazuli be split there with the mason's stone. Don't let your boxwood be chopped up there with the carpenter's wood. Don't let young lady Inana be killed in the Underworld."

57–64 'And if Nanna does not help you in this matter, go to Eridug. In Eridug, when you have entered the house of Enki, lament before Enki: "Father Enki, don't let anyone kill your daughter in the Underworld. Don't let your precious metal be alloyed there with the dirt of the Underworld. Don't let your precious lapis lazuli be split there with the mason's stone. Don't let your boxwood be chopped up there with the carpenter's wood. Don't let young lady Inana be killed in the Underworld."

65–7 'Father Enki, the lord of great wisdom, knows about the life-giving plant and the life-giving water. He is the one who will restore me to life.'

68–72 When Inana travelled on towards the Underworld, her minister Ninšubura travelled on behind her. She said to her minister Ninšubura: 'Go now, my Ninšubura, and pay attention. Don't neglect the instructions I gave you.'

73–7 When Inana arrived at the palace Ganzer, she pushed aggressively on the door of the Underworld. She shouted aggressively at the gate of the Underworld: 'Open up, doorman, open up. Open up, Neti, open up. I am all alone and I want to come in.'

78–80 Neti, the chief doorman of the Underworld, answered holy Inana: 'Who are you?'

81 'I am Inana going to the east.'

82–4 'If you are Inana going to the east, why have you travelled to the land of no return? How did you set your heart on the road whose traveller never returns?'

85–9 Holy Inana answered him: 'Because lord Gud-gal-ana, the husband of my elder sister holy Ereškigala, has died; in order to have his funeral rites observed, she offers generous libations at his wake—that is the reason.'

90–3 Neti, the chief doorman of the Underworld, answered holy Inana: 'Stay here, Inana. I will speak to my mistress. I will speak to my mistress Ereškigala and tell her what you have said.'

94–101 Neti, the chief doorman of the Underworld, entered the house of his mistress Ereškigala and said: 'My mistress, there is a lone girl outside. It is Inana, your sister, and she has arrived at the palace Ganzer. She pushed aggressively on the door of the Underworld. She shouted aggressively at the gate of the Underworld. She has abandoned E-ana and has descended to the Underworld.

102–7 'She has taken the seven divine powers. She has collected the divine powers and grasped them in her hand. She has come on her way with all the good divine powers. She has put a turban, headgear for the open country, on her head. She has taken a wig for her forehead. She has hung small lapis lazuli beads around her neck.

108–13 'She has placed twin egg-shaped beads on her breast. She has covered her body with the *pala* robe of ladyship. She has placed mascara which is called "Let a man come" on her eyes. She has pulled the pectoral which is called "Come, man, come" over her breast. She has placed a golden ring on her hand. She is holding the lapis lazuli measuring rod and measuring line in her hand.'

114–22 When she heard this, Ereškigala slapped the side of her thigh. She bit her lip and took the words to heart. She said to Neti, her chief doorman: 'Come Neti, my chief doorman of the Underworld, don't neglect the instructions I will give you. Let the seven gates of the Underworld be bolted. Then let each door of the palace Ganzer be opened separately. As for her, after she has entered, and crouched down and had her clothes removed, they will be carried away.'

123–28 Neti, the chief doorman of the Underworld, paid attention to the instructions of his mistress. He bolted the seven gates of the Underworld. Then he opened each of the doors of the palace Ganzer separately. He said to holy Inana: 'Come on, Inana, and enter.'

129–30 And when Inana entered,° the turban, headgear for the open country, was removed from her head.

131 'What is this?'

132–3 'Be satisfied, Inana, a divine power of the Underworld has been fulfilled. Inana, you must not open your mouth against the rites of the Underworld.'

134–5 When she entered the second gate, the small lapis lazuli beads were removed from her neck.

136 'What is this?'

137–8 'Be satisfied, Inana, a divine power of the Underworld has been fulfilled. Inana, you must not open your mouth against the rites of the Underworld.'

139–40 When she entered the third gate, the twin egg-shaped beads were removed from her breast.

141 'What is this?'

142–3 'Be satisfied, Inana, a divine power of the Underworld has been fulfilled. Inana, you must not open your mouth against the rites of the Underworld.'

144–5 When she entered the fourth gate, the 'Come, man, come' pectoral was removed from her breast.

146 'What is this?'

147–8 'Be satisfied, Inana, a divine power of the Underworld has been fulfilled. Inana, you must not open your mouth against the rites of the Underworld.'

149–50 When she entered the fifth gate, the golden ring was removed from her hand.

151 'What is this?'

152–3 'Be satisfied, Inana, a divine power of the Underworld has been fulfilled. Inana, you must not open your mouth against the rites of the Underworld.'

154–5 When she entered the sixth gate, the lapis lazuli measuring rod and measuring line were removed from her hand.

156 'What is this?'

157–8 'Be satisfied, Inana, a divine power of the Underworld has been
fulfilled. Inana, you must not open your mouth against the rites of
the Underworld.'

159–60 When she entered the seventh gate, the *pala* robe, the garment of
ladyship, was removed from her body.

FIG. 12. 'The *pala* robe, the garment of ladyship, was removed
from her body'—Inana in the Underworld, depicted on an Old
Babylonian terracotta plaque

161 'What is this?'

162–3 'Be satisfied, Inana, a divine power of the Underworld has been
fulfilled. Inana, you must not open your mouth against the rites of
the Underworld.'

164–72 After she had crouched down and had her clothes removed, they
were carried away. Then she made her sister Ereškigala rise from her
throne, and instead she sat on her throne. The Anuna, the seven
judges, rendered their decision against her. They looked at her—it
was the look of death. They spoke to her—it was the speech of anger.

They shouted at her—it was the shout of heavy guilt. The afflicted woman was turned into a corpse. And the corpse was hung on a hook.

173–5 After three days and three nights had passed, her minister Ninšubura° carried out the instructions of her mistress°.

176–82 She made a lament for her in her ruined (*houses*). She beat the drum for her in the sanctuaries. She made the rounds of the houses of the gods for her. She lacerated her eyes for her, she lacerated her nose. In private she lacerated her buttocks for her. Like a pauper, she clothed herself in a single garment, and all alone she set her foot in the E-kur, the house of Enlil.

183–9 When she had entered the E-kur, the house of Enlil, she lamented before Enlil: 'Father Enlil, don't let anyone kill your daughter in the Underworld. Don't let your precious metal be alloyed there with the dirt of the Underworld. Don't let your precious lapis lazuli be split there with the mason's stone. Don't let your boxwood be chopped up there with the carpenter's wood. Don't let young lady Inana be killed in the Underworld.'

190–4 In his rage Father Enlil answered Ninšubura: 'My daughter craved the great heaven and she craved the great below as well. Inana craved the great heaven and she craved the great below as well. The divine powers of the Underworld are divine powers which should not be craved, for whoever gets them must remain in the Underworld. Who, having got to that place, could then expect to come up again?'

195–203 Thus Father Enlil did not help in this matter, so she went to Urim. In the E-mud-kura at Urim, when she had entered the E-kiš-nuĝal, the house of Nanna, she lamented before Nanna: 'Father Nanna, don't let your daughter be killed in the Underworld. Don't let your precious metal be alloyed there with the dirt of the Underworld. Don't let your precious lapis lazuli be split there with the mason's stone. Don't let your boxwood be chopped up there with the carpenter's wood. Don't let young lady Inana be killed in the Underworld.'

204–8 In his rage Father Nanna answered Ninšubura: 'My daughter craved the great heaven and she craved the great below as well. Inana craved the great heaven and she craved the great below as well. The divine powers of the Underworld are divine powers which should not be craved, for whoever gets them must remain in the Underworld. Who, having got to that place, could then expect to come up again?'

209–16 Thus Father Nanna did not help her in this matter, so she went to Eridug. In Eridug, when she had entered the house of Enki, she lamented before Enki: 'Father Enki, don't let anyone kill your daughter in the Underworld. Don't let your precious metal be alloyed there with the dirt of the Underworld. Don't let your precious lapis lazuli be split there with the mason's stone. Don't let your boxwood be chopped up there with the carpenter's wood. Don't let young lady Inana be killed in the Underworld.'

217–21 Father Enki answered Ninšubura: 'What has my daughter done? She has me worried. What has Inana done? She has me worried. What has the mistress of all the lands done? She has me worried. What has the Mistress of heaven done? She has me worried.'°

222–5 He removed some dirt from the tip of his fingernail and created the *kurĝara*. He removed some dirt from the tip of his other fingernail and created the *galatura*. To the *kurĝara* he gave the life-giving plant. To the *galatura* he gave the life-giving water.

226–35 Then father Enki spoke out to the *galatura* and the *kurĝara*:° 'Go and direct your steps to the Underworld. Flit past the door like flies. Slip through the door pivots like phantoms. The mother who gave birth, Ereškigala, on account of her children, is lying there. Her holy shoulders are not covered by a linen cloth. Her breasts are not full like a *šagan* vessel. Her nails are like a pickaxe (?) upon her. The hair on her head is bunched up as if it were leeks.

236–45 'When she says: "Oh my heart", you are to say: "You are troubled, our mistress, oh your heart". When she says: "Oh my liver", you are to say: "You are troubled, our mistress, oh your liver". (*She will then ask:*) "Who are you? Speaking to you from my heart to your heart, from my liver to your liver—if you are gods, let me talk with you; if you are mortals, may a destiny be decreed for you." Make her swear this by heaven and earth. (*1 line fragmentary*)

246–53 'They will offer you a riverful of water—don't accept it. They will offer you a field with its grain—don't accept it. But say to her: "Give us the corpse hanging on the hook." (*She will answer:*) "That is the corpse of your queen." Say to her: "Whether it is that of our king, whether it is that of our queen, give it to us." She will give you the corpse hanging on the hook. One of you sprinkle on it the life-giving plant and the other the life-giving water. And so let Inana arise.'

254–62 The *galatura* and the *kurĝara* paid attention to the instructions of Enki. They flitted through the door like flies. They slipped through the door pivots like phantoms. The mother who gave birth, Ereškigala, because of her children, was lying there. Her holy shoulders were not covered by a linen cloth. Her breasts were not full like a *šagan* vessel. Her nails were like a pickaxe (?) upon her. The hair on her head was bunched up as if it were leeks.

263–72 When she said: 'Oh my heart', they said to her: 'You are troubled, our mistress, oh your heart'. When she said: 'Oh my liver', they said to her: 'You are troubled, our mistress, oh your liver'. (*Then she asked:*) 'Who are you? I tell you from my heart to your heart, from my liver to your liver—if you are gods, I will talk with you; if you are mortals, may a destiny be decreed for you.' They made her swear this by heaven and earth. They . . . .

273–5 They were offered a river with its water—they did not accept it. They were offered a field with its grain—they did not accept it. They said to her: 'Give us the corpse hanging on the hook.'

276–7 Holy Ereškigala answered the *galatura* and the *kurĝara*: 'The corpse is that of your queen.'

278 They said to her: 'Whether it is that of our king or that of our queen, give it to us.'

279–81 They were given the corpse hanging on the hook. One of them sprinkled on it the life-giving plant and the other the life-giving water. And so Inana arose.

282–3 Ereškigala said to the *galatura* and the *kurĝara*: 'Bring your queen . . . , your . . . has been seized.'

284–9 Inana, because of Enki's instructions, was about to ascend from the Underworld. But as Inana was about to ascend from the Underworld, the Anuna seized her: 'Who has ever ascended from the Underworld, has ascended unscathed from the Underworld? If Inana is to ascend from the Underworld, let her provide a substitute for herself.'

290–4 So when Inana left the Underworld, the one in front of her, though not a minister, held a sceptre in his hand; the one behind her, though not an escort, carried a mace at his hip, while the small demons, like a reed enclosure, and the big demons, like the reeds of a fence, restrained her on all sides.

295–305 Those who accompanied her, those who accompanied Inana, know no food, know no drink, eat no flour offering and drink no libation. They accept no pleasant gifts. They never enjoy the pleasures of the marital embrace, never have any sweet children to kiss. They tear away the wife from a man's embrace. They snatch the son from a man's knee. They make the bride leave the house of her father-in-law.°

306–10 After Inana had ascended from the Underworld, Ninšubura threw herself at her feet at the door of the Ganzer. She had sat in the dust and clothed herself in a filthy garment. The demons said to holy Inana: 'Inana, proceed to your city, we will take her back.'

311–21 Holy Inana answered the demons: 'This is my minister of fair words, my escort of trustworthy words. She did not forget my instructions. She did not neglect the orders I gave her. She made a lament for me on the ruin mounds. She beat the drum for me in the sanctuaries. She made the rounds of the gods' houses for me. She lacerated her eyes for me, lacerated her nose for me.° In private, she lacerated her buttocks for me. Like a pauper, she clothed herself in a single garment.

322–8 'All alone she directed her steps to the E-kur, to the house of Enlil, and to Urim, to the house of Nanna, and to Eridug, to the house of Enki.° She brought me back to life. How could I turn her over to you? Let us go on. Let us go on to the Sig-kur-šaga in Umma.'

329–33 At the Sig-kur-šaga in Umma, Šara, in his own city, threw himself at her feet. He had sat in the dust and dressed himself in a filthy garment. The demons said to holy Inana: 'Inana, proceed to your city, we will take him back.'

334–8 Holy Inana answered the demons: 'Šara is my singer, my manicurist and my hairdresser. How could I turn him over to you? Let us go on. Let us go on to the E-muš-kalama in Bad-tibira.'

339–43 At the E-muš-kalama in Bad-tibira, Lulal, in his own city, threw himself at her feet. He had sat in the dust and clothed himself in a filthy garment. The demons said to holy Inana: 'Inana, proceed to your city, we will take him back.'

344–7 Holy Inana answered the demons: 'Outstanding Lulal follows me at my right and my left. How could I turn him over to you? Let us go on. Let us go on to the great apple tree in the plain of Kulaba.'

348–53 They followed her to the great apple tree in the plain of Kulaba. There was Dumuzid clothed in a magnificent garment and seated magnificently on a throne. The demons seized him there by his thighs. The seven of them poured the milk from his churns. The seven of them shook their heads like . . . . They would not let the shepherd play the pipe and flute before her (?).

354–8 She looked at him, it was the look of death. She spoke to him (?), it was the speech of anger. She shouted at him (?), it was the shout of heavy guilt: 'How much longer? Take him away.' Holy Inana gave Dumuzid the shepherd into their hands.

359–67 Those who had accompanied her, who had come for Dumuzid, know no food, know no drink, eat no flour offering, drink no libation. They never enjoy the pleasures of the marital embrace, never have any sweet children to kiss. They snatch the son from a man's knee. They make the bride leave the house of her father-in-law.

368–75 Dumuzid let out a wail and turned very pale. The lad raised his hands to heaven, to Utu: 'Utu, you are my brother-in-law. I am your relation by marriage. I brought butter to your mother's house. I brought milk to Ningal's house. Turn my hands into snake's hands and turn my feet into snake's feet, so I can escape my demons, let them not keep hold of me.'

376–83 Utu accepted his tears.° Utu turned Dumuzid's hands into snake's hands. He turned his feet into snake's feet. Dumuzid escaped his demons.° They seized . . . . (2 lines fragmentary) Holy Inana . . . her heart.

384–93 Holy Inana wept bitterly for her husband. (4 lines fragmentary) She tore at her hair like esparto grass, she ripped it out like esparto grass. 'You wives who lie in your men's embrace, where is my precious husband? You children who lie in your men's embrace, where is my precious child? Where is my man? Where . . . ? Where is my man? Where . . . ?'

394–5 A fly spoke to holy Inana: 'If I show you where your man is, what will be my reward?'

396–8 Holy Inana answered the fly: 'If you show me where my man is, I will give you this gift: I will cover . . . .'

399–403 The fly helped (?) holy Inana. The young lady Inana decreed the destiny of the fly: 'In the beer-house and the tavern (?), may there . . . for you. You will live (?) like the sons of the wise.' Now Inana decreed this fate and thus it came to be.

404–10 . . . was weeping. She came up to the sister (?) and . . . by the hand: 'Now, alas, my . . . . You for half the year and your sister for half the year: when you are demanded, on that day you will stay, when your sister is demanded, on that day you will be released.' Thus holy Inana gave Dumuzid as a substitute . . . .

411–12 Holy Ereškigala, it is sweet to praise you!

Notes

6–13 After 'to the Underworld.' 1 MS adds 8 lines: 'She abandoned the Ibgal in Umma, and descended to the Underworld. She abandoned the E-Dilmuna in Urim, and descended to the Underworld. She abandoned the Amaš-e-kug in Kisiga, and descended to the Underworld. She abandoned the E-ešdam-kug in Ĝirsu, and descended to the Underworld. She abandoned the E-sig-meše-du in Isin, and descended to the Underworld. She abandoned the Anzagar in Akšak, and descended to the Underworld. She abandoned the Niĝin-ĝar-kug in Šuruppag, and descended to the Underworld. She abandoned the E-šag-ḫula in Kazallu, and descended to the Underworld.'

28–31 Instead of 'my minister who speaks fair words, my escort who speaks trust-worthy words' 1 MS has: 'I am going to give you instructions: my instructions must be followed; I am going to say something to you: it must be observed'.

37–40 After 'lacerate your nose for me.' 1 MS adds 1 line: 'Lacerate your ears for me, in public.'

129–30 After 'And when Inana entered,' 1 MS adds 2 lines: 'the lapis lazuli measuring rod and measuring line were removed from her hand, when she entered the first gate,'.

173–5 After 'Ninšubura' 2 MSS add 2 lines: ', her minister who speaks fair words, her escort who speaks trustworthy words,'. Instead of 'carried out the instructions of her mistress' 1 MS has 2 lines: 'did not forget her orders, she did not neglect her instructions'.

217–21 After '"She has me worried."' 1 MS adds 1 line: 'Thus father Enki helped her in this matter.'

226–35 Instead of 'Then father Enki spoke out to the *galatura* and the *kurĝara*:' 1 MS has the line: ' "One of you sprinkle the life-giving plant over her, and the other the life-giving water".'

295–305 Instead of 'They accept no pleasant gifts. They never enjoy the pleasures of the marital embrace, never have any sweet children to kiss. They tear away the wife from a man's embrace. They snatch the son from a man's knee. They make the bride leave the house of her father-in-law.' 1 MS has 2 lines: 'They take the wife away from a man's embrace. They take away the child hanging on a wet-nurse's breasts.' 1 MS adds 3 lines here: 'They crush no bitter garlic. They eat no fish, they eat no leeks. They, it was, who accompanied Inana.'

311–21 After 'lacerated her nose for me.' 1 MS adds 1 line: 'She lacerated her ears for me in public.'

322–8 After 'to the house of Enki.' 1 MS adds 1 line: 'She wept before Enki.'

376–83 After 'Utu accepted his tears.' 1 MS adds 1 line: 'Dumuzid's demons could not keep hold of him.' After 'Dumuzid escaped his demons.' 1 MS adds 1 line: 'Like a *saĝkal* snake he . . . .'

Dumuzid's dream

This composition is one of a complex of related narratives focusing on the goddess Inana's journey to the Underworld, her rescue and return, and her pact with the Underworld gods, whereby she is replaced in the Underworld by her lover, the god Dumuzid.

In *Dumuzid's dream* Dumuzid is being hunted down by the demons of the Underworld, who, we have to assume, have just been promised him by Inana. He has a disturbing dream with presentiments of death, whose meaning his sister Ĝeštin-ana woefully confirms. Immediately she notices the demons approaching and warns Dumuzid to hide, swearing to tell no one where he is.

When the demons catch Ĝeštin-ana and demand Dumuzid, she refuses to tell them where he is hiding. They turn instead to Dumuzid's friend, who reveals his whereabouts, and Dumuzid is captured. Dumuzid pleads with the sun-god Utu to help him escape. Utu turns him into a gazelle and Dumuzid runs away. When the demons find Dumuzid, he pleads with Utu a second time. Once more Dumuzid is transformed into a gazelle, and this time he takes shelter in the house of an old woman. The demons catch Dumuzid a third time. A third time Dumuzid prays to Utu, and Dumuzid again takes the form of a gazelle, finding refuge at his sister's sheepfold. But Ĝeštin-ana gives herself away by the fear on her face. When the demons come for Dumuzid they wreck the sheepfold, killing Dumuzid and fulfilling his portentous dream.

The composition exploits the powerful image of the sheepfold as a centre of warmth, well-being, prosperity, and stability: contented sheep and cattle in their byres are a common motif on cylinder seals and monumental art, especially of the Uruk and Early Dynastic periods. In the city laments too, the cities are often characterized as deserted sheepfolds or cattle-pens which have been abandoned by the gods. When the comfortable, ordered world of the sheepfold is attacked and disordered, as first in Dumuzid's dream and second when the demons enter, nothing but misery and death can come of it.

Translation

1–4   His heart was full of tears as he went out into the countryside. The lad's heart was full of tears as he went out into the countryside. Dumuzid's heart was full of tears as he went out into the countryside.

He carried with him his° stick on his shoulder, sobbing all the time:

5–14 'Grieve, grieve, O countryside, grieve! O countryside, grieve! O marshes, cry out! O . . . crabs of the river, grieve! O frogs of the river, cry out! My mother will call to me, my mother, my Durtur, will call to me, my mother will call to me for five things, my mother will call to me for ten things: if she does not know the day when I am dead, you, O countryside, can inform my mother who bore me. Like my little sister may you weep for me.'

15–18 In ancient times he lay down, in ancient times he lay down, in ancient times the shepherd lay down. When in ancient times the shepherd lay down, he lay down to dream. He woke up—it was a dream! He shivered—it was sleep! He rubbed his eyes, he was terrified.

19–24 'Bring, bring, bring my sister! Bring my Ĝeštin-ana, bring my sister! Bring my scribe proficient in tablets, bring my sister! Bring my singer expert in songs, bring my singer! Bring my perspicacious girl, bring my sister! Bring my wise woman who knows the meanings of dreams, bring my sister! I will relate the dream to her.'

FIG. 13. 'My male goats were dragging their dark beards in the dust for me'—Dumuzid receiving offerings of goats and plants, on an Old Akkadian cylinder seal

25–39 'A dream, my sister! A dream! In my dream, rushes were rising up for me, rushes kept growing for me; a single reed was shaking its head at me; twin reeds—one was being separated from me. Tall trees in the forest were rising up together over me. Water was poured over my holy coals° for me, the cover of my holy churn was removed, my holy drinking cup was torn down from the peg where it hung, my shepherd's stick disappeared from me. An owl (?) took a lamb from the sheep house, a falcon caught a sparrow on the reed fence, my male goats were dragging their dark beards in the dust for me, my rams were scratching the earth with their thick legs for me. The churns were lying on their sides, no milk was being poured, the drinking cups were lying on their sides, Dumuzid was dead, the sheepfold was haunted.'

40–55 Ĝeštin-ana answered Dumuzid: 'My brother, your dream is not favourable, don't tell me any more of it! Dumuzid, your dream is not favourable, don't tell me any more of it! The rushes rising up for you, which kept growing for you, are bandits rising against you from their ambush. The single reed shaking its head at you is your mother who bore you, shaking her head for you. The twin reeds of which one was being separated from you are you and I—one will be separated from you. The tall trees in the forest rising up together over you are the evil men catching you within the walls. That water was poured over your holy coals means the sheepfold will become a house of silence. That the cover of your holy churn was removed for you means the evil man will bring it inside in his hands.

56–69 'Your holy drinking cup torn down from the peg where it hung is you falling off the lap of the mother who bore you. That your shepherd's stick disappeared from you means the demons will set fire to it°. The owl (?) taking a lamb from the sheep house is the evil man who will hit you on the cheek°. The falcon catching a sparrow on the reed fence is the big demon coming down° from the sheep house. That the churns were lying on their sides, no milk was being poured, the drinking cups were lying on their sides, that Dumuzid was dead, and the sheepfold haunted, means your hands will be bound in handcuffs, your arms will be bound in fetters. That your male goats were dragging their dark beards in the dust for you means that my hair will whirl around in the air like a hurricane for you. That your rams were scratching the earth with their thick legs for you means that I shall lacerate my cheeks with my fingernails for you as if with a boxwood needle.'

70–82 Hardly had she spoken these words when he said: 'Sister, go up onto the mound, sister, go up onto the mound! Sister, when you go up onto the mound, do not go up onto the mound like an ordinary person, but lacerate your heart° and your liver, lacerate your clothes and your crotch, sister, and then go up onto the mound! Sister, when you go up onto the mound, look out from on the mound! The evil . . . , hated by men, . . . a river barge! They hold in their hands the wood to bind the hands, they are identified (?) from the wood to bind the neck—no man knows how to undo it!'

83–6 Ama-ĝeštin-ana went up onto the mound and looked around, Ĝeštin-ana craned her neck. Her girlfriend Ĝeštin-dudu advised her: 'The big men who bind the neck are already coming for him, they are . . . coming for him!'

87 'My adviser and girlfriend! Are they coming?'

88 'Yes, I will point out to you those who bind the neck!'

89–90 'My brother, your demons are coming for you! Duck down your head in the grass! Dumuzid, your demons are coming for you! Duck down your head in the grass!'

91–4 'My sister, I will duck down my head in the grass! Don't reveal my whereabouts to them! I will duck down my head in the short grass! Don't reveal my whereabouts to them! I will duck down my head in the tall grass! Don't reveal my whereabouts to them! I will drop down into the ditches of Arali! Don't reveal my whereabouts to them!'

95–7 'If I reveal your whereabouts to them, may your dog devour me! The black dog, your shepherd dog, the noble dog, your lordly dog, may your dog devour me!'

98–102 She remembered (?): '. . . give your friend instructions about it! O my brother, may you never have a friend or comrade like . . . ! After the demons (?) have searched for you, . . . , if he tells you . . . .'

103–6 'My friend, I will duck down my head in the grass! Don't reveal my whereabouts to them! I will duck down my head in the short grass! Don't reveal my whereabouts to them! I will duck down my head in the tall grass! Don't reveal my whereabouts to them! I will drop down into the ditches of Arali! Don't reveal my whereabouts to them!'

107–9 'If I reveal your whereabouts to them, may your dog devour me! The black dog, your shepherd dog, the noble dog, your lordly dog, may your dog devour me!'

110–38 Those who come for the king are a motley crew, who know no food, who know no drink, who eat no sprinkled flour, who drink no poured water, who accept no pleasant gifts, who do not enjoy a wife's embraces, who never kiss dear little children, who never chew sharp-tasting garlic, who eat no fish, who eat no leeks. There were two men of Adab who came for the king. They were thistles in dried-up waters, they were thorns in stinking waters—'his hand was on the table, his tongue was in the palace'°. Then there were two men of Akšak who came for the king, with . . . carried on their shoulders. Then there were two men of Unug who came for the king. With head-smashing clubs tied to their waists, there were two men of

Urim who came for the king. With shining° clothes on the quayside, there were two men of Nibru who came for the king. Crying 'Man run after man!', they came to the sheepfold and cattle-pen. They caught Ĝeštin-ana at the sheepfold and cattle-pen. They offered a river of water, but she wouldn't accept it. They offered her a field of grain, but she wouldn't accept it. The little demon spoke to the big demon, the wise demon, the lively demon, and the big demon who was between them, wise like . . . destroying a . . . , like . . . barring a . . . , they spoke:

139–40 'Who since the most ancient times has ever known a sister reveal a brother's whereabouts? Come! Let us go to his friend!'

141–3 Then they offered his friend a river of water, and he accepted it. They offered him a field of grain, and he accepted it.

144 'My friend ducked down his head in the grass, but I don't know his whereabouts.'°

145 They looked for Dumuzid's head in the grass, but they couldn't find him.

146 'He ducked down his head in the short grass, but I don't know his whereabouts.'

147 They looked for Dumuzid's head in the short grass, but they couldn't find him.

148 'He ducked down his head in the tall grass, but I don't know his whereabouts.'

149 They looked for Dumuzid's head in the tall grass, but they couldn't find him.

150 'He has dropped down into the ditches of Arali, but I don't know his whereabouts.'

151–5 They caught Dumuzid in the ditches of Arali. Dumuzid began to weep and turned very pale: 'In the city my sister saved my life, my friend caused my death. If a sister leaves (?) a child in the street, someone should kiss it. But if a friend leaves (?) a child in the street, no one should kiss it.'

156–63 The men surrounded him and drained the standing waters. They twisted a cord for him, they knotted a net for him. They wove a reed hawser for him, they cut sticks for him. The one in front of him threw missiles at him, the one behind him . . . one cubit°. His hands were bound in handcuffs, his arms were bound in fetters.

164–73 The lad raised his hands heavenward to Utu: 'Utu, you are my brother-in-law, I am your sister's husband! I am he who carries food to E-ana, I am he who brought the wedding gifts to Unug, I am he who kisses the holy lips, I am he who dances on the holy knees, the knees of Inana. Please change my hands into gazelle hands, change my feet into gazelle feet, so I can evade my demons. Let me escape with my life to Ku-bireš-dildareš.'

174–80   Utu accepted his tears°. Like a merciful man he showed him mercy. He changed his hands into gazelle hands, he changed his feet into gazelle feet, and so he evaded the demons, and escaped with his life to Ku-bireš-dildareš. The demons searched for him, but didn't find him.

181   'Come, let us go to Ku-bireš.'°

182–90   They caught Dumuzid at Ku-bireš. The men surrounded him and drained the standing waters. They twisted a cord for him, they knotted a net for him. They wove a reed hawser for him, they cut sticks for him, the one in front of him threw missiles at him, the one behind him . . . . His hands were bound in handcuffs, his arms were bound in chains.

191–9   The lad raised his hands heavenward to Utu: 'Utu, you are my brother-in-law, I am your sister's husband! I am he who carries food to E-ana, I am he who brought the wedding gifts to Unug, I am he who kisses the holy lips, I am he who dances on the holy knees, the knees of Inana. Please change my hands into gazelle° hands, change my feet into gazelle° feet, so I can escape to the house of Old Woman Belili.'

200–5   Utu accepted his tears. He changed his hands into gazelle° hands, he changed his feet into gazelle° feet, so he evaded the demons and escaped with his life to the house of Old Woman Belili. He approached the house of Old Woman Belili.

206–8   'Old woman! I am not just a man, I am the husband of a goddess! Would you pour water—please—so I can drink water. Would you sprinkle flour—please—so I can eat flour.'

209–12   She poured water, and she sprinkled flour, and he sat down inside the house. The old woman left the house. When the old woman left the house, the demons saw her.

213–16   'Unless the old woman is aware of Dumuzid's whereabouts, she is indeed looking frightened! She is indeed screaming in a frightened way! Come, let us go to the house of Old Woman Belili!'

217–25   They caught Dumuzid at the house of Old Woman Belili. The men surrounded him and drained the standing waters. They twisted a cord for him, they knotted a net for him. They wove a reed hawser for him, they cut sticks for him, the one in front of him threw missiles at him, the one behind him . . . . His hands were bound in handcuffs, his arms were bound in chains.

226–34 The lad raised his hands heavenward to Utu: 'Utu, you are my brother-in-law, I am your sister's husband! I am he who carries food to E-ana, I am he who brought the wedding gifts to Unug, I am he who kisses the holy lips, I am he who dances on the holy knees, the knees of Inana. Please change my hands into gazelle hands, change my feet into gazelle feet, so I can escape to the holy sheepfold, my sister's sheepfold.'

235–44 Utu accepted his tears. He changed his hands into gazelle° hands, he changed his feet into gazelle° feet, so he evaded the demons, and escaped with his life to the holy sheepfold, his sister's sheepfold. He approached the holy sheepfold, his sister's sheepfold. Ĝeštin-ana cried toward heaven, cried toward earth. Her cries covered the horizon completely like a cloth, they were spread out like linen. She lacerated her eyes, she lacerated her face, she lacerated her ears in public; in private she lacerated her buttocks.

245 'My brother, I will go round in the streets . . . .'

246–9 'Unless Ĝeštin-ana is aware of Dumuzid's whereabouts, she is indeed looking frightened! She is indeed screaming in a frightened way! Come, let us go to the sheepfold and cattle-pen!'

250–5 When the first demon entered the sheepfold and cattle-pen, he set fire to the bolt°. When the second entered the sheepfold and cattle-pen, he set fire to the shepherd's stick. When the third entered the sheepfold and cattle-pen, he removed the cover of the holy churn.

256–60 When the fourth entered the sheepfold and cattle-pen, he tore down the drinking cup from the peg where it hung. When the fifth entered the sheepfold and cattle-pen, the churns lay on their sides, no milk was poured, the drinking cups lay on their sides, Dumuzid was dead, the sheepfold was haunted.°

261 A *šir-kalkal* of the dead Dumuzid.

Notes

1–4 After 'his' 1 MS adds: 'shepherd's'.

25–39 Instead of 'coals' 1 MS has: 'brazier'.

56–69 Instead of 'will set fire to it' 1 MS has: 'will smash it'. Instead of 'who will hit you on the cheek' 1 MS has: 'who will destroy the sheep house'. Instead of 'down' 1 MS has: 'out'.

70–82   Instead of 'your heart' 1 MS has: 'your hair'.

110–38   'his hand was on the table, his tongue was in the palace': alludes to a proverb. Instead of 'shining' 1 MS has: 'clean'.

144   After 'his whereabouts.' 1 MS adds: 'Dumuzid ducked down his head in the grass, but I don't know his whereabouts.'

156–63   One cubit is about half a metre.

174–80   After 'tears' 1 MS adds: 'as a gift'.

181   After 'go to Ku-bireš.'' 1 MS adds: '. . . like a net . . .'.

191–9   Instead of 'gazelle' 1 MS has: 'snake'.

200–5   Instead of 'gazelle' 1 MS has: 'snake'.

235–44   Instead of 'gazelle' 1 MS has: 'snake'.

250–5   Instead of 'he set fire to the bolt' 1 MS has: 'he shouted . . .'.

256–60   Instead of these lines 1 MS has: 'When the fourth entered the sheepfold and cattle-pen, he poured water on my holy brazier. When the fifth demon entered the sheepfold and cattle-pen, he tore down my holy drinking cup from the peg where it hung. When the sixth demon entered the sheepfold and cattle-pen, the churns lay on their sides, and no milk was poured. When the seventh demon entered the sheepfold and cattle-pen, the drinking cups lay on their sides, Dumuzid was dead, the sheepfold was haunted.'

Ploughing with the jewels

This love song, anciently ascribed to the *kungar* genre (see Group H), represents an intimate episode between Inana and Dumuzid, here referred to by his name Ama-ušumgal-ana. In the first two paragraphs, first Inana and then Dumuzid speak in tones which suggest a quarrel about the propriety of their relationship and the relative merits of their families.

But the rest of the song is a lyrical outpouring about the act of sexual intercourse, referred to by the metaphor of ploughing. The '*šuba* stones' seem both to be a metaphor for Dumuzid's semen and, understood more literally, to refer to jewels worn by Inana: *šuba* is a precious stone, perhaps cornelian. (*A* šir-gida *to Ninisina*, Group H, relates how Ninisina invented them for Inana.) In the last paragraph, the 'beard of lapis lazuli' is a conventional reference to a dark-coloured beard (as if made from a precious stone), perhaps alluding to the false lapis lazuli beards actually made for representations of bulls in works of art of the third millennium BCE.

The wide range of divine names, including alternative names for Dumuzid and Inana, and the references to Inana as a 'priestess' and as 'the mistress' (*nugig*) suggest that this song is not a simple love song but has a religious cultic context.

Translation

1–6 'If it were not for our mother, he would be chasing me along the dark (?) paths of the desert! If it were not for our mother, this young man would be chasing me along the dark (?) paths of the desert! If it were not for my mother Ningal, he would be chasing me along the dark (?) paths of the desert! If it were not for Ningikuga, he would be chasing me along the dark (?) paths of the desert! If it were not for Father Suen, he would be chasing me along the dark (?) paths of the desert! If it were not for my brother Utu, he would be chasing me along the dark (?) paths of the desert!'

7–22 'Young woman, don't provoke a quarrel! Inana, let us talk it over! Inana, don't provoke a quarrel! Ninegala, let us discuss it together! My father is just as good as your father; Inana, let us talk it over! My mother is just as good as your mother; Ninegala, let us discuss it together! Ĝeštin-ana is just as good as . . . ; Inana, let us talk it over! I am just as good as Utu; Ninegala, let us discuss it together! Enki is just as good as Suen; Inana, let us talk it over! Durtur is just as good as Ningal; Ninegala, let us discuss it together!'

23–4 The words they speak are words towards desire; provoking a quarrel is the desire of his heart!

25–30 He of the *šuba* stones, he of the *šuba* stones is indeed ploughing with the *šuba* stones! Ama-ušumgal-ana, he of the *šuba* stones, is indeed ploughing with the *šuba* stones! He lays down like seeds the little jewels among his jewels. He piles up (?) like grain piles the large jewels among his jewels. He will carry them to the roof for his . . . who is leaning towards him from the roof; he will carry them to the wall for Inana who is leaning towards him from the wall.

31–5 . . . calls out to Ama-ušumgal-ana: 'Ploughing with the jewels, ploughing with the jewels, for whom is he ploughing? Ama-ušum-gal-ana, ploughing with the jewels, for whom is he ploughing? May the little jewels among his jewels be on our throat! May the large jewels among his jewels be on our holy breast!'

36–40 Ama-ušumgal-ana answers the mistress: 'It is for the mistress, it is for my spouse the mistress—I am ploughing with them for her! For holy Inana, the priestess—I am ploughing with them for her!' He of the *šuba* stones, he of the *šuba* stones will indeed plough with the *šuba* stones! Ama-ušumgal-ana, he of the *šuba* stones, will indeed plough with the *šuba* stones!

41–5 'Ploughing with the jewels, ploughing with the jewels, for whom is
he ploughing? Ama-ušumgal-ana, ploughing with the jewels, for
whom is he ploughing? The beard of the one whom he will create for
me, the one whom he will create for me, is of lapis lazuli, the beard of
the . . . whom An will create for me is lapis lazuli, the beard of the
. . . is of lapis lazuli, his beard is of lapis lazuli.'
46 A *kungar* of Inana.

Dumuzid and Enkimdu

The poem *Dumuzid and Enkimdu* is similar in some ways to the compositions which have been called 'debates' (see Group G), and is even described
by the same ancient term. However, there are important differences. This is
a debate between Dumuzid, the shepherd, and Enkimdu, a minor deity
associated with cultivation and here representing the interests of the farmer.
(Enkimdu has no connection to Enkidu, the slave of Gilgameš.) Shepherds
and farmers coexisted in the Mesopotamian economy and, while they
may have had their differences, in many ways their interests were comple-
mentary.

Here the debate is put into a dramatic context, since Inana's brother the
sun-god Utu is urging her to marry Dumuzid the shepherd (11–19), whereas
Inana is more inclined to marry Enkimdu the farmer (7–10, 20–34). The
shepherd insists that nothing which the farmer can offer—woven garments,
beer, bread, or beans—is superior to the sheep, milk, curds, cheeses or butter
that he, the shepherd, can produce (40–64).

But just at the point when the debate might have become heated, following provocation from the shepherd, the farmer declines to argue, and good-
naturedly allows the shepherd to graze his sheep on the stubble of the fields,
and to water his flocks in the farm's canal. The two end up as friends, and the
farmer will provide the shepherd with wheat, beans, and barley. He will also
continue to bring presents for Inana, even when she is married to Dumuzid.
The poem ends with praise to Inana.

Translation

1–6 'Maiden, the cattle-pen . . . ; maiden Inana, the sheepfold . . . .
bending in the furrows. Inana, let me stroll with you; . . . the emmer
wheat . . . . Young lady, let me . . . .'

7–10 'I am a woman and I won't do that, I won't! I am a star . . . , and I won't! I won't be the wife of a shepherd!'

11–19 Her brother, the warrior youth Utu, said to holy Inana: 'My sister, let the shepherd marry you! Maiden Inana, why are you unwilling? His butter is good, his milk is good°—all the work of the shepherd's hands is splendid. Inana, let Dumuzid marry you. You who wear jewellery, who wear *šuba* stones, why are you unwilling?° He will eat his good butter with you. Protector of the king, why are you unwilling?'

20–34 'The shepherd shall not marry me! He shall not make me carry his garments of new wool. His brand new wool will not influence me. Let the farmer marry me, the maiden. With the farmer who grows colourful flax, with the farmer who grows dappled grain . . . .' (*1 line fragmentary; approximately 7 lines missing*) 'The shepherd shall not marry me!'

35–9 These words . . . . the farmer to the shepherd. My king . . . , the shepherd, Dumuzid . . . . to say . . . :

40–54 'In what is the farmer superior to me, the farmer to me, the farmer to me? Enkimdu, the man of the dykes and canals—in what is that farmer superior to me? Let him give me his black garment, and I will give the farmer my black ewe for it. Let him give me his white garment, and I will give the farmer my white ewe for it. Let him pour me his best beer, and I will pour the farmer my yellow milk for it. Let him pour me his fine beer, and I will pour the farmer my soured (?) milk for it. Let him pour me his brewed beer, and I will pour the farmer my whipped milk for it. Let him pour me his beer shandy, and I will pour the farmer my . . . milk for it.

55–64 'Let him give me his best filtered beer, and I will give the farmer my curds (?). Let him give me his best bread, and I will give the farmer my . . . milk for it. Let him give me his little beans, and I will give the farmer my small cheeses for them.° After letting him eat and letting him drink, I will even leave extra butter for him, and I will leave extra milk for him. In what is the farmer superior to me?'

65–73 He was cheerful, he was cheerful, at the edge of the riverbank, he was cheerful. On the riverbank, the shepherd on the riverbank, now the shepherd was even pasturing the sheep on the riverbank. The farmer approached the shepherd there, the shepherd pasturing the sheep on the riverbank; the farmer Enkimdu approached him there. Dumuzid . . . the farmer, the king of dyke and canal. From the plain where he was, the shepherd from the plain where he was provoked a quarrel with him; the shepherd Dumuzid from the plain where he was provoked a quarrel with him.

74–9 'Why should I compete against you, shepherd, I against you, shepherd, I against you? Let your sheep eat the grass of the riverbank, let your sheep graze on my stubble. Let them eat grain in the jewelled (?) fields of Unug, let your kids and lambs drink water from my Surungal canal.'

80–3 'As for me, the shepherd: when I am married, farmer, you are going to be counted as my friend. Farmer Enkimdu, you are going to be counted as my friend, farmer, as my friend.'

84–7 'I will bring you wheat, and I will bring you beans; I will bring you two-row barley from the threshing-floor. And you, maiden, I will bring you whatever you please, maiden Inana, . . . barley or . . . beans.'

88–9 The debate between the shepherd and the farmer: maiden Inana, it is sweet to praise you!

90 A *balbale*.

Notes

11–19 Instead of 'His butter is good, his milk is good' 2 MSS have: 'He of good butter, he of good milk'. After 'unwilling?' 1 MS adds 2 lines: 'His butter is good, his milk is good—all the work of the shepherd's hands is splendid.'

55–64 After 'cheeses for them.' 1 MS adds 2 lines: 'Let him give me his large beans, and I will give the farmer my big cheeses for them.'

A love song for Šu-Suen

Most Sumerian love songs are written in the female voice, even if they were composed by male singers. This one is put into the mouth of the goddess Inana, cast as a young girl still living at home with her parents. The object of her desire is Šu-Suen, who was historically the fourth king of the Third Dynasty of Urim, but who is presented both as a young lad who has fallen in love with Inana and as the king.

This is one of several love songs composed for this king which articulate a belief in his very close and personal relationship with the goddess of love. In some songs of this type, the king's name seems to have been merely substituted for that of Dumuzid. Almost certainly they were performed in the context of certain religious rituals which have been referred to as the 'sacred marriage', but the precise details are unknown. The belief that the king could in some sense actually have sexual intercourse with the goddess is intimately connected to the belief in the divinity of the kings of this period. There is evidence of a similar belief in elaborate songs composed for Išme-Dagan, king of Isin (see *Inana and Išme-Dagan*). These kings received divine honours in the cult, and their names were written with the same symbol to indicate divine status as those of the gods.

This song may surprise us by its intimate tone and sexually explicit words, but it is typical of Mesopotamian love poetry of this period. The sticky sweetness of honey is used as a vivid metaphor for Inana's sexual arousal.

Translation

1–4 Man of my heart, my beloved man, your allure is a sweet thing, as sweet as honey. Lad of my heart, my beloved man, your allure is a sweet thing, as sweet as honey.

5–8 You have captivated me (?), of my own free will I shall come to you. Man, let me flee with you—into the bedroom. You have captivated me (?); of my own free will I shall come to you. Lad, let me flee with you—into the bedroom.

9–14 Man, let me do the sweetest things to you. My precious sweet, let me bring you honey. In the bedchamber dripping with honey let us enjoy over and over your allure, the sweet thing. Lad, let me do the sweetest things to you. My precious sweet, let me bring you honey.

15–21 Man, you have become attracted to me. Speak to my mother and I will give myself to you; speak to my father and he will make a gift of me. I know where to give physical pleasure to your body—sleep, man, in our house till morning. I know how to bring heart's delight to your heart—sleep, lad, in our house till morning.

22–3 Since you have fallen in love with me, lad, if only you would do your sweet thing to me.

24–7 My lord and god, my lord and guardian angel, my Šu-Suen who cheers Enlil's heart, if only you would handle your sweet place, if only you would grasp your place that is sweet as honey.

28–9 Put your hand there for me like the cover (?) on a measuring cup. Spread (?) your hand there for me like the cover (?) on a cup of wood shavings.

30 A *balbale* of Inana.

FIG. 14. 'Man, let me do the sweetest things to you'—
a love scene on an Old Babylonian terracotta model of a bed

Inana and Išme-Dagan

This is a song of praise for the goddess Inana, in which she is presented as the
wife of Išme-Dagan, king of Isin. The first paragraph invokes Inana, emphasizing briefly her character as a young woman of marriageable age, her
ambitious control of divine powers, and her aspect as Venus, the morning
and evening star.

In the next section Inana's martial qualities as a goddess of war are
described (7–18). Then her sexual qualities are emphasized (19–31), including
her mysterious power 'to turn a man into a woman and a woman into a man',
perhaps alluding to the ambivalent sexual characteristics of some of her
votaries. In both cases, it is stated that the divine couple Enlil and Ninlil,
deities of the city of Nibru, have endowed her with these various powers.

Next, the song tells how Enlil and Ninlil have given her king Išme-Dagan
as her husband, and that together the couple have a range of duties to serve
the gods (36–42). The same king enjoys a more bucolic relationship with

Inana in *A love song for Išme-Dagan* (Group F), while his predecessor's association with the goddess is explored in *A šir-namursaĝa to Inana for Iddin-
Dagan* (Group H).

Finally, the location of Nibru (where Enlil and Ninlil had their main
temples) is directly addressed, which suggests the song originally had a cultic
context. The king's name occurs again in the last line.

Translation

1–6 Young woman Inana, Suen's daughter, who makes the divine
powers of the Land supreme, who achieves everything, who seizes
the divine powers in heaven and gathers them up on earth, who proceeds proudly with her head reaching the heavens, whose radiance
makes the night-time secure like a fire which lights up into the
distance—no god can stand up as her opposition, ...

7–18 Holy Inana was endowed by Enlil and Ninlil with the capacity to
make the heavens shake, to make the earth tremble, to hold the four
directions in her hand and to act grandly as their lady, to shout with
wide open mouth in battle and combat and to wreak carnage (?), to
butt all at once valiantly (?) like a wild bull, to make the earth drink
the blood of enemies like water and to pile up their bodies, to take
captive their overwhelmed (?) troops and to make them serve, to
make the people ascend from below to above, to make the foreign°
people change their place, and to turn light to darkness and darkness
to light. They made her without rival in heaven and on earth. They
bestowed on her the power to establish a woman's domain in . . . .
They determined as her fate to . . . , to make them content together.

19–31 Inana was entrusted by Enlil and Ninlil with the capacity to gladden
the heart of those who revere her in their established residences, but
not to soothe the mood of those who do not revere her in their well-
built houses; to turn a man into a woman and a woman into a man,
to change one into the other, to make young women dress as men on
their right side, to make young men dress as women on their left side,
to put spindles into the hands of men . . . , and to give weapons to the
women; to see that women amuse themselves by using children's
language, to see that children amuse themselves by using women's
language, to . . . skill, to . . . . They built a palace, her house of ladyship, for the Mistress of heaven, and invested it with fearsome
radiance. They made it into the neck-stock of all the foreign countries, and imbued it with awe-inspiring, terrifying splendour.

32–5 To clamp down (?) on the black-headed people, to . . . , to decide justly the lawsuits of the numerous people, to select the just, . . . , to . . . who speaks (?) violently—all these were entrusted into Inana's hands by them.

36–42 Enlil and Ninlil gave her Išme-Dagan, the constant attendant, . . . as her husband . . . . The duty to build temples for the gods, to furnish their daily portions, to purify their raised temples and to sanctify their daises, to secure their daily liquor, syrup, and choice beer in their dining halls—all this was bestowed on Inana and Išme-Dagan by Enlil and Ninlil.

43–5 August Nibru, no god excels like your lord and lady! In your midst they have bestowed the divine powers on the young woman Inana. I, Išme-Dagan, have put this° in everyone's mouth for all time.

Notes

7–18   Instead of 'the foreign' 1 MS has: 'numerous'.
43–5   'this': i.e. this composition.

A hymn to Inana

The text of this important and extensive hymn to the goddess Inana is preserved in a partly fragmentary state, with a number of serious gaps. The tone of the hymn is so emphatic as to Inana's superiority to all other gods that the composition can only have issued from a religious milieu fanatically devoted to her cult. All hymns to a single deity emphasize the powers of that deity, but generally they acknowledge the status of the deity in relation to the other great gods. Here it is stated that the supreme god An 'dares not proceed' against Inana's command, that the great god Enlil determines no destinies without Inana, and that Inana is like a falcon preying on the other gods. A large part of the hymn (18–72) is concerned with Inana's martial qualities, as she stirs up war and joyfully sings her battle-song on the field of combat. An obscure passage mentions various personnel of her cult, with ambiguous sexual characteristics (80–90).

The long middle section (91–218) addresses the goddess directly and enumerates the many powers, both positive and negative, which the goddess exercises, again emphasizing her superiority to all other deities. Her violent campaign against Mount Ebiḫ is alluded to (109 ff.; see *Inana and Ebiḫ*,

Group J). Her role as Venus, the morning star and evening star, is also mentioned (209 ff.).

The last section of the hymn (part of which is, unfortunately, not preserved) is spoken in the first person as if by En-ḫedu-ana, a historical personage who was the daughter of king Sargon of Agade and held the role of *en* (high priestess) of Nanna at the city of Urim in southern Mesopotamia (219–74). Whether this is evidence that En-ḫedu-ana composed the hymn, or whether this section was added later, or her name inserted in the Old Babylonian period from a desire to attribute the hymn to her, is not clear. It is difficult to believe that the language of the hymn dates from the Old Sumerian phase of the language. However, this last section seems to allude to some historical events which cannot at present be elucidated. (See too *The exaltation of Inana*, Group J.)

Translation

1–10   The great-hearted mistress, the impetuous lady, proud among the Anuna gods and pre-eminent in all lands, the great daughter of Suen, exalted among the Great Princes°, the magnificent lady who gathers up the divine powers of heaven and earth and rivals great An, is mightiest among the great gods—she makes their verdicts final. The Anuna gods crawl before her august word whose course she does not let An know; he dares not proceed against her command. She changes her own action, and no one knows how it will occur. She makes perfect the great divine powers, she holds a shepherd's crook, and she is their magnificent pre-eminent one. She is a huge shackle clamping down upon the gods of the Land. Her great awesomeness covers the great mountain and levels the roads.

11–17   At her loud cries, the gods of the Land become scared. Her roaring makes the Anuna gods tremble like a solitary reed. At her rumbling, they hide all together. Without Inana great An makes no decisions, and Enlil determines no destinies. Who opposes the mistress who raises her head and is supreme over the mountains? Wherever she . . . , cities become ruin mounds and haunted places, and shrines become waste land. When her wrath makes people tremble, the burning sensation and the distress she causes are like an *ulu* demon ensnaring a man.

18–28   She stirs confusion and chaos against those who are disobedient to her, speeding carnage and inciting the devastating flood, clothed in terrifying radiance. It is her game to speed conflict and battle, untiring, strapping on her sandals. Clothed (?) in a furious storm, a whirlwind, she . . . the garment of ladyship. When she touches . . . there is despair, a south wind which has covered . . . . Inana sits on harnessed (?) lions, she cuts to pieces him who shows no respect. A leopard of the hills, entering (?) the roads, raging (?), . . . , the mistress is a great bull trusting in its strength; no one dares turn against her. . . . , the foremost among the Great Princes, a pitfall for the disobedient, a trap for the evil, a . . . for the hostile, wherever she casts her venom . . . .

29–38 Her wrath is . . . , a devastating flood which no one can withstand. A great watercourse, . . . , she abases those whom she despises. The mistress, an eagle who lets no one escape, . . . , Inana, a falcon preying on the gods, Inana rips to pieces the spacious cattle-pens. The fields of the city which Inana has looked at in anger . . . . The furrows of the field which the mistress . . . grass. An opposes her, ... Setting on fire, in the high plain the mistress . . . . Inana . . . . The mistress . . . fighting, . . . , conflict . . . .

39–48 . . . she performs a song. This song . . . its established plan, weeping, the food and milk of death. Whoever eats . . . Inana's food and milk of death will not last. Gall will give a burning pain to those she gives it to eat, . . . in their mouth . . . . In her joyful heart she performs the song of death on the plain. She performs the song of her heart. She washes their weapons with blood and gore, ... Axes smash heads, spears penetrate and maces are covered in blood. Their evil mouths . . . the warriors . . . . On their first offerings she pours blood, filling them with blood.

49–59 On the wide and silent plain, darkening the bright daylight, she turns midday into darkness. People look upon each other in anger, they look for combat. Their shouting disturbs the plain, it weighs on the pasture and the waste land. Her howling is like Iškur's and makes the flesh of all the lands tremble. No one can oppose her murderous battle—who rivals her? No one can look at her fierce fighting, the carnage, the . . . . Engulfing (?) water, raging, sweeping over the earth, she leaves nothing behind. The mistress, a breaking plough opening hard ground, ... The braggarts do not lift their necks, ... Her great heart performs her bidding, the mistress who alone fashions (?) . . . . Exalted in the assembly, she occupies the seat of honour, . . . to the right and left.

60–72 Humbling huge mountains as if they were piles of litter, she immobilizes . . . . She brings about the destruction of the mountain lands from east to west. Inana . . . wall . . . *gulgul* stones, she obtains victory. She . . . the *kalaga* stone . . . as if it were an earthenware bowl, she makes it like sheep's fat. The proud mistress holds a dagger in her hand, a radiance which covers the Land; her suspended net piles up fish in the deep, ... As if she were a clever fowler no bird escapes the mesh of her suspended net. The place she has pulverized . . . , . . . the divine plans of heaven and earth. The intention of her word does not . . . to An. The context of her confusing advice in the great gods' assembly is not known. (*2 lines fragmentary*)

73–9   The mistress, a leopard among the Anuna gods, full of pride, has been given authority. Not having . . . struggle . . . , Inana . . . . She . . . the adolescent girl in her chamber, receiving her, . . . heart . . . charms. She evilly . . . the woman she rejects. In the entire (?) country she . . . . She lets her run around in the street . . . . of a house the wife sees her child.

80–90   When she had removed the great punishment from her body, she invoked blessings upon it; she caused it to be named the *pilipili* priest. She broke the spear and as if she were a man . . . gave her a weapon. When she had . . . punishment, it is not . . . . She . . . the door of the house of wisdom, she makes known its interior. Those who do not respect her suspended net do not escape . . . when she suspends the meshes of her net. The man she has called by name she does not hold in esteem. Having approached the woman, she breaks the weapon and gives her a spear. The male *ĝišgisaĝkeš*, the *nisub* and the female *ĝišgi* officiants, after having . . . punishment, moaning . . . . The ecstatic, the transformed *pilipili*, *kurĝara* and *saĝursaĝ* priests . . . . Lament and song . . . . They exhaust themselves with weeping and grief, they . . . laments.

91–8   Weeping daily your heart does not . . . . 'Alas' . . . heart . . . knows no relaxation. Beloved lady of holy An, your . . . in weeping . . . . In heaven . . . . On your breast . . . . You alone are majestic, you have renown, heaven and earth . . . not . . . . You rival An and Enlil, you occupy their seat of honour. You are pre-eminent in the cult places, you are magnificent in your course.

99–108 Ezina . . . august dais . . . . Iškur who roars from the sky . . . . His thick clouds . . . . When . . . the great divine powers of heaven and earth, Inana, your victory is terrifying . . . . The Anuna gods bow down in prostration, they abase themselves. You ride on seven great beasts as you come forth from heaven. Great An feared your precinct and was frightened of your dwelling-place. He let you take a seat in the dwelling-place of great An and then feared you no more, saying: 'I will hand over to you the august royal rites and the great divine rites.'

109–14 The great gods kissed the earth and prostrated themselves. The high mountain land, the land of cornelian and lapis lazuli, bowed down before you, but Ebiḫ did not bow down before you and did not greet you. Shattering it in your anger, as desired, you smashed it like a storm. Lady, pre-eminent through the power of An and Enlil, ... Without you no destiny at all is determined, no clever counsel is granted favour.

115–31 To run, to escape, to quiet and to pacify are yours, Inana. To rove around, to rush, to rise up, to fall down and to . . . a companion are yours, Inana. To open up roads and paths, a place of peace for the journey, a companion for the weak, are yours, Inana. To keep paths and ways in good order, to shatter earth and to make it firm are yours, Inana. To destroy, to build up, to tear out and to settle are yours, Inana. To turn a man into a woman and a woman into a man are yours, Inana. Desirability and arousal, goods and property are yours, Inana. Gain, profit, great wealth and greater wealth are yours, Inana. Gaining wealth and having success in wealth, financial loss and reduced wealth are yours, Inana. Observation°, choice, offering, inspection and approval are yours, Inana. Assigning virility, dignity, guardian angels, protective deities and cult centres are yours, Inana. (*6 lines fragmentary*)

132–54 . . . mercy and pity are yours, Inana. . . . are yours, Inana. To cause the . . . heart to tremble, . . . illnesses are yours, Inana. To have a wife, . . . , to love . . . are yours, Inana. To rejoice, to control (?), . . . are yours, Inana. Neglect and care, raising and bowing down are yours, Inana. To build a house, to create a woman's chamber, to possess implements, to kiss a child's lips are yours, Inana. To run, to race, to desire and to succeed are yours, Inana. To interchange the brute and the strong and the weak and the powerless is yours, Inana. To interchange the heights and valleys and the . . . and the plains (?) is yours, Inana. To give the crown, the throne and the royal sceptre is yours, Inana. (*12 lines missing*)

155–7 To diminish, to make great, to make low, to make broad, to . . . and to give a lavish supply are yours, Inana. To bestow the divine and royal rites, to carry out the appropriate instructions, slander, untruthful words, abuse, to speak inimically and to overstate are yours, Inana.

158–68 The false or true response, the sneer, to commit violence, to extend derision, to speak with hostility, to cause smiling and to be humbled or important, misfortune, hardship, grief, to make happy, to clarify and to darken, agitation, terror, fear, splendour and great awesomeness in radiance, triumph, pursuit, *imbasur* illness, sleeplessness and restlessness, submission, gift, . . . and howling, strife, chaos, opposition, fighting and carnage, . . . , to know everything, to strengthen for the distant future a nest built . . . , to instil fear in the . . . desert like a . . . poisonous snake, to subdue the hostile enemy, . . . and to hate . . . are yours, Inana.

169–73 To . . . the lots . . . , to gather the dispersed people and restore them to their homes, to receive . . . , to . . . are yours, Inana. (*1 line fragmentary*)

174–81 . . . the runners, when you open your mouth, . . . turns into . . . . At your glance a deaf man does not . . . to one who can hear. At your angry glare what is bright darkens; you turn midday into darkness. When the time had come you destroyed the place you had in your thoughts, you made the place tremble. Nothing can be compared to your purposes (?); who can oppose your great deeds? You are the lady of heaven and earth! Inana, in (?) the palace the unbribable judge, among the numerous people . . . decisions. The invocation of your name fills the mountains, An (?) cannot compete with your . . . .

182–96 Your understanding . . . all the gods . . . . You alone are magnificent. You are the great cow among the gods of heaven and earth, as many as there are. When you raise your eyes they pay heed to you, they wait for your word. The Anuna gods stand praying in the place where you dwell. Great awesomeness, glory . . . . May your praise not cease! Where is your name not magnificent? (*9 lines missing*)

197–202 Your song is grief, lament . . . . Your . . . cannot be changed, your anger is crushing. Your creation cannot be . . . , An has not diminished your . . . orders. Woman, with the help of An and Enlil you (?) have granted . . . as a gift in the assembly. Unison . . . An and Enlil . . . , giving the Land into your hand. An does not answer the word you have uttered to him.

203–8 Once you have said 'So be it', great An does not . . . for him. Your 'So be it' is a 'So be it' of destruction, to destroy . . . . Once you have said your . . . in the assembly, An and Enlil will not disperse it. Once you

FIG. 15. 'You alone are magnificent'—an Ur III cylinder seal from
Nibru showing a king making an offering to Inana as warrior, who
offers him the rod and ring, symbols of kingship, in return

have made a decision . . . , it cannot be changed in heaven and earth.
Once you have specified approval of a place, it experiences no
destruction. Once you have specified destruction for a place, it
experiences no approval.

209–18 Your divinity shines in the pure heavens like Nanna or Utu. Your
torch lights up the corners of heaven, turning darkness into light.
. . . with fire. Your . . . refining . . . walks like Utu in front of you. No
one can lay a hand on your precious divine powers; all your divine
powers . . . . .. You exercise full ladyship over heaven and earth; you
hold everything in your hand. Mistress, you are magnificent, no one
can walk before you. You dwell with great An in the holy resting-
place. Which god is like you in gathering together . . . in heaven and
earth? You are magnificent, your name is praised, you alone are
magnificent!

219–42 I am En-ḫedu-ana, the high priestess of the moon-god. . . . ; I am the
. . . of Nanna. (22 *lines missing or fragmentary*)

243–53 Advice . . . , grief, bitterness . . . , 'alas' . . . . My lady, . . . mercy . . .
compassion . . . I am yours! This will always be so! May your heart be
soothed towards me! May your understanding . . . compassion. May
. . . in front of you, may it be my offering. Your divinity is resplendent in the Land! My body has experienced your great punishment.
Lament, bitterness, sleeplessness, distress, separation . . . , mercy,
compassion, care, lenience and homage are yours, and to cause
flooding, to open hard ground and to turn darkness into light.

254–63 My lady, let me proclaim your magnificence in all lands, and your glory! Let me praise your ways and greatness! Who rivals you in divinity? Who can compare with your divine rites? May great An, whom you love, say for you 'It is enough!' May the great gods calm your mood. May the lapis lazuli dais, fit for ladyship, ... May your magnificent dwelling place say to you: 'Be seated.' May your pure bed say to you: 'Relax.' Your . . . , where Utu rises, ...

264–71 They proclaim your magnificence; you are the lady . . . . An and Enlil have determined a great destiny for you throughout the entire universe. They have bestowed upon you ladyship in the *guena* hall. Being fitted for ladyship, you determine the destiny of noble ladies. Mistress, you are magnificent, you are great! Inana, you are magnificent, you are great! My lady, your magnificence is resplendent. May your heart be restored for my sake!

272–4 Your great deeds are unparallelled, your magnificence is praised! Young woman, Inana, it is sweet to praise you!

Notes

1–10 'Great Princes': a name of the Igigi gods.

115–31 Instead of 'Observation' 1 MS has: 'Everything'.

C. ENLIL AND NINLIL

Enlil, the dominant deity in the Sumerian pantheon, also went by the name Nunamnir and the epithet 'Great Mountain'. He played a central role in royal ideology as the god who bestowed 'kingship of the Land' in his temple at Nibru, the religious centre of the Land. Sumer was rarely politically united—under Sargon and his successors in the late twenty-fourth century; by Šulgi and his descendants throughout the twenty-first century; and by Ḫammurabi in the mid-eighteenth century BCE—but the image of divinely sanctioned unity remained powerful (for instance in *A praise poem of Lipit-Eštar*, Group J). In *The cursing of Agade* Enlil's support is withheld from king Naram-Suen, who takes destructive revenge on Enlil's temple E-kur and then watches helplessly as his magnificent capital city is destroyed in turn. *The lament for Sumer and Urim* (Group D) explains the collapse of the Third Dynasty of Urim precisely as the natural termination of Enlil's backing:

From time immemorial, since the Land was founded, until people multiplied, who has ever seen a reign of kingship that would take precedence for ever?

The functioning of Enlil's temple is described in literary works such as *Enlil in the E-kur* (Group J) and can be reconstructed through contemporary administrative records. At the top of the hierarchy was the *en* priestess, chosen by divination from the entrails of sacrificed animals, and the *lagar*, about whom relatively little is known. In the middle ranks were several *nueš*, in charge of food offerings; *išib*, who maintained the cultic purity of the temple purification; and *gudug*, who took care of clothing. *Nueš* priests were especially associated with Enlil, but it is a *gudug* who encounters Enlil in the street in *Enlil and Nam-zid-tara*.

The human workforce surrounding Enlil was mirrored by the divine entourage which occupied the E-kur. His minister Nuska acted as messenger and intermediary (see *Enlil and Ninlil* and *Enlil and Sud*), while a large number of other gods also had shrines there and subordinate roles to Enlil. Deities with cult centres in other cities could also come and visit, in real life as well as in literature—see *Enki's journey to Nibru* (Group J) and *Nanna-Suen's journey to Nibru* (Group D)—to receive Enlil's blessing.

Enlil's spouse Ninlil had her own cult centre downstream from Nibru, at Tummal, as well as a sanctuary in the E-kur (see *Šulgi and Ninlil's barge*). Two conflicting literary images are painted of the relationship between the two. *Enlil and Sud*, whose aim is to equate Ninlil with Sud, the goddess of Šuruppag, tells of a decorous courtship. The suitor woos his beloved through her family and the outcome is a big white wedding. *Enlil and Ninlil*, by contrast, narrates a series of highly charged illicit sexual encounters whose outcome is the birth of several divine offspring. There is no mention of marriage.

FURTHER READING

Gibson, M., 'Nippur, Sacred City of Enlil, Supreme God of Sumer and Akkad', *Al-Rafidan*, 14 (1993), and <http://www-oi.uchicago.edu/OI/PROJ/NIP/PUB93/NSC/NSC.html>.

Michalowski, P., 'The Unbearable Lightness of Enlil', in J. Prosecky (ed.), *Intellectual Life of the Ancient Near East* (Oriental Institute: Prague, 1998, pp. 237–47) argues that the traditional scholarly interpretation of Enlil as 'Lord Air' should be abandoned and then compares *Enlil and Ninlil* with *Enlil and Sud*.

Westenholz, J. G., 'The Clergy of Nippur: The Priestess of Enlil', in M. de J. Ellis, *Nippur at the Centennial* (University Museum: Philadelphia, 1992, pp. 297–310) surveys the different types of priests attached to Enlil's temple E-kur in Nibru.

OTHER COMPOSITIONS FEATURING ENLIL AND/OR NINLIL INCLUDE

Group A The building of Ninĝirsu's temple
         The death of Ur-Namma
Group B Inana and Išme-Dagan
Group D The lament for Sumer and Urim
         A *balbale* to Nanna
         The herds of Nanna
Group E An *adab* to Nergal for Šu-ilišu
Group F A *tigi* to Nintud-Aruru
Group G The debate between Sheep and Grain
Group H An *adab* to Bau for Išme-Dagan
         A *šir-gida* to Ninisina
         A *šir-namgala* to Ninisina for Lipit-Eštar
         A *šir-namšub* to Utu
         A *šir-namursaĝa* to Inana for Iddin-Dagan
         A *tigi* to Enki for Ur-Ninurta
         An *ululumama* to Suen for Ibbi-Suen

Enlil and Ninlil

Unusually, the beginning of this narrative attempts to normalize the setting, location, and actors: everything is just ordinary, and (unlike many other mythical narratives) it takes place in the city of Nibru, a real, known location. The first person pronoun 'we' is introduced, to involve the audience.

'At that time' (it is implied that this was recent), a goddess warns her daughter about the danger along the river bank from the lusty and irresponsible god Enlil. As the story unfolds, the daughter, Ninlil, resists Enlil's first advance, with various excuses. Enlil relies on his minister Nuska to transport him across the river so he can have sex with Ninlil. Their encounter takes place by the river, as they bathe, float downstream by boat, or cross over by ferry.

Next, Enlil is walking in the Ki-ur, the courtyard of his temple in Nibru, and is forced by the other gods to leave the city, as being ritually impure. The youthful Ninlil, emotionally captive, follows him. In three parallel episodes, Enlil speaks first to the keeper of the city gate, then—as the location becomes more sombre—the man who guards the river of the Underworld, and finally the Underworld ferryman, saying 'Don't tell Ninlil where I am'. Each time, when she asks after Enlil, he answers, disguised as each man in turn, that he does not know where the god is. Ninlil then offers to have sex with him, telling him excitedly, 'The great god Enlil has had sex with me already'. He then has sex again with her: whether he reveals his identity or not is unclear.

The psychology of this is complex. Enlil seems to want to escape from Ninlil. Ninlil seems willing to have sex with anyone. Or is it all a complex sexual game? Successively Ninlil becomes pregnant with the moon-god Suen, two gods associated with the Underworld (Nergal and Ninazu), and Enbilulu, a deity connected with irrigation. The poem ends with praise of the fertility of Enlil and Ninlil.

There seems to be no concern over the obvious problem of serial pregnancy and multiple births, which here seem to override natural laws. Although Enlil is ritually impure from having sex (perhaps in a holy location), there are no moral overtones; and Ninlil seems to be just as promiscuous as he is. On a straightforward level the poem explains the parentage of various deities.

Translation

1–12   There was a city, there was a city — the one we live in. Nibru was the city, the one we live in. Dur-ĝišnimbar was the city, the one we live in. Sala is its holy river, Kar-ĝeština is its quay. Kar-asar is its quay where boats make fast. Pu-lal is its freshwater well. Nunbir-tum is its branching canal, and if one measures from there, its cultivated land is fifty *sar°* each way. Enlil was one of its young men, and Ninlil was one of its young women. Nun-bar-še-gunu was one of its wise old women.

13–21   At that time the maiden was advised by her own mother, Ninlil was advised by Nun-bar-še-gunu: 'The river is holy, woman! The river is holy — don't bathe in it! Ninlil, don't walk along the bank of the Nunbir-tum! His eye is bright, the lord's eye is bright, he will look at you! The Great Mountain, Father Enlil — his eye is bright, he will look at you! The shepherd who decides all destinies — his eye is bright, he will look at you! Straight away he will want to have sex, he will want to kiss! He will be happy to pour lusty semen into your womb, and then he will leave you to it!'

22–30   She advised her from the heart, she gave wisdom to her. The river is holy; the woman bathed in the holy river. As Ninlil walked along the bank of the Nunbir-tum, his eye was bright, the lord's eye was bright, he looked at her. The Great Mountain, Father Enlil — his eye was bright, he looked at her. The shepherd who decides all destinies — his eye was bright, he looked at her. The king said to her: 'I want to have sex with you!', but he could not make her let him. Enlil said to her: 'I want to kiss you!', but he could not make her let him.

31–4   'My vagina is small, it does not know pregnancy. My lips are young, they do not know kissing. If my mother learns of it, she will slap my hand! If my father learns of it, he will lay hands on me! But right now, no one will stop me from telling this to my girl friend!'

35–6   Enlil spoke to his minister Nuska: 'Nuska, my minister!'
'At your service! What do you wish?'

37   'Master builder of the E-kur!'
'At your service, my lord!'

38–40 'Has anyone had sex with, has anyone kissed a maiden so beautiful, so radiant — Ninlil, so beautiful, so radiant?'

41–53 The minister brought his master across by boat, bringing him over with the rope of a small boat, bringing him over in a big boat. The lord, floating downstream to . . . — he was actually to have sex with her, he was actually to kiss her! — father Enlil, floating downstream to . . . — he was actually to have sex with her, he was actually to kiss her! — he grasped hold of her whom he was seeking — he was actually to have sex with her, he was actually to kiss her! — so as to lie with her on a small bank . . . . He actually had sex with her, he actually kissed her. At this one intercourse, at this one kissing he poured the seed of Suen-Ašimbabbar into her womb.

54–64 Enlil was walking in the Ki-ur. As Enlil was going about in the Ki-ur, the fifty great gods and the seven gods who decide destinies had Enlil arrested in the Ki-ur. Enlil, the ritually impure, left the city. Nunamnir, the ritually impure, left the city.° Enlil, in accordance with what had been decided, Nunamnir, in accordance with what had been decided, Enlil went. Ninlil followed. Nunamnir went, the maiden chased him.

65–70 Enlil spoke to the man at the city gate: 'City gatekeeper! Keeper of the barrier! Porter! Keeper of the holy barrier! When your lady Ninlil comes, if she asks after me, don't you tell her where I am!'

71–4 Ninlil addressed the city gatekeeper: 'City gatekeeper! Keeper of the barrier! Porter! Keeper of the holy barrier! When did your lord Enlil go by?' she said to him.

75–7 Enlil answered as the city gatekeeper: 'My lord has not talked with me at all, O loveliest one. Enlil has not talked with me at all, O loveliest one.'

78–81 'I will make clear my aim and explain my intent. You can fill my womb once it is empty — Enlil, lord of all the lands, has had sex with me! Just as Enlil is your lord, so am I your lady!'

82 'If you are my lady, let my hand touch your . . . !'

83–4 'The seed of your lord, the bright seed, is in my womb. The seed of Suen, the bright seed, is in my womb.'

85–6 'My master's seed can go up to the heavens! Let my seed go downwards! Let my seed go downwards, instead of my master's seed!'

87–90 Enlil, as the city gatekeeper, got her to lie down in the chamber. He had sex with her there, he kissed her there. At this one intercourse, at this one kissing he poured the seed of Nergal-Mešlamta-eda into her womb.

91–3   Enlil went. Ninlil followed. Nunamnir went, the maiden chased him. Enlil approached the man of the Id-kura ('River of the Under-world'), the man-eating river.

94–7   'My man of the Id-kura, the man-eating river! When your lady Ninlil comes, if she asks after me, don't you tell her where I am!'

98–100   Ninlil approached the man of the Id-kura, the man-eating river. 'My man of the Id-kura, the man-eating river! When did your lord Enlil go by?', she said to him.

101–3   Enlil answered as the man of the Id-kura: 'My lord has not talked with me at all, O loveliest one. Enlil has not talked with me at all, O loveliest one.'

104–7   'I will make clear my aim and explain my intent. You can fill my womb once it is empty — Enlil, lord of all the lands, has had sex with me! Just as Enlil is your lord, so am I your lady!'

108   'If you are my lady, let my hand touch your . . . !'

109–10   'The seed of your lord, the bright seed, is in my womb. The seed of Suen, the bright seed, is in my womb.'

111–13   'My master's seed can go up to the heavens! Let my seed go downwards! Let my seed go downwards, instead of my master's seed!'

114–16   Enlil, as the man of the Id-kura, got her to lie down in the chamber. He had sex with her there, he kissed her there. At this one inter-course, at this one kissing he poured into her womb the seed of Ninazu, the king who stretches measuring lines over the fields.

117–19   Enlil went. Ninlil followed. Nunamnir went, the maiden chased him. Enlil approached Silu-igi (?), the man of the ferryboat.

120–3   'Silu-igi (?), my man of the ferryboat! When your lady Ninlil comes, if she asks after me, don't you tell her where I am!'

124–6   Ninlil approached the man of the ferryboat. 'Man of the ferryboat! When did your lord Enlil go by?', she said to him.

127–9   Enlil answered as the man Silu-igi (?): 'My lord has not talked with me at all, O loveliest one. Enlil has not talked with me at all, O loveliest one.'

130–3   'I will make clear my aim and explain my intent. You can fill my womb once it is empty — Enlil, king of all the lands, has had sex with me! Just as Enlil is your lord, so am I your lady!'

134   'If you are my lady, let my hand touch your . . . !'

135–6 'The seed of your lord, the bright seed, is in my womb. The seed of
Suen, the bright seed, is in my womb.'

137–8 'My master's seed can go up to the heavens! Let my seed go downwards! Let my seed go downwards, instead of my master's seed!'

139–42 Enlil, as Silu-igi (?), got her to lie down in the chamber. He had sex
with her there, he kissed her there. At this one intercourse, at this one
kissing he poured into her womb the seed of Enbilulu, the inspector
of canals.

143–54 You are lord! You are king! Enlil, you are lord! You are king!
Nunamnir, you are lord! You are king! You are supreme lord, you are
powerful lord! Lord who makes flax grow, lord who makes barley
grow, you are lord of heaven, Lord Plenty, lord of the earth! You
are lord of the earth, Lord Plenty, lord of heaven! Enlil in heaven,
Enlil is king! Lord whose utterances° cannot be altered at all! His
primordial utterances will not be changed! For the praise spoken for
Ninlil the mother, praise be to° Father Enlil!

Notes

1–12 Fifty *sar* is equivalent to just under 2,000 square metres.

54–64 Instead of 'Enlil, the ritually impure, left the city. Nunamnir, the ritually
impure, left the city.' 2 MSS have: 'Enlil, ritually impure, leave the city!
Nunamnir, ritually impure, leave the city!'

143–54 Instead of 'whose utterances' 2 MSS have: 'whose pronouncements'. After
'praise be to' 1 MS adds: 'the Great Mountain,'.

Enlil and Sud

The poem of *Enlil and Sud* has a simple narrative for its theme: the courtship
of Sud, the goddess of Šuruppag and daughter of Nisaba, goddess of Ereš, by
the powerful Enlil, god of Nibru, and their subsequent marriage. Sud
becomes Enlil's consort Ninlil. It is difficult to see this as anything other than
a mythological explanation of a fact of religious history—the absorption of
the local cult of Šuruppag into the pantheon of Nibru. The independent cult
of Sud seems to have died down after the Early Dynastic period. Because at
an even earlier period a relation had been established between the cults of
Ereš and Šuruppag, with their patron deities being represented as mother
and daughter, Sud appears in the poem as a young, shy, unmarried girl living
in her mother's house. Sud's birth and growth to womanhood are described.

This very straightforward narrative is articulated into five sections, of which the second and fourth (a repeated 13-line speech) report the reply of Sud's mother to Enlil's minister Nuska, and Nuska's repetition of the reply to Enlil. Enlil, a bachelor in search of a wife, meets Sud in Ereš 'standing in the street', and—here the story is given an amusing twist—takes her, whether flirtatiously or by genuine mistake, for a prostitute. She repudiates him, and responds to his repeated advances by turning on her heels and retreating into her mother's house. He dispatches his minister Nuska to visit Sud's mother, Nisaba (who also goes by the names Nanibgal and Nun-bar-še-gunu), with an official proposal of marriage and a secret present for Sud. Nisaba is apparently appeased of the outrage implied by Enlil's initial remarks to Sud, and accepts the proposal. Sud's father Ḫaia is not consulted. Nisaba calls Sud into the room to offer hand-washing and a drink to their visitor, when Nuska is able to slip her Enlil's secret present. Then Nuska reports back to Enlil, who is delighted and immediately collects together lavish bridal gifts to shower on Sud's mother: wild and domestic animals, foods and precious stones. Enlil's sister Aruru (here also call Ninmaḫ, Nintud, and perhaps En-Batibira) accompanies the gifts to Ereš, and speaks in a sisterly way with Sud to prepare her for the wedding and to wish her well. After the marriage is consummated, Enlil 'decrees the destiny' of his new wife, who is henceforth to be called Ninlil. The poem ends by praising Enlil and Ninlil.

Manuscripts of this poem are mainly small fragments from Nibru, also Susa and elsewhere. In addition, the story survived into the first millennium BCE, and bilingual versions were found in Assyrian libraries at Nineveh and at Sultantepe (ancient Huzirina).

Translation

A1–8   ... she was faithfully sitting (?) on ..., admirable and full of charms. ..., the noble son—who like him can compare with An and Enlil? Ḫaia, the ..., put the holy semen into her womb. Nun-bar-še-gunu faithfully gave birth to ..., she brought her up in her ... and suckled her at her breasts full of good milk. The ... of the young girl burgeoned, and she became full of flourishing beauty. In the ... of Nisaba, at the gate of the E-zagin, ... she stood, the object of admiration, like a tall, beautifully shaped cow.

A9–14   At that time Enlil had not yet been given a wife in the E-kur; Ninlil's name was not yet famous in the Ki-ur. After travelling through Sumer and to the ends of the universe, he ...; in his search throughout the Land, Enlil, the Great Mountain, stopped at Ereš. As he looked around there, he found the woman of his choice. He approached her and, overflowing with joy, engaged her in conversation.

A15–16   'I will make you perfect in a queen's dress; after standing in the street, you will be . . . . How impressed I am by your beauty, even if you are a shameless person!'

A17–21   In her youthful inexperience Sud answered Enlil: 'If I want to stand proudly at our gate, who dares to give me a bad reputation? What are your intentions? Why have you come here? . . . from my sight!' Others (?) had already tried to deceive . . . , and made her (?) angry.

A22–5   Enlil . . . answered Sud, . . . standing closer to her: 'Come, I want to speak to you! I will have a talk with you about your becoming my wife. Kiss me, my lady of most beautiful eyes—the matter rests in your hands.'

A26   But the words had barely left his mouth when, right in front of him, she went into the house.

A27–8   The heart of the wise lord pounded. He called for Nuska. 'What is your wish?' He gave the following instructions to him:

A29–43   'I want you to go back to Ereš, the city of Nisaba, the city whose foundations are august. Do not delay! Repeat to her what I am going to tell you: "I am a young man, I have sent this message to you because of my wish: I want to take your daughter as wife. Give me your consent. I will send you presents in my name, . . . my marriage gifts. I am Enlil, the descendant and offspring of Anšar, the noble, the lord of heaven and earth. The name of your daughter shall become Ninlil, and all the foreign countries shall . . . it. I will present her with the Ga-ĝiš-šua as her storehouse. I will give her the Ki-ur to be her beloved private quarters. She shall sit° with me in the E-kur, my° august dais. She shall determine fates. She shall apportion the divine powers among the Anuna, the great gods. And as for you, I will place in your hands the lives of the black-headed people." When you get there, let the woman I have chosen for her beauty . . . her mother. Do not go to her empty-handed, but take her some jewellery in your left hand. Waste no time. Return with her answer quickly.'

A44–57   When Nuska, the head of the assembly, had received Enlil's instructions, he wasted no time . . . ; he directed his steps to Ereš. He entered E-zagin, the residence of Nanibgal, and prostrated himself before

Nanibgal on her dais. . . . of Enlil . . . , and she (?) asked him . . . :
'. . . what . . . ?' (*7 lines missing; 1 line fragmentary*)

A58–9   (*Nuska speaks:*) '. . . Sud . . . . What you have told me . . . .'

A60–73   Then Nanibgal went on speaking flatteringly to the minister:
'Adviser, fit for his (?) king, ever observant (?)! Who like you could
give counsel daily to the Great Mountain? How could I contest the
king's message which his slave has received? If there is truth in what
you have told me—and may there be no falsehood—who could
reject one who bestows such exceedingly great favours? . . . makes our
mood and hearts happy. Let us consider that amends have been
made. By bringing the marriage gifts and the presents in his name the
insult is wiped away. Tell him: "You shall become my son-in-law; do
as you wish!" Tell Enlil, the Great Mountain: "Do as you wish!" Let
his sister come from her side, and she shall accompany Sud from
here. Aruru shall become Sud's sister-in-law: let her be shown the
household. Inform your lord thus in his august Ki-ur. Repeat this to
Enlil in the privacy of his holy bedchamber.'

A74–7   After . . . had instructed . . . , . . . and Nuska took his seat on it. (*1 line
missing*) Nanibgal called . . . and gave her advice.

A78–81   'My little one, asleep indoors (?) . . . your pure . . . , the pleasant
private quarters . . . . leave the House of Nisaba's Wisdom. . . . ,
Nuska is knowing and wise. . . . to his presence and pour him beer.'

A82–9   According to the instructions of her mother, she washed his hands
and placed a tankard in his hands. The minister opened his left hand
and gave her the jewellery, ... everything . . . and set it before her.
She received the gifts . . . . directed his steps to Nibru. . . . kissed
the ground before Enlil. . . . the great Lady had said . . . , as she had
instructed him, he repeated (?) . . . . :

A90–102   '(*She said:*) "Adviser, fit for his (?) king, ever observant (?)! Who like
you could give counsel daily to the Great Mountain? How could I
contest the king's message which his slave has received? If there is
truth in what you have told me—and may there be no falsehood—
who could reject one who bestows such exceedingly great favours?
. . . makes our mood and hearts happy. Let us consider that amends
have been made. By bringing the marriage gifts and the presents in
his name the insult is wiped away. Tell him: 'You shall become my
son-in-law; do as you wish!' Tell Enlil, the Great Mountain: 'Do as
you wish!' Let his sister come from her side, and she shall accompany
Sud from here. Aruru shall become Sud's sister-in-law: let her be

shown the household. Inform your lord thus in his august Ki-ur. Repeat this to Enlil in the privacy of his holy bedchamber." '

A103–13 . . . made . . . feel good, brought great rejoicing in Enlil's heart. He raised his head . . . , and animals came running. . . . herds of four-legged animals that graze together in the desert. He caught . . . living in the mountains, he made wild bulls, red deer, elephants, fallow deer, gazelles, bears, wild sheep and rams, lynxes, foxes, wild cats, tigers, mountain sheep, water buffalo, monkeys, and thick-horned fat cattle jostle together noisily. Cows and their calves, wild cattle with wide-spread horns, . . . rope, ewes and lambs, goats and kids, romping°, large kids with long beards, scratching with their hooves, lambs, . . . , and majestic sheep were dispatched by Enlil toward Ereš.

A114–17 Large cheeses, mustard-flavoured cheeses, small cheeses, . . . , milk, cold hard-boiled eggs, butter (?), the sweetest dry honey and white honey, . . . , and thick and large . . . were dispatched by Enlil toward Ereš.

A118–23 . . . , dates, figs, large pomegranates, . . . , ĝipar fruits, plums (?), ḫalub nuts, almonds, acorns, Dilmun dates packed in baskets, dark-coloured date spadices, large pomegranate seeds squeezed out from their rinds, big clusters of early grapes, . . . trees in fruit, trees from orchards, . . . grown in winter, and fruits from orchards were dis-patched by Enlil toward Ereš.

A124–36 Ores (?) from Ḫarali, the faraway land, ... storehouses, . . . , rock crystal, gold, silver, . . . , the yield of the uplands . . . , heavy loads of them, were dispatched by Enlil toward Ereš. After the personal presents, the transported goods . . . , Ninmaḫ and the minister . . . . The dust from their march reached high into the sky like rain clouds. Enormous marriage gifts were being brought for Nanibgal to Ereš; the city was getting full inside and out, . . . it was to be replete. The rest . . . on the outlying roads . . . . blue sky . . . . (1 line missing; 2 lines fragmentary)

A137–45 Nanibgal, the mother-in-law of Enlil, the woman who had been slandered, was treated kindly by Nuska (?)°—but the lady dis-regarded the flatterer, and spoke to her daughter: 'May you be Enlil's favourite wife°, and may he speak to you sweetly. May he embrace you, the most beautiful of all, and tell you: "Beloved, open wide!" May the two of you never lose the pleasure (?) of excitement; make it last (?) a long time.° You two . . . on the hill, and have children after-wards! When you enter the house to live there, may abundance precede you, and may joy follow you. May the people line up for you wherever you go, and may all the people . . . for you. The fate I have determined for you should be fulfilledº! Go with head held high into the E-maḫ.'

A146–55 Then Aruru grasped her by the hand and led her away into the Eš-maḫ. She brought her into the E-kur, the house of Enlil, and . . . . In the sleeping quarters, in the flowered bed . . . like a cedar forest, Enlil made (?) love to his wife and took great pleasure in it. (*1 line fragmentary*) The lord whose statements are . . . the lady; . . . Nintud, the 'Lady who gives birth' . . . . En-Batibira's countenance, ... He presented her with . . . , everything . . . , and . . . .

A156–70 (*Enlil speaks:*) 'From now on, a woman shall be the . . . ; a foreign woman shall be the mistress of the house. May my beautiful wife, who was born of holy Nisaba, be Ezina, the growing grain, the life of Sumer. When you appear in the furrows like a beautiful young girl, may Iškur, the canal inspector, be your provider, supplying you with water from the ground. The height of the year is marked with your new prime flax and your new prime grain; Enlil and Ninlil procreate them (?) as desired. (*1 line unclear*) The harvest crop raises its head high for the great festival of Enlil. The scribal art, the tablets decorated with writing, the stylus, the tablet board, the computing of accounts, adding and subtracting, the shining measuring rope, the . . . , the head of the surveyor's peg, the measuring rod, the marking of the boundaries, and the . . . are fittingly in your hands. The farmer (?) . . . . Woman, the proudest among the Great Princes, . . . , from now on, Sud . . . Ninlil . . . .' (*unknown number of lines missing*)

B1 A holy song of praise . . . . Enlil and Ninlil . . . !

Notes

A29–43 Instead of 'sit' 1 MS has: 'live'. Instead of 'my' 1 MS has: 'the'.

A103–13 Instead of 'ewes and lambs, goats and kids, romping . . .' 1 later MS from Susa has: '. . . and fighting'.

A137–45 Instead of 'Nanibgal, the mother-in-law of Enlil, the woman who had been slandered, was treated kindly by Nuska (?)' 1 MS has: '. . . the mother-in-law of Enlil, the woman . . . Ezina . . .'. Instead of 'Enlil's favourite wife' 1 MS has: 'the wife of Enlil's heart'. Instead of 'May the two of you never lose the pleasure (?) of excitement; make it last (?) a long time.' 1 MS has: 'May it be that the pleasure (?) of excitement will never be lost.' Instead of 'should be fulfilled' 1 MS has: 'cannot be altered'.

Enlil and Nam-zid-tara

The short narrative poem *Enlil and Nam-zid-tara* is like a fable or a folk-tale. Nam-zid-tara is a *gudug* priest. Mesopotamian temples had elaborate and complex hierarchies of staff, from temple administrators to courtyard sweepers, and including a bewildering variety of religious practitioners with particular specialities, such as diviners, magicians, snake charmers, musicians and dancers, not to mention the butchers, cooks, and brewers who were responsible for preparing the daily meals offered regularly to the gods. The *gudug* priests were not a very elevated rank of religious personnel, and were not specialized to the cult of a particular deity but served in many temples.

Nam-zid-tara has been performing his priestly duties at a temple and is walking home. The god Enlil disguises himself as a raven before accosting the priest and engaging him in conversation. In their exchange, Nam-zid-tara is able to recognize that the raven really is Enlil, and is not merely claiming to be. Replying to the god, he alludes to a rather obscure myth about the captivity of En-me-šara, an ancient god known from other sources as an ancestor of Enlil. Enlil is evidently impressed by the priest's knowledge and in return assigns a blessing of some sort to Nam-zid-tara and the *gudug* priests in general, to 'come and go regularly' in the temple of Enlil.

Clearly the narrative is rather abbreviated, and the full details would have been known to the original audience. The motif of a god disguising his true appearance as an animal before speaking to a human is well known from folk-tales from around the world, as is the contrast between a supremely powerful god and a humble human. Similarly the motif of an animal that can speak with a human voice is a feature of other Sumerian narratives (for instance the fly who addresses Inana at the end of *Inana's descent to the Underworld*, Group B). The idea that the *gudug* priests were rewarded in perpetuity because of a clever response by one of their number might suggest that this little tale originated in the milieu of these temple servants.

Translation

1–3 Nam-zid-tara walked by Enlil, who said to him: 'Where have you come from, Nam-zid-tara?'

4–10 'From Enlil's temple. My turn of duty is finished. I serve at the place of the *gudug* priests, with their sheep. I am on my way home. Don't stop me; I am in a hurry. Who are you who asks me questions?'

11–14 'I am Enlil.' But Enlil had changed his appearance: he had turned into a raven and was croaking.

15 'But you are not a raven, you are really Enlil!'

16 'How did you recognize that I am Enlil, who decrees the destinies?'

17–18 'When your uncle En-me-šara was a captive, after taking for himself the rank of Enlil, he said: "Now I shall know the fates, like a lord." '

19–23 'You may acquire precious metals, you may acquire precious stones, you may acquire cattle or you may acquire sheep; but the day of a human being is always getting closer, so where does your wealth lead? Now, I am indeed Enlil, who decrees the fates. What is your name?'

24 'My name is Nam-zid-tara (Well-blessed).'

25–7 'Your fate shall be assigned according to your name: leave the house of your master, and your heirs shall come and go regularly in my temple.'

Šulgi and Ninlil's barge

This exuberant praise song describes a historical event, a festival which took place during king Šulgi's reign (in c.2143 BCE) and which is commemorated by the official name of his eighth year: 'Year the barge of Ninlil was caulked'. We can assume that the song was publicly performed at some ceremonial occasion associated with the festival. Just as the gods lived in houses ('temples') and were fed and provided with furniture and clothes, so some of them also had ceremonial barges on which their statues were transported for festivals. In this case, Šulgi has a barge built for the goddess Ninlil, and has her and other deities transported on an overnight trip to a location near Nibru where a banquet is held. Such splendid ceremonial progresses were a feature of the cultic life of the Third Dynasty of Urim and, to a lesser extent, of its successor dynasties. They helped to aestheticize and ritualize the public lives of the ruler and the elites.

The song is divided into two musical sections, marked *sa-gida* and *sa-g̃ara*. The *sa-gida* comprises an initial paragraph addressing the barge which Šulgi is going to have built. Precious cedar logs from distant forests will be used in its construction. This is followed (10–39) by an elaborate description of the different parts of the vessel, delighting in the technical nautical terms and using a whole series of vivid and extravagant metaphors.

The *sa-g̃ara* section falls into four episodes. First (41–63), the gods' statues are brought out from their shrines and embarked onto the barge, and the vessel is launched. It is rowed and punted to the Tummal, a cultic site associated with Ninlil downstream from Nibru. Then a celebratory banquet takes place, which lasts into the night (64–70); the gods decree a good destiny for the king. In the third episode (71–81), the barge returns next morning to Nibru, escorted by river fish, and is moored at the quay. Finally (82–90), Ninlil herself blesses the king, bestowing on him a long life and assured kingship, and implying the close personal relationship with the gods which rulers of this epoch claimed for themselves.

Unfortunately the text is preserved only in a slightly damaged form.

Translation

1–9   O barge, Enki assigned the quay of abundance to you as your fate. Father Enlil looked at you with approval. Your lady, Ninlil, commanded your construction. She entrusted it to the faithful provider, king Šulgi the shepherd, who is of broad intelligence and who will not rest day and night in thinking deeply about you. He, the wise one, who is proficient in planning, he, the omniscient one, will fell large cedars in the huge forests for you. He will make you perfect and you will be breathtaking to look upon.

FIG. 16. 'You will be breathtaking to look upon'—a goddess travels in a divine barge on an Old Akkadian cylinder seal

10–22   Your woven . . . is . . . . Your covering reed-mats are the daylight spreading wide over the holy settlements. Your timbers are sniffing (?) . . . reptiles crouching on their paws. Your punting poles are dragons sleeping a sweet sleep in their lair. Your strakes (?) are . . . snakes, ... Your floor-planks are flood-currents, sparkling altogether in the pure Euphrates. Your side-planks, which are fastened into their fixed places (?) with wooden rings (?), are a stairway leading to a mountain spring (?), a . . . filled with . . . . Your holy . . . are persisting and firmly founded abundance. Your bench is a lofty dais erected in the midst of the Abzu. Your . . . is Aratta, full-laden with treasures. Your door, facing the sunrise, is a . . . bird, carrying a . . . in its talons while spreading wide its wings.

23–31 Your glittering golden sun-disc, fastened with leather straps, is the brilliant moonlight, shining brightly upon all the lands. Your banner, adorned with the divine powers of kingship, is a woodland of cypress trees irrigated with clean water, giving a pleasant shade. Your small reed mats are the evening sky, illuminated with stars, imbued with terrible awesomeness. In the midst of your carefully tended small *gizi* reeds with numerous twigs (?), swarms of birds twitter as in a holy swamp. Their chirping, as pleasing to the heart as the sound of the churn's shaking, makes Enlil and Ninlil extremely happy (?).

32–9 Your rudder is a large *kiĝ* fish in the broad waters at the mouth of the Kisala canal. Your . . . are a bison, inspiring terror on the great earth. Your tow-rope is the gliding Niraḫ extended over the land. Your mooring pole is the heavenly bond, which . . . . Your longside beams are a warrior striking straight against another warrior. Your prow is Nanna . . . fair sky. Your stern is Utu . . . at the horizon. Your hold (?) is . . . .

40 *Sa-gida.*

41–7 The faithful shepherd Šulgi established the holy festival and the great rituals. The great gods bathe in holy water in Nibru. He assigns the fates to their places in the city and allocates the right divine powers. The mother of the Land, Ninlil the fair, comes out (?) from the house, and Enlil embraces her like a pure wild cow. They take their seats on the barge's holy dais, and provisions are lavishly prepared.

48–63 The lofty barge . . . , the ornament of the Tigris, enters the rolling river; . . . on the shining water. The ritually washed five-headed mace, *mitum* mace, lance and standard . . . at the bow. Enlil's warrior, Ninurta, goes at their front, directing the . . . of your wide ferry-boat (?) straight. He . . . the holy punting pole of the barge, the holy raft. The ferrymen (?) . . . holy songs; they (?) . . . the great exaltedness of the lady. The good woman, Ninlil, . . . joyfully with (?) Šulgi. Sumer and Urim . . . joy and happines. The barge bobs at the quay Ornament of the Waves; it sails off into the reed-beds of Enlil's Tummal. Like a goring (?) ox, it raises, then lowers its head. It strikes its breast against the rising waves; it stirs up (?) the encircling waters. When it thrusts within the waters, the fishes of the subterranean waters become frightened; as it glides (?) upon them, it makes the waters sparkle (?) luxuriantly.

64–70 . . . the holy raft; . . . the lady of Tummal . . . prayer. Enlil's ancestors and An the king, the god who determines the fates, greet her. With Ninlil, they take their seats at the banquet, and Šulgi the shepherd brings along his great food-offerings for them. They pass the day in abundance, they give praise throughout night. They decree a fate, a fate to be pre-eminent forever, for the king who fitted out the holy barge.

71–81 Then light shines up at the edge of the Land as Utu rises dazzlingly. As the barge is travelling upstream, it . . . radiates (?) and creaks (?). . . . in the Ninmutum, the canal of the year of abundance . . . . As the carp make their bellies (?) sparkle, Enlil rejoices. As the *mušu* fish play noisily there, Ninlil rejoices. As the . . . fish . . . , Enki rejoices. As the *suḫurmaš* carp dart about, Nanna rejoices. The Anuna gods rejoice at . . . . lifts its head in the Euphrates; it . . . . In the midst of . . . ever-flowing water is carried. In joyous Nibru, he moors the holy barge at the quay.

82–90 With joyful eyes and shining forehead, Ninlil, . . . , looks upon king Šulgi: 'Shepherd . . . , Šulgi, who has a lasting name, king of jubilation! I will prolong the nights of the crown that was placed upon your head by holy An, and I will extend the days of the holy sceptre that was given to you by Enlil. May the foundation of your throne that was bestowed on you by Enki be firm! Shepherd who brings about perfection, may Nanna, the robust calf, the seed of Enlil, to whom I gave birth, cover your life with . . . which is full of exuberance as if it were my holy *ma* garment!'

91 *Sa-ĝara.*

The cursing of Agade

After the fall first of Kiš and then of Unug, according to *The cursing of Agade*, Enlil accorded the recognized sovereignty over the Land of Sumer to Sargon, king of Agade. At that time Inana set up her shrine at Ulmaš in Agade and worked to bring success and prosperity to the city. Naram-Suen succeeded to the kingship of Agade. Offerings continued to pour into the shrine and Inana was overwhelmed by them. However, no word of approval came from the great god Enlil in his temple E-kur at Nibru. Inana, uneasy, withdrew her patronage and went off to pursue another favourite activity, warfare. The gods Ninurta, Enki, and An all withdrew their marks of favour.

Naram-Suen, in a dream, saw what all this meant and fell into a depression. Eventually he consulted the sacrificial omens twice in succession with the same result: 'the omen had nothing to say about the building of the temple'. Presumably if Enlil's recognition of his 'sovereignty' had been granted, Naram-Suen would have expected to contribute to the beautification of E-kur. Emboldened to a desperate attempt to reverse the implied judgment of Enlil, Naram-Suen set about attacking and savagely plundering E-kur, the holiest shrine in Sumer. Enlil's terrible revenge was to loose upon the Land the violence of the barbarian people of Gutium, an invading horde which left the people decimated and all civilized activities cut short. Enlil himself was deeply affected. In an attempt to calm him, the great gods Suen, Enki, Inana, Ninurta, Iškur, Utu, Nuska, and Nisaba pronounced a terrible curse according to which Agade was destined to lie forever in ruins. 'And before Utu on that very day, so it was!' Agade was destroyed.

The narrative of *The cursing of Agade* is not complex, but the poem juxtaposes a series of vivid, highly-wrought images artfully linked internally by repeated elements. Direct repetition is used much less freely than in some other works. Dialogue is entirely absent, and the only direct speech is the final curses.

The idea of Agade certainly had a hold on the imagination of later Mesopotamian empires. It was known to have been once great, yet with the possible exception of a small religious settlement it seemed to have been completely eclipsed, a striking testament to the mutability of things. (Even its location is unknown to us today.) Interestingly, the literary tradition about the Sargonic dynasty diverges considerably from the historical record revealed by archaeology and contemporary documents. All the Sargonic kings were forgotten except for the names of Sargon and Naram-Suen (see *Sargon and Ur-Zababa*, Group A). Later traditions about Naram-Suen vary in their evaluation of him. In fact he did rebuild part of the E-kur, as we learn from his own inscriptions found there. The story of its destruction may originate in a rebellion in southern Sumer which he quelled. The devastation of Sumer by Gutium was certainly real enough. These discrepancies show that the composition cannot have been composed all that close to the events it purports to describe, yet there are manuscripts from the period of the Third Dynasty of Urim which confirm its origin in the last century of the third millennium BCE. It was widely copied in Old Babylonian schools.

It can be interpreted on one level as a vindication of the idea, current in southern Mesopotamia from at least the time of Sargon's predecessor, Lugal-zage-si of Unug, onwards, that there could be only one authentic king of the Land at any one time. (In the poem, Agade is regarded as part of the Land: there is no Sumerian-Akkadian antipathy.) This seems to have grown up exactly as the earlier warring city-states of the Early Dynastic period were replaced by large empires. The same theory is also found, for instance, in the *Lament for Sumer and Urim* (Group D). Crucial to this authenticity was the approval of the god Enlil in Nibru, and this allowed Nibru to become a sort of Holy City, whose inhabitants enjoyed special freedoms.

On a more general level, the poem is a statement of the impermanence of good fortune, and the subjugation of mankind to the divine will, the changes of which appear to humans as largely arbitrary. Unusually explicit in the poem are the statements that the invasion of Gutium and the cursing of Agade are specifically in revenge for the destruction of E-kur (lines 151, 212 ff.), reinforcing the rule that sacrilegious behaviour can expect retribution.

Translation

1–9   After Enlil's frown had slain Kiš as if it were the Bull of Heaven, had slaughtered the house of the land of Unug in the dust as if it were a mighty bull, and then Enlil had given the rulership and kingship from the south as far as the highlands to Sargon, king of Agade—at that time, holy Inana established the sanctuary of Agade as her celebrated woman's domain; she set up her throne in Ulmaš.

10–24   Like a young man building a house for the first time, like a girl establishing a woman's domain, holy Inana did not sleep as she ensured that the warehouses would be provisioned; that dwellings would be founded in the city; that its people would eat splendid food; that its people would drink splendid beverages; that those bathed for holidays would rejoice in the courtyards; that the people would throng the places of celebration; that acquaintances would dine together; that foreigners would cruise about like unusual birds in the sky; that even Marḫaši would be re-entered on the tribute rolls; that monkeys, mighty elephants, water buffalo, exotic animals, as well as thoroughbred dogs, lions, mountain ibexes°, and *alum* sheep with long wool would jostle each other in the public squares.

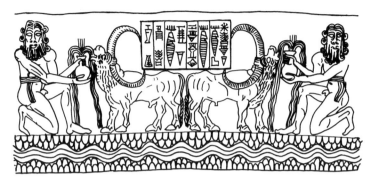

FIG. 17. 'Water buffalo . . . would jostle each other in the public squares'—
water buffalo on the cylinder seal of an Old Akkadian royal scribe

25–39   She then filled Agade's stores for emmer wheat with gold, she filled
its stores for white emmer wheat with silver; she delivered copper,
tin, and blocks of lapis lazuli to its granaries and sealed its silos from
outside. She endowed its old women with the gift of giving counsel,
she endowed its old men with the gift of eloquence. She endowed its
young women with the gift of entertaining, she endowed its young
men with martial might, she endowed its little ones with joy. The
nursemaids who cared for° the general's children played the drumsticks (?). Inside the city *tigi* drums sounded; outside it, flutes and
zamzam instruments. Its harbour where ships moored was full of joy.
All foreign lands rested contentedly, and their people experienced
happiness.

40–56   Its king, the shepherd Naram-Suen, rose as the daylight on the holy
throne of Agade. Its city wall, like a mountain°, reached the heavens.
It was like the Tigris going to° the sea as holy Inana opened the
portals of its city gates and made Sumer bring its own possessions
upstream by boats. The highland Mardu, people ignorant of agriculture, brought spirited cattle and kids for her. The Meluhans, the
people of the black land, brought exotic wares° up to her. Elam and
Subir loaded themselves with goods for her as if they were pack-asses.
All the governors, the temple administrators°, and the accountants
of the Gu-edina regularly supplied the monthly and New Year offerings. What a weariness all these caused at Agade's city gates! Holy
Inana could hardly receive all these offerings. As if she were a citizen
there, she could not restrain (?) the desire (?) to prepare the ground
for a temple.

57–65   But the statement coming from the E-kur was disquieting. Because of Enlil (?) all Agade was reduced (?) to trembling, and terror befell Inana in Ulmaš. She left the city, returning to her home. Holy Inana abandoned the sanctuary of Agade like someone abandoning the young women of her woman's domain. Like a warrior hurrying to arms, she removed° the gift of battle and fight from the city and handed them over to the enemy.

66–76   Not even five or ten days had passed and Ninurta brought the jewels of rulership, the royal crown, the emblem and the royal throne bestowed on Agade, back into his E-šumeša. Utu took away the eloquence of the city. Enki took away its wisdom. An took up° into the midst of heaven its fearsomeness that reaches heaven. Enki tore out its well-anchored holy mooring pole from the Abzu. Inana took away its weapons.

77–82   The life of Agade's sanctuary was brought to an end as if it had been only the life of a tiny carp in the deep waters, and all the cities were watching it. As a mighty elephant, it bent its neck to the ground while they all raised their horns like mighty bulls. As a dying dragon, it dragged its head on the earth and they jointly deprived it of honour as in a battle.

83–93   Naram-Suen saw in a nocturnal vision that Enlil would not let the kingdom of Agade occupy a pleasant, lasting residence, that he would make its future altogether unfavourable, that he would make its temples shake and would scatter its treasures°. He realized what the dream was about, but did not put it into words, and did not discuss it with anyone.° Because of the E-kur, he put on mourning clothes, covered his chariot with a reed mat°, tore the reed canopy off his ceremonial barge°, and gave away his royal paraphernalia. Naram-Suen persisted for seven years! Who has ever seen a king burying his head in his hands for seven years?°

94–9   Then he went to perform extispicy on a kid regarding the temple, but the omen had nothing to say about the building of the temple. For a second time he went to perform extispicy on a kid regarding the temple, but the omen again had nothing to say about the building of the temple. In order to change what had been inflicted (?) upon him, he tried to alter Enlil's pronouncement.

100–19   Because his subjects were dispersed, he now began a mobilization of his troops. Like a wrestler who is about to enter the great courtyard, he . . . his hands towards (?) the E-kur. Like an athlete bent to start a contest, he treated the *giguna* shrine as if it were worth only thirty shekels°. Like a robber plundering the city, he set tall ladders against the temple. To demolish E-kur as if it were a huge ship, to break up its soil like the soil of mountains where precious metals are mined, to splinter it like the lapis lazuli mountain, to prostrate it, like a city inundated by Iškur—although the temple was not a mountain where cedars are felled, he had large axes cast, he had double-edged *agasilig* axes sharpened to be used against it. He set spades against its roots and it sank as low as the foundation of the Land. He put axes against its top, and the temple, like a dead soldier, bowed its neck before him, and all the foreign lands bowed their necks before him.

120–48 He ripped out its drain pipes, and all the rain went back to the heavens. He tore off its upper lintel and the Land was deprived of its ornament°. From its 'Gate from which grain is never diverted', he diverted grain, and the Land was deprived of grain. He struck the 'Gate of Well-Being' with the pickaxe, and well-being was subverted in all the foreign lands. As if they were for great tracts of land with wide carp-filled waters, he cast large spades° to be used against the E-kur. The people could see the bedchamber, its room which knows no daylight. The Akkadians could look into the holy treasure chest of the gods. Though they had committed no sacrilege, its *laḫama* deities of the great pilasters standing at the temple were thrown into the fire by Naram-Suen. The cedar, cypress, juniper, and boxwood, the woods of its *giguna* shrine, were . . . by him. He put its gold in containers and put its silver in leather bags. He filled the docks with its copper, as if it were a huge transport of grain. The silversmiths were reshaping its silver, jewellers were reshaping its precious stones, smiths were beating its copper. Large ships were moored at the temple, large ships were moored at Enlil's temple and its possessions were taken away from the city, though they were not the goods of a plundered city. With the possessions being taken away from the city, good sense left Agade. As the ships moved away from° the docks, Agade's intelligence° was removed.

149–75 Enlil, the roaring (?) storm that subjugates the entire land, the rising deluge that cannot be confronted, was considering what should be destroyed in return for the wrecking of his beloved E-kur. He lifted his gaze towards the Gubin mountains, and made all the inhabitants of the broad mountain ranges descend (?). Enlil brought out of the mountains those who do not resemble other people, who are not reckoned as part of the Land, the Gutians, an unbridled people, with human intelligence but canine instincts° and monkeys' features. Like small birds they swooped on the ground in great flocks. Because of Enlil, they stretched their arms out across the plain like a net for animals. Nothing escaped their clutches, no one left their grasp. Messengers no longer travelled the highways, the courier's boat no longer passed along the rivers. The Gutians drove the trusty (?) goats of Enlil out of their folds and compelled their herdsmen to follow them, they drove the cows out of their pens and compelled their cowherds to follow them. Prisoners manned the watch. Brigands occupied° the highways. The doors of the city gates of the Land lay dislodged in° mud, and all the foreign lands uttered bitter cries from the walls of their cities. They established gardens for themselves° within the cities, and not as usual on the wide plain outside. As if it had been before the time when cities were built and founded, the large° arable tracts yielded no grain, the inundated° tracts yielded no fish, the irrigated orchards yielded no syrup or wine, the thick clouds (?) did not rain, the *mašgurum* tree did not grow.

176–92 In those days, oil for one shekel° was only half a *sila*°, grain for one shekel was only half a *sila*, wool for one shekel was only one mina°, fish for one shekel filled only one *ban* measure°—these sold at such prices in the markets of the cities! Those who lay down on the roof, died on the roof; those who lay down in the house were not buried. People were flailing at themselves from hunger. By the Ki-ur, Enlil's great place, dogs were packed together in the silent streets; if two men walked there they would be devoured by them, and if three men walked there they would be devoured by them. Noses were punched (?), heads were smashed (?), noses (?) were piled up, heads were sown like seeds. Honest people were confounded with traitors, heroes lay dead on top of heroes, the blood of traitors ran upon the blood of honest men.

193–209 At that time, Enlil rebuilt his great sanctuaries into small reed (?) sanctuaries and from east to west he reduced their storehouses. The old women who survived those days, the old men who survived those days and the chief lamentation singer who survived those years set up seven *balaĝ* drums, as if they stood at the horizon, and together with *ub*, *meze*, and *lilis*° drums made them resound to Enlil like Iškur for seven days and seven nights. The old women did not restrain the cry 'Alas for my city!' The old men did not restrain the cry 'Alas for its people!' The lamentation singer did not restrain the cry 'Alas for the E-kur!' Its young women did not restrain from tearing their hair. Its young men did not restrain from sharpening their knives. Their laments were as if Enlil's ancestors were performing a lament in the awe-inspiring Holy Mound by the holy knees of Enlil. Because of this, Enlil entered his holy bedchamber and lay down fasting.

210–21 At that time, Suen, Enki, Inana, Ninurta, Iškur, Utu, Nuska, and Nisaba, the great gods°, cooled° Enlil's heart with cool water and prayed to him: 'Enlil, may the city that destroyed your city be treated as your city has been treated! May the one that defiled your *giguna* shrine be treated as Nibru! In this city, may heads fill the wells! May no one find his acquaintances there, may brother not recognize brother! May its young woman be cruelly killed in her woman's domain, may its old man cry in distress for his slain wife! May its pigeons moan on their window ledges, may its small birds be smitten in their nooks, may it live in constant anxiety like a timid pigeon!'

222–44 Again, Suen, Enki, Inana, Ninurta, Iškur, Utu, Nuska, and Nisaba, all the gods whosoever, turned their attention to the city, and cursed Agade severely: 'City, you pounced on E-kur: it is as if you had pounced on Enlil! Agade, you pounced on E-kur: it is as if you had pounced on Enlil! May your holy walls, to their highest point, resound with mourning! May your *giguna* shrine be reduced to a pile of dust! May your pilasters with the standing *lahama* deities fall to the ground like tall young men drunk on wine! May your clay be returned to its Abzu, may it be clay cursed by Enki! May your grain be returned to its furrow, may it be grain cursed by Ezina! May your timber be returned to its forest, may it be timber cursed by Ninilduma! May the° cattle slaughterer slaughter his wife, may your° sheep butcher butcher his child! May water wash away your pauper as he is looking for . . . ! May your prostitute hang herself at the entrance to her brothel! May your pregnant (?) *nugig* priestesses and cult prostitutes abort (?) their children! May your gold be bought for the price of silver, may your silver be bought for the price of pyrite (?), and may your copper be bought for the price of lead!

245–55 'Agade, may your strong man be deprived of his strength, so that he will be unable to lift his sack of provisions and . . . , and will not have the joy of controlling your superior asses; may he lie idle all day! May this make the city die of hunger! May your citizens, who used to eat fine food, lie hungry in the grass and herbs, may your . . . man eat the coating on his roof, may he chew (?) the leather hinges on the main door of his father's house! May depression descend upon your palace, built for joy°! May the evils of the desert, the silent place, howl continuously!

256–71 'May foxes that frequent ruin mounds brush with their tails your fattening-pens (?), established for purification ceremonies! May the *ukuku*, the bird of depression, make its nest in your gateways, established for the Land! In your city that could not sleep because of the *tigi* drums, that could not rest from its joy, may the bulls of Nanna that fill the pens bellow like those who wander in the desert, the silent place! May the grass grow long on your canal-bank tow-paths, may the grass of mourning grow on your highways laid for waggons! Moreover, may . . . wild rams (?) and alert snakes of the mountains allow no one to pass on your tow-paths built up with canal sediment! In your plains where fine grass grows, may the reed of lamentation grow! Agade, may brackish water flow° where fresh water flowed for you! If someone decides: "I will dwell in this city!", may he not enjoy the pleasures of a dwelling place! If someone decides: "I will rest in Agade!", may he not enjoy the pleasures of a resting place!'

272–80 And before Utu on that very day, so it was! On its canal-bank tow-paths, the grass grew long. On its highways laid for waggons, the grass of mourning grew. Moreover, on its tow-paths built up with canal sediment, . . . wild rams (?) and alert snakes of the mountains allowed no one to pass. On its plains, where fine grass grew, now the reeds of lamentation grew. Agade's flowing fresh water flowed as brackish water. When someone decided: 'I will dwell in that city!', he could not enjoy the pleasures of a dwelling place. When someone decided: 'I will rest in Agade!', he could not enjoy the pleasures of a resting place!

281 Praise be to Inana for the destruction of Agade!

Notes

10–24 Instead of 'mountain ibexes' some MSS have: 'mountain beasts (?)'; others have: 'horses'.

25–39 Instead of 'who cared for' some MSS have: 'of'.

40–56 Instead of 'like a mountain' 1 MS has: 'a great mountain'. Instead of 'going to' some MSS have: 'flowing into'. Instead of 'exotic wares' some MSS have: 'wares of foreign countries'. Instead of 'temple administrators' 1 MS has: 'generals'.

57–65 Instead of 'removed' some MSS have: 'tore away'.

66–76 Instead of 'up' some MSS have: 'out'; 1 MS has: 'away'.

83–93 Instead of 'scatter its treasures' 1 MS has: 'destroy its treasuries'. After 'discuss it with anyone.' 1 MS adds 2 lines: '. . . temples shake . . . , . . . perform (?) extispicy regarding (?) his temple . . . .'. Instead of 'covered his chariot with a reed mat' 1 MS has: 'pulled out the outside pin of his chariot'. Instead of 'his ceremonial barge' 1 MS has: 'the prow of his ceremonial barge'; another MS has: 'the cabin of his ceremonial barge'. After 'for seven years?' some MSS add the line: 'He realized what the dream was about, but did not put it into words, and did not discuss it with anyone.'

100–19 Thirty shekels are equivalent to about 250 grams.

120–48 Instead of 'the Land was deprived of its ornament' 1 MS has: 'the ornament of the Land disappeared'. Instead of 'spades' 1 MS has: 'axes'. Instead of 'moved away from' some MSS have: 'juddered'. Instead of 'intelligence' 1 MS has: 'sanctuary'.

149–75 Instead of 'instincts' some MSS have: 'feelings'. Instead of 'occupied' 1 MS has: 'attacked'. Instead of 'lay dislodged in' 1 MS has: 'were covered with'. Instead of 'established gardens for themselves' 1 MS has: 'made gardens grow'. After 'the large' some MSS add: 'fields and'. After 'the inundated' some MSS add: 'fields and'.

176–92 A shekel is equivalent to a little over 8 grams; a *sila* is equivalent to about a litre; a mina is equivalent to about 500 grams; a *ban* is equivalent to about 10 litres.

193–209 Instead of '*meze*, and *lilis*' some MSS have: '*šem*, and *lilis*'; 1 MS has: 'and bronze *šem*'.

210–21 Instead of 'the great gods' 1 MS has: 'all the gods whosoever'. Instead of 'cooled' 1 MS has: 'sprinkled'.

222–44 Instead of 'the' 1 MS has: 'your'. Instead of 'your' 1 MS has: 'the'.

245–55 Instead of 'palace, built for joy' 1 MS has 'joyous palace'.

256–71 Instead of 'Agade, may brackish water flow' 1 MS has: 'May brackish water flow in the river'.

D. THE MOON-GOD
NANNA-SUEN

In Mesopotamian belief, all the major celestial bodies were envisaged as visible manifestation of deities. The sun, the moon, the stars and comets were a source of never-ending wonder. Utu (the sun) sheds a brilliant light during each day, and returns again each new day to illuminate the life of human beings, as well as bringing about the fertility of vegetation with his beneficial warmth. Utu was believed to emerge from a set of doors at the eastern horizon at dawn each day and make a daily journey across the skies, driven by his charioteer Bunene. Finally he entered 'the interior of heaven' once more at dusk, through a corresponding doorway on the western horizon. At night, when the sun's light was absent, the moon took over the duty of illuminating the skies. Given the absence of artificial light in ancient times, and the limited amount of fires, torches, or candles shining upwards from the earth, the skies would regularly have been brilliantly bright with the moon and stars, dimmed only by cloud cover. The waxing and waning of the moon, and its varying positions in the sky depending on the time of year, were keenly observed (see *A šir-namgala to Nanna*), and as with all astronomical observations were interpreted as omens of the future. The calendar year was a lunar year, divided into twelve months each of thirty days. This necessitated the occasional intercalation of an extra month at the end of the lunar year to bring the calendar back into rhythm with the solar cycle.

Both the moon and the sun were envisaged as male deities. This is different from the Graeco-Roman belief according to which the sun was a male deity but the moon a female. In Sumerian, the names of the moon-god were Suen or Nanna, and sometimes he was called by both together, Nanna-Suen. Often he is referred to either as 'youthful Suen' or 'Father Nanna', making it clear that these names were assigned respectively to the minimal and maximal phases of the lunar cycle. Sometimes Nanna is represented as a cowherd who is responsible for the herds of heaven: the stars (see *The herds of Nanna*). He was generally considered a benign deity who might provide assistance and to whom one might turn in prayer.

Other names included Ašimbabbar and the Glory of Heaven. In

Akkadian, Suen was later pronounced Sîn. Nanna was the son of the deities Enlil and Ninlil; his wife was the goddess Ningal, and their children were the sun-god Utu and the goddess Inana. The most important shrine of Nanna was the temple E-kiš-nugal at Urim, and this meant that Nanna was regarded as an important deity in the very capital city of the empire of the Third Dynasty of Urim (see *The lament for Sumer and Urim*).

Although he was a very popular deity in the early second millennium BCE, the position of Nanna always remained subordinate to that of the chief gods of the pantheon (see *A balbale to Nanna* and *Nanna-Suen's journey to Nibru*). A symbol of Nanna was a recumbent crescent (which is how the new moon appears in the latitudes of Iraq). Probably because of the similarity of this to the horns of a bull, his associated animal was a bull.

FURTHER READING

Colbow, G., 'More Insights into Representations of the Moon God: The Third and Second Millennia BC', in I. L. Finkel and M. J. Geller (eds.), *Sumerian Gods and their Representations* (Styx: Groningen, 1997, pp. 19–31) explores the iconography of Nanna-Suen.

Klein, J., 'The Genealogy of Nanna-Suen and its Historical Background', in T. Abusch *et al.* (eds.), *Historiography in the Cuneiform World* (CDL Press: Bethesda, MD, 2001, pp. 279–302) examines literary traditions about the divine family of Nanna-Suen.

Michalowski, P., *The Lamentation over the Destruction of Sumer and Ur* (Eisenbrauns: Winona Lake, Ind., 1989) is an in-depth study of *The lament for Sumer and Urim*.

OTHER COMPOSITIONS FEATURING
NANNA-SUEN INCLUDE

Group A   Lugalbanda in the mountain cave
Group B   Ploughing with the jewels
Group C   Enlil and Ninlil
          Šulgi and Ninlil's barge
Group G   The home of the fish
Group H   An *ululumama* to Suen for Ibbi-Suen
Group J   The exaltation of Inana

The lament for Sumer and Urim

This long poem is representative of a group of compositions whose central theme is the fall and destruction of cities and states, commonly grouped together under the label of 'city laments'. Although formally heterogeneous, they share some fundamental themes: destruction as a result of divine decision, abandonment of the city by the tutelary god, restoration, and return of the tutelary god. City laments may vary widely in the emphasis given to these themes: in the poem translated here the largest part is taken up with the dramatic, vivid, and exhaustive account of the calamity that affects Sumer and the city of Urim together with its tutelary deity Nanna. There is evidence that the similarities among the city laments were also perceived by the scribes, as in lines 32–4 of the *Literary catalogue from Nibru* (Group J) three of the five known city laments are listed together. The poem *The cursing of Agade* (Group C) shows extensive thematic similarities to the city laments.

The historical background behind the poem is the fall of the Third Dynasty of Urim, whose last ruler Ibbi-Suen is mentioned by name. However, the poem uses these events as an opportunity to convey what could be taken as its main message: the fickleness of fortune, the inherent mortality of all things: 'Who has ever seen a reign of kingship that would take precedence for ever?'

The composition is divided into five *kirugus*, each followed by a very short *ğišğiğal* except for the last. The first *kirugu* (1–112) begins with the divine decision to destroy Urim, followed by the actual destruction. The second *kirugu* (115–281) contains a long litany of gods who are forced to leave and so lament their destroyed cities and temples. The third (285–357) details once more the destruction of Urim. It ends with Nanna's plea for Enlil to relent. The fourth *kirugu* (360–478) begins with Enlil's reply in which he attributes responsibility to the divine assembly and instructs Nanna to leave Urim. It continues with a portrayal of the dreadful conditions within the city, and concludes with Nanna's second plea. This time Enlil has mercy on Nanna and orders Urim to be restored. The last *kirugu* (483–519) is a prayer in the voice of the narrator wishing that the great gods will never again change the fate of the restored city.

Translation

1–2 To overturn the appointed times, to obliterate the divine plans, the storms gather to strike like a flood.

3–11 An, Enlil, Enki, and Ninḫursaĝa° have decided its fate—to overturn the divine powers of Sumer, to lock up the favourable reign in its home, to destroy the city, to destroy the house, to destroy the cattle-pen, to level the sheepfold; that the cattle should not stand in the pen, that the sheep should not multiply in the fold, that watercourses should carry brackish water, that weeds should grow in the fertile fields, that mourning plants should grow in the open country,

12–21 that the mother should not seek out her child, that the father should not say 'O my dear wife!', that the junior wife should take no joy in his embrace, that the young child should not grow vigorous on his knee, that the wet-nurse should not sing lullabies; to change the location of kingship, to defile the seeking of oracles, to take kingship away from the Land, to cast the eye of the storm on all the land, to obliterate the divine plans by the order of An and Enlil;

22–6 after An had frowned upon all the lands, after Enlil had looked favourably on an enemy land, after Nintud had scattered the creatures that she had created, after Enki had altered the course of the Tigris and Euphrates, after Utu had cast his curse on the roads and highways;

27–37 so as to obliterate the divine powers of Sumer, to change its pre-ordained plans, to alienate the divine powers of the reign of kingship of Urim, to humiliate the princely son in his house E-kiš-nuĝal, to break up the unity of the people of Nanna, numerous as ewes; to change the food offerings of Urim, the shrine of magnificent food offerings; that its people should no longer dwell in their quarters, that they should be given over to live in an inimical place; that Šimaški and Elam, the enemy, should dwell in their place; that its shepherd, in his own palace, should be captured by the enemy, that Ibbi-Suen should be taken to the land of Elam in fetters, that from Mount Zabu on the edge of the sea to the borders of Anšan, like a swallow that has flown from its house, he should never return to his city;

38–46 that on the two banks of the Tigris and of the Euphrates bad weeds should grow, that no one should set out on the road, that no one should seek out the highway, that the city and its settled surround-ings should be razed to ruin-mounds; that its numerous black-headed people should be slaughtered; that the hoe should not attack the fertile fields, that seed should not be planted in the ground, that the melody of the cowherds' songs should not resound in the open country, that butter and cheese should not be made in the cattle-pen, that dung should not be stacked on the ground, that the shepherd should not enclose the sacred sheepfold with a fence, that the song of the churning should not resound in the sheepfold;

47–55 to decimate the animals of the open country, to finish off all living things, that the four-legged creatures of Šakkan should lay no more dung on the ground, that the marshes should be so dry as to be full of cracks and have no new seed, that sickly-headed reeds should grow in the reed-beds, that they should be covered by a stinking morass, that there should be no new growth in the orchards, that it should all collapse by itself—so as quickly to subdue Urim like a roped ox, to bow its neck to the ground: the great charging wild bull, confident in its own strength, the primeval city of lordship and kingship, built on sacred ground.

56–7 Its fate cannot be changed. Who can overturn it? It is the command of An and Enlil. Who can oppose it?

58–68 An frightened the very dwellings of Sumer, the people were afraid. Enlil blew an evil storm, silence lay upon the city. Nintud bolted the door of the storehouses of the Land. Enki blocked the water in the Tigris and the Euphrates. Utu took away the pronouncement of equity and justice. Inana handed over victory in strife and battle to a rebellious land. Ninĝirsu poured Sumer away like milk to the dogs. Turmoil descended upon the Land, something that no one had ever known, something unseen, which had no name, something that could not be fathomed. The lands were confused in their fear. The god of the city turned away, its shepherd vanished.

69–78 The people, in their fear, breathed only with difficulty. The storm immobilized them, the storm did not let them return. There was no return for them, the time of captivity did not pass. What did Enlil, the shepherd of the black-headed people, do? Enlil, to destroy the loyal households, to decimate the loyal men, to put the evil eye on the sons of the loyal men, on the first-born, Enlil then sent down Gutium from the mountains. Their advance was as the flood of Enlil that cannot be withstood. The great wind of the countryside filled the countryside, it advanced before them. The extensive countryside was destroyed, no one moved about there.

79–92 The dark time was roasted by hailstones and flames. The bright time was wiped out by a shadow.° On that day, heaven rumbled, the earth trembled, the storm worked without respite. Heaven was darkened, it was covered by a shadow; the mountains roared. Utu lay down at the horizon, dust passed over the mountains. Nanna lay at the zenith, the people were afraid. The city . . . stepped outside. The foreigners in the city even chased away its dead. Large trees were uprooted, the forest growth was ripped out. The orchards were stripped of their fruit, they were cleaned of their offshoots. The crop drowned while it was still on the stalk, the yield of the grain diminished. (*3 lines fragmentary*)

93–103 They piled . . . up in heaps, they spread . . . out like sheaves. There were corpses floating in the Euphrates, brigands roamed the roads. The father turned away from his wife without saying 'O my wife!' The mother turned away from her child without saying 'O my child!' He who had a productive estate neglected his estate without saying 'O my estate!' The rich man took an unfamiliar path away from his possessions. In those days the kingship of the Land was defiled. The tiara and crown that had been on the king's head were both spoiled. The lands that had followed the same path were split into disunity. The food offerings of Urim, the shrine of magnificent food offerings, were changed for the worse. Nanna traded away his people, numerous as ewes.

104–11 Its king sat immobilized in the palace, all alone. Ibbi-Suen was sitting in anguish in the palace, all alone. In E-namtila, his place of delight, he wept bitterly. The devastating flood was levelling everything. Like a great storm it roared over the earth—who could escape it?—to destroy the city, to destroy the house, so that traitors would lie on top of loyal men and the blood of traitors flow upon loyal men.

112 1st *kirugu*.

113 The storms gather to strike like a flood.

114 *Ḡišḡiḡal* to the *kirugu*.

115–22 The house of Kiš, Ḫursaĝ-kalama, was destroyed. Zababa took an unfamiliar path away from his beloved dwelling. Mother Bau was lamenting bitterly in her E-Iri-kug. 'Alas, the destroyed city, my destroyed house,' she cried bitterly. (*1 line fragmentary; 2 lines missing*) 'Alas, the destroyed city, my destroyed house,' she cried bitterly.

123–32 Kazallu, the city of teeming multitudes, was cast into confusion. Numušda took an unfamiliar path away from the city, his beloved dwelling. His wife Namrat, the beautiful lady, was lamenting bitterly. 'Alas, the destroyed city, my destroyed house,' she cried bitterly. Its river bed was empty, no water flowed. Like a river cursed by Enki its opening channel was dammed up. On the fields fine grains grew no more, people had nothing to eat. The orchards were scorched like an oven, its open country was scattered. The four-

legged wild animals did not run about. The four-legged creatures of
Šakkan could find no rest.

133–42 Lugal-Marda stepped outside his city. Ninzuana took an unfamiliar
path away from her beloved dwelling. 'Alas, the destroyed city, my
destroyed house,' she cried bitterly. Isin, the shrine that was not a
quay, was split by onrushing waters. Ninisina, the mother of the
Land, wept bitter tears. 'Alas, the destroyed city, my destroyed
house,' she cried bitterly. Enlil struck Dur-an-ki with a mace. Enlil
made lamentation in his city, the shrine Nibru. Mother Ninlil, the
lady of the Ki-ur shrine, wept bitter tears. 'Alas, the destroyed city,
my destroyed house,' she cried bitterly.

143–54 Keš, built all alone on the high open country, was haunted. Adab,
the settlement which stretches out along the river, was treated
as a rebellious land.° The snake of the mountains made his lair
there, it became a rebellious land. The Gutians bred there, issued
their seed. Nintud wept bitter tears over her creatures. 'Alas, the
destroyed city, my destroyed house,' she cried bitterly. In Zabalam
the sacred Giguna was haunted. Inana abandoned Unug and went
off to enemy territory. In the E-ana the enemy set eyes upon the
sacred g̃ipar shrine. The sacred g̃ipar of en priesthood was defiled.
Its en priest was snatched from the g̃ipar and carried off to enemy
territory. 'Alas, the destroyed city, my destroyed house,' she cried
bitterly.

155–62 A violent storm blew over Umma, brickwork in the midst of the
highlands. Šara took an unfamiliar path away from the E-maḫ, his
beloved dwelling. Ninmul cried bitter tears over her destroyed city.
'Oh my city, whose charms can no longer satisfy me,' she cried
bitterly. G̃irsu, the city of heroes, was afflicted with a lightning
storm. Nin-g̃irsu took an unfamiliar path away from the E-ninnu.
Mother Bau wept bitter tears in her E-Iri-kug. 'Alas, the destroyed
city, my destroyed house,' she cried bitterly.

163–73 On that day the word of Enlil was an attacking storm. Who could
fathom it? The word of Enlil was destruction on the right, was . . . on
the left. What did Enlil do in order to decide the fate of mankind?
Enlil brought down the Elamites, the enemy, from the highlands.
Nanše, the noble daughter, was settled outside the city. Fire
approached Ninmarki in the shrine Gu-aba. Large boats were carrying off its silver and lapis lazuli. The lady, sacred Ninmarki, was
despondent because of her perished goods. Then the day . . . ,

burning like . . . . The province of Lagaš was handed over to Elam. And then the queen also reached the end of her time.

174–84 Bau, as if she were human, also reached the end of her time: 'Woe is me! Enlil has handed over the city to the storm. He has handed it over to the storm that destroys cities. He has handed it over to the storm that destroys houses.' Dumuzid-abzu was full of fear in the house of Kinirša. Kinirša, the city of her noble youth, was ordered to be plundered. The city of Nanše, Nigin, was delivered to the foreigners. Sirara, her beloved dwelling, was handed over to the evil ones. 'Alas, the destroyed city, my destroyed house,' she cried bitterly. Its sacred ĝipar of en priesthood was defiled. Its en priest was snatched from the ĝipar and carried off to enemy territory.

185–92 Mighty strength was set against the banks of the Nuna-Nanna canal. The settlements of the E-danna of Nanna, like substantial cattle-pens, were destroyed. Their refugees, like stampeding goats, were chased (?) by dogs. They destroyed Gaeš like milk poured out to dogs, and shattered its finely fashioned statues. 'Alas, the destroyed city, my destroyed house,' he cried bitterly. Its sacred ĝipar of en priesthood was defiled. Its en priestess was snatched from the ĝipar and carried off to enemy territory.

193–205 A lament was raised at the dais that stretches out toward heaven. Its heavenly throne was not set up, was not fit to be crowned (?). It was cut down as if it were a date palm and tied together. Aššu, the settlement that stretches out along the river, was deprived of water. At the place of Nanna where evil had never walked, the enemy walked. How was the house treated like that? The E-puhruma was emptied. Ki-abrig, which used to be filled with numerous cows and numerous calves, was destroyed like a mighty cattle-pen. Ningublaga took an unfamiliar path away from the Ga-bur. Niniagar wept bitter tears all alone. 'Alas, the destroyed city, my destroyed house,' she cried bitterly. Its sacred ĝipar of en priesthood was defiled. Its en priestess was snatched from the ĝipar and carried off to enemy territory.

206–13 Ninazu deposited his weapon in a corner in the E-gida. An evil storm swept over Ninhursaĝa at the E-nutura. Like a pigeon she flew from the window, she stood apart in the open country. 'Alas, the destroyed city, my destroyed house,' she cried bitterly. In Ĝišbanda, the house that was filled with lamentation, lamentation reeds grew. Ninĝišzida took an unfamiliar path away from Ĝišbanda. Azimua, the queen of the city, wept bitter tears. 'Alas, the destroyed city, my destroyed house,' she cried bitterly.

214-20 On that day, the storm forced people to live in darkness. In order to destroy Kuara, it forced people to live in darkness. Nineḥama in her fear wept bitter tears. 'Alas the destroyed city, my destroyed house,' she cried bitterly. Asarluḫi put his robes on with haste and . . . . Lugalbanda took an unfamiliar path away from his beloved dwelling.° 'Alas the destroyed city, my destroyed house,' she (*Nineḥama*) cried bitterly.

221-4 Eridug, floating on great waters, was deprived (?) of drinking water. In its outer environs, which had turned into haunted plains, ... The loyal man in a place of treachery . . . . Ka-ḫeg̃ala and Igi-ḫeg̃ala . . . .

225-33 'I, a young man whom the storm has not destroyed, ... I, not destroyed by the storm, my attractiveness not brought to an end, ... We have been struck down like beautiful boxwood trees. We have been struck down like . . . with coloured eyes. We have been struck down like statues being cast in moulds. The Gutians, the vandals, are wiping us out. We turned to Father Enki in the Abzu of Eridug. . . . what can we say, what more can we add? . . . what can we say, what more can we add?

234-42 '. . . we have been driven out of Eridug. We who were in charge of . . . during the day are eclipsed (?) by shadows. We who were in charge of . . . during the night are . . . by the storm. How shall we receive among our weary ones him who was in charge during the day? How shall we let him who was in charge by night go astray among our sleepless ones? Enki, your city has been cursed, it has been given to an enemy land. Why do they reckon us among those who have been displaced from Eridug? Why do they destroy us like palm trees, us who were not violent? Why do they break us up, like a new boat that has not . . . ?'

243-50 After Enki had cast his eyes on a foreign land, (*1 line unclear*) . . . have risen up, have called on their cohorts. Enki took an unfamiliar path away from Eridug. Damgalnuna, the mother of the E-maḫ, wept bitter tears. 'Alas the destroyed city, my destroyed house,' she cried bitterly. Its sacred g̃ipar of en priesthood was defiled. Its en priestess was snatched from the g̃ipar and carried off to enemy territory.

251-9 In Urim no one went to fetch food, no one went to fetch water. Those who went to fetch food, went away from the food and will not return. Those who went to fetch water, went away from the water and will not return. To the south, the Elamites stepped in, slaughtering . . . . In the uplands, the vandals, the enemy, ... The Tidnum daily strapped the mace to their loins. To the south, the Elamites, like an onrushing wave, were . . . . In the uplands, like chaff blowing in the wind, they . . . over the open country. Urim, like a great charging wild bull, bowed its neck to the ground.

260–71 What did Enlil, who decides the fates, then do? Again he sent down the Elamites, the enemy, from the mountains. The foremost house, firmly founded, ... In order to destroy Kisiga, ten men, even five men . . . . Three days and three nights did not pass, . . . the city was raked by a hoe. Dumuzid left Kisiga like a prisoner of war, his hands were tied. (*5 lines fragmentary*)

272–80 She rode away from her possessions, she went to the mountains. She loudly sang out a lament over those brightly lit mountains: 'I am queen, but I shall have to ride away from my possessions, and now I shall be a slave in those parts. I shall have to ride away from my silver and lapis lazuli, and now I shall be a slave in those parts. There, slavery, . . . people, who can . . . it? There, slavery, Elam . . . , who can . . . it? Alas, the destroyed city, my destroyed house,' she cried bitterly. My queen, though not the enemy, went to enemy land. Ama-ušumgal-ana . . . Kisiga. Like a city . . . .

281 2nd *kirugu*. (*1 line fragmentary; 1 line missing*)

284 *Ĝišgiĝal* to the *kirugu*. (*7 lines missing or fragmentary*)

292–302 Enlil threw open the door of the grand gate to the wind. In Urim no one went to fetch food, no one went to fetch water. Its people rushed around like water being poured from a well. Their strength ebbed away, they could not even go on their way. Enlil afflicted the city with an evil famine. He afflicted the city with that which destroys cities, that which destroys houses. He afflicted the city with that which cannot be withstood with weapons. He afflicted the city with dissatisfaction and treachery. In Urim, which was like a solitary reed, there was not even fear. Its people, like fish being grabbed in a pond, sought to escape. Its young and old lay spread about, no one could rise.

303–17 At the royal station (?) there was no food on top of the platform (?). The king who used to eat marvellous food grabbed at a mere ration. As the day grew dark, the eye of the sun was eclipsing, the people experienced hunger. There was no beer in the beer-hall, there was no more malt for it. There was no food for him in his palace, it was unsuitable to live in. Grain did not fill his lofty storehouse, he could not save his life. The grain-piles and granaries of Nanna held no grain. The evening meal in the great dining hall of the gods was defiled. Wine and syrup ceased to flow in the great dining hall. The butcher's knife that used to slay oxen and sheep lay hungry in the grass. Its mighty oven no longer cooked oxen and sheep, it no longer emitted the aroma of roasting meat. The sounds of the *bursaĝ* building, the pure . . . of Nanna, were stilled. The house which used to bellow like a bull was silenced. Its holy deliveries were no longer fulfilled, its . . . were alienated. The mortar, pestle, and grinding stone lay idle; no one bent down over them.

318–27 The Shining Quay of Nanna was silted up. The sound of water against the boat's prow ceased, there was no rejoicing. Dust piled up in the *unuribanda* of Nanna. The rushes grew, the rushes grew, the mourning reeds grew. Boats and barges ceased docking at the Shining Quay. Nothing moved on your watercourse which was fit for barges. The plans of the festivals at the place of the divine rituals were altered. The boat with first-fruit offerings of the father who begot Nanna no longer brought first-fruit offerings. Its food offerings could not be taken to Enlil in Nibru. Its watercourse was empty, barges could not travel.

328–39 There were no paths on either of its banks, long grass grew there. The reed fence of the well-stocked cattle-pen of Nanna was split open. The reed huts were overrun, their walls were breached. The cows and their young were captured and carried off to enemy territory. The *munzer*-fed cows took an unfamiliar path in an open country that they did not know. Gayau, who loves cows, dropped his weapon in the dung. Šuni-dug, who stores butter and cheese, did not store butter and cheese. Those who are unfamiliar with butter were churning the butter. Those who are unfamiliar with milk were curdling (?) the milk. The sound of the churning vat did not resound in the cattle-pen. Like mighty fire that once burnt, its smoke is extinguished. The great dining hall of Nanna . . . .

340–9 Suen wept to his father Enlil: 'O father who begot me, why have you turned away from my city which was built (?) for you? O Enlil, why have you turned away from my Urim which was built (?) for you? The boat with first-fruit offerings no longer brings first-fruit offerings to the father who begot him. Your food offerings can no longer be brought to Enlil in Nibru. The *en* priests and priestesses of the countryside and city have been carried off by phantoms. Urim, like a city raked by a hoe, is to be counted as a ruin-mound. The Ki-ur, Enlil's resting-place, has become a haunted shrine. O Enlil, gaze upon your city, an empty wasteland. Gaze upon your city Nibru, an empty wasteland.

350–6 'The dogs of Urim no longer sniff at the base of the city wall. The man who used to drill large wells scratches the ground in the market place. My father who begot me, enclose in your embrace my city which is all alone. Enlil, return to your embrace my Urim which is all alone. Enclose in your embrace my E-kiš-nuĝal which is all alone. May you bring forth offspring in Urim, may you multiply its people. May you restore the divine powers of Sumer that have been forgotten.'

357 3rd *kirugu*.

358 O good house, good house! O its people, its people!

359 *Ĝišgiĝal.*

360–70 Enlil then answered his son Suen: 'There is lamentation in the haunted city, reeds of mourning grow there.° In its midst the people pass their days in sighing.° Oh Nanna, the noble son . . . , why do you concern yourself with crying? The judgment uttered by the assembly cannot be reversed. The word of An and Enlil knows no overturning. Urim was indeed given kingship but it was not given an eternal reign. From time immemorial, since the Land was founded, until people multiplied, who has ever seen a reign of kingship that would take precedence for ever? The reign of its kingship had been long indeed but had to exhaust itself. O my Nanna, do not exert yourself in vain, abandon your city.'

371–7 Then my king, the noble son, became distraught. Lord Ašimbabbar, the noble son, grieved. Nanna who loves his city left his city. Suen took an unfamiliar path away from his beloved Urim. In order to go as an exile from her city to foreign territory, Ningal quickly clothed herself and left the city. The Anuna stepped outside of Urim.

378–88 . . . approached Urim. The trees of Urim were sick, its reeds were sick. Laments sounded all along its city wall. Daily there was slaughter before it. Large axes were sharpened in front of Urim. The spears, the arms of battle, were prepared. The large bows, javelin and shield gathered together to strike. The barbed arrows covered its outer side like a raining cloud. Large stones, one after another, fell with great thuds.° Urim, confident in its own strength, stood ready for the murderers. Its people, oppressed by the enemy, could not withstand their weapons.

389–402 In the city, those who had not been felled by weapons succumbed to hunger. Hunger filled the city like water, it would not cease. This hunger contorted people's faces, twisted their muscles. Its people were as if drowning in a pond, they gasped for breath. Its king breathed heavily in his palace, all alone. Its people dropped their weapons, their weapons hit the ground. They struck their necks with their hands and cried. They sought counsel with each other, they searched for clarification: 'Alas, what can we say about it? What more can we add to it? How long until we are finished off by this catastrophe? Inside Urim there is death, outside it there is death. Inside it we are to be finished off by famine. Outside it we are to be finished off by Elamite weapons. In Urim the enemy oppresses us, oh, we are finished.'

403–10 The people took refuge (?) behind the city walls. They were united in fear. The palace that was destroyed by onrushing water was defiled, its doorbolts were torn out. Elam, like a swelling flood wave, left (?) only the ghosts. In Urim people were smashed as if they were clay pots. Its refugees were unable to flee, they were trapped inside the walls.° The statues that were in the treasury were cut down. The great stewardess Niniagar ran away from the storehouse. Its throne was cast down before it, she threw herself down into the dust.

411–19 Its mighty cows with shining horns were captured, their horns were cut off. Its unblemished oxen and grass-fed sheep were slaughtered.° The palm-trees, strong as mighty copper, the heroic strength, were torn out like rushes, were plucked like rushes, their trunks were turned sideways. Their tops lay in the dust, there was no one to raise them. The midriffs of their palm fronds were cut off and their tops were burnt off. Their date spadices that used to fall (?) on the well were torn out. The fertile reeds, which grew in the sacred . . . , were defiled. The great tribute that they had collected was hauled off to the mountains.

420–34 The house's great door ornament fell down, its parapet was destroyed. The wild animals that were intertwined on its left and right lay before it like heroes smitten by heroes. Its gaping-mouthed dragons and its awe-inspiring lions were pulled down with ropes like captured wild bulls and carried off to enemy territory. The fragrance of the sacred seat of Nanna, formerly like a fragrant cedar grove, was destroyed.° The glory of the house, whose glory was once so lovely, was extinguished. Like a storm that fills all the lands, it was built there like twilight in the heavens; its doors adorned with the heavenly stars, its . . . . Great bronze latches . . . were torn out. Its hinges . . . . Together with its door fittings it (?) wept bitterly like a fugitive. The bolt, the holy lock and the great door were not fastened for it. The noise of the door being fastened had ceased; there was no one to fasten it. The . . . and was put out in the square.

435–48 The food offerings . . . of his royal dining place were altered. In its sacred place (?) the *tigi*, *šem*, and *ala* drums did not sound. Its mighty *tigi* . . . did not perform its sacred song. Verdicts were not given at the Dubla-maḫ, the place where oaths used to be taken. The throne was not set up at its place of judgment, justice was not administered. Alamuš threw down his sceptre, his hands trembling. In the sacred bedchamber of Nanna musicians no longer played the *balaǧ* drum. The sacred box that no one had set eyes upon was seen by the enemy. The divine bed was not set up, it was not spread with clean hay. The statues that were in the treasury were cut down. The cook, the dream interpreter, and the seal keeper did not perform the ceremonies properly. They stood by submissively and were carried off by the foreigners. The holy *uzga* priests of the sacred lustrations, the linen-clad priests, forsook the divine plans and sacred divine powers, they went off to a foreign city.

449–59 In his grief Suen approached his father. He went down on his knee in front of Enlil, the father who begot him: 'O father who begot me, how long will the enemy eye be cast upon my account, how long . . . ? The lordship and the kingship that you bestowed . . . , Father Enlil, the one who advises with just words, the wise words of the Land . . . , your inimical judgment . . . , look into your darkened heart, terrifying like waves. O Father Enlil, the fate that you have decreed cannot be explained, the . . . of lordship, my ornament.' . . . he put on a garment of mourning.

460–74 Enlil then provided a favourable response to his son Suen: 'My son, the city built for you in joy and prosperity was given to you as your reign. The destroyed city, the great wall, the walls with broken battlements: all this too is part of that reign. . . . the black, black days of the reign that has been your lot. As for dwelling in your home, the E-temen-ni-guru, that was properly built—indeed Urim shall be rebuilt in splendour, the people shall bow down to you. There is to be bounty at its base, there is to be grain. There is to be splendour at its top, the sun shall rejoice there. Let an abundance of grain embrace its table. May Urim, the city whose fate was pronounced by An, be restored for you.' Having pronounced his blessing, Enlil raised his head towards the heavens: 'May the land, south and highland, be organized for Nanna. May the roads of the mountains be set in order for Suen. Like a cloud hugging the earth, they shall submit to him. By order of An and Enlil it shall be conferred.'

475–7 Father Nanna stood in his city of Urim with head raised high again. The youth Suen could enter again into the E-kiš-nuĝal. Ningal refreshed herself in her sacred living quarters.°

478 4th *kirugu*.

479–81 There is lamentation in the haunted city, mourning reeds grew there. In its midst there is lamentation, mourning reeds grew there. Its people spend their days in moaning.

482 *Ĝišgiĝal*.

483–92 O bitter storm, retreat! O storm, storm return to your home. O storm that destroys cities, retreat! O storm, storm return to your home. O storm that destroys houses, retreat! O storm, storm return to your home. Indeed the storm that blew on Sumer, blew also on the foreign lands. Indeed the storm that blew on the land, blew on the foreign lands. It has blown on Tidnum, it has blown on the foreign lands. It has blown on Gutium, it has blown on the foreign lands. It has blown on Anšan, it has blown on the foreign lands. It levelled Anšan like a blowing evil wind. Famine has overwhelmed the evildoer; those people will have to submit.

493–504 May An not change the divine powers of heaven, the divine plans for treating the people with justice. May An not change the decisions and judgments to lead the people properly. To travel on the roads of the Land: may An not change it. May An and Enlil not change it, may An not change it. May Enki and Ninmaḫ not change it, may An not change it. That the Tigris and Euphrates should again carry water: may An not change it. That there should be rain in the skies and on the ground speckled barley: may An not change it. That there should be watercourses with water and fields with grain: may An not change it. That the marshes should support fish and fowl: may An not change it. That old reeds and fresh reeds should grow in the reed-beds: may An not change it. May An and Enlil not change it. May Enki and Ninmaḫ not change it.

505–18 That the orchards should bear syrup and grapes, that the high plain should bear the *mašgurum* tree, that there should be long life in the palace, that the sea should bring forth every abundance: may An not change it. The land densely populated from south to uplands: may An not change it. May An and Enlil not change it, may An not change it. May Enki and Ninmaḫ not change it, may An not change it. That cities should be rebuilt, that people should be numerous, that in the whole universe the people should be cared for; O Nanna, your kingship is sweet, return to your place. May a good abundant reign be long-lasting in Urim. Let its people lie down in safe pastures, let them reproduce. O mankind . . . , princess overcome by lamentation and crying! O Nanna! O your city! O your house! O your people!

519 5th *kirugu*.

Notes

3–11 Instead of 'Ninḫursaĝa' 2 MSS have: 'Ninmaḫ'.

79–92 After 'by a shadow.' 2 MSS add 2 lines: 'On that bloody day, mouths were crushed, heads were crashed. The storm was a harrow coming from above, the city was struck by a hoe.'

143–54 Instead of 'was treated as a rebellious land.' 1 MS has: 'was deprived of water.'

214–20 After 'his beloved dwelling' 1 MS adds: 'Ninsumun . . . .'

360–70 After 'reeds of mourning grow there.' 1 MS adds 1 line: 'In its midst there is lamentation, reeds of mourning grow there.' After 'days in sighing.' 1 MS adds the line: 'My son, the noble son . . . , why do you concern yourself with crying?'

378–88 After 'fell with great thuds.' 1 MS adds 1 line: 'Daily the evil wind returned in the city.'

403–10 After 'trapped inside the walls.' 1 MS adds 3 lines: 'Like fish living in a pond, they tried to escape. The enemy seized the E-kiš-nuĝal of Nanna. They ripped out its heavy . . . .'

411–19 After 'sheep were slaughtered.' 1 MS adds 1 line: 'They were cut down like date palms and were tied together.'

420–34 After 'was destroyed.' 1 MS adds 1 line: 'Its architrave . . . gold and lapis lazuli.'

475–7 After 'living quarters.' 1 MS adds 1 line: 'In Urim she could enter again into her E-kiš-nuĝal.'

A *balbale* to Nanna

The main theme of this most beautiful song is Nanna's relationship with his divine parents, Enlil and Ninlil of Nibru. As Nanna was also the tutelary god of the southern city Urim, whose rulers during the Third Dynasty of Urim controlled the whole of Mesopotamia, the poem may support a reading that reflects this. Nanna's portrayal as the favourite and elevated son who fulfils his filial duties in an exemplary way somehow mirrors the harmonious relationship between the rulers of Urim and sacred Nibru which was seen to be a guarantee of Urim's continuing prosperity.

The opening passage (1–14) praises Nanna as a herdsman tending his cows. It alludes to both his celestial and pastoral aspects by projecting the image of a cowherd upon the heavenly bodies in the sky (see also *The herds of Nanna*). In the main part of the composition Ninlil gives Nanna three blessings, each of increasing length (15–20, 25–36, and 41–60). They depict a warm, loving relationship between Nanna and his parents, imitating those which exist within an ideal human family. The allusion to Urim's political hegemony is most tangible in the third, longest blessing, in which Ninlil reminds Nanna that An, another supreme deity, bestowed on him the roles of both shepherd and king of the Land and chose Urim as his favourite city.

Translation

1–14 How many there are! How many cows there are! How many cattle of Suen there are! The dark ones are translucent lapis lazuli; the pale cows are the light of the risen moon. The little ones trickle down like barleycorns for you; the large ones throng together like wild bulls for you. The Glory of Heaven has undone the halters of the numerous cows in his teeming herd. He has poured out milk from the beautiful cows at the offering table; his bright hands ever pour the milk. After my king has completed the work, Suen . . . the shining halter . . . the cows, he . . . the cows, he . . . the cows. He acts as the herder of the cows.

15–20 His own mother, the lady of Nibru, speaks a prayer to the lord in his desert: 'A prayer, O shepherd! A prayer! May the cows be numerous for you in the good desert. When you arrive at nightfall, may you renew the E-kur, the highly prized sanctuary.'

21–4 He is its lover, he is its lover, he is the lord, the E-kur's lover! He is the man of delight to Enlil, he is Suen, the cry of joy of his own mother.

FIG. 18. 'The large ones throng together like wild bulls for you'—
a procession of bull calves on a frieze from Early Dynastic Ubaid

25–36 The mother who bore him speaks kindly from her loving heart to
Suen: 'You are the beloved of the heart who calms the heart, Suen,
shining calf who grew fat on the holy lap; you can wish in your heart
for anything! You can desire everything precious to the heart! . . . ,
splendour of the E-kur, make your wish on Enlil's lap. May you
create glory in heaven! May the E-kur sing a song of joy about you,
may the people call upon your life, Suen, may you be supreme in
heaven and earth!'

37–40 He has poured out milk from the . . . cows at the offering table, Suen
has ordained the purification rites: 'Everything that I produce is
brilliant! May my father Enlil consume them with delight.'

41–9 His mother speaks kindly in joy to the king, the holy barge which
travels across the sky: 'My wild bull whom An has well called, your
name is respected in all lands. Lord of the holy herd who consecrates
the purification rites, seed engendered in a holy shrine, shining
halter, heroic child born of Ninlil! Nanna, seed engendered in the
fields, beloved of holy An! An has conferred on you the shepherding
of the Land!

50–60 'Enlil has named you with a good renown—you are the son of Enlil
whose speech is just. In his elevated heart An has bestowed kingship
on you. He has chosen your city Urim in his heart. For you he has
brought fish and birds to the princely river. First-born of Enlil, who
. . . the rank of lord, he has bestowed on you the kingship of heaven.
You are a god dressed in beauty in the heavens. Your moonlight is
holy and bright, and because like Utu you are a shepherd of the
Land, Nanna, it shines forth for the king like the daylight.'

61 A *balbale* of Suen.

A *šir-namgala* to Nanna

The moon, whose changes in shape and position are the easiest to observe and chart among the celestial bodies, played an important role in ancient Mesopotamia as the basis for reckoning time in days, months, and years. Accordingly, this poem portrays Nanna as the organizer of time, who thereby also provides abundance in the country and stability for the dynasty.

The composition is divided into sections, which are, however, marked only with rulings on one of the two existing manuscripts and not by rubrics as usual. The significance of the divisions must have been obvious to the scribes, but we can only guess that the two sections (1–5 and 8–15) preceding the two short *ĝišgiĝal* sections may have been *kirugu*s. Another section of three lines (18–20) without rubric was separated by rulings before the last *kirugu* (21–46). The concluding section is an *uru*. Unfortunately the poem is preserved in a partly fragmentary state.

Translation

1–5 Princely son, respected one in heaven spreading amply over the high mountains, inspiring awe as he casts a glowing radiance, majestic . . . , his head reaching the sky, fixing the new moon and the months, shining forth, Nanna! Versed in numbers, may you look down graciously!

6 Ašimbabbar, great light of holy An, mighty one (?) spreading wide, you cover (?) the numerous people.

7 Its *ĝišgiĝal*.

8–15 . . . light, prince lifting his head with (?) the crown, not changing . . . , making the Land firm forever, august . . . who . . . in abundance, . . . kingship . . . , . . . with shining horns, in the sky . . . , . . . the month . . . Sumer, on earth . . . , . . . of (?) the E-kur, radiance . . . . on the other side, holy glow which he alone . . . .

16 True light, filling the wide sky, Ašimbabbar . . . greatly.

17 Its *ĝišgiĝal*.

18–20 Nanna, dragon of heaven and earth, standing . . . , fixing the months and the new moon, sets the year in its place. Suen, lord, in heaven you alone are majestic.

21–30 Lord, light of heaven, you are positioned forever. To prolong years of abundance, causing the early flood and unceasing abundance, to make firm the quays, to regulate the nipples of heaven, to establish celebration, ... to bring speckled grain, to ..., ..., to make firm the lofty dais of E-kiš-nuĝal, Nanna, to make firm the seat of kingship of the Land, (*3 lines fragmentary*)

31–40 ... with (?) a remote heart ..., ... Urim, the city you have chosen, in the ... of An and Enlil ..., his lofty ..., may he (?) look favourably upon you. ... when you reside in the place where you find rest, ... in the Agrun-kug a just destiny is determined. The Great Mountain Enlil has set his mind on lord Ašimbabbar. ... in his Ḫursaĝ-kalama, ... as he bears radiance and inspires terrifying awe, in the ... of the shrine Urim he determines favourable destinies.

41–6 ... widespread people ... may he until distant times make the power majestic. ... speckled grain ..., ... abundance ... ; may he raise his head ... like .... May ... the restored place. May he bestow ... unapproachable ....

47 ... *kirugu.*

48–51 Majestic ..., born of Ninlil, ..., lord Ašimbabbar, holy son of An, ... luxuriance, majestic ... whose just word cannot be changed, ..., Nanna, may you exert great power!

52 Its *uru.*

53 A *šir-namgala* of Nanna.

The herds of Nanna

Beside his obvious celestial aspect, the moon-god Nanna was commonly portrayed in literary works as a bull. He was associated with cattle herds, and on a general level with agricultural fertility. The image of Nanna as a bull may be connected with viewing the crescent of the waxing moon, which in the latitude of Mesopotamia lies almost horizontally like the horns of a bull. The connection between the moon's ever returning cycles and women's menstrual cycles may have created another link between Nanna and fertility.

The opening passage (1–8) praises Nanna as the rising moon. It is followed by a short section (9–13) which shows him as the favourite son who determines the fates together with his omnipotent father, Enlil (see also *A balbale to Nanna*). The longest part of the composition (14–41) enumerates the cattle in Nanna's herd. It starts with the number and size of the cattle-pens, then the various types of livestock are listed in impressive numbers. All of the figures are simple multiples of 3,600, the archetypical large number in the

Sumerian sexagesimal (base 60) system. The goddess of accounting, Nisaba, records the number of livestock on a tablet. The long and detailed enumeration gives the impression of inexhaustible abundance and perpetual fertility, whose ultimate source is Nanna. The composition ends with a line of praise to both Nanna and his spouse Ningal.

Translation

1–8   The lord has burnished (?) the heavens; he has embellished the night°. Nanna has burnished the heavens; he has embellished the night°. When he comes forth from the turbulent mountains, he stands as Utu stands at noon. When Ašimbabbar comes forth from the turbulent mountains, he stands as Utu stands at noon.

9–13   His father, whose word is true, speaks with him day and night. Enlil, whose word is true, speaks with him day and night, and in decision determines the fates with him.

14–17   His lofty *ĝipar* shrines number four. There are four platforms° which he has established for him. His great temple cattle-pens, one *eše*° in size, number four. They play for him with drumsticks (?)°.

18–25   The cows are driven together in herds for him. His various types of cow number 39,600. His young (?) cows and calves° number 108,000. His young bulls number 126,000. The sparkling-eyed cows number 50,400. The white cows number 126,000. The cows for the evening meal (?) are in four groups of five each (?). Such are the various types of cow of Father Nanna.

26–30   His wild cows number 180,000. The . . . cows are four. Their herds of cattle are seven. Their . . . herdsmen are seven. There are four of those who dwell among the cows (?).

31–6   They give praise to the lord, singing paeans (?) as they move into the *ĝipar* shrine. Nisaba has taken their grand total; Nisaba has taken their count, and she is writing it on clay. Praise be to the holy cows of Nanna, cherished by the youth Suen!

37–41   He is ever able to increase the butter of abundance in the holy animal pens of . . . and goats. He is able to provide abundantly the great liquor of the mountains, and syrup, and alcoholic drink for the king on his lofty pure platform.

42–5   Mighty one, trusted one of Enlil, youth, god of living creatures, leader of the Land, and Ningal, lady of the *ĝipar* shrine—praise be to Father Nanna!

FIG. 19. 'Ningal, lady of the *ḡipar* shrine—praise be to father Nanna!'—Ur-Namma makes offerings to the patron deities of Urim on a fragmentary stone stela

Notes

1–8   Instead of 'the night' 1 MS has: 'the earth'.

14–17   Instead of 'platforms' 1 MS has: 'cattle-pens'. One *eše* is equivalent to just over 2 hectares. Instead of 'with drumsticks (?)' 1 MS has: 'on the churn'.

18–25   Instead of 'His young (?) cows and calves' 1 MS has: 'His fattened cows'.

Nanna-Suen's journey to Nibru

A number of compositions describe a deity's journey to the city of his or her divine father (see for instance *Ninurta's return to Nibru*, Group E, and *Enki's journey to Nibru*, Group J). In *Nanna-Suen's journey to Nibru* the purpose of Nanna's visit is to present his father Enlil with various offerings, and in return to obtain blessings for the fertility and prosperity of Urim. As cultic processions of various deities are repeatedly mentioned in administrative documents, we have every reason to believe that there are real cultic events behind the composition and performance of divine journey poems.

This straightforward narrative divides into three parts. The first and longest describes the preparations for the journey (1–197). It starts with Nanna's declared wish to visit the city of 'his mother and father', followed by a short hymnic passage on Nibru. A long passage then relates the building and outfitting of the processional boat from timber, reeds, and pitch fetched from various locations (see also *Šulgi and Ninlil's barge*, Group C). About 60 lines are missing at this point, and after the gap the text enumerates meticulously the numerous gifts Nanna takes with him on the boat, manifesting

Nanna's association with agricultural and animal fertility. The description of animal fertility has numerous close parallels in the poem *A balbale to Ninurta* (Group E).

In the second part (198–257) Nanna sets off from Urim and makes a stop at each of five cities with his boat. The itinerary of Nanna's journey no doubt reflects a real upstream route from Urim to Nibru. In each of the cities Nanna is received and greeted by a local goddess.

The third part of the composition relates the events in Nibru (258–352). After his arrival Nanna recites the inventory of his gifts and offers them to Enlil. Enlil rejoices and arranges a banquet for his son. At the end of the meal Nanna makes his request for the prosperity of Urim; Enlil grants his request and blesses his son.

Translation

1–8   The heroic Nanna-Suen fixed his mind on the city of his mother. Suen Ašimbabbar fixed his mind on the city of his mother. Nanna-Suen fixed his mind on the city of his mother and his father. Ašimbabbar fixed his mind on the city of Enlil and Ninlil:

9–16   'I, the hero, will set off for my city. I will set off for my city, I will set off to my father. I, Suen, will set off for my city. I will set off for my city, I will set off to my father. I will set off to my father Enlil. I will set off for my city, I will set off to my mother. I will set off to my mother Ninlil. I will set off to my father.

17–27   'The shining city, the pure place . . . . (*6 lines missing*) . . . very great, . . . very great, . . . very great, . . . very great.

28–36   'My Nibru, where black birch trees grow in a good place, my sanctuary Nibru, where white birch trees grow in a pure place—my Nibru's shrine is built in a good place. The sanctuary Nibru's name is a good name. My Nibru's shrine is built in a good place. The sanctuary Nibru's name is a good name. Before Dilmun existed, palm trees grew in my city. Before Dilmun existed, palm trees grew in Nibru and the great mother Ninlil was clothed in fine linen.'

37–8   Suen set about constructing (?) a barge. He set about constructing (?) a barge and sent for reed matting.

39–48   Nanna-Suen dispatched people to Tummal for the barge's reeds. Ašimbabbar dispatched people to the Abzu for the barge's pitch. Nanna-Suen dispatched people to Du-ašaga for its rushes. Ašimbabbar dispatched people to the cypress forest for its strakes (?).

Nanna-Suen dispatched people to the forests of Kug-nuna for its ribbing (?).°

49–58 Ašimbabbar dispatched people to the forests of Ebla for its planking. Nanna-Suen dispatched people to the fragrant cedar forest for its fir wood. Ašimbabbar dispatched people to the junipers of Langi for its . . . . Ašimbabbar dispatched people to . . . for its . . . . Nanna-Suen dispatched people to the mound of . . . for its . . . .

59–82 When the barge's reeds were brought to Nanna-Suen from Tummal, when the barge's pitch was brought to Ašimbabbar from the Abzu, when its rushes were brought to Nanna-Suen from Du-ašaga, when its strakes (?) were brought to Ašimbabbar from the cypress forest; when its ribbing (?) was brought to Nanna-Suen from the forests of Kug-nuna,° when its planking was brought to Ašimbabbar from the forests of Ebla, when its fir wood was brought to Nanna-Suen from the fragrant cedar forest; when its . . . was brought to Ašimbabbar from the junipers of Langi, when its . . . was brought to Ašimbabbar from . . . , when its . . . was brought to Nanna-Suen from the mound of . . . , (*1 line fragmentary*) Utu rejoiced at him and put . . . . Gibil rejoiced at him. (*lines 83–146 missing or fragmentary*)

147–56 (*He declared:*) 'I am Nanna-Suen, I . . . , I will . . . to the house of Enlil. I am Ašimbabbar, and I will . . . to the house of Enlil.' (*6 lines missing*)

157–66 Nanna-Suen will gather bulls for the cattle-pen for the house of Enlil. Ašimbabbar will collect (?) fattened sheep for the house of Enlil. Nanna-Suen will purify the cattle-pen for the house of Enlil. Ašimbabbar will feed meal to the goats for the house of Enlil. Nanna-Suen will . . . porcupines for the house of Enlil.

167–75 Ašimbabbar will . . . long-tailed bush-rats for the house of Enlil. Nanna-Suen will gather (?) little *kuda* birds for the house of Enlil. Ašimbabbar will bring small *ubi* birds from the pond for the house of Enlil. Nanna-Suen will bring small *azagun* birds from the . . . for the house of Enlil.

176–85 Ašimbabbar will . . . *suḫur* carp for the house of Enlil. Nanna-Suen will . . . *eštub* carp for the house of Enlil. Ašimbabbar will pour the oil of rushes onto the water for the house of Enlil. Nanna-Suen will fill baskets with eggs for the house of Enlil. Ašimbabbar will cause old reed and fresh reed to thrive for the house of Enlil.

186–97 Nanna-Suen will cause six hundred ewes to give birth to lambs for the house of Enlil, for he will cause their rams to be let loose among them, and he will distribute them along the banks of the Surungal canal. Ašimbabbar will cause six hundred nanny-goats to give birth to kids for the house of Enlil, for he will cause their billy-goats to be let loose among them, and he will distribute them along the banks of the Surungal canal. Nanna-Suen will cause six hundred cows to give birth to calves for the house of Enlil, for he will cause their bulls to be let loose among them, and he will distribute them along the banks of the Surungal canal.

FIG. 20. 'O boat of Suen, welcome, welcome O boat!'—a banquet is preceded by a boat journey on a stone plaque from Early Dynastic Nibru

198–202 Enegir lay ahead of the offerings, Urim lay behind them. She brought out of the house what should not come out of the house, what should not come out of the house—Ningirida brought out of the house what should not come out of the house: 'Welcome, welcome, welcome O boat! O boat of Suen, welcome, welcome O boat!'

203–8 She laid out flour before the barge and spread bran. At her feet stood a covered bronze *gakkul* vat.° 'I shall rub precious oil on this peg.

May ghee, syrup, and wine be abundant in your midst, may the *suḫur* carp and the *eštub* carp rejoice at the prow of your boat!' But the boat did not give her its cargo: 'I am going to Nibru!'

209–13 Larsa lay ahead of the offerings, Enegir lay behind them. She brought out of the house what should not come out of the house, what should not come out of the house—the lovely Šerida brought out of the house what should not come out of the house: 'Welcome, welcome, welcome O boat! O boat of my father, welcome, welcome O boat!'

214–19 She laid out flour before the barge and spread bran. At her feet stood a covered bronze *gakkul* vat.° 'I shall rub precious oil on this peg. May ghee, syrup, and wine be abundant in your midst, may the *suḫur* carp and the *eštub* carp rejoice at the prow of your boat!' But the boat did not give her its cargo: 'I am going to Nibru!'

220–4 Unug lay ahead of the offerings, Larsa lay behind them. She brought out of the house what should not come out of the house, what should not come out of the house—holy Inana brought out of the house what should not come out of the house: 'Welcome, welcome, welcome O boat! O boat of my father welcome, welcome O boat!°'

225–30 She laid out flour before the barge and spread bran. At her feet stood a covered bronze *gakkul* vat.° 'I shall rub precious oil on your peg. May ghee, syrup and wine be abundant in your midst, may the *suḫur* carp and the *eštub* carp rejoice at the prow of your boat!' But the boat did not give her its cargo: 'I am going to Nibru!'

231–5 Šuruppag lay ahead of the offerings, Unug lay behind them. She brought out of the house what should not come out of the house, what should not come out of the house—Ninunuga brought out of the house what should not come out of the house: 'Welcome, welcome, welcome O boat! O boat of Suen welcome, welcome O boat!'

236–41 She laid out flour before the barge and spread bran. At her feet stood a covered bronze *gakkul* vat.° 'I shall rub precious oil on this peg. May ghee, syrup, and wine be abundant in your midst, may the *suḫur* carp and the *eštub* carp rejoice at the prow of your boat!' But the boat did not give her its cargo: 'I am going to Nibru!'

242–6 Tummal lay ahead of the offerings, Šuruppag lay behind them. She brought out of the house what should not come out of the house, what should not come out of the house—the fair Ninlil brought out of the house what should not come out of the house: 'Welcome, welcome, welcome O boat! O boat of the princely son welcome, welcome O boat!'

247–52 She laid out flour before the barge and spread bran. At her feet stood a covered bronze *gakkul* vat.° 'I shall rub precious oil on this peg. May ghee, syrup, and wine be abundant in your midst, may the *suḫur* carp and the *eštub* carp rejoice at the prow of your boat!' But the boat did not give her its cargo: 'I am going to Nibru!'

253–7 Nibru lay ahead of the offerings, Tummal lay behind them. At the Shining Quay, the quay of Enlil, Nanna-Suen finally docked the boat. At the White Quay, the quay of Enlil, Ašimbabbar finally docked the boat.

258–64 He stepped up to the cultic building of his father who begot him and called out to the porter of his father who begot him: 'Open the house, porter, open the house! Open the house, Kalkal, open the house! Kalkal, doorkeeper, open the house! Doorman, doorkeeper, open the house! Porter, open the house! Kalkal, open the house!

265–74 'I, Nanna-Suen, have gathered bulls for the cattle-pen for the house of Enlil; porter, open the house. I, Ašimbabbar, have collected (?) fattened sheep for the house of Enlil; porter, open the house. I, Nanna-Suen, shall purify the cattle-pen for the house of Enlil; porter, open the house. I, Ašimbabbar, shall feed meal to the goats for the house of Enlil; porter, open the house. I, Nanna-Suen, have . . . porcupines for the house of Enlil; porter, open the house.

275–83 'I, Ašimbabbar—I, Ašimbabbar—have . . . long-tailed bush-rats for the house of Enlil; porter, open the house. I, Nanna-Suen, have gathered (?) little *kuda* birds for the house of Enlil; porter, open the house. I, Ašimbabbar, have brought small *ubi* birds from the pond for the house of Enlil; porter, open the house. I, Nanna-Suen, have brought small *azagun* birds from the pond for the house of Enlil; porter, open the house.

284–93 'I, Ašimbabbar, . . . *suḫur* carp for the house of Enlil; porter, open the house. I, Nanna-Suen, . . . *eštub* carp for the house of Enlil; porter, open the house. I, Ašimbabbar, shall pour the oil of rushes onto the water for the house of Enlil; porter, open the house. I, Nanna-Suen, have filled baskets with eggs for the house of Enlil; porter, open the house. I, Ašimbabbar, have caused old reed and fresh reed to thrive for the house of Enlil; porter, open the house.

294–305 'I, Nanna-Suen, have caused six hundred ewes to give birth to lambs for the house of Enlil, for I have caused their rams to be let loose among them, and I have distributed them along the banks of the Surungal canal; porter, open the house. I, Ašimbabbar, have caused six hundred nanny-goats to give birth to kids for the house of Enlil, for I have caused their billy-goats to be let loose among them, and I have distributed them along the banks of the Surungal canal; porter, open the house. I, Nanna-Suen, have caused six hundred cows to give birth to calves for the house of Enlil, for I have caused their bulls to be let loose among them, and I have distributed them along the banks of the Surungal canal; porter, open the house.

306–8 'Porter, open the house! Kalkal, open the house! I will give you that which is in the prow of the boat as a first offering, and I will give you that which is in the stern of the boat as a last offering.'

309–18 Rejoicing, the porter rejoicing, the porter rejoicing opened the house. Kalkal, the doorkeeper, rejoicing, the porter rejoicing opened the house. Kalkal, in charge of the bolt-handle, rejoicing, the porter rejoicing opened the house. At the house of Enlil, . . . , Nanna-Suen made the offerings. Enlil, rejoicing over the offerings, offered bread to Suen, his son.

319–25 Enlil rejoiced over Suen and spoke kindly: 'Give sweet cakes to my little fellow who eats sweet cakes. Give sweet cakes to my Nanna who loves eating sweet cakes. Bring out from the E-kur the bread allotment and first-quality bread for him. Pour out for him the finest beer, my pure . . . . May the . . . of the towering *tilimda* vessels, standing on the ground, ... Order pure sweet cake, syrup, crescent (?) cake and clear water for him.'

326–30 Suen replied to his father who begot him: 'Father who begot me, I am indeed satisfied with what you have given me to eat. O Great Mountain, father who begot me, I am indeed satisfied with what you have given me to drink. Wherever you lift your eyes, there is kingship. O Enlil, your abundance is . . . .

331–9 'Give to me, Enlil, give to me—I want to set off for Urim! In the river give me the carp-flood—I want to set off for Urim! In the fields give me speckled barley—I want to set off for Urim! In the marshes give me *kuda* carp and *suḫur* carp—I want to set off for Urim! In the reedbeds give me old reed and fresh reed—I want to set off for Urim! In the forests give me the ibex and wild ram—I want to set off for Urim! In the high plain give me the *mašgurum* tree—I want to set off for Urim! In the orchards give me syrup and wine—I want to set off for Urim! In the palace give me long life—I want to set off for Urim!'

340–8 He gave to him, Enlil gave to him—and he set off for Urim. In the river he gave him the carp-flood—and he set off for Urim. In the field he gave him speckled barley—and he set off for Urim. In the pond he gave him *kuda* carp and *suḫur* carp—and he set off for Urim. In the reed-beds he gave him old reed and fresh reed—and he set off for Urim. In the forests he gave him the ibex and wild ram—and he set off for Urim. In the high plain he gave him the *mašgurum* tree—and he set off for Urim. In the orchards he gave him syrup and wine—and he set off for Urim. In the palace he gave him long life—and he set off for Urim.

349–52 My king, on your throne, for Enlil, may Nanna-Suen make you be born for seven days. On your holy throne, for the great mother Ninlil, may the lord Ašimbabbar make you be born for seven days.

Notes

39–48 After 'for its ribbing (?).' 3 MSS add 2 lines: 'Ašimbabbar dispatched people to the mountain of fragrant cedar for its beams.'

59–82 After 'Kug-nuna,' 3 MSS add 2 lines: 'when its beams were brought to Ašimbabbar from the mountain of fragrant cedar,'

203–8, 214–19, 225–30, 236–41, 247–52 After '*gakkul* vat.' 1 MS adds 1 line: 'With her fingers she pulled out the boxwood bung (?) for him (*declaring:*)'

220–4 After 'boat!' 1 MS adds 1 line: 'O boat of Suen welcome, welcome O boat!'

E. THE WARRIOR GODS NERGAL, NUMUŠDA, AND NINURTA

War was an inescapable aspect of urban life from the time of the earliest Sumerian cities in the mid-fourth millennium BCE. Inter-city warfare was gradually replaced by inter-state warfare as the great kingdoms of Agade, Urim, Isin, Larsa, and ultimately Babylon developed through the late third and early second millennia. Active and defensive campaigns against the often hostile peoples of the Iranian mountains to the east of the Mesopotamian plain also featured both in reality and in legend.

Despite the gradual growth of warfare using armies, the figure of the single champion who fights on behalf of the group that he protects persisted in the religious sphere. Savage warrior deities were consequently common among the pantheons of various cities. With the exception of the goddess Inana, all were male. In some cases their warrior aspect was only one characteristic of their cultic personalities. The god Nergal, sometimes under the title Mešlamta-eda, 'Warrior who comes forth from the Underworld', was worshipped at temples called E-mešlam, considered to be entrances to the Underworld. Certainly in one aspect he was regarded as a deity of the Underworld (see *The dedication of an axe to Nergal*). But he was also associated with plagues and fevers and was described in rather gory terms as a gruesome warrior, who could nevertheless be engaged as an ally by rulers (see *An adab to Nergal for Šu-ilišu*). In art he was often depicted holding a curved scimitar.

Numušda was a much less important deity, whose cult was mainly associated with the city of Kazallu in northern Babylonia. He was considered to be a son of the moon-god Nanna. His wife was the goddess Namrat (see *A hymn to Numušda for Sîn-iqīšam*).

By contrast, the god Ninurta was one of the most important gods in the Sumerian pantheon and continued to be very prominent in religious cults down to the first millennium BCE, largely because he was claimed as a protector of the king and the institution of kingship. This became especially important in the later Assyrian empire and may have developed from one of Ninurta's own titles, 'the King'. Ninurta was also identified with Ningirsu, the principal deity of the city-state of Lagaš (see *The building of Ningirsu's temple*, Group A). First and foremost, Ninurta was a warrior, a son of Enlil and Ninlil, who fought at his father's behest in defence of the great gods. His most important shrine was the E-šumeša in Nibru. Often he fights against the 'rebel lands' to the east of Sumer and Akkad (see *Ninurta's return to Nibru*). Ninurta has a characteristic armoury of weapons including several battle-maces with many spikes, and battle-nets, which are often enumerated in literary contexts: among his maces are the Šar-ur ('Mows-down-a-myriad') and the Šar-gaz ('Crushes-a-myriad'). The god had defeated a range of fearsome monsters, who were regarded as his trophies: these included the Anzud bird (see *Lugalbanda and the Anzud bird*, Group A). Historically Ninurta is an ancestor of the Greek Herakles with his club.

In another aspect Ninurta was an agricultural deity who gave advice on the cultivation of crops and stimulated the fecundity of animals and the growth of crops (see *A balbale to Ninurta*). Both the warrior and agricultural aspects are seen in *Ninurta's exploits*, where the warrior god proceeds to facilitate agriculture for humans by rebuilding the stone warriors he has defeated into a mountain range.

FURTHER READING

Annus, A., *The God Ninurta in the Mythology and Royal Ideology of Ancient Mesopotamia* (Neo-Assyrian Text Corpus Project: Helsinki, 2002).

Black, J. A., 'Some Structural Features of Sumerian Narrative Poetry', in M. E. Vogelzang and H. L. J. Vanstiphout (eds.), *Mesopotamian Epic Literature: Oral or Aural?* (The Edwin Mellen Press: Lewiston/Queenston/Lampeter, 1992, pp. 71–101) deals especially with *Ninurta's exploits*.

Wiggermann, F. A. M., 'Nergal', *Reallexikon der Assyriologie*, 9 (2001), 215–26.

OTHER COMPOSITIONS FEATURING WARRIOR GODS INCLUDE

Group B   A hymn to Inana
Group C   Enlil and Ninlil
Group F   Inana and Šu-kale-tuda
Group H   A *balbale* to Ningišzida
Group J   The exaltation of Inana
          Inana and Ebiḫ

The dedication of an axe to Nergal

This short composition gives the impression that it was originally inscribed on an actual axe offered to the god Nergal as a dedicatory gift. However, it is known only from manuscripts written on clay tablets which originate in the context of scribal education. Although it might have functioned as a kind of 'model' dedicatory inscription that was learned and copied as part of the curriculum, in fact its structure is completely different from dedications on surviving archaeological artefacts (see the Introduction to this book).

The function of a dedicatory gift was to secure the benevolence of the god to whom it was offered. This composition serves the same purpose by verbal means. It divides into three parts. After naming the donor and the receiving god, the first part calls the deity's attention to the quality of the dedicated object by detailing its excellence. The second contains an unparalleled promise in case of damage or loss of the axe. The composition concludes with an appeal to Nergal asking him to care for the donor in his life as well as after his death. The request for clean water reflects the fear of the inhabitants of ancient Mesopotamia that the Underworld was a place where the spirits of the dead lived on dust and foul water. The miserable existence of the dead is portrayed in the compositions *Gilgameš, Enkidu, and the Underworld* and *The death of Ur-Namma* (both Group A).

Nergal, the god of inflicted death, who also had a warrior aspect, was frequently depicted carrying a weapon. It is therefore not accidental that the gift dedicated to Nergal is a weapon. Numerous mace-heads with a dedicatory inscription to Nergal have been found in Mesopotamia as well as a single stone axe-head from the early first millennium BCE.

Translation

1–9 Nibruta-lu, the son of the merchant Lugal-šuba, has had this tin axe made for Nergal. Its wooden part is of *arganum* tree of the mountains, a wood which is superior even to the *alal* stone; its stone part is of *antasura*, a stone which has no equal. The arm of the man who strikes with it will never get tired.

10–11 Should it break, I will repair it for Nergal. Should it disappear, I will replace it for him.

12–16 May Nergal look after me during my life, and may he provide me with clean water in the Underworld after my death.

Fig. 21. 'Nibruta-lu . . . has had this tin axe made
for Nergal'—a terracotta votive figure from
Old Babylonian Ĝirsu

An *adab* to Nergal for Šu-ilišu

This hymn is addressed to Nergal on behalf of Šu-ilišu, second king of the
Dynasty of Isin. It both praises and celebrates Nergal's martial qualities, and
calls on him to use them for Šu-ilišu's benefit. Indeed, the historical evidence
shows that Šu-ilišu had occasion to draw on Nergal's support, when he led a
military campaign to Anšan in the highlands of western Iran. He succeeded
in capturing the moon-god Nanna's statue and returning it to its rightful
home in Urim, from where it had been stolen during the collapse of the
Third Dynasty of Urim a few decades before. He thereby further legitimated
his dynasty's right to rule the land as the divinely supported successor state
to the Third Dynasty of Urim (see also *The lament for Sumer and Urim*,
Group D).

The hymn was qualified with a subscript as an *adab* by the ancient scribes, and accordingly it divides into two longer sections, a *sa-gida* and a *sa-g̃ara*, and concludes with a three-line *uru* section. The *sa-gida* is constructed from subsections, called *barsud* and *šagbatuku*, and is followed by a one-line *g̃išg̃i-g̃al* of the *sa-gida*. Both the *sa-gida* and the *sa-g̃ara* sections conclude with prayers for the king, imploring Nergal to help Šu-ilišu in defeating and destroying his enemies.

Translation

1–4   Lord, furiously raging storm, confusing the enemies and unleashing (?) great terror over the Land, Nergal, mighty quay of heaven and earth, who . . . all living things, lord who guards (?) the teeming people when he looks up furiously, turning (?) his weapons against the wicked: Nergal, powerful in heaven and earth, who . . . the people in heaps!

5   *Barsud.*

6–11   Lord, mighty storm, raging with your great powers, south storm which covers the Land, Nergal, who smites the enemy whom he has cursed . . . , exalted lord, strong one with a powerful wrist, whom no one can withstand, Nergal, rising broadly, full of furious might, great one praised for his accomplishments, pre-eminent among the great youthful gods, whose valour is . . . of valour, Nergal, whose greatness covers heaven and earth to their uttermost limits!

12   *Šagbatuku.*

13–16   Warrior with head held high, respected lord, son who rises up to protect his father, Nergal, angry sea, inspiring fearsome terror, whom no one knows how to confront, youth whose advance is a hurricane and a flood battering the lands, Nergal, dragon covered with gore, drinking the blood of living creatures!

17   2nd *barsud.*

18–23   Lord who, like his own father Nunamnir, has the power to create life, Nergal, in (?) the eternal home, the Underworld, you are the junior Enlil! It is in your power to determine destinies, to render judgments and to make decisions, Nergal, your great hands are filled with mighty actions and terrible powers! Great rites which are revealed to no one are organized for you! Nergal, among this people it is you who take charge of the divine plans and the purification rites!

24   2nd *šagbatuku.*

25–8   In the west, Utu has shone forth for you, and an awe-inspiring dais

has been erected for you! Nergal, you, lord, are one who has the
power to carry off and to bring back (?)! In the east, lord, . . . , you are
imbued with a terrible great awesomeness; Nergal, your praise and
renown are such as to unleash awe and terror!

29 3rd *barsud.*

30–5 Shepherd who organizes, giving just verdicts like the noble youth
Utu! Nergal, pile up his malefactors in heaps for him, for Šu-ilišu,
the prince who displays lasting divine powers among the Anuna
gods! May Šu-ilišu rely on you, may he be made joyful by you! May
he walk as the shepherd whose name is extolled among this people
like that of Utu! May all lands and the teeming people bless (?) the
life of Šu-ilišu!

36 *Barsud.*

37 Nergal, may you be the trust of prince Šu-ilišu until distant days!

38 *Ĝišgiĝal* and its *sa-gida.*

39–53 Lord of the Underworld, who acts swiftly in everything, whose terrifying anger smites the wicked, Nergal, single-handed crusher, who
tortures the disobedient, fearsome terror of the Land, respected lord
and hero, established offspring of Nunamnir . . . ! Nergal, who
sprinkles cool water on the angry heart of Enlil, great lord . . . !
Nergal, standing ready for battle, superior with head lifted high, lord
who overpowers all the wicked like a lion, . . . , unwilling to turn back
at the door-pivot! Nergal, great battle-net for malefactors, covering
all enemies! Warrior, you are a great and furious storm upon the land
which disobeys your father! Nergal, you terrify the walled cities and
the settlements as you stand in your path like a wild bull, smiting
them with your great horns! Nergal, you have consumed their brickwork as if it were chaff in the air. When you lift your furious face, no
one dares look at it. When you have . . . in the Land°, Nergal, you
pour their blood down the wadis like rain. You afflict all the wicked
peoples with woe, and deprive all of them of their lives.

54–62 Youthful Nergal, those who are saved with your help magnify you
with praise! Lord, you have avenged Enlil! He has calmed the heart
of his father! Nergal the strong, son who subdues the foreign lands
for Nunamnir: may you assist in battle, furious fight and combat the
shepherd whom An has chosen among the numerous people, the
good and exalted youth of the Great Mountain—Šu-ilišu, who
publicly performs the purification rites, born of Ninlil! Nergal, catch
his malefactors for him like small birds! You cover the land which is

disobedient to him with a raging storm; may you be the weapon of slaughter! Heap up in piles for Šu-ilišu the inhabitants of the city that does not support him.

63 *Sa-ḡara.*

64–6 Powerful (?) lord of his own father, entrusted with authority, Nergal, the lord to whom Nunamnir has entrusted authority! Šu-ilišu will forever pray to you in the shrine E-mešlam for his long life and good health.

67 Its *uru.*

68 An *adab* of Nergal.

Note

39–53 Instead of 'in the Land' 1 MS has: 'among that people'.

A hymn to Numušda for Sîn-iqīšam

Numušda, son of the moon-god Suen, was the tutelary god of Kazallu, a northern Babylonian city whose exact location is unknown. The hymn may been composed during the second regnal year of Sîn-iqīšam, seventh king of the Dynasty of Larsa, when he had statues of Numušda, his wife Namrat, and another minor god fashioned and brought to Kazallu.

The hymn divides into two parts (1–33 and 34–60) both of which conclude with a short prayer for Sîn-iqīšam. After an unusual reference to the god's birth and infancy (but see *A balbale* to *Ninḡišzida*, Group H), the first part extols Numušda as a violent, forceful, and fearsome god. Fittingly the prayer at the end of this section implores the god's help in defeating the king's enemies. The second part describes how Enlil instructed Sîn-iqīšam to restore Numušda's city Kazallu and temple Kun-satu. The concluding prayer asks Numušda to bestow a long life on the king.

The hymn might have originally been composed in the form of an *adab*. The sections which distinguish this form are, however, marked in an inconsistent and partial way. Many of the expected rubrics are missing. This carelessness may be related to the fact that the text of the hymn is known from a single manuscript which is characterized by an unusually high number of corrections and erasures.

Translation

1–11 Exalted lord, for whom a favourable destiny was determined while he was still in the good womb! Numušda, exalted lord, for whom a favourable destiny was determined while he was still in the good womb! Ningal formed . . . the holy seed . . . engendered by Suen. Born amid plenty in the holy mountains, eating fruits from a green garden, named with a good name by An and Enlil, carefully cherished by the great lady Ninlil! Numušda, son of the prince, whose appearance is full of awe-inspiring radiance! Great wild bull battering the enemy country, great lord Numušda!

12 *Šagbatuku.*

13–23 Snarling lion fiercely poised for the fight, . . . snake spitting roaring at the enemy, great dragon . . . holy incantations, whose knees never cease from running! Fearsome flood which no one can withstand, overflowing high water engulfing the banks! (*1 line unclear*) God, creative (?) personage who has no rival, foremost in heroism, who can rival you? Numušda, your face is that of a lion, and you have a muzzle like that of a fearsome *mušḫuš* serpent.

24 2nd (?) *šagbatuku.*

25–32 Your arm is a battle-net in (?) the land of those who do not practise agriculture; your claws are the claws of an *urin* bird, grasping the wicked. No one dares to oppose your authority. Your greatness and magnitude, surpassing all praise, and your utterances which cannot be dismissed (*1 line unclear*). My god, hand over to the king the disobedient lands! Numušda, hand over to prince Sîn-iqīšam the disobedient lands!

33 *Sa-gida* of the *ĝišgiĝal.*

34–41 Warrior, powerful in strength, who perfectly controls the complex divine powers! Warrior Numušda, powerful in strength, who perfectly controls the complex divine powers! God with the limbs of a bison, decorous to behold, like your father Suen you love to bestow life. Choosing truth and annihilating wickedness, in E-kiš-nuĝal, the holy and princely dwelling, your divine powers are most precious divine powers, and your purification rites are resplendent. Numušda, hero, powerful in strength, who perfectly controls the complex divine powers!

42–56 Nunamnir, the lord who determines the destinies, has made your name august throughout the wide extent of foreign lands. He has assigned as a cult place for you the city of abundance, founded in a favourable place: Kazallu, the mountain of plenty. By his unchangeable command he has ordered the fashioning of Kun-satu, your lordly dais. Father Enlil, the good shepherd who loves your plans, has desired to make its forgotten layout visible again, and to restore its abandoned cities; he has ordered prince Sîn-iqīšam to accomplish it, and he has made (?) your cities and settlements peaceful dwelling places. He has dredged your canals, and cleared up the levees and irrigation ditches, so that abundant water will never be lacking there. He has put in your . . . and made manifest all that is proper.

57–60 Regard with favour his commendable prayers! Regard Prince Sîn-iqīšam with favour! May the king's joyous days be prolonged, O Numušda!

Ninurta's exploits

This poem is one of the longest Sumerian narrative compositions with its 726 lines. It links together a number of episodes from the mythology of Ninurta in a connected narrative, presenting him both as an irresistible warrior god and as a farmer god associated with agricultural fertility. It falls neatly into two halves, each of which consists of three sections (two short ones framing one long middle section), followed by some concluding lines of praise. The first half deals with Ninurta's physical actions and is therefore dramatic (concerned with actions), while the second half deals with his verbal activities and is therefore rhetorical (concerned with words).

The poem starts with an introductory hymn praising Ninurta (1–16), followed by a long narrative that relates Ninurta's battles and victory over the Asag, a monstrous demon, and its army of stone warriors (17–333). He is supported by the Šar-ur, his staunchly faithful divine mace, and by the bodies of previously defeated demonic enemies, suspended from his chariot like trophies. The first half ends with a short passage which describes Ninurta's building of the hills and invention of agriculture (334–67).

The second half (368–410) begins with Ninurta renaming his mother Ninmaḫ ('Great Lady') as Ninḫursaĝa ('Lady of the mountain') in celebration of his victory. In its long middle section (411–644) Ninurta passes judgment on nineteen groups of stones, which are blessed or cursed according to whether they aided or fought him in the conflict with the Asag. The judgments of the stones are full of puns which are difficult to render into English but in Sumerian this passage is a rhetorical *tour de force*. At another level, it serves as an aetiology, explaining how each stone came to have its particular physical properties, technological functions, and cultural associations. Then Ninurta returns to Nibru by his boat Ma-kar-nunta-eda while his boatmen, the Anuna gods, and Enlil himself take it in turns to sing his praise (645–97). The composition concludes with praise to the goddess Nisaba containing also a summary of the events in the poem (698–723), and with praise to Ninurta (724–5).

Ninurta's martial exploits and return to Nibru are also the subject of *Ninurta's return to Nibru*.

Translation

1–16   °O King°, storm of majestic splendour, peerless Ninurta, possessing superior strength; who pillages the Mountains all alone; deluge, indefatigable serpent hurling yourself at the rebel land, Hero striding formidably into battle; Lord whose powerful arm is fit to bear the mace, reaping like barley the necks of the insubordinate; Ninurta, King, son in whose strength his father rejoices; Hero whose awesomeness covers the Mountains like a south storm; Ninurta, who makes the good tiara, the rainbow (?), flash like lightning; grandly begotten by him who wears the princely beard; dragon who turns on himself, strength of a lion snarling at a snake, roaring hurricane; Ninurta, King, whom Enlil has exalted above himself; Hero, great battle-net flung over the foe; Ninurta, with the awesomeness of your shadow extending over the Land; releasing fury on the rebel lands, overwhelming their assemblies! Ninurta, King, son who has forced homage to his father far and wide!

17–23   Inspiring great numinous power, he had taken his place on the throne, the august dais, and was sitting gladly at his ease at the festival celebrated in his honour, rivalling An and Enlil in drinking his fill, while Bau was pleading petitions in a prayer for the king, and he, Ninurta, Enlil's son, was handing down decisions. At that moment the Lord's battle-mace looked towards the Mountains, the Šar-ur cried out aloud to its master:

24–47   'Lord of lofty station, foremost one, who presides over all lords from the throne dais, Ninurta, whose orders are unalterable, whose decisions are faithfully executed; my master! Heaven copulated with the verdant Earth, Ninurta: she has borne him a warrior who knows no fear—the Asag, a child who sucked the power of milk without ever staying with a wet-nurse, a foster-child, O my master—knowing no father, a murderer from the Mountains, a youth who has come forth from . . . , whose face knows no shame; impudent of eye, an arrogant male, Ninurta°, rejoicing in his stature. My Hero, you who are like a bull, I will take my stand beside you. My master, who turns sympathetically towards his own city, who is effective in carrying out his mother's wishes: it has sired offspring in the Mountains, and spread its seeds far and wide. The plants have unanimously named it king over them; like a great wild bull, it tosses its horns amongst them. The *šu*, the *saĝkal*, the diorite, the *usium*, the haematite, and the heroic *nu* stones, its warriors, constantly come raiding the cities. For them a shark's tooth has grown up in the Mountains; it has stripped the trees. Before its might the gods of those cities bow towards it. My master, this same creature has erected a throne dais: it is not lying idle. Ninurta, Lord, it actually decides the Land's lawsuits, just as you do. Who can compass the Asag's dread glory? Who can counteract the severity of its frown? People are terrified, fear makes the flesh creep; their eyes are fixed upon it. My master, the Mountains have taken their offerings to it.

48–56   'Hero! They have appealed to you, because of your father; son of Enlil, Lord, because of your superior strength they are looking to you here; since you are strong, my master, they are calling for your help, saying, Ninurta, that not a single warrior counts except for you! They wanted to advise you about . . . . Hero, there have been consultations with a view to taking away your kingship. Ninurta, it is confident that it can lay hands on the powers received by you in the Abzu. Its face is deformed, its location is continually changing; day by day, the Asag adds territories to its domain.

57–69   'But you will force it into the shackles of the gods. You, Antelope of Heaven, must trample the Mountains beneath your hooves, Ninurta, Lord, son of Enlil. Who has so far been able to resist its assault? The besetting Asag is beyond all control, its weight is too heavy. Rumours of its armies constantly arrive, before ever its soldiers are seen. This thing's strength is massive, no weapon has been able to overturn it. Ninurta, neither the axe nor the all-powerful spear can penetrate its flesh, no warrior like it has ever been created against you. Lord, you who reach out towards the august divine powers, splendour, jewel of the gods, you bull with the features of a wild bull, with a prominent backbone, . . . this fellow is clever! My Ninurta, whose form Enki contemplates with favour, my Uta-ulu, Lord, son of Enlil, what is to be done?'

70–95 The Lord cried 'Alas!' so that Heaven trembled, and Earth huddled at his feet and was terrified (?) at his strength. Enlil became confused and went out of the E-kur. The Mountains were devastated. That day the earth became dark, the Anuna gods trembled. The Hero beat his thighs with his fists. The gods dispersed; the Anuna disappeared over the horizon like sheep. The Lord arose, touching the sky; Ninurta went to battle, with one step (?) he covered a *danna°*, he was an alarming storm, and rode on the eight winds towards the rebel lands. His arms grasped the lance. The mace snarled at the Mountains, the club began to devour all the enemy. He fitted the evil wind and the sirocco on a pole (?), he placed the quiver on its hook (?). An enormous hurricane, irresistible, went before the Hero, stirred up the dust, caused the dust to settle, levelled high and low, filled the holes. It caused a rain of coals and flaming fires; the fire consumed men. It overturned tall trees by their trunks, reducing the forests to heaps, Earth put her hands on her heart and cried harrowingly; the Tigris was muddied, disturbed, cloudy, stirred up. He hurried to battle on the boat Ma-kar-nunta-eda; the people there did not know where to turn, they bumped into (?) the walls. The birds there tried to lift their heads to fly away, but their wings trailed on the ground. The storm flooded out the fish there in the subterranean waters, their mouths snapped at the air. It reduced the animals of the open country to firewood, roasting them like locusts. It was a deluge rising and disastrously ruining the Mountains.

96–118 The Hero Ninurta led the march through the rebel lands. He killed their messengers in the Mountains, he crushed (?) their cities, he smote their cowherds over the head like fluttering butterflies, he tied together their hands with *ḫirin* grass, so that they dashed their heads against walls. The lights of the Mountains did not gleam in the distance any longer. People gasped for breath (?); those people were ill, they hugged themselves, they cursed the Earth, they considered the day of the Asag's birth a day of disaster. The Lord caused bilious poison to run over the rebel lands. As he went the gall followed, anger filled his heart, and he rose like a river in spate and engulfed all the enemies. In his heart he beamed at his lion-headed weapon, as it flew up like a bird, trampling the Mountains for him. It raised itself on its wings to take away prisoner the disobedient, it spun around the horizon of heaven to find out what was happening. Someone from afar came to meet it, brought news for the tireless one, the one who never rests, whose wings bear the deluge, the Šar-ur. What did it gather there . . . for Lord Ninurta? It reported the deliberations of the Mountains, it explained their intentions to Lord Ninurta, it outlined (?) what people were saying about the Asag.

119–21 'Hero, beware!' it said concernedly. The weapon embraced him whom it loved, the Šar-ur addressed Lord Ninurta:

122–34 'Hero, pitfall (?), net of battle, Ninurta, King, celestial mace . . . irresistible against the enemy, vigorous one, tempest which rages against the rebel lands, wave which submerges the harvest, King, you have looked on battles, you have . . . in the thick of them. Ninurta, after gathering the enemy in a battle-net, after erecting a great reed-altar, Lord, heavenly serpent, purify your pickaxe and your mace! Ninurta, I will enumerate the names of the warriors you have already slain: the Mermaid, the Dragon, the Gypsum, the Strong Copper, the hero Six-headed Wild Ram, the Magilum Barge, Lord Saman-ana, the Bison, the Palm-tree King, the Anzud bird, the Seven-headed Serpent—Ninurta, you slew them in the Mountains.

135–50 'But Lord, do not venture again to a battle as terrible as that. Do not lift your arm to the smiting of weapons, to the festival of the young men, to Inana's dance! Lord, do not go to such a great battle as this! Do not hurry; fix your feet on the ground. Ninurta, the Asag is waiting for you in the Mountains. Hero who is so handsome in his crown, first-born son whom Ninlil has decorated with numberless charms, good Lord, whom a princess bore to an *en* priest, Hero who wears horns like the moon, who is long life for the king of the Land, who opens the sky by great sublime strength, inundation who engulfs the banks . . . , Ninurta, Lord, full of fearsomeness, who will hurry towards the Mountains, proud Hero without fellow, this time you will not equal the Asag! Ninurta, do not make your young men enter the Mountains.'

151–67 The Hero, the son, pride of his father, the very wise, rising from profound deliberation, Ninurta, the Lord, the son of Enlil, gifted with broad wisdom, the . . . god, the Lord stretched his leg to mount the onager, and joined the battalions . . . . He spread over the Mountains his great long . . . , he caused . . . to go out among its people like the . . . . He reached . . . . He went into the rebel lands in the vanguard of the battle. He gave orders to his lance, and attached it . . . by its cord; the Lord commanded his mace, and it went to its belt. The Hero hastened to the battle, he . . . heaven and earth. He prepared the throw-stick and the shield, the Mountains were struck and cringed beside the battle legions of Ninurta. When the hero was girding on his mace, the sun did not wait, the moon went in; they were forgotten, as he marched towards the Mountains; the day became like pitch.

168–86   The Asag leapt up at the head of the battle. For a club it uprooted the sky, took it in its hand; like a snake it slid its head along the ground. It was a mad dog attacking to kill the helpless, dripping with sweat on its flanks. Like a wall collapsing, the Asag fell on Ninurta the son of Enlil. Like an accursed storm, it howled in a raucous voice; like a gigantic snake, it roared at the Land. It dried up the waters of the Mountains, dragged away the tamarisks, tore the flesh of the Earth and covered her with painful wounds. It set fire to the reed-beds, bathed the sky in blood, turned it inside out; it dispersed the people there. At that moment, on that day, the fields became black potash, across the whole extent of the horizon, reddish like purple dye— truly it was so! An was overwhelmed, crouched, wrung his hands against his stomach; Enlil groaned and hid himself in a corner, the Anuna flattened themselves against walls, the house was full of fearful sighing as of pigeons. The Great Mountain Enlil cried to Ninlil:

187–90   'My wife, my son is no longer there; what is there to support me? The Lord, the authority of the E-kur, the King who imposes the strong shackle for his father, a cedar rooted in the Abzu, a crown with broad shade, my son, my security—he is not here any more: who will take me by the hand?'

191–214   The weapon which loved the Lord, obedient to its master, the Šar-ur . . . for Lord Ninurta to his father in Nibru . . . . The awesome splendour enveloped Ninurta like a garment, ... bound him: therefore the Lord . . . . The weapon . . . said to Enlil: (*8 lines missing, fragmentary, or unclear*)

215–24   '. . . Ninurta, having confidence in himself; . . . he will be standing; the waters will be dried up as if by the sun's heat; . . . he will breathe again, he will be standing full of joy. I shall cause horrid storms to rise against . . . of the Hero Ninurta . . . . as for him who resisted (?) the Mountains, he has been amazed by his strength. Now I shall give my orders, you are to follow these instructions: (*1 line unclear*) . . . in

FIG. 22. 'The weapon which loved the Lord, obedient
to its master'—a lion-headed stone mace from Early
Dynastic Sippar

the fields, let him not diminish the population. . . . let him not cause
a lack of posterity. Let him not cause to perish the name of all the
kinds of species whose destinies I, Enlil, have decreed.'

225–7   The weapon, its heart . . . , was reassured: it slapped its thighs, the
Šar-ur began to run, it entered the rebel lands, joyfully it reported the
message to Lord Ninurta:

228–43   'My master, . . . for you, Enlil has said: "As the Deluge°, before whom
the venom has piled up, attacks the enemy, let him take the Asag by
the shoulder, let him pierce its liver, let my son enter with it into the
E-kur. Then, Ninurta, to the limits of the earth my people will
deservedly praise your power. You, Lord who trusts in the word of
his father, do not tarry, great strength of Enlil. Storm of the rebel
lands, who grinds the Mountains like flour, Ninurta, Enlil's seal-
bearer, go to it! Do not tarry." My master: the Asag has constructed
a wall of stakes on an earthen rampart; the fortress is too high and
cannot be reached, . . . its fierceness does not diminish. (*3 lines
unclear*) My master, ...'

244–50   Ninurta opened his mouth to speak to the mace . . . . He aimed the lance at the Mountains . . . . The Lord stretched out an arm towards the clouds. Day became a dark night. He yelled like a storm, ... (*2 lines unclear*)

251–64 The Lord . . . clouds of dust. In his battle he struck down the Mountains with a cudgel. The Šar-ur made the storm-wind rise to heaven, scattering the people; like . . . it tore. Its venom alone destroyed the townspeople. The destructive mace set fire to the Mountains, the murderous weapon smashed skulls with its painful teeth, the club which tears out entrails gnashed its teeth. The lance was stuck into the ground and the crevasses filled with blood. In the rebel lands dogs licked it up like milk. The enemy rose up, crying to wife and child: 'You did not lift your arms in prayer to Lord Ninurta.' The weapon covered the Mountains with dust, but did not shake the heart of the Asag. The Šar-ur threw its arms around the neck of the Lord:

265–80 'Hero, ah, what further awaits you? Do not on any account meddle with the hurricane of the Mountains. Ninurta, Lord, son of Enlil, I tell you again, it is made like a storm. It is a blister whose smell is foul, like mucus which comes from the nose it is unpleasant, Lord, its words are devious, it will not obey you. My master, it has been created against you as a god; who can help you? Hero, it falls on the land as a whirlwind, it scrubs it as if with saltwort, Ninurta, it chases the onagers before it in the Mountains. Its terrifying splendour sends the dust into clouds, it causes a downpour of potsherds. In the rebel lands it is a lion striking with savage teeth; no man can catch it. After reducing everything to nothing in the north wind, it . . . . The sheep-folds have been closed by ghostly demons. It has dried up the waters in the ground. In the whirlwind storm, the people are finished, they have no solution (?). From an implacable enemy, great Hero, Lord, turn away,' he said quietly.

281–99 But the Lord howled at the Mountains, could not withhold a roar. The Hero did not address the rebel lands, he . . . . He reversed the evil that it had done . . . . He smashed the heads of all the enemies, he made the Mountains weep. The Lord ranged about in all directions, like a soldier saying 'I will go on the rampage'. Like a bird of prey the Asag looked up angrily from the Mountains. He commanded the rebel lands to be silent and . . . . Ninurta approached the enemy and flattened him like a wave (?). The Asag's terrifying splendour was contained, it began to fade, it began to fade. It looked wonderingly upwards. Like water he agitated it, he scattered it into the Mountains, like weeds he pulled it up, like rushes he ripped it up. Ninurta's splendour covered the Land, he pounded the Asag like roasted barley, he . . . its genitals (?), he piled it up like a heap of broken bricks, he heaped it up like flour, as a potter does with coals; he piled it up like stamped earth whose mud is being stirred. The Hero had achieved his heart's desire. Ninurta, the Lord, the son of Enlil, . . . began to calm down.

300–9 In the Mountains, the day came to an end. The sun bade it farewell. The Lord . . . his belt and mace in water, he washed the blood from his clothes, the Hero wiped his brow, he made a victory-chant over the dead body. When he had brought the Asag which he had slain to the condition of a ship wrecked by a tidal wave, the gods of the Land came to him. Like exhausted wild asses they prostrated themselves before him, and for this Lord, because of his proud conduct, for Ninurta, the son of Enlil, they clapped their hands in greeting. The Šar-ur addressed these flattering words aloud to its master°:

310–30 'Lord, great *mes* tree in a watered field, Hero, who is like you? My master, beside you there is no one else, nor can anyone stand like you, nor is anyone born like you. Ninurta, from today no one in the Mountains will rise against you. My master, if you give but one roar, . . . how they will praise you! (*1 line unclear*) Lord Ninurta . . . .' (*7 lines fragmentary*) After he had pulled up the Asag like a weed in the rebel lands, torn it up like a rush, Lord Ninurta . . . his club: '(*1 line unclear*) From today forward, do not say Asag: its name shall be Stone. Its name shall be *zalag* stone, its name shall be Stone. This, its entrails, shall be the Underworld. Its valour shall belong to the Lord.'

331–3 The blessing of the club, laid to rest in a corner: 'The mighty battle which reduces the Land (*1 line missing*).'

334–46 At that time, the good water coming forth from the earth did not pour down over the fields. The cold water (?) was piled up everywhere, and the day when it began to . . . it brought destruction in the Mountains, since the gods of the Land were subject to servitude, and had to carry the hoe and the basket—this was their corvée work—people called on a household for the recruitment of workers. The Tigris did not bring up its flood in its fullness. Its mouth did not finish in the sea, it did not carry fresh water. No one brought (?) offerings to the market. The famine was hard, as nothing had yet been born. No one yet cleaned the little canals, the mud was not dredged up. Ditch-making did not yet exist. People did not work (?) in furrows, barley was sown broadcast°.

347–59 The Lord applied his great wisdom to it. Ninurta°, the son of Enlil, set about it in a grand way. He made a pile of stones in the Mountains. Like a floating cloud he stretched out his arms over it. With a great wall he barred the front of the Land. He installed a sluice (?) on the horizon. The Hero acted cleverly, he dammed in the cities together. He blocked (?) the powerful waters by means of stones. Now the waters will never again go down from the Mountains into the earth. That which was dispersed he gathered together. Where in the Mountains scattered lakes had formed, he joined them all together and led them down to the Tigris. He poured carp-floods of water over the fields.

360–7 Now, today, throughout the whole world, kings of the Land far and wide rejoice at Lord Ninurta. He provided water for the speckled barley in the cultivated fields, he raised up° the harvest of fruits in garden and orchard. He heaped up the grain piles like mounds. The Lord caused trading colonies to go up from the Land of Sumer. He contented the desires of the gods. They duly praised Ninurta's father.

368–71 At that time he also reached a woman with compassion. Ninmaḫ was sleepless from remembering the place where she had conceived him. She covered her outside with a fleece, like an unshorn ewe, she made a great lament about the now inaccessible Mountains:

372–86 'The Mountains could not bear the Lord's great strength. The great Hero—the force of whose rage no one can approach, like heaven itself; the savage storm which walks on earth, spilling poison in the earth's breast; the Lord, the life-breath of Enlil, whose head is worthy of the tiara, . . . who knows nothing of . . . : in triumph he hurried by me, he with whom my husband made me pregnant (?). I bore him for my husband. He was close . . . ; but the son of Enlil passed by and did not lift his glance to me. For the good youth'— thus the good lady said, as she went to him in E-šumeša, his chosen place, —'I will cut the knot. Now I, yes I, shall go to the presumptuous Lord, to gaze upon the precious Lord. I will go directly to him, to my son, Enlil's judge, the great Hero, favoured by his father.'

387–9 The lady performed the song in a holy manner. Ninmaḫ recited it to Lord Ninurta. He looked at her with his life-giving looks and spoke to her:

390–410   'Lady, since you came to the Mountains, Ninmaḫ ('Great Lady'),
since you entered the rebel lands for my sake, since you did not keep
far from me when I was surrounded by the horrors of battle—let the
name of the pile which I, the Hero, have piled up be 'Mountain'
(ḫursaĝ) and may you be its lady (nin): now that is the destiny
decreed by Ninurta. Henceforth people shall speak of Ninḫursaĝa.
So be it. Let its meadows produce herbs for you. Let its slopes
produce honey and wine for you. Let its hillsides grow cedars,
cypress, juniper, and box for you. Let it make abundant for you ripe
fruits, as a garden. Let the Mountains supply you richly with divine
perfumes. Let them mine gold and silver for you, make . . . for you.
Let them smelt copper and tin for you, make their tribute for
you. Let the Mountains make wild animals teem for you. Let the
Mountains increase the fecundity of quadrupeds for you. You, O
Queen, become equal to An, wearing a terrifying splendour. Great
goddess who detests boasting, good lady, maiden Ninḫursaĝa,
Nintud, . . . approach me. Lady, I have given you great powers: may
you be exalted.'

411–13   While the Lord was fixing the destiny of the Mountains, as he walked
about in the sanctuary of Nibru, the good lady whose powers excel
all powers, 'Lady-creatrix-of-the-womb', Aruru, Enlil's elder sister,
stood before him:

414–15   'Great Hero whose word like that of his father is unalterable, Lord:
you have not fixed the destinies of the warriors that you have slain.'

416–18   The Lord then addressed the emery. He defined (?) its typical
behaviour. The Lord spoke to it in anger in the Land, Ninurta son of
Enlil cursed it:

419–34   'Emery, since you rose against me in the Mountains, since you
barred the way° so as to detain me, since you swore to put me to
death, since you frightened me, Lord Ninurta, on my great throne;
you are powerful, a youth of outstanding strength: may your size be
diminished. A mighty lion, confident in its strength, will tear you
into pieces, the strong man will fling you in his hand in combat°.
Young emery, your brothers will heap you up like flour. You will lift
your hand against your offspring, sink your teeth into their corpses.
You, young man, though you may cry out, will end as . . . . Like a
great wild bull killed by many people, be divided into portions.
Emery, you will be hounded from the battlefield with clubs, like a
dog chased by shepherd boys. Because I am the Lord: since cornelian

is polished by you, you shall be called by its name. And now, according to the destiny fixed by Ninurta, henceforth when emery touches it, there will be pierced cornelian. Let it be so.'

435–7 The Hero addressed the *šu* and *gasura* stones. The Lord enumerated their characteristics. Ninurta son of Enlil fixed their destiny:

438–47 '*Šu* stones, since you attacked against my weapons; *gasura* stones, since you stood fiercely against me like bulls, since you tossed (?) your horns in the dust at me like wild bulls, you shall be . . . like butterflies. My terrifying splendour will cover you. Since you cannot escape from my° great strength, the goldsmith shall puff and blow on you with his breath. You shall be shaped by him to form a matrix for his creations. People shall place the first fruits of the gods on you at the time of the new moon.'

448–50 My King stood before the *saĝkal* stone, he addressed the *gulgul* and *saĝĝar* stones. Ninurta son of Enlil fixed their destiny:

451–62 '*Saĝkal* stone, since you flew up against me . . . ; *gulgul* stone, since you sparked lightning against me . . . ; *saĝĝar* stone, since you shook your head at me, since you ground your teeth at me, the Lord! The *saĝkal* stone will smash you, *saĝĝar* stone, young brave, and the *gulgul* stone will destroy (*gul*) you. You will be discarded as contemptible and valueless (*saĝ nukala*). Be a prey to the famine (*šaĝĝar*) of the Land; you shall be fed by the charity of your city. You shall be accounted a common person, a warrior among slave-girls. They shall say to you: "Be off with you, hurry!", it shall be your name. And now, by the destiny fixed by Ninurta, henceforth you shall be called a bad lot in the Land. So be it.'

463–5 My King stood before the diorite. . . . he spoke in hymnic language. Ninurta son of Enlil fixed its destiny:

466–78 'Diorite, your army in battle changed sides separately (?). You spread before me like thick smoke. You did not raise your hand. You did not attack me. Since you said: "It is false. The Lord is alone the Hero. Who can vie with Ninurta, son of Enlil?"—they shall extract you from the highland countries. They shall bring (?) you from the land of Magan. You shall shape (?) Strong Copper like leather and then you shall be perfectly adapted for my heroic arm, for me, the Lord. When a king who is establishing his renown for perpetuity has had its statues sculpted for all time, you shall be placed in the place of libations—and it shall suit you well—in my temple E-ninnu, the house full of grace.'

479–81 My King turned to the *na* stone. He . . . the body from the *na* stone. Ninurta son of Enlil cursed it:

482–6 'Stone, since you said: "If only it had been me"; *na* stones, since you bewitched my powers—lie down there, you, to be worked on like a pig. Be discarded, be used for nothing, end up by being reduced to tiny fragments. He who knows you shall reduce you to liquid.'

487–8 My King turned to the *elel* stone. Ninurta son of Enlil fixed its destiny:

489–96 '*Elel*, intelligently you caused terror of me to descend on the Mountains where discord had broken out. In the rebel lands you proclaimed my name among my people who had banded together. Nothing of your wholeness shall be diminished (?). It shall be difficult to reduce your mass to small pieces. My divine ordinances shall be set out in straight lines on your body. You shall be greatly suited to the clash of weapons, when I have heroes to slay. You shall be set up on a pedestal in my great courtyard. The Land shall praise you in wonder, the foreign lands shall speak your praises°.'

497–9 The Hero turned to the haematite, he addressed it for its hardness. Ninurta son of Enlil fixed its destiny:

500–11 'Young man worthy of respect, whose surface reflects the light, haematite, when the demands of the rebel lands reached you, I did not conquer you . . . . I did not notice you among the hostile ones. I shall make room for you in the Land. The divine rites of Utu shall become your powers. Be constituted as a judge in the foreign lands. The craftsman, expert in everything, shall value you as if gold. Young man of whom I have taken possession, because of you I shall not sleep until you come to life. And now, according to the destiny fixed by Ninurta, henceforth haematite shall live! So shall it be.'

512–13 The Hero stood before the great alabaster. Ninurta son of Enlil fixed its destiny:

514–21 'Alabaster, whose body shines like the daylight! Purified silver, youth destined for the palace, since you alone held out your hands to me, and you prostrated yourself before me in your Mountains, I did not smite you with the club, and I did not turn my strength against you. Hero, you stood firm by me when I yelled out. Your name shall be called benevolence. The treasury of the Land shall be subject to your hand, you shall be its seal-keeper.°'

522–4 My King turned to the *algameš* stone and frowned. The Lord spoke to it angrily in the Land. Ninurta son of Enlil cursed it:

525–7 'What provision did you make to assist my progress? Be the first to go into my forge. *Algameš*, you shall be the regular sacrifice offered daily by the smiths.'

528–33 My King turned to the *dušia* stone. He addressed the *nir*, the cornelian, and the lapis lazuli; the *amaš-pa-ed*, the *šaba*, the *ḫurizum*, the *gug-gazi*, and the *marḫali*; the *egi-zaga*, the *girin-ḫiliba*, the *anzugulme*, and the *nir-mušgir* stones°. The Lord Ninurta, son of Enlil, fixed their destinies for . . . the waterskin:

534–42 'How you came to my side, male and female in form, and in your own way! You committed no fault, and you supported me with strength. You exalted me in public. Now in my deliberation, I shall exalt you. Since you made yourself general of the assembly, you, *nir*, shall be chosen for syrup and for wine. You shall all be decorated with precious metal. The principal among the gods shall cause the foreign lands to prostrate themselves before you, putting their noses to the ground.'

543–65 My King turned to the flint, and frowned. The Lord spoke to it angrily in the Land. Ninurta son of Enlil cursed it:

546–53 'Ah, duplicitous flint, what then? They shall split your horns, wild bull, in your Mountains. Lie down before the . . . . You were not equal to me who supported you. I shall rip you like a sack, and people will smash you into tiny pieces. The metalworker shall deal with you, he shall use his chisel on you. Young man, massive, bearer of hatred: the carpenter, saying "I wish to buy the work", shall wet you with water . . . and shall crush you like malt.'

554–6 My King turned to the *iman* stones, he addressed the *alliga* stones. Ninurta son of Enlil fixed their destiny:

557–65 '*Iman* stones, in the Mountains you cried out against me. You fiercely uttered battle-yells. I shall enflame you like fire. Like a storm I shall overturn you. I shall strip you like rushes. I shall rip you up like weeds. Who will assist you then? *Iman* stone: your cries shall not be valued, no attention shall be paid to them. *Iman* stone, *alliga* stone: your path shall not lead to the palace.'

566–8 My King turned to the *mašda* stone. He addressed the *dubban* and *urutum* stones. Ninurta son of Enlil defined (?) their characteristic behaviour:

569–78 '*Mašda* stone, *dubban* stone, blazing fires; *urutum* stone, which nothing resists; when the *gasura* stone . . . and you were set ablaze, you burnt against me in the rebel lands like a brazier. Since you all stood against me in the land of Saba: *mašda* stone, they shall slaughter you like a sheep. *Dubban* stone, they shall crunch you for pulverizing. *Urutum* stone, they shall sharpen you for the battle-mace; with bronze, the arrowheads of the gods, they shall smash you with the axe, stinging with fierce swords.'

579–80 My King turned to the *šagara* stone. Ninurta son of Enlil fixed its destiny:

581–91 '*Šagara* stone, who smash (?) your head against anyone travelling alone in the desert, in the Mountains when my arms were occupied you tried to trample on me. Since you glutted yourself in the battle, the reed-worker shall make the reeds jump with you. You shall be thrown onto your couch; the appearance (?) of your mother and father who bore you shall be forgotten (?). No one shall say to you: "Get up", no one shall have the feeling that he misses you, the people shall not complain about your loss. In praise of the eternally created powers in Ninḫursaĝa's resting place, you shall be discarded on the dais there. They shall feed you on malt, as they do for sheep; you shall content yourself with a portion of scattered flour. This shall be the explanation for you.'

592–3 My King turned to the *marḫuša* stone, Ninurta the son of Enlil pronounced its destiny:

594–9 '*Marḫuša*, . . . the string in my place, . . . you were taken, since you did not participate in the crimes of your city, . . . ; you shall be the bowl under the filter-jug, the water shall filter into you. *Marḫuša*, you shall be used for inlay-work, ... You shall be the perfect ornament for sacred brooches. *Marḫuša*, you shall be duly praised in the temples of the gods.'

600–2 The Hero turned to the *ḫaštum* stone and frowned. In the Land the Lord addressed it angrily; Ninurta the son of Enlil pronounced its destiny:

603–8 '*Ḫaštum* stone, you cried out against me in the Mountains. You yelled fiercely with wild battle-yells. With your yelling, you fixed a *lila* demon in the Mountains. Young man, because of your digging, 'ditch' (*ḫaštum*) shall be your name. And now, according to the destiny of Ninurta, henceforth they shall say *ḫaštum*. So be it.'

609–10 My King turned to the *durul* stone. Ninurta son of Enlil fixed its destiny:

611–17 '*Durul* stone, holy garment of mourning, blinded youth whom people carve, in the Mountains you prostrated yourself before me.

Since you said to me: "If only it had been me who broke the bars of the gates, if only I had stood before him, before my King, Lord Ninurta", your name shall be magnified of its own accord wherever it is mentioned. As the connoisseur says of precious metal: "I will buy it", so the foreign nations, like musicians playing the reed-pipe, shall pursue you.'

618–23 My King turned to the *šigšig* stone, he addressed the *engen* and *ezinum* stones. For the *ug-gun*, the *ḫem*, the *madanum*, the *saĝgirmud*, the . . . and the *mursuḫ* stones, Ninurta son of Enlil fixed their destiny:

624–33 '(*2 lines unclear*) with ribs drawn in, balancing on the haunches, heart elated, legs bent like a bear, . . . : I shall come to you; now, being an ally, you come forward from all of them; who shall extend the hand to them? You were the club, you stood as the doorway. (*3 lines unclear*) In the Land, the champion shall always look (?) with favour on you.'

634–7 The Hero turned to the *kurgaranum* stone. He addressed the *bal* stone; the Lord Ninurta, son of Enlil, fixed the destiny for the yellow-coloured kohl:

638–44 'Since you said: "I will bring forth the people", (*1 line unclear*) you . . . as if . . . the young man who has obtained (?) glory for you; the young artisan shall sing your praises. You shall be favoured for the festival of spirits of the dead; on the ninth day of the month, at the new moon, the young men shall . . . for you.' He assigned . . . them to the cult of Ninḫursaĝa.

645–51 The Hero had conquered the Mountains. As he moved across the desert, he . . . . Through the crowd, he came forth among their acclamations (?), majestically he . . . . Ninurta joyfully went to his beloved barge, the Lord set foot in the boat Ma-kar-nunta-eda. The boatmen sang a pleasant song, for the Lord they sang his praise. They addressed an eternal greeting to Ninurta son of Enlil:

652–61 'God who outstrips the heroes, Lord Ninurta, king of the Anuna gods, holding a cudgel in his right hand, bearded, you fall as a torrent on all enemies; who can rival your great works? Hero, deluge, without equal, the *enki* and *ninki* deities do not dare to resist (?) you. Hero who pillages the cities, who subjugates the Mountains, son of Enlil, who will rise up against you? Ninurta, Lord, son of Enlil, Hero, who is like you?

662–8 'My King: there is a hero who is devoted to you and to your offerings, he is as just as his reputation, he walks in your ways; since he has brilliantly accomplished all that is proper for you in your temple, since he has made your shrine rise from the dust for you, let him do everything magnificently for your festival. Let him accomplish perfectly for you your holy rites. He has formulated a vow for his life. May he praise you in the Land.

669–71 'May An's heart be appeased for the Lord, may the maiden mother Bau shine like the daylight for Ninurta, Enlil's strength.'

672–80 They sang to the Lord in the ceremonial (?) boat. The boat, floating of its own accord, was piled up with riches. The boat Ma-kar-nunta-eda proceeded shiningly. To greet the Hero from the smiting of weapons, the Anuna . . . came to meet him. They pressed their noses to the ground, they placed their hands on their chests. They addressed a prayer and a supplication to the Lord: 'May your anger be appeased . . . . Ninurta, King, Uta-ulu, lift your head to heaven.'

681 His father Enlil blessed him:

682–97 '. . . , pre-eminent with your great name, you have established your habitation . . . . Chest, fittingly . . . , King of battle, I presented the storm of heaven to you for use against the rebel lands. O Hero of heaven and earth I presented to you the club, the deluge which sets the Mountains on fire. King, ahead of your storm the way was narrow. But, Ninurta, I had confidence in your march to the Mountains. Like a wolf (?) set free to seize his prey, in your storm you adventured into the rebel lands from above. The Mountains that you have handed over shall not be restored. You have caused their cities to be counted as ruin-mounds. Their mighty rulers have lost their breath before you. A celestial mace, a prosperous and unchanging rule, eternal life, the good favour of Enlil, O King, and the strength of An: these shall be your reward.'

698–711 Since the Hero had killed the Asag, since the Lord had made that pile of stones, since he had given the order 'Let it be called Stone', since he had . . . the roaring dragon, since the Hero had traced the way of the waters . . . down from above, since he had brought them to the fertile fields, since he had made famous the plough of abundance, since the Lord had established it in regular furrows, since Ninurta son of Enlil had heaped up grain-piles and granaries—Ninurta son of Enlil entrusted their keeping to the care of the lady who possesses the divine powers which exist of themselves, who is eminently worthy of praise, to Nisaba, good lady, greatly wise, pre-eminent in the lands, to her who possesses the principal tablet with the obligations of *en* priest and king, endowed by Enki on the Holy Mound with a great intelligence.

712–23 To the lady, the celestial star, made magnificently beautiful by the prince in the Abzu, to the lady of knowledge who gladdens hearts, who alone has the gift of governing, endowed with prudence, . . . , who rules the black-headed, who possesses the tablet with all the names (?), from whose suspended nets the birds which are caught do not escape, whose every work accomplished meets with complete success, to her . . . which is not unravelled, to her for whom the days are counted according to the phases of the moon, to her who is unassailable as if a fortress of copper . . . , who is . . . in counsels, and wise in all manner of things, . . . who cares for the black-headed, who rules the people justly, . . . , the replica of Enlil, to the bright good lady who takes counsel with An—praise be to Nisaba!

724–5 Enlil's mighty Lord, Ninurta, great son of the E-kur, heroic one of the father who bore him: it is sweet to praise you!

726 A *šir-gida* of Ninurta.

Notes

1–16 1 MS adds before line 1: 'An, king of the gods, majestic one:'. 'King', 'Lord', and 'Hero' are titles of Ninurta.

24–47 Instead of 'Ninurta' 1 MS has: 'Ninĝirsu'.

70–95 A *danna* is about 11 kilometres.

228–43 'the Deluge': i.e. Ninurta.

300–9 Instead of 'aloud to its master' 1 MS has: 'to Lord Ninurta'.

334–46 'barley was sown broadcast': i.e. scattered by hand instead of released through a seeder plough.

347–59 Instead of 'Ninurta' 1 MS has: 'Ninĝirsu'.

360–7 Instead of 'raised up' 2 MSS have: 'piled up'.

419–34 Instead of 'barred the way' 2 MSS have: 'seized me'. Instead of 'in combat' 1 MS has: 'for strength'.

438–47 Instead of 'my' 1 MS has: 'his'.

489–96 Instead of 'speak your praises' 2 MSS have: 'elevate you'.

514–21 After 'seal-keeper.' 1 MS adds the line: 'The Anuna . . . .'.

528–33 Instead of 'the *anzugulme* and the *nir-mušĝir* stones' 1 MS has: 'the . . . and the *gazi-musud* stones'.

Ninurta's return to Nibru

Ninurta's return relates in more detail than *Ninurta's exploits* the heroic god's triumphal journey to Nibru after his conquest of the hostile mountains and the rebel lands. It falls neatly into five major parts of varying length alternating hymnic and narrative content: the hymnic passages (1 and 5) frame the narratives (2 and 4), within which a hymn (3) is embedded. The introductory hymn enumerates Ninurta's attributes and qualities and praises his strength and great achievements (1–29). That passage is followed by a long narrative section describing Ninurta's return to Nibru on his chariot decorated with battle trophies. In Nibru he proceeds to the E-kur with his trophies and booty, where he is received by his divine family and the Anuna gods (30–112). He approaches his mother, Ninlil, with a hymn of self-praise, in which he demands both his and his city's elevation as a result of his accomplishments (113–174). Leaving the E-kur Ninurta moves to the E-šumeša, his temple in Nibru, where he joins his wife, Ninnibru, and blesses the king of the city on her request (175–98). The composition concludes with praise to Ninurta (199–207). It was qualified with a subscript as a *šir-gida* (lit. 'long song') by the ancient scribes.

Translation

1–6 Created like An, O son of Enlil, Ninurta, created like Enlil, born of Nintud, mightiest of the Anuna gods, who came forth from the mountain range, imbued with terrible awesomeness, son of Enlil, confident in his strength, my sovereign, you are magnificent—let your magnificence therefore be praised. Ninurta, you are magnificent—let your magnificence therefore be praised.

7–12 King of all the lands, in your massive might, warrior of Enlil, in your great might, fierce warrior, you have taken up the divine powers which are like heaven, son of Enlil, you have taken up the divine powers which are like the earth, you have taken up the divine powers of the mountains, which are heavy as heaven, you have taken up the divine powers of Eridug, which are huge as the earth.

13–15 You have made the gods prostrate (?) themselves before you. You have made the Anuna salute (?) you. Ninurta, you are made complete by heroic strength.

16–17 The utterance of the sovereign is a storm . . . . The word of Lord Ninurta is a storm . . . .

18–23 To the hostile mountains . . . . To the fortress of the rebellious land
. . . . (*1 line unclear*) Lord, frighteningly fierce, ... Fierce in heaven
and earth, ... (*1 line unclear*)

24–5 His angry utterance made a corpse of the mountains. His fierce
countenance . . . .

26–9 Horned wild bull . . . . Wild ram and stag . . . . The great wild bull of
the mountains . . . from its . . . . He put his . . . , the strength in
battle, in his belt.

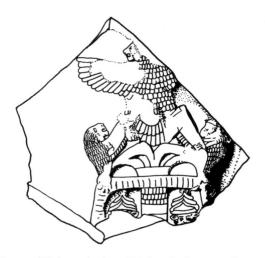

FIG. 23. 'He hung the Anzud bird on the front guard'—
a chariot adorned with the Anzud bird, on a fragmentary
stone stela from Ḡirsu

30–40 The sovereign, with his heroic arms, Ninurta, son of Enlil, in his
great might, brought forth the Six-headed Wild Ram from the
shining, lofty house. He brought forth the Warrior Dragon from the
great fortress of the mountains. He brought forth the Magilum
Barge from . . . his Abzu. He brought forth the Bison from his battle
dust. He brought forth the Mermaid from the limits of heaven and
earth. He brought forth the Gypsum from the soil of the mountain
range. He brought forth the Strong Copper from the shattered
mountain range. He brought forth the Anzud bird from the *ḫalub-
ḫaran* tree. He brought forth the Seven-headed Serpent from the . . .
of the mountains.

41–6 He mustered them all before him . . . . He spoke . . . . He was
unhappy . . . . He spoke . . . . He seized the axe . . . . He took his . . . .

47–51 The warrior ... made a corpse of the mountains. Lord Ninurta, who destroys (?) ..., made a corpse of the mountains. He piled up .... The King, with his heroic strength, wreaked his vengeance (?). The warrior Ninurta, with his heroic strength, wreaked his vengeance (?).

52–4 On his shining chariot, which inspires terrible awe, he hung his captured wild bulls on the axle and hung his captured cows on the cross-piece of the yoke.

55–63 He hung the Six-headed Wild Ram on the dust-guard. He hung the Warrior Dragon on the seat. He hung the Magilum Barge on the .... He hung the Bison on the beam. He hung the Mermaid on the foot-board. He hung the Gypsum on the forward part of the yoke. He hung the Strong Copper on the inside pole pin (?). He hung the Anzud bird on the front guard. He hung the Seven-headed Serpent on the shining ....

64–9 Lord Ninurta stepped into his battle-worthy chariot. Ud-ane, the all-seeing god, and Lugal-anbara, the bearded (?) lord, went before him, and the awesome one of the mountains, Lugal-kur-dub, the ... of Lord Ninurta, followed behind him.

70–2 The lion who ... from the Abzu, who ... An's awesomeness and radiance—the Anuna, the great gods ....

73–5 As the King swept on like the deluge, as Ninurta, storm of the rebellious land, swept on like the deluge, he rumbled like a storm on the horizon.

76–9 When, at Enlil's command, he was making his way towards E-kur, the warrior of the gods was levelling the Land; and before he had yet approached Nibru from afar, Nuska, the chancellor of Enlil, came forth from the E-kur to meet him.

80–2 He greeted Lord Ninurta: 'My sovereign, perfect warrior, heed yourself. Ninurta, perfect warrior, heed yourself.

83–6 'Your radiance has covered Enlil's temple like a cloak. When you step into your chariot, whose creaking is a pleasant sound, heaven and earth tremble. When you raise your arm ....

87–91 'The Anuna, the great gods .... Do not frighten your father in his residence. Do not frighten Enlil in his residence. May your father give you gifts because of your heroic strength. May Enlil give you gifts because of your heroic strength.

92–7 'O King, shackle of An, first among the gods, seal-bearer of Enlil, inspired by E-kur, O warrior, because you have toppled the mountains your father need send out no other god beside you. Ninurta, because you have toppled the mountains Enlil need send out no other god beside you.'

98–101 While these words were still in Nuska's mouth, Ninurta put the whip and goad away in the rope-box. He leaned his mace, the strength in battle, against the box and entered into the temple of Enlil.

102–7 He directed his captive wild bulls into the temple. He directed his captive cows, like the wild bulls, into the temple. He laid out the booty of his plundered cities. The Anuna were amazed. . . . Enlil the Great Mountain made obeisance to him, and Ašimbabbar prayed to him.

108–12 The great mother Ninlil, from within her Ki-ur, spoke admiringly to Lord Ninurta: 'O wild bull, with fierce horns raised, son of Enlil, you have struck blows in the mountains. Warrior, Lord Ninurta, you have . . . . You have . . . the rebellious land.'

113–18 Lord Ninurta answered her: 'My mother, I alone cannot . . . with you . . . . Ninlil, I alone cannot . . . with you, for me alone . . . . Battle arrayed like heaven—no one can rival me (?). Like the deluge . . . . Smashing the mountains like reed huts . . . .

119–24 'My battle, like an onrushing flood, overflowed in the mountains. With a lion's body and lion's muscles, it rose up in the rebellious land. The gods have become worried and flee (?) to the mountain ranges. They beat their wings like a flock of small birds. They stand hiding in the grass like wild bulls . . . . No one can confront my radiance, heavy as heaven.

125–7 'Because I am the Lord of the terraced mountain ranges, in every direction . . . . Because I have subjugated these mountain ranges of alabaster and lapis lazuli, the Anuna hide like mice.

128–34 'Now I have re-established my heroic strength in the mountains. On my right, I bear my Šar-ur. On my left, I bear my Šar-gaz. I bear my Fifty-toothed Storm, my heavenly mace. I bear the hero who comes down from the great mountains, my No-resisting-this-storm. I bear the weapon which devours corpses like a dragon, my *agasilig* axe. I bear my . . . .

135–9 'I bear my . . . . I bear the *alkad* net of the rebellious land, my *alkad* net. I bear that from which the mountains cannot escape, my *šušgal* net. I bear the seven-mouthed *mušmah* serpent, the slayer, my spike (?). I bear that which strips away the mountains, the sword, my heavenly dagger.

140-5 'I bear the deluge of battle, my fifty-headed mace. I bear the storm that attacks humans, my bow and quiver. I bear those which carry off the temples of the rebellious land, my throw-stick and shield. I bear the helper of men, my spear. I bear that which brings forth light like the day, my Obliterator-of-the-mountains. I bear the maintainer of the people in heaven and earth, my The-enemy-cannot-escape.

146-51 'I bear that whose awesome radiance covers the Land, which is grandly suited for my right hand, finished in gold and lapis lazuli, whose presence is amazing, my Object-of-trust. I bear the perfect weapon, exceedingly magnificent, trustworthy in battle, having no equal, well-suited for my wrist on the battlefield, my fifty-headed mace, I bear the weapon which consumes the rebellious land like fire, my fifty-headed club.

152-8 'Let my father therefore bring in my battle trophies and weapons for me. Let Enlil bathe my heroic arms. Let him pour holy water on the fierce arms which bore my weapons. Let him set up a holy dais in the throne room for me. Let him set my heavenly chariot upon a pedestal. Let him tether my captured warriors there like butting bulls. Let him have my captured kings make obeisance to me there, as to the light of heaven.

159-63 'I am the strong one, unopposed in the mountains, I am Ninurta— let them prostrate themselves at my name. I am the exceedingly mighty lion-headed one of Enlil, whom he engendered in his strength. The storm of heaven, shackle of the gods, I am the one whom An in his great might has chosen.

164-7 'I am the . . . , the creature of Inana. I am the warrior, destined with Enki to be suited for the fearsome divine powers. Let my kingship be manifest unto the ends of heaven and earth. I am most able among the gods—let me be imbued with great awesomeness.

168-74 'Let my beloved city, the sanctuary Nibru, raise its head as high as heaven. Let my city be pre-eminent among the cities of my brothers. Let my temple rise (?) the highest . . . among the temples of my brothers. Let the territory of my city be the freshwater well of Sumer. Let the Anuna, my brother gods, bow down there. Let their flying birds establish nests in my city. Let their refugees refresh themselves in my shade.'

175-9 As Ninurta went out from Enlil's temple, the most bright-faced of warriors, Ninkarnuna, having heard the favourable pronouncement of Ninurta, stepped before Lord Ninurta and prayed to him:

180–6   'My sovereign, may you be well disposed towards your beloved city. Lord Ninurta, may you be well disposed towards your beloved city. May you be well disposed towards the sanctuary Nibru, your beloved city. When you enter E-šumeša, your beloved temple, alone, tell your wife, young lady Ninnibru, what is in your heart, tell her what is on your mind. Make an enduring favourable pronouncement to her for the king.'

187–94   The content of that prayer of the offspring of a prince, Ninkarnuna, his sprinkling Ninurta's heart with an offering of cool water, and the matter of prosperity about which he spoke were pleasing to Ninurta's heart as he went in procession to E-šumeša to manifest the eternal divine powers. Lord Ninurta gazed approvingly at Ninkarnuna.

195–8   When Ninurta entered E-šumeša, his beloved temple, alone, he told his wife, young lady Ninnibru, what was in his heart, he told her what was on his mind and he made an enduring favourable pronouncement to her for the king.

199–201   The warrior, whose heroism is manifest, Ninurta, son of Enlil, has firmly grounded his greatness in Enlil's sanctuary.

202–7   Lord who has destroyed the mountains, who has no rival, who butts angrily in that magnificent battle, great warrior who goes forth in his . . . might, strong one, deluge of Enlil, Ninurta, magnificent child of E-kur, pride of the father who engendered him, it is sweet to praise you!

208   A *šir-gida* of Ninurta.

A *balbale* to Ninurta

This short song-like composition is devoted to the god Ninurta, whose complex character had two main aspects: the fierce warrior and the farmer. The composition is devoted to the latter one, depicting him as the god of agricultural and animal fertility.

The poem is carefully constructed, even though it is brief and composed largely of phrases drawn from the common stock of images invoking plenitude. (Sumerian poets often aimed for an effect of abundance by listing many commodities or animals in sequence.) The composition falls into two sections, a division that was made visible by a scribal ruling in one of the

two existing manuscripts. The opening invocation is followed by a passage
(8–21) that falls into five parallel groups of lines which move up the scale from
the fecundity of sheep through that of goats, cattle, and asses to the fertility
of humans, implying Ninurta's responsibility for all this by the juxtaposition
of devotional addresses to the god.

The second section (22–31) presents a survey that starts from flax and
barley, moves through the cultivated landscape of river fisheries and agriculture, the uncultivated but exploited landscape of marsh lagoons, the wild
scene of forests and deserts, and then concludes with the cultivated gardens
and the palace.

Both halves of the poem thus exhibit a parallel movement towards the
human sphere, and the final mention of the 'palace' and 'long life' suggests a
nod, at least, in the direction of the conventional prayer for long life for the
king.

Translation

1–21 Good semen, good seed, King chosen by Enlil! Very good semen,
very good seed, Ninurta, chosen by Enlil! My King, I shall call upon
your name. Ninurta, I am your man, your man; I shall call upon your
name. My King, ewes give birth to lambs, ewes give birth to lambs,
the sheep of the fold are born; I shall call upon your name. My King,
goats give birth to kids, goats give birth to kids, billy goats are born;
I shall call upon your name. My King, cows give birth to calves, cows
give birth to calves, cows and breed-bulls are born; I shall call upon
your name. My King, she-asses give birth to foals, she-asses give birth
to foals, donkeys . . . are born; I shall call upon your name. My King,
humans give birth to children, humans give birth to children.
Ninurta, King . . . .

22–31 Through the King, flax is born; through the King, barley is born.
Through him, carp floods are made plentiful in the river. Through
him, fine grains are made to grow in the fields. Through him, carp
are made plentiful in the lagoons. Through him, dead and fresh reed
are made to grow in the reed thickets. Through him, fallow deer
and wild sheep are made plentiful in the forests. Through him,
mašgurum trees are made to grow in the high desert. Through him,
syrup and wine are made plentiful in the watered gardens. Through
him, life which is long is made to grow in the palace.

32 A *balbale* of Ninurta.

F. LOVE AND SEX

The whole spectrum of heterosexual love is explored and celebrated in Sumerian literature, as well as the bonds of family and friendship. Neither male nor female homosexuality is recognized (though homoeroticism is a defining feature of Gilgameš and Enkidu's relationship in the Babylonian *Epic of Gilgameš*, largely absent in the Sumerian Gilgameš narratives). The intense attachments between mother and child are given voice in many different ways. That giving birth is hair-raisingly dangerous and distressing as well as overpoweringly joyful is acknowledged in *A tigi to Nintud-Aruru*, the birth goddess. In *A lullaby for a son of Šulgi* the infant prince is lulled to sleep with maternal hopes and fears for his future life. By contrast, in *Lu-digira's message to his mother* an adult son waxes so lyrical about his mother's beauty and goodness that he forgets to say anything meaningful to her in the message itself. The contrast between his eloquent adoration of her, as expressed to the messenger, and his gruff acknowledgement of her need to know of his well-being that constitutes the message, poignantly and humorously encapsulates the difficulty of directly expressing love to other adult family members.

Sibling affection (and disaffection) is explored in *Inana's descent to the Underworld* (Group B), in which Dumuzid and Ĝeštin-ana's close bond contrasts strongly with the rivalry of the sisters Inana and Ereškigala. In *A balbale to Inana and Dumuzid* Inana's brother Utu tenderly offers to prepare her linen bridal sheets—though Inana's thoughts are too fixed on her lover to spare a word of sisterly thanks. Sexual desire can be overwhelming and inconstant compared to the steadfast certainties of family ties.

A large number of very beautiful and tender love poems of the divine couple Inana and Dumuzid survive, in some of which, like *A love song for Išme-Dagan*, Dumuzid is represented by a human king. They romanticize the shepherd's life as do many later European traditions, from Virgil's *Eclogues* to Thomas Hardy's *Tess of the D'Urbervilles*. Their erotic charge comes through pastoral and agricultural imagery: 'ploughing' as a metaphor for penetrative sex, 'honey' for female sexual arousal (see *Ploughing with the jewels* and *A love song for Šu-Suen*, both Group B). Layered repetition of short phrases produces the effect of murmured endearments, often in the female voice: 'Lad, let me do the sweetest things to you.'

The headiness of sex has its downside in lover's quarrels, which may themselves be arousing (in *Ploughing with the jewels*) or absolutely devastating (at the end of *Inana's descent to the Underworld*). Or the relationship itself may be ambiguous: in *Enlil and Ninlil* (Group C) it is not clear whether the young goddess is infatuated with Enlil or with the adult status that being sexually active imparts. Enlil himself has no qualms about taking advantage of her innocent gullibility as often as possible, and in disguise. When, in *Inana and Šu-kale-tuda*, the goddess discovers she has been raped in her sleep, she is clearly furious. But is she enraged by her violation *per se* or by the temerity of her rapist—who turns out to be a mere spotty gardener's boy?

FURTHER READING

Alster, B., 'Sumerian Love Songs', *Revue d'Assyriologie*, 79 (1985), 127–59.

Cooper, J., 'Gendered Sexuality in Sumerian Love Poetry', in I. L. Finkel and M. J. Geller (eds.), *Sumerian Gods and their Representations* (Styx: Groningen, 1997), pp. 85–97.

Leick, G., *Sex and Eroticism in Mesopotamian Literature* (Routledge: London, 1994).

Stol, M., *Birth in Babylonia and the Bible: its Mediterranean Setting* (Styx: Groningen, 2000).

OTHER COMPOSITIONS ON THIS THEME INCLUDE

Group A   The death of Ur-Namma
Group B   Ploughing with the jewels
          Dumuzid and Enkimdu
          A love song for Šu-Suen
          Inana and Išme-Dagan
Group C   Enlil and Ninlil
          Enlil and Sud
Group E   A *balbale* to Ninurta
Group H   A *kuĝar* to Inana and Dumuzid
          A *šir-namursaĝa* to Inana for Iddin-Dagan
          An *ululumama* to Suen for Ibbi-Suen
Group I   The instructions of Šuruppag

Lu-digira's message to his mother

Lu-digira's message to his mother is an engaging composition based around the very simple idea of sending a letter home. Lu-digira is no one special, indeed no one in particular, as it is one of the commonest Sumerian personal names. The dramatic situation is presupposed that Lu-digira, who is away for some unexplained reason in another city, wishes to communicate with his mother who (we are told) has been worrying about him. Lu-digira instructs a messenger (rather grandly addressed as 'royal courier') to take a message to the city of Nibru to his mother, who has been asking other travellers for news of him.

The main part of the composition consists of five paragraphs of description of Lu-digira's mother, ostensibly to enable the messenger to recognize her when he delivers the hand-written tablet into her hands. In fact this is an excuse for Lu-digira to express his affection for his mother, and each section focuses on a different aspect. In the first, we are told her name (Šat-Eštar, literally 'She of the goddess Ištar') and her social role as a mistress of the family household is stressed. In the second her physical appearance is compared to various precious stones or metals and, interestingly, she is said to resemble a fine statue. The third section uses botanical metaphors to evoke the mother's bounty; the fourth describes her joyous nature. Finally the fifth paragraph employs a range of images most of which are luxury objects to emphasize the mother's refinement and kindness. These include ostrich eggs, which were made into vessels in ancient Mesopotamia, some of which survive. By the time he begins the message itself, we are expecting something equally elaborate and flowery: its simplicity and brevity—'Your beloved son Lu-digira is in good health'—are a very funny anticlimax.

This composition was quite popular in the schools of Nibru, although there is no evidence that the young pupils were themselves living apart from their families. Several hundred years later it was known in Ugarit on the Mediterranean coast of Syria, and was also translated into the Hittite language.

Translation

1–8 Royal courier, start the journey! I want to send you to Nibru— deliver this message! You are going on a long journey. My mother is worried, she cannot sleep°. Although the way to her° woman's domain is blocked, deliver my letter of greeting into her hands, as she keeps asking° the travellers° about my well-being. Then my mother will be delighted, and will treat you most kindly (?) for it.

9–20 In case you should not recognize my mother, let me describe her to you. Her name is Šat-Eštar°, . . . by her words . . . . Her body, face and limbs, and outer appearance are . . . . She is the fair goddess of her city-quarter. Her fate has been decided since the days of her youth. Single-handed she keeps in order the house of her father-in-law. She serves humbly before her divine mistress. She knows how to look after Inana's place. She never disobeys the orders° of the king. She is energetic and causes possessions to multiply. She is loving, gentle, and lively. By nature she is a lamb, sweet butter, honey, flowing ghee.

21–31 Let me give you another description of my mother: My mother is like the bright light in the sky°, a doe on the hillsides. She is the morning star, shining even at noon-time°. She is precious cornelian, a topaz from Marḫaši. She is the jewellery of a king's brother, full of beauty. She is a cylinder seal of *nir* stone, an ornament like the sun°. She is a bracelet of tin, a ring of *antasura* stone. She is a nugget of shining gold and silver, but which is living and draws breath . . .°. She is an alabaster statuette of a protective goddess standing on a pedestal of lapis lazuli. She is a polished rod of ivory°, with limbs full of beauty°.

32–9 Let me give you a third description of my mother: My mother is rain from heaven°, water for the finest seeds. She is a bountiful harvest of fully-grown fine barley°. She is a garden of . . .°, full of laughter°. She is a well-irrigated pine tree, an adorned juniper°. She is early fruit, the products° of the first month. She is an irrigation ditch bringing fertilizing water to the garden plots. She is a sweet Dilmun date, a prime date much sought after.

40–6 Let me give you a fourth description of my mother: My mother fills the festivals and offerings with joy. She is an *akitum* offering°, awesome (?) to look upon. She is . . . child° of the king, a song of abundance. She is a place of entertainment set up for delights.° She is a lover, a loving heart who never becomes sated with pleasure. She is the good news that the captive will return to his mother°.

47–52 Let me give you a fifth description of my mother: My mother is a palm tree, with the sweetest fragrance. She is a chariot of juniper wood, a waggon of boxwood. She is a fine cloth° perfumed with refined oil. She is a bunch of grapes, a garland (?) growing

luxuriantly°. She° is a phial made from an ostrich egg, overflowing°
with finest° oil.°

53–4 When, thanks to the descriptions I have given you, you stand in her
(?) radiant presence, tell her: 'Your beloved son Lu-digira is in good
health.'°

Notes

1–8 Instead of 'is worried, she cannot sleep' 1 MS has: 'is too (?) . . . to sleep'.
Instead of 'her' 1 MS has: 'the closed'. Instead of 'as she keeps asking' 1 MS has:
'and then she will not keep asking'. Instead of 'travellers' 1 MS has: 'wayfarers'.

9–20 Instead of 'Šat-Eštar' 1 MS has: 'Šimat-Eštar'. Instead of 'orders' 1 MS has:
'wishes'.

21–31 Instead of 'in the sky' 1 MS has: 'on the horizon'. Instead of 'shining even at
noon-time' 1 MS has: 'providing plenty of light'. Instead of 'a cylinder seal of
nir stone, an ornament like the sun' 1 MS has: 'a delightful cornelian jewel, an
ornament'; 1 MS has: 'a cornelian . . . , an ornament of *nir* stone'; 1 MS has: 'a
. . . jewel, delightful and beautiful'. Instead of 'but which is living and draws
breath . . .' 1 MS has: '. . . and breathing'; 1 MS has: '. . . place . . .'. Instead of
'a polished rod of ivory' 2 MSS have: 'a living figurine (?)'. Instead of 'with
limbs full of beauty' 1 MS has: 'full of pleasure'.

32–9 Instead of 'rain from heaven' 1 MS has: 'timely rain'. Instead of 'fully-grown
fine barley' 1 MS has: 'ripe, exceedingly fine barley'; 1 MS has: 'heavenly . . .';
1 MS has: 'ripe . . .'. Instead of '. . .' 1 MS has 'delights'. Instead of 'full of
laughter' 1 MS has: 'filled with rejoicing'. Instead of 'an adorned juniper' 1 MS
has: 'adorned with pine-cones'. Instead of 'products' 1 MS has: 'garden's
yield'.

40–6 Instead of 'an *akitum* offering' 1 MS has: 'the *akitum* festival'. Instead of 'child'
1 MS has 'daughter'. After 'delights.' 1 MS adds: '. . . fruit . . . abundance'.
Instead of 'to his mother' 1 MS has: 'to celebrate'.

47–52 Instead of 'a fine cloth' 1 MS has: 'a good . . .'. Instead of 'growing luxuriantly'
1 MS has: 'perfect in luxuriant growth'. Instead of 'She' 1 MS has: 'My
mother'. Instead of 'overflowing' 1 MS has: 'full'. Instead of 'finest' 1 MS has
'perfumed'. After 'oil.' 1 MS adds: 'She is a fair woman, accompanied by a protective goddess . . . . She is a woman who will show you compassion like (?)
Aruru, . . . born . . . .'.

53–4 Instead of these lines 1 MS has: 'The descriptions I have given you describe (?)
her (?) appearance. A most fair woman accompanied by many protective
goddesses, she is my mother. Pay attention, . . . joyfully . . . : 'Your beloved son
Lu-digira is in good health . . .', tell her . . . . (*1 line fragmentary*).'

A lullaby for a son of Šulgi

This composition is cast in the voice of a wife of the famous king Šulgi, singing their baby son to sleep. The song is quite literary in its style and language. The metaphors of plants are reminiscent of some of the praise poems composed for the adult Šulgi, but in general the tone and content of this composition are unparalleled in Sumerian literature. What its social context might have been is unknown. Unfortunately part of it is preserved only in a fragmentary state.

The mother imagines the child's adulthood, and wishes that he may in due course marry happily and have a son of his own. As she sits guarding him while he sleeps beneath the moon and stars, she frightens him with a suggestion of some terrible accident, humorously defused as she describes how the various small animals that surround the cradle—the mongoose, the gecko, the fly, the lizard—would mourn for him.

The names of three wives of Šulgi are known: Tarām-Uram, his first wife and the mother of Amar-Suen, who was to succeed Šulgi as king; Amat-Suen, whom Šulgi married during the middle of his long reign; and Šulgi-simtī, whom he married around his twenty-ninth year of kingship and who remained his queen until the end of his life. In addition to his three wives, Šulgi had at least six 'consorts' who did not have the full rank of queen. Altogether the names of eighteen sons and thirteen daughters of Šulgi are known.

Translation

1–5 Ah, ah, may he grow sturdy through my crooning, may he flourish through my crooning! May he put down strong foundations as roots, may he spread branches wide like a *šakir* plant!

6–11 Lord, from this you know our whereabouts; among those resplendent apple trees overhanging the river, may someone who passes by (?) reach out his hand, may someone lying there raise his hand. My son, sleep will overtake you, sleep will settle on you.

12–18 Sleep come, sleep come, sleep come to my son, sleep hasten (?) to my son! Put to sleep his open eyes, settle your hand upon his sparkling eyes—as for his murmuring tongue, let the murmuring not spoil his sleep.

19–23 May he fill your lap with emmer wheat while I sweeten miniature

FIG. 24. 'My son, sleep will overtake you'—a nursing
mother on an Old Babylonian terracotta plaque from Ĝirsu

cheeses for you, those cheeses that are the healer of mankind, that are
the healer of mankind, and of the lord's son, the son of lord Šulgi.

24-30 In my garden, it is the lettuces that I have watered, and among the
lettuces it is the *gakkul* lettuce that I have chopped. Let the lord eat
this lettuce! Through my crooning let me give him a wife, let me give
him a wife, let me give him a son! May a happy nursemaid chatter
with him, may a happy nursemaid suckle him!

31-8 Let me . . . a wife for my son, and may she bear him a son so sweet.
May his wife lie in his warm embrace, and may his son lie in his outstretched arms. May his wife be happy with him, and may his son be
happy with him. May his young wife be happy in his embrace, and
may his son grow vigorously on his gentle knees.

39-48 You are restless—I am troubled, I am quite silent (?), gazing at the
stars, as the crescent moon shines on my face. Your bones might be
arrayed on the wall! The man of the wall might shed tears for you!
The mongoose might beat the *balaĝ* drums for you! The gecko might
gouge its cheeks for you! The fly might gash its lips for you! The
lizard might tear out (?) its tongue for you!

49-56 May the lullaby (?) make us flourish! May the lullaby (?) make us
thrive! When you flourish, when you thrive, when you . . . the

shaking of churns, sweet sleep . . . , the sweet bed . . . . (*2 lines fragmentary*)

57–63 May a wife be your support, and may a son . . . . May a son be your fortune. May winnowed grain be your lover, and may Ezina-Kusu be your aid. May you have an eloquent protective goddess. May you be brought up to a reign of favourable days. May you smile upon festivals.

64–6 My son is . . . ; he knows nothing. He does not know the length of his old age (?). He does not know the dwelling of the . . . .

67–73 May you discover . . . . May you eat . . . . (*3 lines fragmentary*) May you be . . . . May you be . . . .

74–91 (*7 lines fragmentary*) . . . goats, sheep and donkeys . . . (*1 line fragmentary*) Ninkasi . . . in her vat . . . (*5 lines fragmentary*) The shepherd's wife . . . He . . . the . . . of the date palm. He brings date shoots among the offerings.

92–114 As for you, lie in sleep! May your palm tree, extending its fronds, spread joy like a fig tree (?). Place coals (?) beside Urim! Place charcoal beside Unug! Seize the enemy's mouth like . . . ! Bind his arms like reed bundles! Make the enemy cower before you, lest he rip open your back like a sack, (*14 lines fragmentary or missing; unknown number of lines missing*)

A *tigi* to Nintud-Aruru

This song addressed to the 'mother goddess' Nintud is a tightly structured 42-line composition divided, in the typical format of *tigi* songs, into *sa-gida* and *sa-ĝara* sections (see Group H), and is followed in the ancient sources by the subscript: 'A *tigi* of Nintud'. Nintud is often referred to as the mother goddess of Mesopotamian tradition, that is to say, a goddess associated not only with human pregnancy but also with the original creation of mankind; and sometimes a mother of the gods. Throughout this song, she is referred to repeatedly as Nintud but also twice (in lines 1 and 4) as Aruru, evidently synonymously; the subject-matter primarily concerns her role as symbolic creator of two priestly ranks, *en* and *lagar*, and of the king. The city of Keš, which is known chiefly as the centre of the cult of the mother goddess, is also mentioned several times (see *The Keš temple hymn*, Group J).

In fact there were various goddesses associated with aspects of motherhood. The ancient Mesopotamian lists of gods refer to them under various names, including Aruru, Digirmaḫ ('August Deity'), Mama/Mami, Nindigirene and Bēlet-ilī (both meaning 'Lady of the Gods'), Ninḫursaga ('Lady of the Hills'), Ninmaḫ ('August Lady'), Ninmena ('Lady of the Crown'), Nintud (possibly 'Lady of Giving Birth'), and so on. There exists a vestigial tradition of Aruru as an independent powerful goddess associated with vegetation; this tradition is preserved exclusively in certain difficult songs in the Emesal register of Sumerian. However, it seems that from a relatively early date her cult was assimilated to that of the other mother goddesses.

This mainstream Sumerian composition also survived into later Mesopotamian tradition. An almost identical version of it exists from the first millennium BCE, on a tablet from the library of the Assyrian king Assurbanipal (ruled 668– c.631 BCE) at Nineveh.

Translation

1–12 Lady Aruru of the house Keš, born in the mountains, the pure place! Nintud, supreme mother of all lands, mother Nintud, lady Aruru of the house Keš, born in the mountains, the pure place! Nintud, supreme mother of all lands, has appeared with the hair-raising fearsomeness of a lion. She has given birth to the *en* priest, has given birth to the *lagar* priest. On the holy throne-dais, Nintud has given birth to the king. Nintud has appeared with the hair-raising fearsomeness of a lion. She has given birth to the *en* priest, has given birth to the *lagar* priest. On the holy throne-dais, Nintud has given birth to the king.

13–18 Nintud has placed upon his head the . . . that excels all; . . . , who has established giving birth in joy. Mother Nintud, Nintud, has placed upon his head the . . . that excels all; Nintud, who has established giving birth in joy.

19 *Sa-gida*.

20–35 Forceful lady with the nobility of heaven and earth, . . . born . . . Nintud! . . . , which the prince has put in the Abzu, she who has contended with the Great Mountain Enlil! Nintud, forceful lady with the nobility of heaven and earth, . . . born . . . Nintud! . . . , which the prince has put in the Abzu, she who has contended with the Great Mountain Enlil! The cow cries aloud to her about her calf and, because of her distress, mother Nintud looks for him, mother Nintud, the august lady of Keš, she who has contended with the Great Mountain Enlil. The cow cries aloud to her about her calf and, because of her distress, Nintud—mother Nintud—looks for him, mother Nintud, the august lady of Keš, she who has contended with the Great Mountain Enlil.

36–43 When mother Nintud sat upon the throne-dais on the holy seat of joy, the seat from which she has made everything numerous, it was then that the highest divine powers, which are golden, the glory of the numerous people—the *en* priesthood and the kingship—were created for Enlil. When Nintud, mother Nintud, sat upon the throne-dais on the seat of joy, the seat from which she has made everything numerous, it was then that the highest divine powers, which are golden, the glory of the numerous people—the *en* priesthood and the kingship—were created for Enlil.

44 *Sa-g̃ara.*

45 A *tigi* of Nintud.

Inana and Šu-kale-tuda

This mythical narrative relates an encounter between the great goddess Inana and a humble gardener's boy whose name, Šu-kale-tuda, appears to mean 'Spotty'. (He is the precursor of one of the goddess's lovers whose inhumane treatment by her is the subject of Gilgameš's taunting in Tablet VI of the Babylonian *Epic of Gilgameš*.) Although it may be possible to interpret the narrative on one level as a political allegory recalling the conquests of the mountain areas lying to the east of Mesopotamia by the kings of the Agade dynasty, the simplest and most direct reading of it describes a rural agricultural landscape in Sumer—a vegetable garden. The repeated refrain 'Now, what did one say to another? What further did one add to the other in detail?' creates an informal style evoking an orally transmitted story.

A short subplot (42–90) seems to describe how the wise god Enki teaches a raven to do some gardening tasks, including planting a vegetable like a leek which turns into the first palm tree. Šu-kale-tuda is working in the garden, but seems not to be a very efficient gardener's boy, since none of his vegetable plots thrive, and he has the habit of pulling up the plants which he has sown earlier. A sudden dust-storm blows up, during which he catches sight of the goddess Inana. In the hot sun, the exhausted goddess looks for somewhere to rest, and lights on a corner of Šu-kale-tuda's vegetable garden. As she lies sleeping under a shady Euphrates poplar, Šu-kale-tuda has sex with her. He goes back to work afterwards; but by the following sunrise the goddess is fully aware of exactly what has happened, and is enraged at the indignity of her situation. She sends a plague of blood on the Land, swearing to find the man who has taken advantage of her.

Šu-kale-tuda tells his father the whole story. His father advises him that in the country he will be easily tracked down and identified; the best thing will be to go to the nearby town, where he can quickly become invisible among the crowds. A second plague follows, and a third in which the highways of the Land are blocked.

Finally, Inana tracks down the gardener's boy and threatens him mercilessly with death. But she tells him that at least his name will be remembered in the songs sung about him, in palaces and in the countryside by shepherds.

Translation

1–8 The mistress who, having all the great divine powers, deserves the throne-dais; Inana, who, having all the great divine powers, occupies a holy throne-dais; Inana, who stands in E-ana as a source of wonder—once, the young woman went up into the mountains, holy Inana went up into the mountains. To detect falsehood and justice, to inspect the Land closely, to identify the criminal against the just, she went up into the mountains.

9–10 Now, what did one say to another? What further did one add to the other in detail?

11–12 My lady stands among wild bulls at the foot of the mountains, she possesses fully the divine powers. Inana stands among stags in the mountain tops, she possesses fully the divine powers.

13–14 Now, what did one say to another? What further did one add to the other in detail?

15–20 Then the . . . left heaven, left the earth and climbed up into the mountains. Inana left heaven, left the earth and climbed up into the mountains. She left E-ana in Unug and climbed up into the mountains. She left the Giguna in Zabalam and climbed up into the mountains. As she had gone up from E-ana, . . . ĝipar shrine . . . . Inana . . . her cloak . . . and climbed up into the mountains.

21–2 Now, what did one say to another? What further did one add to the other in detail?

23–39 (15 lines missing or fragmentary) After . . . had tired . . . with questions and searching, may . . . come alone (?) to the back-room of my shrine.

40–1 Now, what did one say to another? What further did one add to the other in detail?

42–56 (*5 lines missing or fragmentary*) 'He will . . . its feet,' he (Enki) says. Full of wisdom he adds the following words: 'Raven, I shall give you instructions. Pay attention to my instructions. Raven, in the shrine I shall give you instructions. Pay attention to my instructions. First, chop up (?) and chew (?) the kohl for the incantation priests of Eridug with the oil and water which are to be found in a lapis lazuli bowl and are placed in the back-room of the shrine. Then plant them in a trench for leeks in a vegetable plot; then you should pull out (?) . . . .'

57–8 Now, what did one say to another? What further did one add to the other in detail?

59–71 The raven paid exact attention to the instructions of his master. It chopped up (?) and chewed (?) the kohl for the incantation priests of Eridug with the oil and water which were to be found in a lapis lazuli bowl and were placed in the back-room of the shrine. It planted them in a trench for leeks in a vegetable plot; then it pulled out (?) . . . . A plant growing in a plot like leeks, an oddity standing up° like a leek stalk—who had ever seen such a thing before? (*1 line unclear*) That a bird like the raven, performing the work of man, should make the counterweight blocks of the shadouf bump up and settle down; that it should make the counterweight blocks of the shadouf bump down and rise up—who had ever seen such a thing before?

72–88 Then the raven rose up from this oddity, and climbed up it—a date palm!—with a harness. It rubbed off the kohl (?) . . . which it had stuffed into its beak onto the pistils (?). . . . just as with a date palm, which . . . , a tree growing forever—who has ever seen such a thing before? Its scaly leaves surround its palmheart. Its dried palm-fronds serve as weaving material. Its shoots are like a surveyor's gleaming line; they are fit for the king's fields. Its (?) branches are used in the king's palace for cleaning. Its dates, which are piled up near purified barley, are fit for the temples of the great gods. That a bird like the raven, performing the work of man, makes the counterweight blocks of the shadouf bump up and settle down; that it makes the counter-weight blocks of the shadouf bump down and rise up—who had ever seen such a thing before? At his master's command, the raven stepped into the Abzu.

89–90 Now, what did one say to another? What further did one add to the other in detail?

91–111 ... Šu-kale-tuda was his name. ..., a son (?) of Igi-sigsig, the ..., was to water garden plots and build the installation for a well among the plants, but not a single plant remained there, not even one: he had pulled them out by their roots and destroyed them. Then what did the storm-wind bring? It blew the dust of the mountains into his eyes. When he tried to wipe the corner of his eyes with his hand, he got some of it out, but was not able to get all of it out. He raised his eyes to the lower land and saw the exalted gods of the land where the sun rises. He raised his eyes to the highlands and saw the exalted gods of the land where the sun sets. He saw a solitary ghost. He recognized a solitary god by her appearance. He saw someone who possesses fully the divine powers. He was looking at someone whose destiny was decided by the gods. In that plot—had he not approached it five or ten times before?—there stood a single shady tree at that place. The shady tree was a Euphrates poplar with broad shade. Its shade was not diminished in the morning, and it did not change either at midday or in the evening.

112–28 Once, after my lady had gone around the heavens, after she had gone around the earth, after Inana had gone around the heavens, after she had gone around the earth, after she had gone around Elam and Subir, after she had gone around the intertwined horizon of heaven, the mistress became so tired that when she arrived there she lay down by its roots. Šu-kale-tuda noticed her from beside his plot. Inana ... the loincloth (?) of the seven divine powers over her genitals .... the girdle of the seven divine powers over her genitals .... with the shepherd Ama-ušumgal-ana .... over her holy genitals .... Šu-kale-tuda undid the loincloth (?) of seven divine powers and got her to lie down in her resting place. He had sex with her and kissed her there. After he had sex with her and kissed her, he went back to beside his plot. When day had broken and Utu had risen, the woman inspected herself closely, holy Inana inspected herself closely.

129–36 Then the woman was considering what should be destroyed because of her genitals; Inana was considering what should be done because of her genitals. She filled the wells of the Land with blood, so it was blood that the irrigated orchards of the Land yielded, it was blood that the slave who went to collect firewood drank, it was blood that the slavegirl who went out to draw water drew, and it was blood that

the black-headed people drank. No one knew when this would end.
She said: 'I will search everywhere for the man who had sex with me.'
But nowhere in all the lands could she find the man who had sex with
her.

137-8 Now, what did one say to another? What further did one add to the
other in detail?

FIG. 25. 'He had sex with her'—an erotic scene
on an Old Babylonian terracotta plaque

139-40 The boy went home to his father and spoke to him; Šu-kale-tuda
went home to his father and spoke to him:

141-59 'My father, I was to water garden plots and build the installation for
a well among the plants, but not a single plant remained there, not
even one: I had pulled them out by their roots and destroyed them.
Then what did the storm-wind bring? It blew the dust of the mountains into my eyes. When I tried to wipe the corner of my eyes with
my hand, I got some of it out, but was not able to get all of it out. I
raised my eyes to the lower land, and saw the high gods of the land
where the sun rises. I raised my eyes to the highlands, and saw the
exalted gods of the land where the sun sets. I saw a solitary ghost. I
recognized a solitary god by her appearance. I saw someone who
possesses fully the divine powers. I was looking at someone whose
destiny was decided by the gods. In that plot—had I not approached
it five or ten° times before?—there stood a single shady tree at that

place. The shady tree was a Euphrates poplar with broad shade. Its shade was not diminished in the morning, and it did not change either at midday or in the evening.

160–7 'Once, after my lady had gone around the heavens, after she had gone around the earth, after Inana had gone around the heavens, after she had gone around the earth, after she had gone around Elam and Subir, after she had gone around the intertwined horizon of heaven, the mistress became so tired that when she arrived there she lay down by its roots. I noticed her from beside my plot. I had sex with her and kissed her there. Then I went back to beside my plot.

168–76 'Then the woman was considering what should be destroyed because of her genitals; Inana was considering what should be done because of her genitals. She filled the wells of the Land with blood, so it was blood that the irrigated orchards of the Land yielded, it was blood that the slave who went to collect firewood drank, it was blood that the slavegirl who went out to draw water drew, and it was blood that the black-headed people drank. No one knew when this would end. She said: "I will search everywhere for the man who had sex with me." But nowhere could she find the man who had sex with her.'

177–81 His father replied to the boy; his father replied to Šu-kale-tuda: 'My son, you should join the city-dwellers, your brothers°. Go at once to the black-headed people, your brothers! Then this woman will not find you among the mountains.'

182–4 He joined the city-dwellers, his brothers all together. He went at once to the black-headed people, his brothers, and the woman did not find him among the mountains.

185–93 Then the woman was considering a second time what should be destroyed because of her genitals; Inana was considering what should be done because of her genitals. She mounted on a cloud, took (?) her seat there and . . . . The south wind and a fearsome storm flood went before her. The *pilipili* priest and a dust storm followed her. Abba-šušu, Inim-kur-dugdug, . . . adviser . . . . Seven times seven helpers (?) stood beside her in the high desert. She said: 'I will search everywhere for the man who had sex with me.' But nowhere could she find the man who had sex with her.

194–5 The boy went home to his father and spoke to him; Šu-kale-tuda went home to his father and spoke to him:

196–205 'My father, the woman of whom I spoke to you, this woman was considering a second time what should be destroyed because of her genitals; Inana was considering what should be done because of her genitals. She mounted on a cloud, took (?) her seat there and . . . . The south wind and a fearsome storm flood went before her. The *pilipili* priest and a dust storm followed her. Abba-šušu, Inim-kur-dugdug, . . . adviser . . . . Seven times seven helpers (?) stood beside her in the high desert. She said: "I will search everywhere for the man who had sex with me." But nowhere could she find the man who had sex with her.'

206–10 His father replied to the boy; his father replied to Šu-kale-tuda: 'My son, you should join the city-dwellers, your brothers. Go at once to the black-headed people, your brothers! Then this woman will not find you among the mountains.'

211–13 He joined the city-dwellers, his brothers all together. He went at once to the black-headed people, his brothers, and the woman did not find him among the mountains.

214–20 Then the woman was considering a third time what should be destroyed because of her genitals; Inana was considering what should be done because of her genitals. She took a single . . . in her hand. She blocked the highways of the Land with it. Because of her, the black-headed people . . . . She said: 'I will search everywhere for the man who had sex with me.' But nowhere could she find the man who had sex with her.

221–2 The boy went home to his father and spoke to him; Šu-kale-tuda went home to his father and spoke to him:

223–30 'My father, the woman of whom I spoke to you, this woman was considering a third time what should be destroyed because of her genitals; Inana was considering what should be done because of her genitals. She took a single . . . in her hand. She blocked the highways of the Land with it. Because of her, the black-headed people . . . . She said: "I will search everywhere for the man who had sex with me." But nowhere could she find the man who had sex with her.'

231–5 His father replied to the boy; his father replied to Šu-kale-tuda: 'My son, you should join the city-dwellers, your brothers. Go at once to the black-headed people, your brothers! Then this woman will not find you among the mountains.'

236–8 He joined the city-dwellers, his brothers all together. He went at once to the black-headed people, his brothers, and the woman did not find him among the mountains.

239–44 When day had broken and Utu had risen, the woman inspected herself closely, holy Inana inspected herself closely. 'Ah, who will compensate me? Ah, who will pay (?) for what happened to me? Should it not be the concern of my own father, Enki?'

245-9 Holy Inana directed her steps to the Abzu of Eridug and, because of this, prostrated herself on the ground before him and stretched out her hands to him. 'Father Enki, I should be compensated! What's more, someone should pay (?)° for what happened to me! I shall only re-enter my shrine E-ana satisfied after you have handed over that man to me from the Abzu.'

250 Enki said 'All right!' to her. He said 'So be it!' to her.

251-5 With that holy Inana went out from the Abzu of Eridug. She stretched herself like a rainbow across the sky and thereby reached as far as the earth. She let the south wind pass across, she let the north wind pass across. From fear,° Šu-kale-tuda tried to make himself as tiny as possible, but the woman had found him among the mountains.

256-61 Holy Inana now spoke to Šu-kale-tuda: 'How...?...dog...!... ass...!...pig...!' (1 line missing)

262-81 Šu-kale-tuda replied to holy Inana: 'My lady (?), I was to water garden plots and build the installation for a well among the plants, but not a single plant remained there, not even one: I had pulled them out by their roots and destroyed them. Then what did the storm-wind bring? It blew the dust of the mountains into my eyes. When I tried to wipe the corner of my eyes with my hand, I got some of it out, but was not able to get all of it out. I raised my eyes to the lower land, and saw the exalted gods of the land where the sun rises. I raised my eyes to the highlands, and saw the exalted gods of the land where the sun sets. I saw a solitary ghost. I recognized a solitary god by her appearance. I saw someone who possesses fully the divine powers. I was looking at someone whose destiny was decided by the gods. In that plot—had I not approached it three or six hundred times before?—there stood a single shady tree at that place. The shady tree was a Euphrates poplar with broad shade. Its shade was not diminished in the morning, and it did not change either at midday or in the evening.

282-9 'Once, after my lady had gone around the heavens, after she had gone around the earth, after Inana had gone around the heavens, after she had gone around the earth, after she had gone around Elam and Subir, after she had gone around the intertwined horizon of heaven, the mistress became so tired that when she arrived there she lay down by its roots. I noticed her from beside my plot. I had sex with her and kissed her there. Then I went back to beside my plot.'

290–5 When he had spoken thus to her, . . . hit . . . . added (?) . . . . changed (?) him . . . . She (?) determined his destiny . . . , holy Inana spoke to Šu-kale-tuda:

296–306 'So! You shall die! What is that to me? Your name, however, shall not be forgotten. Your name shall exist in songs and make the songs sweet. A young singer shall perform them most pleasingly in the king's palace. A shepherd shall sing them sweetly as he tumbles his butter churn. A shepherd boy shall carry your name to where he grazes the sheep. The palace of the desert shall be your home.' (5 *lines unclear*)

307–10 Šu-kale-tuda . . . (*1 line missing*) Because . . . destiny was determined, praise be to . . . Inana!

Notes

59–71   Instead of 'standing up' 1 MS has: 'sticking up'.
141–59   Instead of 'five or ten' 1 MS has: 'three or six hundred'.
177–81   Instead of 'your brothers' 1 MS has: 'who are your brothers'.
245–9   Instead of 'pay (?)' 1 MS has: 'make up'.
251–5   After 'From fear,' 1 MS adds: 'solitary'.

A love song for Išme-Dagan

This purports to be a song of the goddess Inana expressing her love for the youthful god Dumuzid, portrayed as a herdsman. The rustic details are sketched, as if she were visiting the cattle-pen and sheepfold: the bleating of the sheep and the lowing of the cattle, and the pleasant noise made by the butter churn as it is rocked. However, a prayer for long life for Išme-Dagan, king of Isin, suggests that the social context of this pastoral idyll may in fact be the royal court, and places the song against the background of rituals in which the king was considered himself to be the spouse of the goddess Inana.

A slightly longer version of this composition exists in which Dumuzid himself, not Išme-Dagan, is the male protagonist (*A balbale to Inana and Dumuzid*, ETCSL 4.08.a; see also *Inana and Išme-Dagan*, Group B).

Translation

1–8 Lady, going to the sweet-voiced cows and gentle-voiced calves in the cattle-pen, young woman, when you arrive there, Inana, may the churn sound! May the churn of your spouse sound, Inana, may the churn sound! May the churn of Dumuzid sound, Inana, may the churn sound!

9–14 The rocking of the churn will sing (?) for you, Inana, may it thus make you joyous! The good shepherd, the man of sweet songs, will loudly (?) sing songs for you; lady, with all the sweetest things, Inana, may he make your heart joyous!

15–20 Lady, when you enter the cattle-pen, Inana, the cattle-pen indeed will rejoice over you. Mistress, when you enter the sheepfold, Inana, the sheepfold indeed will rejoice over you. When you enter the feeding-pen, healthy ewes will spread out their wool for you.

21–4 May the holy sheepfold provide (?) you with butter abundantly, may the cattle-pen produce butter and cream for you! May abundance endure in the sheepfold, may the days of Išme-Dagan be numerous!

25–6 May my spouse, a ewe cherishing its lamb, be praised with sweet admiration!

A *balbale* to Inana and Dumuzid

The term *balbale* was used for a variety of short song-like compositions, though the exact criteria for its use are not clear. It has been proposed that it might refer to conversational or other exchanges of speech, and this would certainly make good sense in this particular case. This song has considerable similarity in tone to various strophic folk-songs known from other cultures which refer to their subject matter only obliquely. Interest is built up through repetitious lines, and the true topic of the dialogue revealed at the end.

The song forms a dialogue between the goddess Inana and her brother, the sun-god Utu. It eventually transpires that the real topic of their exchange is Inana's lover, the shepherd-god Dumuzid, here referred to by his name Ama-ušumgal-ana. As in many such songs, Inana is presented as a shy but infatuated young girl. The sequence of the verses follows the whole sequence of the linen-making process, from flax growing as a plant, through harvesting, retting, spinning, twining, warping (i.e. setting up the threads on a loom), weaving, and bleaching. Finally the purpose of the linen sheets—to cover the bridal bed—is revealed.

Translation

1–11 The brother speaks gently to his sister, Utu speaks gently to his sister, he speaks tenderly to holy Inana: 'Young lady, the flax in the garden beds is full of loveliness, Inana, the flax in the garden beds is full of loveliness, like the barley in the furrows, overflowing with loveliness and delight. Sister°, you took a fancy to a grand length of linen; Inana, you took a fancy to a grand length of linen. I will dig up the plants for you and give them to you. Young lady°, I will bring you flax from the garden beds. Inana, I will bring you flax from the garden beds.'

12–14 'Brother°, when you have brought me flax from the garden beds, who will ret it for me? Who will ret it for me? Who will ret that flax for me?'

15–16 'My sister, I will bring it to you already retted! Inana, I will bring it to you already retted!'

17–19 'Brother°, when you have brought it to me already retted, who will spin it for me? Who will spin it for me? Who will spin that flax for me?'

20–1 'My sister, I will bring it to you already spun! Inana, I will bring it to you already spun!'

22–4 'Brother°, when you have brought it to me already spun, who will twine it for me? Who will twine it for me? Who will twine that flax for me?'

25–6 'My sister, I will bring it to you already twined! Inana, I will bring it to you already twined!'

27–9 'Brother, when you have brought it to me already twined, who will warp it for me? Who will warp it for me? Who will warp that flax for me?'

30–1 'My sister, I will bring it to you already warped! Inana, I will bring it to you already warped!'

32–4 'Brother, when you have brought it to me already warped, who will weave for me? Who will weave for me? Who will weave that flax for me?'

35–6 'My sister, I will bring it to you already woven! Inana, I will bring it to you already woven!'

37–9 'Brother, when you have brought it to me already woven, who will bleach it for me? Who will bleach it for me? Who will bleach that linen for me?'

40–1 'My sister, I will bring it to you already bleached! Inana, I will bring it to you already bleached!'

42–4 'Brother, when you have brought it to me already bleached, who will lie down on it with me? Who will lie down on it with me? Who will lie down on that linen with me?'

45–50 'There shall lie down with you, there shall lie down with you, there shall lie down with you your bridegroom! Ama-ušumgal-ana shall lie down with you, the companion of Enlil shall lie down with you, the issue of a noble womb shall lie down with you, the offspring of a ruler shall lie down with you.'

Fig. 26. 'He is the man of my heart!'—a loving couple on an Old Babylonian terracotta plaque

51–6 'Is it true?—He is the man of my heart! He is the man of my heart! Brother, he is the man who has spoken to my heart! He does no hoeing, yet heaps up piles of grain; he delivers grain regularly to the storehouse, a farmer who has numerous piles of grain°; a shepherd whose sheep are heavy (?) with wool.'

57 A *balbale* of Inana.

Notes

1–11 Instead of 'Sister' 1 MS has: 'Young lady'; instead of 'Young lady' 1 MS has: 'My sister'.

12–14, 17–19, 22–4 Instead of 'Brother' 1 MS has: 'My brother'.

51–6 Instead of 'grain' 1 MS has: 'plentiful grain'.

G. THE NATURAL ORDER

How did the world come to be the way it is and what is our place within it? These difficult questions have plagued and stimulated mankind for millennia and the responses found in Sumerian literature are amongst the world's oldest surviving attempts to tackle them.

A multiplicity of Sumerian creation myths address both the formation of the gods and the construction of the human world. At the beginning of *The debate between Sheep and Grain* we are taken back to a time before agriculture, when the gods dwelt together on the Holy Mound, created by An, the supreme deity. In *Enki and the world order* it is Enki who is the creative force, ordering, naming, and allocating responsibility for different aspects of human endeavour to the various gods. In *Ninurta's exploits* (Group E), on the other hand, Ninurta finds uses for the various defeated stones and invents the agricultural basis of Sumerian society.

The fragmentary *Flood story*, by contrast, is about destruction as much as creation, as the original population is wiped out, save for Zi-ud-sura and his followers. The primeval Flood was a powerful motif in Sumerian literature, dividing the past into antediluvian and historical time (see also *The instructions of Šuruppag*, Group I). At another level, it was a way of coming to terms with the potentially catastrophic inundations from the Tigris and Euphrates rivers every spring caused by the snow melting up in the Taurus mountains at their source.

The landscape of Sumer was an extraordinarily flat alluvial plain. Without careful and labour-intensive water management whole cities could be deluged, or major rivers divert their courses overnight. Canals and irrigation ditches crisscrossed the land, enabling intensive grain agriculture. But herding was equally important to the Sumerian economy, on the field boundaries, fallow land, and uncultivated areas beyond the reach of the watercourses. The tension between the two is expressed in *The debate between Sheep and Grain* (as indeed in *Dumuzid and Enkimdu*, Group B, in which the shepherd and the farmer vie for Inana's love).

In the undrained marshland, where thick banks of reeds could grow two metres high, a rich wild flora and fauna flourished. Reeds and other plant products provided essential construction materials for everything from domestic utensils to houses and boats, while the native birds and fish were also hunted and consumed. *The debate between Bird and Fish* vigorously sets out their more unappetizing features (the smell, the droppings) as well as their benefits to humankind. *The heron and the turtle*, on the other hand, is not in the least concerned with human utility but vividly dramatizes the predatory dangers of nature in the raw. The narrator of *The home of the fish* humorously stresses the comforts of the domestic over the hazards of the wild to lure his prey out of the perilous marshland, alive with ravenous fish-eating birds, and into the safety of the homely fish trap.

Hills and mountains were not a feature of the Sumerian local landscape and were therefore seen as particularly magical and thrilling places. (The marshes by contrast, are a familiar environment, of no special danger to human beings.) The cedar forests of Lebanon are inhabited by a spirit, who turns out to be much less threatening than the hero imagines (*Gilgameš and Ḫuwawa*, Group J), while the Zagros mountains of Iran are initially a frightening place in which to be ill, abandoned, and alone (*Lugalbanda in the mountain cave*, Group A). Rebellions and threats to the calm order of Sumer all stem from the mountain lands too (see for instance *Inana and Ebiḫ*, Group J, *The lament for Sumer and Urim*, Group D, *The cursing of Agade*, Group C). But, in the literary tradition at least, there is always the comfort that the gods of Sumer will prevail and order will return to the Land.

FURTHER READING

Black, J. A., 'The Sumerians in their Landscape', in T. Abusch (ed.), *Riches Hidden in Secret Places: Ancient Near Eastern Studies in Memory of Thorkild Jacobsen* (Eisenbrauns: Winona Lake, Ind., 2002), pp. 41–61.

Kramer, S. N., and Maier, J., *Myths of Enki, the Crafty God* (Oxford University Press: New York/Oxford, 1989).

Reinink, G. J., and Vanstiphout, H. L. J. (eds.), *Dispute Poems and Dialogues in the Ancient and Medieval Near East: Forms and Types of Literary Debates in Semitic and Related Literatures* (Departement Oriëntalistiek: Leuven, 1991) places the Sumerian debate poems at the start of a long tradition in the Middle East.

Veldhuis, N., *Religion, Literature and Scholarship: The Sumerian Composition Nanše and the Birds* (Styx: Leiden, 2004) relates *The home of the fish* and other Sumerian literary works to scribal school exercises.

OTHER COMPOSITIONS ON THIS THEME INCLUDE

Group A The death of Ur-Namma
Group B Dumuzid and Enkimdu
        A hymn to Inana
Group C Šulgi and Ninlil's barge
        The cursing of Agade
Group D The lament for Sumer and Urim
        A *balbale* to Nanna
        The herds of Nanna
Group E Ninurta's exploits
        A *balbale* to Ninurta
Group F Lu-digira's message to his mother
        A love song for Išme-Dagan
Group H An *adab* to Bau for Išme-Dagan
        A *šir-namšub* to Utu
        A *šir-namursaga* to Inana for Iddin-Dagan
Group I The instructions of Šuruppag
        A hymn to Nisaba
Group J A praise poem of Šulgi
        A praise poem of Lipit-Eštar
        The song of the hoe
        Enlil in the E-kur
        The Keš temple hymn

The Flood story

The Sumerian story of the universal Flood is preserved in a fragmentary condition. More than two-thirds of it is missing, and because of breaks on the clay tablet which is the only available source, only five disconnected episodes survive. Although these are not sufficient to reconstruct the entire narrative, it resembles the longer version preserved in the Babylonian poems *Atra-ḥasīs* and the *Epic of Gilgameš*. It also bears a strong similarity to the biblical account.

In the first surviving episode of the Sumerian composition, the gods create mankind—the 'black-headed people'—and herds of animals. In the second surviving segment of the story, kingship is instituted and the first cities are built: Eridug, Bad-tibira, Larag, Zimbir, and Šuruppag in sequence. Agriculture supplemented by irrigation is devised.

In the third segment, the gods have decided to send a Flood to exterminate mankind, although the reason why is not preserved. King Zi-ud-sura, who is to survive the Flood, hears a voice speaking to him through the wall, warning him of the impending Flood which will destroy mankind. In the Babylonian versions of the narrative, this is the voice of Enki, who wishes to forewarn Zi-ud-sura but not to break his oath to the other gods by informing the human directly.

In the fourth segment, the Flood and storms have raged for seven days and nights. The sun-god Utu shines, and Zi-ud-sura drills a hole to look out from the boat in which he has taken refuge from the Flood. The sun's rays shine in, revealing that the Flood has abated. Zi-ud-sura sacrifices oxen and sheep in gratitude. He allows the animals he had sheltered in the boat to disembark. He prostrates himself before the gods An and Enlil, who bestow eternal life on Zi-ud-sura in return for preserving the animals and mankind. Apparently they have changed their minds after sending the Flood. Zi-ud-sura is allowed to settle in the distant land of Dilmun, here a legendary location but in reality identified with the area around Bahrain.

Translation

(*approximately 36 lines missing*)

AI–10 . . . sets up . . . . 'I will . . . the perishing of my mankind; for Nintud, I will stop the annihilation of my creatures, and I will return the people from their dwelling grounds. Let them build many cities so that I can refresh myself in their shade. Let them lay the bricks of many cities in pure places, let them establish places of divination in pure places, and when the fire-quenching . . . is arranged, the divine rites and exalted powers are perfected and the earth is irrigated, I will establish well-being there.'

AII–14 After An, Enlil, Enki, and Ninḫursaǧa had fashioned the black-headed people, they also made animals multiply everywhere, and made herds of four-legged animals exist on the plains, as is befitting.

(*approximately 32 lines missing*)

BI–3 (*too fragmentary for translation*)

B4–5 'I will oversee their labour. Let . . . the builder of the Land, dig a solid foundation.'

B6–18 After the . . . of kingship had descended from heaven, after the exalted crown and throne of kingship had descended from heaven, the divine rites and the exalted powers were perfected, the bricks of the cities were laid in holy places, their names were announced and the . . . were distributed. The first of the cities, Eridug, was given to Nudimmud the leader. The second, Bad-tibira, was given to the Mistress. The third, Larag, was given to Pabilsaĝ. The fourth, Zimbir, was given to hero Utu. The fifth, Šuruppag, was given to Sud. And after the names of these cities had been announced and the . . . had been distributed, the river . . . , . . . was watered, and with the cleansing of the small canals . . . were established. (*approximately 34 lines missing*)

C1–17 . . . seat in heaven. . . . flood. . . . mankind. So he made . . . . Then Nintud . . . . Holy Inana made a lament for its people. Enki took counsel with himself. An, Enlil, Enki and Ninḫursaĝa made all the gods of heaven and earth take an oath by invoking An and Enlil. In those days Zi-ud-sura the king, the *gudug* priest, ... He fashioned . . . . The humble, committed, reverent . . . . Day by day, standing constantly at . . . . Something that was not a dream appeared, conversation . . . , . . . taking an oath by invoking heaven and earth. In the Ki-ur, the gods . . . a wall.

C18–28 Zi-ud-sura, standing at its side, heard: 'Side-wall standing at my left side, ... Side-wall, I will speak words to you; take heed of my words, pay attention to my instructions. A flood will sweep over the . . . in all the . . . . A decision that the seed of mankind is to be destroyed has been made. The verdict, the word of the divine assembly, cannot be revoked. The order announced by An and Enlil cannot be overturned. Their kingship, their term has been cut off; their heart should be rested about this. Now . . . . What . . . .' (*approximately 38 lines missing*)

D1–11 All the windstorms and gales arose together, and the flood swept over the . . . . After the flood had swept over the land, and waves and windstorms had rocked the huge boat for seven days and seven nights, Utu the sun-god came out, illuminating heaven and earth. Zi-ud-sura could drill an opening in the huge boat and hero Utu entered the huge boat with his rays. Zi-ud-sura the king prostrated himself before Utu. The king sacrificed oxen and offered innumerable sheep.

D12–17 (*too fragmentary for translation; approximately 33 lines missing*)

E1–2 'They have made you swear by heaven and earth, ... An and Enlil have made you swear by heaven and earth, ...'

E3–11 More and more animals disembarked onto the earth. Zi-ud-sura the king prostrated himself before An and Enlil. An and Enlil treated Zi-ud-sura kindly . . . , they granted him life like a god, they brought down to him eternal life. At that time, because of preserving the animals and the seed of mankind, they settled Zi-ud-sura the king in an overseas country, in the land Dilmun, where the sun rises.

E12 'You . . . .' (*approximately 39 lines missing*)

Enki and the world order

This high-flown hymn of praise to the god Enki identifies him very closely with every aspect of how the world is organized. In the first section Enki's importance among the Anuna gods (the gods of heaven) is emphasized, and it is made clear that he derives his power directly from the god Enlil, the senior deity of the pantheon. This entitles Enki in turn to distribute powers and privileges to other gods and to mankind. In two parallel sections Enki praises himself and is praised by the Anuna (61–139).

The cult of Eridug, Enki's city, is initiated, while the god travels on his ceremonial barge, accompanied by his boatmen and surrounded by his various creatures (140–87). Enki praises and assigns a destiny to the land of Sumer and the city of Urim, then in turn to the distant lands of Meluḫa (the Indus Valley), Dilmun (the area of Bahrain), and finally to the Mardu (the nomadic peoples) (188–249).

In the second half of the hymn, Enki assigns areas of responsibility to various deities covering the whole of the natural order. At this point, in a dramatic turn, the goddess Inana intervenes to complain that no functions have been assigned to her. She complains that Aruru has been assigned midwifery (395–402), Ninisina will have a sacred role (403–5), the goddess Ninmug has been assigned metalworking (406–11), and Nisaba the scribal art (412–17). Nanše is to look after the birds and fish (418–21). But Enki has not forgotten Inana, who is assigned dual roles as a sexual goddess and a deity of warfare (424 ff.).

Translation

1–16 Grandiloquent lord of heaven and earth, self-reliant, father Enki, engendered by a bull, begotten by a wild bull, cherished by Enlil the Great Mountain, beloved by holy An, king, *mes* tree planted in the Abzu, rising over all lands; great dragon who stands in Eridug, whose shadow covers heaven and earth, a grove of vines extending over the Land, Enki, lord of plenty of the Anuna gods, Nudimmud, mighty one of the E-kur, strong one of heaven and earth! Your great house is founded in the Abzu, the great mooring-post of heaven and earth. Enki, from whom a single glance is enough to unsettle the heart of the mountains; wherever bison are born, where stags are born, where ibex are born, where wild goats are born, in meadows . . . , in hollows in the heart of the hills, in green . . . unvisited by man, you have fixed your gaze on the heart of the Land like a *ḫalḫal* reed.

17–31 Counting the days and putting the months in their houses, so as to complete the years and to submit the completed years to the assembly for a decision, taking decisions to regularize the days: father Enki, you are the king of the assembled people. You have only to open your mouth for everything to multiply and for plenty to be established. Your branches . . . green with their fruit . . . , . . . do honour to the gods. . . . in its forests is like a fleecy garment. Good sheep and good lambs do honour to . . . . When . . . the prepared fields, . . . will accumulate stockpiles and stacks. . . . there is oil, there is milk, produced by the sheepfold and cattle-pen. The shepherd sweetly sings his rustic song, the cowherd spends the day rocking his churns. Their products would do honour to the late lunches in the gods' great dining hall.

32–7 Your word fills the young man's heart with vigour, so that like a thick-horned bull he butts about in the courtyard. Your word bestows loveliness on the young woman's head, so that the people in their settled cities gaze at her in wonder. (*2 lines unclear*)

38–49 Enlil, the Great Mountain, has commissioned you to gladden the hearts of lords and rulers and wish them well. Enki, lord of prosperity, lord of wisdom, lord, the beloved of An, the ornament of Eridug, who establishes commands and decisions, who well understands the decreeing of fates: you close up the days . . . , and make the months enter their houses. You bring down . . . , you have reached their number. You make the people dwell in their dwelling places . . . , you make them follow their herdsman . . . . (*2 lines unclear*)

50–1 You turn weapons away from their houses . . . , you make the people safe in their dwellings . . . .

52–60 When father Enki goes forth to the inseminated people, good seed will come forth. When Nudimmud goes forth to the good pregnant ewes, good lambs will be born; when he goes forth to the fecund cows, good calves will be born; when he goes forth to the good pregnant goats, good kids will be born. If you go forth to the cultivated fields, to the good germinating fields, stockpiles and stacks can be accumulated on the high plain. If you go forth to the parched areas of the Land, (*2 lines missing or unclear*)

61–80 Enki, the king of the Abzu, justly praises himself in his majesty: 'My father, the king of heaven and earth, made me famous in heaven and earth. My elder brother, the king of all the lands, gathered up all the divine powers and placed them in my hand. I brought the arts and crafts from the E-kur, the house of Enlil, to my Abzu in Eridug. I am the good semen, begotten by a wild bull, I am the first-born of An. I am a great storm rising over the great earth, I am the great lord of the Land. I am the principal among all rulers, the father of all the foreign lands. I am the big brother of the gods, I bring prosperity to perfection. I am the seal-keeper of heaven and earth. I am the wisdom and understanding of all the foreign lands. With An the king, on An's dais, I oversee justice. With Enlil, looking out over the lands, I decree good destinies. He has placed in my hands the decreeing of fates in the "Place where the sun rises". I am cherished by Nintud. I am named with a good name by Ninḫursaḡa. I am the leader of the Anuna gods. I was born as the first-born son of holy An.'

81–3 After the lord had proclaimed his greatness, after the great prince had eulogized himself, the Anuna gods stood there in prayer and supplication:

84–5 'Praise be to Enki, the much-praised lord who controls all the arts and crafts, who takes decisions!'

86–8 In a state of high delight Enki, the king of the Abzu, again justly praises himself in his majesty: 'I am the lord, I am one whose word is reliable, I am one who excels in everything.

89–99 'At my command, sheepfolds have been built, cattle-pens have been fenced off. When I approach heaven, a rain of abundance rains from heaven. When I approach earth, there is a high carp-flood. When I approach the green meadows, at my word stockpiles and stacks are accumulated. I have built my house, a shrine, in a pure place, and named it with a good name. I have built my Abzu, a shrine, in . . . , and decreed a good fate for it. The shade of my house extends over the . . . pool. By my house the *suḫur* carp dart among the honey plants, and the *eštub* carp wave their tails among the small *gizi* reeds. The small birds chirp in their nests.

FIG. 27. 'I am Enki! They stand before me, praising me'—Enki, his two-faced minister Isimud, and a worshipper on an Old Akkadian cylinder seal

100–22 'The lords . . . to me. I am Enki! They stand before me, praising me. The *abgal* priests and *abrig* officials who . . . stand before me . . . distant days. The *enkum* and *ninkum* priests organize . . . . They purify the river for me, they . . . the interior of the shrine for me. In my Abzu, sacred songs and incantations resound for me. My barge Crown, the Stag of the Abzu, transports me there most delightfully. It glides swiftly for me through the great marshes to wherever I have decided, it is obedient to me. The stroke-callers make the oars pull in perfect unison. They sing for me pleasant songs, creating a cheerful mood on the river. Niĝir-sig, the captain of my barge, holds the golden sceptre for me. I am Enki! He is in command of my boat Stag of the Abzu. I am the lord! I will travel! I am Enki! I will go forth into my Land! I, the lord who determines the fates, . . . , (4 lines unclear)

123–30 'I will admire its green cedars. Let the lands of Meluḫa, Magan, and Dilmun look upon me, upon Enki. Let the Dilmun boats be loaded (?) with timber. Let the Magan boats be loaded sky-high. Let the *magilum* barges of Meluḫa transport gold and silver and bring them to Nibru for Enlil, king of all the lands.'

131–3 He presented animals to those who have no city, to those who have no houses, to the Mardu nomads.

134–9 The Anuna gods address affectionately the great prince who has travelled in his Land: 'Lord who rides upon the great powers, the pure powers, who controls the great powers, the numberless powers, foremost in all the breadth of heaven and earth; who received the supreme powers in Eridug, the holy place, the most esteemed place, Enki, lord of heaven and earth—praise!'

140–61 All the lords and rulers, the incantation priests of Eridug, and the linen-clad priests of Sumer perform the purification rites of the Abzu for the great prince who has travelled in his land; for father Enki they stand guard in the holy place, the most esteemed place. They . . . the chambers . . . , they . . . the emplacements, they purify the great shrine of the Abzu . . . . They bring there the tall juniper, the pure plant. They organize the holy . . . in the great music room . . . of Enki. Skilfully they build the main staircase of Eridug on the Good Quay. They prepare the sacred *uzga* shrine, where they utter endless prayers. (*7 lines missing, fragmentary, or unclear*)

162–5 For Enki, . . . squabbling together, and the *suḫurmaš* carp dart among the honey plants, again fighting amongst themselves for the great prince. The *eštub* carp wave their tails among the small *gizi* reeds.

166–81 The lord, the great ruler of the Abzu, issues instructions on board the Stag of the Abzu—the great emblem erected in the Abzu, providing protection, its shade extending over the whole land and refreshing the people, the principal foundation (?), the pole planted in the . . . marsh, rising high over all the foreign lands. The noble captain of the lands, the son of Enlil, holds in his hand the sacred punt-pole, a *mes* tree ornamented in the Abzu which received the supreme powers in Eridug, the holy place, the most esteemed place. The hero proudly lifts his head towards the Abzu. (*6 lines missing or unclear*)

182–7 Sirsir . . . , the boatman of the barge, . . . the boat for the lord. Niĝir-sig, the captain of the barge, holds the holy sceptre for the lord. The fifty *laḫama* deities of the subterranean waters speak affectionately to him. The stroke-callers, like heavenly *gamgam* birds, ...

188–91 The intrepid king, father Enki . . . in the Land. Prosperity was made to burgeon in heaven and on earth for the great prince who travels in the Land. Enki decreed its fate:

192–209 'Sumer, Great Mountain, land of heaven and earth, trailing glory, bestowing powers on the people from sunrise to sunset: your powers are superior powers, untouchable, and your heart is complex and inscrutable. Like heaven itself, your good creative force (?), in which gods too can be born, is beyond reach. Giving birth to kings who put on the good diadem, giving birth to lords who wear the crown on their heads—your lord, the honoured lord, sits with An the king on An's dais. Your king, the Great Mountain, father Enlil, the father of all the lands, has blocked you impenetrably (?) like a cedar tree. The Anuna, the great gods, have taken up dwellings in your midst, and consume their food in your *giguna* shrines with their single trees. Household Sumer, may your sheepfolds be built and your cattle multiply, may your *giguna* shrines touch the skies. May your good temples reach up to heaven. May the Anuna determine the destinies in your midst.'

210–11 Then he proceeded to the sanctuary of Urim. Enki, lord of the Abzu, decreed its fate:

212–18 'City which possesses all that is fitting, bathed by water! Sturdy bull, altar of abundance that strides across the mountains, rising like the hills, forest of *ḫašur* cypresses with broad shade, self-confident! May your perfect powers be well directed. The Great Mountain Enlil has pronounced your name great in heaven and on earth. City whose fate Enki has decreed, sanctuary of Urim, you shall rise high to heaven!'

219–20 Then he proceeded to the land of Meluḫa. Enki, lord of the Abzu, decreed its fate:

221–37 'Black land, may your trees be great trees, may your forests be forests of highland *mes* trees! Chairs made from them will grace royal palaces! May your reeds be great reeds, may they . . . ! Heroes shall . . . them on the battlefield as weapons! May your bulls be great bulls, may they be bulls of the mountains! May their bellowing be the bellowing of wild bulls of the mountains! The great powers of the gods shall be made perfect for you! May the francolins of the mountains wear cornelian beards! May your birds all be peacocks! May their cries grace royal palaces! May all your silver be gold! May all your copper be tin-bronze! Land, may all you possess be plentiful! May your people . . . ! May your men go forth like bulls against their fellow men!' (*2 lines unclear*)

238–47 He cleansed and purified the land of Dilmun. He placed Ninsikila in charge of it. He gave . . . for the fish spawn, ate its . . . fish, bestowed palms on the cultivated land, ate its dates. . . . Elam and Marḫaši . . . . to devour . . . . The king endowed with strength by Enlil destroyed their houses, demolished (?) their walls. He brought their silver and lapis lazuli, their treasure, to Enlil, king of all the lands, in Nibru.

248–9 Enki presented animals to those who have no city, who have no houses, to the Mardu nomads.

250–66 After he had turned his gaze from there, after father Enki had lifted his eyes across the Euphrates, he stood up full of lust like a rampant bull, lifted his penis, ejaculated and filled the Tigris with flowing water. He was like a wild cow mooing for its young in the wild grass, its scorpion-infested cattle-pen. The Tigris . . . at his side like a rampant bull. By lifting his penis, he brought a bridal gift. The Tigris rejoiced in its heart like a great wild bull, when it was born . . . . It brought water, flowing water indeed: its wine will be sweet. It brought barley, mottled barley indeed: the people will eat it. It filled the E-kur, the house of Enlil, with all sorts of things. Enlil was delighted with Enki, and Nibru was glad. The lord put on the diadem as a sign of lordship, he put on the good crown as a sign of kingship, touching the ground on his left side. Plenty came forth out of the earth for him.

267–73 Enki, the lord of the destinies, Enki, the king of the Abzu, placed in charge of all this him who holds a sceptre in his right hand, him who with glorious mouth submits to verification the devouring force of the Tigris and Euphrates, while prosperity pours forth from the palace like oil—Enbilulu, the inspector of waterways.

274–7 He called the marshes and gave them the various species of carp, he spoke to the reed beds and bestowed on them the old and new growths of reeds. (*2 lines missing*)

278–84 He issued a challenge . . . . Enki placed in charge of all this him from whose net no fish escapes, him from whose trap no living thing escapes, him from whose bird-net no bird escapes, (*1 line unclear*)— . . . , who loves fish.

285–98 The lord established a shrine, a holy shrine, whose interior is elaborately constructed. He established a shrine in the sea, a holy shrine, whose interior is elaborately constructed. The shrine, whose interior is a tangled thread, is beyond understanding. The shrine's emplacement is situated by the constellation the Field, the holy upper shrine's emplacement faces towards the Chariot constellation. Its terrifying awesomeness is a rising wave, its splendour is fearsome. The Anuna gods dare not approach it. . . . to refresh their hearts, the palace rejoices. The Anuna stand by with prayers and supplications. They set up a great altar for Enki in the E-Engur, for the lord . . . . The great prince . . . . the pelican of the sea. (*1 line unclear*)

299–308 He filled the E-kur, the house of Enlil, with goods of all sorts. Enlil was delighted with Enki, and Nibru was glad. Enki placed in charge of all this, over the wide extent of the sea, her who sets sail . . . in the holy shrine, who induces sexual intercourse . . . , who . . . over the

enormous high flood of the subterranean waters, the terrifying
waves, the inundation of the sea . . . , who comes forth from the . . . ,
the mistress of Sirara, . . .—Nanše.

309-17   He called to the rain of the heavens. He . . . as floating clouds. He
made . . . rising at the horizon. He turned the mounds into fields
. . . . Enki placed in charge of all this him who rides on the great
storms, who attacks with lightning bolts, the holy bar which blocks
the entrance to the interior of heaven, the son of An, the canal
inspector of heaven and earth—Iškur, the bringer of plenty, the son
of An.

318-25   He organized ploughs, yokes, and teams. The great prince Enki
bestowed the horned oxen that follow . . . , he opened up the holy
furrows, and made the barley grow on the cultivated fields. Enki
placed in charge of them the lord who wears the diadem, the ornament of the high plain, him of the implements, the farmer of Enlil—
Enkimdu, responsible for ditches and dykes.

326-34   The lord called the cultivated fields, and bestowed on them mottled
barley. Enki made chickpeas, lentils, and . . . grow. He heaped up
into piles the early, mottled, and *innuḫa* varieties of barley. Enki
multiplied the stockpiles and stacks, and with Enlil's help he
enhanced the people's prosperity. Enki placed in charge of all this
her whose head and body are dappled, whose face is covered in syrup,
the mistress who causes sexual intercourse, the power of the Land,
the life of the black-headed—Ezina, the good bread of the whole
world.

335-40   The great prince fixed a string to the hoe, and organized brick
moulds. He penetrated the . . . like precious oil. Enki placed in
charge of them him whose sharp-bladed hoe is a corpse-devouring
snake that . . . , whose brick mould in place is a tidy stack of hulled
grain for the ewes—Kulla, who . . . bricks in the Land.

341-8   He tied down the strings and coordinated them with the foundations, and with the power of the assembly he planned a house and
performed the purification rituals. The great prince put down the
foundations, and laid the bricks. Enki placed in charge of all this him
whose foundations once laid do not sag, whose good houses once
built do not collapse (?), whose vaults reach up into the heart of the
heavens like a rainbow—Mušdama, Enlil's master builder.

349-57   He raised a holy crown over the upland plain. He fastened a lapis
lazuli beard to the high plain, and made it wear a lapis lazuli head-

dress. He made this good place perfect with grasses and herbs in abundance. He multiplied the animals of the high plain to an appropriate degree, he multiplied the ibex and wild goats of the pastures, and made them copulate. Enki placed in charge of them the hero who is the crown of the high plain, who is the king of the countryside, the great lion of the high plain, the muscular, the hefty, the burly strength of Enlil—Šakkan, the king of the hills.

358–67 He built the sheepfolds, carried out their cleaning, made the cattlepens, bestowed on them the best fat and cream, and brought luxury to the gods' dining places. He made the plain, created for grasses and herbs, achieve prosperity. Enki placed in charge of all this the king, the good provider of E-ana, the friend of An, the beloved son-in-law of the youth Suen, the holy spouse of Inana the mistress, the lady of the great powers who allows sexual intercourse in the open squares of Kulaba—Dumuzid-ušumgal-ana, the friend of An.

368–80 He filled the E-kur, the house of Enlil, with possessions. Enlil was delighted with Enki and Nibru was glad. He demarcated borders and fixed boundaries. For the Anuna gods, Enki situated dwellings in cities and disposed agricultural land into fields. Enki placed in charge of the whole of heaven and earth the hero, the bull who comes out of the ḫašur forest bellowing truculently, the youth Utu, the bull standing triumphantly, audaciously, majestically, the father of the Great City, the great herald in the east of holy An, the judge who searches out verdicts for the gods, with a lapis lazuli beard, rising from the horizon into the holy heavens—Utu, the son born of Ningal.

381–6 He picked out the tow from the fibres, and adapted it for rags (?). Enki greatly perfected the task of women. For Enki, the people . . . in suluḫu garments. Enki placed in charge of them the honour of the palace, the dignity of the king—Uttu, the conscientious woman, the silent one.

387–90 Then, alone lacking any functions, the great woman of heaven, Inana, lacking any functions—Inana came in to see her father Enki in his house, weeping to him, and making her complaint to him:

391–4 'Enlil left it in your hands to confirm the functions of the Anuna, the great gods. Why did you treat me, the woman, in an exceptional manner? I am holy Inana—where are my functions?

395–402 'Aruru, Enlil's sister, Nintud, the lady of giving birth, is to get the holy birth-bricks as her prerogative. She is to carry off the lancet for umbilical cords, the special sand and leeks. She is to get the *sila-ğara* bowl° of translucent lapis lazuli. She is to carry off the holy consecrated *ala* vessel. She is to be the midwife of the land! The birthing of kings and lords is to be in her hands.

403–5 'My illustrious sister, holy Ninisina, is to get the jewellery of *šuba* stones. She is to be An's mistress. She is to stand beside An and speak to him whenever she desires.

406–11 'My illustrious sister, holy Ninmug, is to get the golden chisel and the silver burin. She is to carry off her big flint *antasura* blade. She is to be the metal-worker of the Land. The fitting of the good diadem when a king is born and the crowning with the crown when a lord is born are to be in her hands.

412–17 'My illustrious sister, holy Nisaba, is to get the measuring-reed. The lapis lazuli measuring tape is to hang over her arm. She is to proclaim all the great powers. She is to demarcate boundaries and mark borders. She is to be the scribe of the Land. The planning of the gods' meals is to be in her hands.

418–21 'Nanše, the august lady, who rests her feet on the holy pelican, is to be the fisheries inspector of the sea. She is to be responsible for accepting delectable fish and delicious birds from there to go to Nibru for her father Enlil.

422–3 'But why did you treat me, the woman, in an exceptional manner? I am holy Inana—where are my functions?'

424–36 Enki answered his daughter, holy Inana: 'How have I disparaged you? Goddess, how have I disparaged you? How can I enhance you? Maiden Inana, how have I disparaged you? How can I enhance you? I made you speak as a woman with pleasant voice. I made you go forth . . . . I covered . . . with a garment. I made you exchange its right side and its left side. I clothed you in garments of women's power. I put women's speech in your mouth. I placed in your hands the spindle and the hairpin. I . . . to you women's adornment. I settled on you the staff and the crook, with the shepherd's stick beside them.

437–44 'Maiden Inana, how have I disparaged you? How can I enhance you? Amongst the ominous occurrences in the hurly-burly of battle, I shall make you speak vivifying words; and in its midst, although you are not an *arabu* bird°, I shall make you speak ill-omened words also. I made you tangle straight threads; maiden Inana, I made you straighten out tangled threads. I made you put on garments, I made you dress in linen. I made you pick out the tow from the fibres, I

made you spin with the spindle. I made you colour tufted (?) cloth
with coloured threads.

445–50 'Inana, you heap up human heads like piles of dust, you sow heads
like seed. Inana, you destroy what should not be destroyed; you
create what should not be created. You remove the cover from the
šem drum of lamentations, Maiden Inana, while shutting up the *tigi*
drum and *adab* instrument in their homes. You never grow weary
with admirers looking at you. Maiden Inana, you know nothing of
tying the ropes on deep wells.

451–71 'But now, the heart has overflowed, the Land is restored; Enlil's heart
has overflowed, the Land is restored. In his overflowing heart of
mankind, (*4 lines unclear*) . . . lapis lazuli headdress . . . is your
prerogative, . . . is your prerogative, . . . is your prerogative, . . . is your
prerogative.' (*10 lines unclear*)

472 Praise be to Father Enki!

Notes

395–402 'the *sila-g̃ara* bowl': in which to place the afterbirth.
437–44 'an *arabu* bird': a bird of ill omen.

The debate between Sheep and Grain

Formal debates were a popular entertainment at the court of the kings of the
Third Dynasty of Urim. Records survive indicating that payments were
made to the performers who took part. Typically, the contest is between two
natural phenomena, animals, or materials that are significant in human life:
Winter and Summer, Bird and Fish, Sheep and Grain, Tree and Reed, Date
Palm and Tamarisk, Hoe and Plough, Silver and Copper. The debate progresses as each contestant, personified, speaks alternately, often with considerable acrimony. Each tries to persuade the audience that it is more
beneficial to mankind than the other. Consequently, although the debates
give a fascinating insight into Sumerian attitudes to the environment, they
reveal an exclusively human-focused set of assessments. Conventionally one
of the contestants is in due course adjudged the winner by a god or the king.

The debate between Sheep and Grain is of added interest because it begins
with a short ad hoc creation myth (1–42) which portrays a world before sheep
and grain, when the gods lived on the Holy Mound, a mythical location

where heaven and earth were as yet unseparated from each other. Mankind, it seems, lived at the foot of the Mound, and eventually the gods bestowed sheep and grain on them too.

The personifications of Sheep and Grain begin quarrelling after drinking wine and beer. Sheep is useful for its meat, milk, wool, and gut, and its skin can be turned into leather waterskins and sandals. Its oil is used to make perfumes. Grain, of course, produces bread as well as the mash that is used in making beer; and it is also used for feeding—sheep.

The god Enki finally recommends to the god Enlil that Grain should be judged the winner, implying perhaps that mankind could live without domestic animals but not without bread. However, the balance of arguments on each side is in reality fairly equal.

Translation

1–11   When, upon the hill of heaven and earth, An spawned the Anuna gods, since he neither spawned nor created Grain with them, and since in the Land he neither fashioned the yarn of Uttu nor pegged out the loom for Uttu—with no Sheep appearing, there were no numerous lambs, and with no goats, there were no numerous kids, the sheep did not give birth to her twin lambs, and the goat did not give birth to her triplet kids; the Anuna, the great gods, did not even know the names Ezina-Kusu or Sheep.

12–25   There was no *muš* grain of thirty days; there was no *muš* grain of forty days; there was no *muš* grain of fifty days; there was no small grain, grain from the mountains or grain from the holy habitations. There was no cloth to wear; Uttu had not been born—no royal turban was worn; lord Niĝir-sig, the precious lord, had not been born; Šakkan had not gone out into the barren lands. The people of those days did not know about eating bread. They did not know about wearing clothes; they went about with naked limbs in the Land. Like sheep they ate grass with their mouths and drank water from the ditches.

26–36   At that time, at the place of the gods' formation, in their own home, on the Holy Mound, they created Sheep and Grain. Having gathered them in the divine banqueting chamber, the Anuna gods of the Holy Mound partook of the bounty of Sheep and Grain but were not sated; the Anuna gods of the Holy Mound partook of the sweet milk of their holy sheepfold but were not sated. For their own well-being in the holy sheepfold, they gave them to mankind as sustenance.

37–42 At that time Enki spoke to Enlil: 'Father Enlil, now Sheep and Grain have been created on the Holy Mound, let us send them down from the Holy Mound.' Enki and Enlil, having spoken their holy word, sent Sheep and Grain down from the Holy Mound.

43–53 Sheep being fenced in by her sheepfold, they gave her grass and herbs generously. For Grain they made her field and gave her the plough, yoke, and team. Sheep standing in her sheepfold was a shepherd of the sheepfolds brimming with charm. Grain standing in her furrow was a beautiful girl radiating charm; lifting her raised head up from the field she was suffused with the bounty of heaven. Sheep and Grain had a radiant appearance.

54–64 They brought wealth to the assembly. They brought sustenance to the Land. They fulfilled the ordinances of the gods. They filled the store-rooms of the Land with stock. The barns of the Land were heavy with them. When they entered the homes of the poor who crouch in the dust they brought wealth. Both of them, wherever they directed their steps, added to the riches of the household with their weight. Where they stood, they were satisfying; where they settled, they were seemly. They gladdened the heart of An and the heart of Enlil.

65–70 They drank sweet wine, they enjoyed sweet beer. When they had drunk sweet wine and enjoyed sweet beer, they started a quarrel concerning the arable fields, they began a debate in the dining hall.

71–82 Grain called out to Sheep: 'Sister, I am your better; I take precedence over you. I am the glory of the lights of the Land. I grant my power to the saḡursaḡ priest—he fills the palace with awe and people spread his fame to the borders of the Land. I am the gift of the Anuna gods. I am central to all princes. After I have conferred my power on the warrior, when he goes to war he knows no fear, he knows no faltering (?)—I make him leave . . . as if to the playing field.

83–91 'I foster neighbourliness and friendliness. I sort out quarrels started between neighbours. When I come upon a captive youth and give him his destiny, he forgets his despondent heart and I release his fetters and shackles. I am Ezina-Kusu; I am Enlil's daughter. In sheep shacks and milking pens scattered on the high plain, what can you put against me? Answer me what you can reply!'

92–101 Then Sheep answered Grain: 'My sister, whatever are you saying? An, king of the gods, made me descend from the holy place, my most precious place. All the yarns of Uttu, the splendour of kingship, belong to me. Šakkan, king of the mountain, embosses the king's emblems and puts his implements in order. He twists a giant rope against the great peaks of the rebel land. He . . . the sling, the quiver and the longbows.

102–6 'The watch over the elite troops is mine. Sustenance of the workers in the field is mine: the waterskin of cool water and the sandals are mine. Sweet oil, the fragrance of the gods, mixed (?) oil, pressed oil, aromatic oil, cedar oil for offerings are mine.

107–15 'In the gown, my cloth of white wool, the king rejoices on his throne. My body glistens on the flesh of the great gods. After the purification priests, the incantation priests and the bathed priests have dressed themselves in me for my holy lustration, I walk with them to my holy meal. But your harrow, ploughshare, binding, and strap are tools that can be utterly destroyed. What can you put against me? Answer me what you can reply!'

116–22 Again Grain addressed Sheep: 'When the beer dough has been carefully prepared in the oven, and the mash tended in the oven, Ninkasi mixes them for me while your big billy-goats and rams are dispatched for my banquets. On their thick legs they are made to stand separate from my produce.

123–9 'Your shepherd on the high plain eyes my produce enviously; when I am standing in the furrow in the field, my farmer chases away your herdsman with his cudgel. Even when they look out for you, from the open country to the hidden places, your fears are not removed from you: fanged (?) snakes and bandits, the creatures of the desert, want your life on the high plain.

130–42 'Every night your count is made and your tally-stick put into the ground, so your herdsman can tell people how many ewes there are and how many young lambs, and how many goats and how many young kids. When gentle winds blow through the city and strong winds scatter, they build a milking pen for you; but when gentle winds blow through the city and strong winds scatter, I stand up as an equal to Iškur. I am Grain, I am born for the warrior—I do not give up. The churn, the vat on legs (?), the adornments of shepherding, make up your properties. What can you put against me? Answer me what you can reply!'

143–55 Again Sheep answered Grain: 'You, like holy Inana of heaven, love horses. When a banished enemy, a slave from the mountains or a labourer with a poor wife and small children comes, bound with his rope of one cubit°, to the threshing-floor or is taken away from (?) the threshing-floor, when his cudgel pounds your face, pounds your mouth, as a pestle (?) . . . your ears (?) . . . . and you are . . . around by the south wind and the north wind. The mortar . . . . As if it were pumice (?) it makes your body into flour.

156–68 'When you fill the trough the baker's assistant mixes you and throws you on the floor, and the baker's girl flattens you out broadly. You are put into the oven and you are taken out of the oven. When you are put on the table I am before you—you are behind me. Grain, heed yourself! You too, just like me, are meant to be eaten. At the inspection of your essence, why should it be I who come second? Is the miller not evil? What can you put against me? Answer me what you can reply!'

169–79 Then Grain was hurt in her pride, and hastened for the verdict. Grain answered Sheep: 'As for you, Iškur is your master, Šakkan your herdsman, and the dry land your bed. Like fire beaten down (?) in houses and in fields, like small flying birds chased from the door of a house, you are turned into the lame and the weak of the Land. Should I really bow my neck before you? You are distributed into various measuring-containers. When your innards are taken away by the people in the market-place, and when your neck is wrapped with your very own loincloth, one man says to another: "Fill the measuring-container with grain for my ewe!" '

180–91 Then Enki spoke to Enlil: 'Father Enlil, Sheep and Grain should be sisters! They should stand together! Of their threefold metal . . . shall not cease. But of the two, Grain shall be the greater. Let Sheep fall on her knees before Grain. Let her kiss the feet of . . . . From sunrise till sunset, may the name of Grain be praised. People should submit to the yoke of Grain. Whoever has silver, whoever has jewels, whoever has cattle, whoever has sheep shall take a seat at the gate of whoever has grain, and pass his time there.'

192–3 Debate spoken between Sheep and Grain: Sheep is left behind and Grain comes forward—praise be to Father Enki!

Note

143–55 One cubit is equivalent to about half a metre.

The debate between Bird and Fish

Like *The debate between Sheep and Grain*, *The debate between Bird and Fish* also begins with a short creation myth, explaining how the marsh environment characteristic of southern Iraq came into existence. An area of many hundreds of square kilometres, the shallow brackish water extended in broad lagoons and narrow channels running between the immense beds of reeds (growing up to six metres or more in height). Not only was this region of considerable economic importance as a source of fish and game, but it also stimulated the imagination of the ancient Mesopotamians as a locale where fugitives could hide and where secret sexual encounters took place (see *Enlil and Ninlil*, Group C).

This debate is conducted on a highly acrimonious level. Although the various benefits of fish and birds to mankind are discussed by the participants—the personified Fish and Bird—much of their discourse is devoted to insulting each other. Thus Fish does not have a proper body with limbs, and it stinks; while Bird is vain, leaves its droppings everywhere and troubles people with its constant squawking.

A short narrative section in the middle describes how Fish overturns Bird's nest and smashes her eggs. Bird gets her revenge by snatching Fish's spawn from the water. With hostilities raised to this level of tension, the contestants decide to register a formal lawsuit at Eridug, the city of the god Enki who has a special concern for the marsh areas. A formal verdict is finally delivered by king Šulgi, the most illustrious king of the Third Dynasty of Urim, and a role model of just kingship. Despite the arguments on both sides, and perhaps because of Fish's savage attack on Bird's eggs, Bird is adjudged the winner. But in this case, the argument seems to rest as much on the pleasure created to man and the gods by Bird's beautiful plumage and attractive singing, as on any economic reasons.

Translation

1–12   In those ancient days, when the good destinies had been decreed, and after An and Enlil had set up the divine rules of heaven and earth, then the third of them, . . . , the lord of broad wisdom, Enki, the master of destinies, gathered together . . . and founded dwelling places; he took in his hand waters to encourage and create good seed; he laid out side by side the Tigris and the Euphrates, and caused them to bring water from the mountains; he scoured out the smaller

streams, and positioned the other watercourses . . . . Enki made
spacious sheepfolds and cattle-pens, and provided shepherds and
herdsmen; he founded cities and settlements throughout the earth,
and made the black-headed multiply. He provided them with a king
as shepherd, elevating him to sovereignty over them; the king rose as
the daylight over the foreign countries.

13–21 . . . Enki knit together the marshlands, making young and old reeds
grow there; he made birds and fish teem in the pools and lagoons
. . . ; he gave . . . all kinds of living creatures as their sustenance, . . .
placed them in charge of this abundance of the gods. When
Nudimmud, august prince, the lord of broad wisdom, had fashioned
. . . , he filled the reed-beds and marshes with fish and birds, indicated to them their positions and instructed them in their divine
rules.

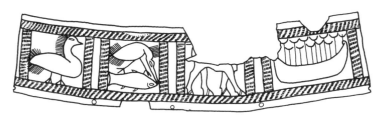

FIG. 28. 'But Bird frightened the Fish of the lagoons'—marshland scenes
on a bitumen vessel from Ĝirsu

22–8 Then Fish laid its eggs in the lagoons; Bird built its nest in a gap in
the reed-beds. But Bird frightened the Fish of the lagoons in its . . . .
Fish took up a stand and cried out. Grandiosely it initiated hostilities. It roused the street by quarrelling in an overbearing manner.
Fish addressed Bird murderously:

29–40 '. . . Bird, . . . there is no insult . . . ! Croaking, . . . noise in the marshes
. . . squawking! Forever gobbling away greedily, while your heart is
dripping with evil! Standing on the plain, you can keep pecking away
until they chase you off! The farmer's sons lay lines and nets for you
in the furrows. The gardener sets up nets against you in gardens and
orchards. He cannot rest his arm from firing his sling; he cannot sit
down because of you. You cause damage in the vegetable plots; you
are a nuisance. In the damp parts of fields, there are your unpleasing

footprints. Bird, you are shameless: you fill the courtyard with your droppings. The courtyard sweeper-boy who cleans the house chases after you with ropes. By your noise the house° is disturbed; your din drives people away.

41–50 'They bring you into the fattening shed. They let you moo like cattle, bleat like sheep. They pour out cool water in jugs for you. They drag you away for the daily sacrifice. The fowler brings you with bound wings.° They tie up your wings and beak. Your squawking is to no profit; what are you flapping about? With your ugly voice you frighten the night; no one can sleep soundly. Bird, get out of the marshes! Get this noise of yours off my back! Go out of here into a hole on the rubbish heap: that suits you!'

51–6 Thus Fish insulted Bird on that day. But Bird, with multicoloured plumage and multicoloured face, was convinced of its own beauty, and did not take to heart the insults Fish had cast at it. As if it was a nursemaid singing a lullaby, it paid no attention to the speech, despite the ugly words that were being uttered. Then Bird answered Fish:°

57–69 'How has your heart become so arrogant, while you yourself are so lowly? Your mouth is flabby (?), but although your mouth goes all the way round, you cannot see behind you. You are bereft of hips, as also of arms, hands, and feet—try bending your neck to your feet! Your smell is awful; you make people throw up, they bare their teeth at you! No trough would hold the kind of prepared food you eat. He who has carried you dares not let his hand touch his skin! In the great marshes and the wide lagoons, I am your persecuting demon. You cannot eat the sweet plants there, as my voice harasses you. You cannot travel with confidence in the river, as my storm-cloud covers you. As you slip through the reed-beds you are always beneath my eyes. Some of your little ones are destined to be my daily offering; you give them to me to allay my hunger. Some of your big ones are just as certainly destined for my banqueting hall . . . in the mud. (*1 line unclear*)

70–9 'But I am the beautiful and clever Bird! Fine artistry went into my adornment. But no skill has been expended on your holy shaping! Strutting about in the royal palace is my glory; my warbling is considered a decoration in the courtyard. The sound I produce, in all its sweetness, is a delight for the person of Šulgi, son of Enlil. Fruits and produce of gardens and orchards are the enormous daily offerings due to me. Groats, flour malt, hulled barley, and emmer wheat (?) are sweet things to my mouth. How do you not recognize my superiority from this? Bow your neck to the ground!'

80–5 Thus Bird insulted Fish on that occasion. Fish became angry, and, trusting in its heroic strength and solidness, swept across the bottom like a heavy rain cloud. It took up the quarrel. It did not take to heart the insults that Bird had cast at it. It could not bring itself to submit, but spoke unrestrainedly. Again Fish replied to Bird:

86–94 'Chopped-off beak and legs, deformed feet, cleft mouth, thin tongue! You clatter away in your ignorance, with never any reflection! Gluttonous, malformed, filling the courtyard with droppings! The little sweeper-boy sets nets in the house and chases you with ropes. The baker, the brewer, the porter, all those who live in the house are annoyed with you. Bird, you have not examined the question of my greatness; you have not taken due account of my nature. You could not understand my weakness and my strength; yet you spoke inflammatory words. Once you have really looked into my achievements, you will be greatly humbled. Your speech contains grave errors; you have not given it due consideration.

95–101 'I am Fish. I am responsibly charged with providing abundance for the pure shrines. For the great offerings at the lustrous E-kur°, I stand proudly with head raised high! Just like Ezina I am here to satisfy the hunger of the Land. I am her helper. Therefore people pay attention to me, and they keep their eyes upon me. As at the harvest festival, they rejoice over me and take care of me. Bird, whatever great deeds you may have achieved, I will teach you their pretentiousness. I shall hand back to you in your turn your haughtiness and mendacious speech.'

102–15 Thereupon Fish conceived a plot against Bird. Silently, furtively, it slithered alongside. When Bird rose up from her nest to fetch food for her young, Fish searched for the most discreet of silent places. It turned her well-built nest of brushwood into a haunted house. It destroyed her well-built house, and tore down her storeroom. It smashed the eggs she had laid and threw them into the sea. Thus Fish struck at Bird, and then fled into the waters. Then Bird came, lion-faced and with an eagle's talons, flapping its wings towards its nest. It stopped in mid-flight. Like a hurricane whirling in the midst of heaven, it circled in the sky. Bird, looking about for its nest, spread wide its limbs. It trampled over the broad plain after its well-built nest of brushwood. Its voice shrieked into the interior of heaven like the Mistress's.

116–21 Bird sought for Fish, searching the marshes. Bird peered into the deep water for Fish, watching closely. Extending its claws, it just snatched from the water Fish's tiny fish-spawn, gathering them all together and piling them up in a heap. Thus Bird took its revenge and . . . its heart. Again Bird replied to Fish:

122–4 'You utter fool! Dumb, muddle-headed Fish, you are out of . . . ! The mouths of those who circle (?) the quay never get enough to eat, and their hunger lasts all day. Swine, rascal, gorging yourself upon your own excrement, you freak!

125–36 'You are like a watchman living on the walls (?), . . . ! Fish, you kindled fire against me, you planted henbane. In your stupidity you caused devastation; you have spattered your hands with blood! Your arrogant heart will destroy itself by its own deeds! But I am Bird, flying in the heavens and walking on the earth. Wherever I travel to, I am there for the joy of its . . . named. . . . , O Fish, . . . bestowed by the Great Princes°. I am of first-class seed, and my young are first-born young! . . . walks with uplifted head . . . to the lustrous E-kur. . . . until distant days. . . . the numerous people say. How can you not recognize my pre-eminence? Bow your neck to the ground.'

137–40 Again Bird had hurled insults at Fish. Then Fish shouted at Bird, eyeing it angrily: 'Do not puff yourself up from your lying mouth! Our judge shall take this up. Let us take our case to Enki, our judge and adjudicator.'

141–7 And so with the two of them jostling and continuing the evil quarrel in order to establish, the one over the other, their grandness and pre-eminence, the litigation was registered within Eridug, and they put forward their argumentation°. . . . thrashing about (?) amid roaring like that of a bull, . . . crept forward like . . . . They requested a verdict . . . from king Šulgi, son of Enlil.

148–57 (*Bird speaks:*) 'You . . . , lord of true speech, pay attention to my words! I had put . . . and laid eggs there. . . . had bestowed . . . and had given as their sustenance. After . . . had started . . . , . . . it destroyed my house. It turned my nest of brushwood into a haunted house. It destroyed my house, and tore down my storeroom. It smashed my eggs and threw them into the sea. . . . examine what I have said. Return a verdict in my favour.' . . . investigating . . . , she prostrated herself to the ground.

158–60 ... announced (?) the word. ... august, spoke from the heart: 'Your words are sterling words, such as delight the heart.'

161 (*Šulgi speaks:*) 'For how long are they° going to persist (?) in quarrelling?'

162–3 Like ... came out supreme. Like butting ..., they jostled each other.

164 (*Fish speaks:*) '..., let it be favourable to me!'

165–77 (*Šulgi speaks:*) 'I shall instruct you in the divine rules and just ordinances of our dwelling-place. Like (?) Enki, king of the Abzu, I am successful in finding solutions, and am wise in words.' He answered Bird and Fish: 'To strut about in the E-kur is a glory for Bird, as its singing is sweet. At Enlil's holy table, Bird ... precedence over you ...! It shall utter its cries in the temple of the great gods. The Anuna gods rejoice at its voice. It is suitable for banquets in the great dining hall of the gods. It provides good cheer in the king's° palace. ... with head high, at the table of Šulgi, son of Enlil. The king ... long life. (*1 line fragmentary*) Fish ... in splendour ....'

178–90 Thereupon Fish ... Bird. (*6 lines missing or fragmentary*) ... Enki ... bestowed. (*1 line fragmentary*) In the Abzu of Eridug ... Bird .... Because Bird was victorious over Fish in the debate between Fish and Bird, praise be to Father Enki!

Notes

29–40 Instead of 'house' 1 MS has: 'palace'.

41–50 After 'with bound wings.' 1 MS adds: 'The fisherman brings you into the palace.'

51–6 Instead of 'Then Bird answered Fish:' 1 MS has: 'It ... insulted Fish; ... said ...:'.

95–101 Instead of 'For the great offerings at the lustrous E-kur' 1 MS has: 'On the august platform of the great offerings of the gods'.

125–36 'the Great Princes': a name for the Igigi.

141–7 Instead of 'put forward their argumentation' 1 MS has: 'stood there in debate'.

161 Instead of 'they' 1 MS has: 'you'.

165–77 Instead of 'the king's' 1 MS has: 'Šulgi's'.

The heron and the turtle

This composition can perhaps best be described as a fable, although one scene, where one of the two protagonists takes her case to the god Enki in Eridug for adjudication, resembles the debates (*The debate between Sheep and*

Grain and *The debate between Bird and Fish*). The last part of the composition is missing completely, and the second half of what survives is damaged and difficult to make sense of.

The turtle and the heron are portrayed as having human characters. The quarrelsome and malicious turtle overturns the heron's nest, tipping out her fledgelings and bloodying the bird herself in the ensuing struggle.

Enki's response is damaged but seems to involve building a construction of some sort, possibly a sluice or gate that would protect the heron's nest from the turtle in future (A107–66). A subsequent damaged episode (A167–208) has Enki creating a vegetable from the dirt under his fingernail (see *Inana's descent to the Underworld*, Group B, lines 222–5). This leads to the growth of the flax plant, which may have been used to make linen cord for a hunting net. The remainder of the fable, which still includes the turtle, is obscure and unrecoverable at present.

The opening section (A1–21) of this composition evokes the tone of an oral folk-tale, setting the location over quite a wide range of areas along the major rivers, wherever there were reed-beds, including Tutub (on the river Diyala), Akšak (on the Tigris), and Eridug and Urim (near the Euphrates). Different types of reeds and aquatic plants typical of these regions are described, with their appearance characterized in human terms. The various plants are repeatedly named through the composition, reinforcing the marshland landscape setting.

Translation

A1–9 What do they say in the reed-beds whose growth is good? In the wide reed-beds of Tutub, whose growth is good? In the marshes of Kiritaba, whose growth is good? In the *adara* thickets of Akšak, whose growth is good? In Enki's interconnecting (?) lagoons, whose growth is good? In the smaller lagoon, Enki's lagoon, whose growth is good? In Enki's *barbar* reeds, whose growth is good? In the little *gizi* reeds of Urim, whose growth is good? In Urim, where cows and calves abound, whose growth is good?

A10–21 At that time, the water was drained away from the reeds . . . , and they were visible at the sheepfold. The *aštaltal* plant, spreading its seeds from the reed-beds, and the little *kumul* plants came out of the earth: they are good as little ones. The small *enbar* reed grooms her hair: it is good as a young maiden. The *ubzal* reed goes about the city: it is good as a young man. The *pela* reed is covered from bottom to top: it is good daughter-in-law. The *pela* reed turns from bottom to top:

it is a good young son. The *gašam* reed digs in the ground: it is good as an old man. The *gizi* reed . . . on its own: it is good as an old woman. The reed-bed lifts its head beautifully: it is a good Gudea. The *ildag* tree lifts its head in the irrigation ditch: it is good as a king. . . . with bright branches: it is a good prince.

A22–5 On that day, beside the reed-beds, someone sitting on the bank prays: 'Let me snatch away the heron's eggs, let me take them away . . . , so that the gift-bringing bird will not be able to make a gift, so that the gift-bringing heron will not be able make a gift!'

A26–31 He catches fish; he collects eggs and crushes them. He crushes the *suḫur* carp in the honey plants. He crushes the *eštub* carp in the little *gizi* reeds. He crushes toads in the *ligiligi* grass. He crushes fish spawn, his offspring, his family. He strikes the heron's eggs and smashes them in the sea.

A32–47 The gift-giving bird made a plea; the heron entered the house of king Enki and spoke to him: 'Give me . . . a wide-open place to lay my eggs in.' He gave her . . . , and did . . . for her. . . . is indeed . . . (*1 line fragmentary*). She laid eggs in the . . . . She laid eggs in the wide reed-beds of Tutub. She laid eggs in the marshes of Kiritaba. She laid eggs in the *adara* thickets of Akšak. She laid eggs in Enki's interconnecting (?) lagoons. She laid eggs in the smaller lagoon, the lagoon of Eridug. She laid eggs in Enki's *barbar* reeds. She laid eggs in the little *gizi* reeds of Urim. She laid eggs in Urim, where cows and calves abound.

A48–59 Then the quarrelsome turtle, he of the troublesome way, said: 'I am going to pick a quarrel with the heron, the heron! I, the turtle, am going to pick a quarrel with the heron! I, whose eyes are snake's eyes, am going to pick a quarrel! I, whose mouth is a snake's mouth, am going to pick a quarrel! I, whose tongue is a snake's tongue, am going to pick a quarrel! I, whose bite is a puppy's bite, am going to pick a quarrel! With my slender hands and slender feet, I am going to pick a quarrel! I, the turtle—an oven brick—am going to pick a quarrel! I, who live in the vegetable gardens, am going to pick a quarrel! I, who like a digging tool spend my time in the mud, am going to pick a quarrel! I, an unwashed refuse-basket, am going to pick a quarrel!'

A60–6 The turtle, the trapper of birds, the setter of nets, overthrew the heron's construction of reeds for her, turned her nest upside down, and tipped her children into the water. The turtle scratched the dark-eyed bird's forehead with his claws, so that her breast was covered in blood from it.°

A67–71 The heron cried out and grew pale: 'If I, a bird, . . . my empty nest and . . .°. Let my king judge my case, and give me verdict! Let Enki judge my case, and give me verdict! May the lord of Eridug . . . my claim.'

A72–3 (*The turtle speaks*:) 'A second time, may the gift-bringing bird not be able to make a gift, may the gift-bringing heron not be able to make a gift!'

A74–9 He catches fish; he collects eggs and crushes them. He crushes the *suḫur* carp in the honey plants°. He crushes the *eštub* carp in the little *gizi* reeds. He crushes toads in the *ligiligi* grass. He crushes fish spawn, his offspring, his family. He dug in the ground, . . . his head upwards . . . .°

A80–9 She° cried out to king Enki: 'My king, you gave me the wide reed-beds, and I laid eggs there. I laid eggs in the wide reed-beds of Tutub. I laid eggs in the marshes of Kiritaba. I laid eggs in the *adara* thickets of Akšak. I laid eggs in Enki's interconnecting (?) lagoons. I laid eggs in the smaller lagoon, the lagoon of Eridug. I laid eggs in Enki's *barbar* reeds. I laid eggs in the little *gizi* reeds of Urim. I laid eggs in Urim, where cows and calves abound.

A90–101 'Then the quarrelsome turtle, he of the troublesome way, he whose eyes are snake's eyes, he of the troublesome way, he whose mouth is a snake's mouth, he of the troublesome way, he whose tongue is a snake's tongue, he of the troublesome way, he whose bite is a puppy's bite, he of the troublesome way, he with the slender hands and slender feet, the turtle—an oven brick—he of the troublesome way, he who lives in the vegetable gardens, he of the troublesome way, he who like a digging tool spends his time in the mud, he of the troublesome way, an unwashed refuse-basket, he of the troublesome way, the turtle, the trapper of birds, the setter of nets, overthrew my heron's construction of reeds.

A102–6 'He turned my nest upside down, and tipped my children into the water. The turtle scratched my forehead—me, the dark-eyed bird—with his claws, so that my breast was covered with my blood°.'

A107–8 The prince called to his minister, Isimud: 'My minister, Isimud, my Sweet Name of Heaven!'

A109 'I stand at Enki's service! What is your wish?'

A110–20 'First . . . is filtered on the left (?) side, then a copper box is made, so that . . . is covered. Then you tie . . . , and you tie the top with string . . . ; then you . . . with a piece of dough, and you irrigate the outer enclosure (?); and you put . . . (?) Enki's interconnecting (?) lagoons. Then let him sit . . .' (*1 line missing, 1 line fragmentary*)

A121–9 Isimud . . . paid attention. First he filtered . . . holy water, then he made a copper box and covered . . . . Then he tied the top with string . . . ; then he . . . with a piece of dough, and he irrigated the outer enclosure (?); and he . . . (?) Enki's interconnecting (?) lagoons. (*Enki speaks:*) 'Then I, the prince, will make . . . stand . . . .'

A130–66 The turtle called to the prince: 'You are a prince! She . . . . from fire. I am not a god; . . . (*1 line fragmentary*) King Enki . . . . You are a prince! She . . . . My heart . . . . You are a prince! She . . . your word. My little one destroyed a wall . . . ; she . . . . You are a prince! You are . . . . brickwork. (*16 lines missing*) Your flax (?) is single (*1 line unclear*) Your . . . is single; . . . . the hero . . . . Your seed is single . . . . a tall tree. My strong copper . . . . good semen . . .'

A167–208 Then, on the ziggurrat . . . . king Enki was . . . on the ziggurrat. The great brickwork of the ziggurrat . . . the Abzu; the brickwork of the Abzu . . . . He took dirt from his fingernail and created the *dimgi* vegetable. He made the *dimgi* . . . in the ground. Your flax came out of the earth . . . . He watered the little ones with his hand; he watered the big ones with his foot. The flax grew large. After the flax had grown tall, after he had bound (?) it . . . (*1 line fragmentary, 6 lines missing*) The king . . . . (*5 lines fragmentary or missing*) They seized . . . for him. They . . . for him. They confronted (?) . . . in the desert. (*1 line unclear*) . . . , they laid out the hunting net. . . . did not catch; he caught in (?) the hunting net, . . . did not catch; he spread out the hunting net. (*5 lines fragmentary*) . . . of Enki (*1 line fragmentary*) May you be . . . ; may you be . . . ; may you be . . . ; may you be . . . (*unknown number of lines missing*)

B1–9 (*2 lines fragmentary*) . . . of Enki. . . . did not catch; . . . the hunting net. The turtle . . . . Enki . . . something from his fingernail. Its inside is five . . . ; its exterior is ten . . . . A crevice . . . (*unknown number of lines missing*)

Notes

A60–6 After 'blood from it.' 1 MS adds 1 line: '. . . in the dust.'

A67–71 After 'my empty nest and . . .' 1 MS adds: 'I, a heron, . . . ; I shall take my case up to my king, . . .'.

A74–9 Instead of 'honey plants' 1 MS has: 'reed-beds'. Instead of 'He dug in the ground, . . . his head upwards. . . .' 1 MS has: 'The heron . . . , ...'

A80–9   After 'She' (the heron) 1 MS adds: 'entered the house and'.
A102–6   After 'with my blood' 1 MS adds: '. . . in the water'.

The home of the fish

This delightful composition is cast in the form of a monologue spoken by a fisherman who has built a fish trap. The fisherman addresses the fish exactly as if they were humans, and describes the trap as if it were a welcoming human house, into which he tries to lure the fish. Many different kinds are specified, and are described in vivid and probably humorous terms. Mostly the varieties cannot be securely identified with modern species, so here their names are left in Sumerian. There is an intimate lexical relationship between the names of the fish enumerated here and those in the traditional list of fish, one among the many word lists which had been learnt for centuries by apprentice scribes in Mesopotamian schools. This strongly suggests that the composition had been adapted for school use by incorporating extra pedagogical material.

Finally the fisherman suggests to the fish that they would actually be safer in the 'home' he has built for them, as if they remain in the river they are in constant danger of being snatched up in the claws of any one of several predatory birds. And by entering the trap, they will actually give pleasure to Nanše, the goddess of fish and fishermen.

As with the pastoral compositions that are set in the world of shepherds and cowherds (see Groups B and F), this evocation of the fisherman's life has a tone characteristic of a whole group of Sumerian literary compositions (see *The debate between Bird and Fish, The heron and the turtle*). We can assume that in reality these rural worlds of fowlers, fishermen, and pastoralists were some distance removed from the everyday experience of the literate copyists and urban consumers of this literature.

Translation

A1–13   My fish, I have built you a home! My fish, I have built you a house, I have built you a store! I have built you a house bigger than a house, in fact a large sheepfold. Inside there is incense, and I have covered it with cloths for you; in this happy place, I . . . water of joy for you; a house not bothered by cords dividing the plots, . . . in the gutters. In the house, there is food, food of the best quality. In the house, there is food, food in good condition. No flies buzz around in your house where beer is poured out. Your reputation . . . cannot be alienated (?). The threshold and the door-bolt, the ritual flour and the incense-burner are all in place. The scent and fragance in the house are like an aromatic cedar forest. In the house, there is beer, there is good beer. There is sweet beer, and honeyed cakes, extending as far as the reed fence.

A14–24 Let your acquaintances come! Let your dear ones come! Let your father and grandfather come! Let the sons of your elder brother and the sons of your younger brother come! Let your little ones come, and your big ones too! Let your wife and your children come! Let your friends and companions come! Let your brother-in-law and your father-in-law come! Let the crowd by the side of your front door come! Don't leave your friends' children outside! Don't leave your neighbours outside, whoever they may be!

A25–33 Enter, my beloved son! Enter, my fine son! Don't let the day go by, don't let the night come! The moonlight should not enter that house! But if the day has gone by and the night comes, enter and I will let you relax there; I have made the grounds suitable for you! Inside, I have fixed up a seat for you. My fish, no one who sleeps there will be disturbed; no one who sits there will get involved in a quarrel.

A34–9 Enter, my beloved son! Enter, my fine son! As if you were in a river with brackish water, don't go investigating any canals! As if you were in silt settled on the riverbed, may you not be able to get up! As if you were in flowing water, you should not fix your bed! The moonlight should not enter that house!

A40–4 And may you not succeed in getting away: face towards me! And may you not succeed in getting away like a . . . to your lair: face towards me! And may you not succeed in getting away like a dog to where you go sniffing: face towards me! And may you not succeed in getting away like a . . . to where you . . . : face towards me! And may you not succeed in getting away like a bull to your cattle-pen, like a sheep to your sheepfold: face towards me!

A45–67 Now, just . . . like a bull to your cattle-pen! Enter for me, and Suen will be delighted with you! Now, just . . . like a sheep to your sheep-fold! Enter for me, and Dumuzid will be delighted with you! When you lift your head like a bull towards your cattle-pen, Lord Ašimbabbar Suen will be delighted with you! When you raise your head like a sheep in the sheepfold, Dumuzid the shepherd will be delighted with you! *(15 lines fragmentary or missing)*

A68–80   The fish who . . . . May all kinds of fishes also enter with you, my fish! The one with handsome barbels who eats the honey plant, my *suḫur-gal* fish: may he also enter with you, my fish! The one who always eats . . . reeds, . . . , my *suḫur-tur* fish: may he also enter with you, my fish! The one with big lips, who sucks the *gizi* reeds, *(1 line fragmentary)* whose food . . . , my *eštub* fish: may he also enter with you, my fish! The black punting-pole, engendered in the fields, the farrowing sow who takes away the dough from the river banks, my *gubi* fish°: may he also enter with you, my fish!

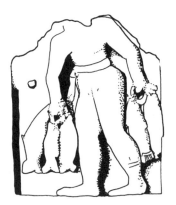

Fig. 29. 'May all kinds of fishes also enter with you, my fish!'—a fisherman with his catch on a fragmentary stone stela from Ǧirsu

A81–95   The one with a spiny (?) tail and a spiny (?) back, who goes . . . , my *še-suḫur-gal* (?) fish: may he also enter with you, my fish! The fish who is like a crying child in its prayers, my *še-suḫur-sig* (?) fish: may he also enter with you, my fish! With a pickaxe as a head, and having a comb for teeth, the branches of a fir-tree as his bones, Dumuzid's water-skin for the skin of his bladder (?), with a dehaired skin that does not need processing, with his slender tail like the fishermen's whip, the jumping fish, with naturally smoothed skin, with no entrails in his nose, the fish who seizes adversaries by arms and legs, whose sting goes across like a nail, who is taboo and is not placed as an offering in the city's shrines, my *mur* fish°: may he also enter with you, my fish!

A96–113 The one whose fins (?) churn the troubled waters, a fish who seizes . . . at a glance (?), my *kiĝ* fish: may he also enter with you, my fish! With a head like a small millstone, . . . a dog's head, (*1 line unclear*) the fish who does not eat the . . . plants, . . . , my *ĝir-gid* fish: may he also enter with you, my fish! With the noise of his entrails . . . , my *gir* fish: may he also enter with you, my fish! The fish who . . . , the fish who knows how to escape through a reed barrier, the fish who despite being tasty is an abomination, my *ab-suḫur* fish: may he also enter with you, my fish! The fish who causes breaches in dykes, with venom in his jaws, my *agargar* fish: may he also enter with you, my fish! The one whom the merchants . . . , my *kamar* fish: may he also enter with you, my fish! The one whom the Mardu fetch away, my *nunbar-gid* (?) fish: may he also enter with you, my fish!

A114–17 The fish who does not eat edible plants, . . . , my *azagur* fish: may he also enter with you, my fish! The one who . . . a heavy skin, . . . , my *muš* fish: may he also enter with you, my fish! (*approximately 7 lines fragmentary or missing*)

B1–7 . . . , spotted (?) . . . , my *ĝiru* (?) fish: may he also enter with you, my fish! The one whom the children bring in . . . , my *salsal* fish: may he also enter with you, my fish! The one with snake's eyes, a . . . mouse's mouth, who . . . on riverbanks, (*approximately 8 lines fragmentary or missing*)

C1–12 The one that utters its sinister cry in the marshes and rivers, my *agane* bird: you would be dangling from its claws, my fish! The one that circles the nets looking for you in the waters where the nets are stretched, my *ubure* bird: you would be dangling from its claws, my fish! The one with long legs, that laughs, the alien from faraway waters, that writes in the mud, my *anše-bar* (?) bird: you would be dangling from its claws, my fish! The one that does not adorn . . . , with the . . . of a bird and webbed (?) feet, my *kib* bird: you would be dangling from its claws, my fish! The one that seizes the quadrupeds that wander into the marshes, my *kuda* crocodile: you would be dangling from its claws, my fish!

C13–17 But you won't be dangling from their claws, you won't be snatched up by their feet! Time is pressing, my fish! Just you come to me! Time is pressing! Just you come to me! Nanše, the queen of the fishermen, will be delighted with you.

Notes

A68–80 '*gubi* fish': probably eel.

A81–95 '*mur* fish': stingray.

H. THE HYMNIC GENRES

Our understanding of the Sumerian literary corpus is greatly hampered by the absence of any ancient tradition of explicit literary interpretation. We classify the corpus with the help of modern categories that post-date the works we are classifying by many centuries and belong to a different literary tradition. The compositions of this group are classified as hymns mainly on the thematic grounds that they are all basically poems praising a god.

The scribes of Sumer, however, did not perceive these compositions as belonging to a single class but categorized them using a set of native labels into a number of groups. Two basic kinds of labels can be distinguished: subscripts and rubrics. Subscripts stand at the end of a composition and refer to the whole of the poem; they may be considered as native generic designations. They have the form *subscript* of *divine name*; for example, the first composition of this chapter is qualified with the subscript 'An *adab* of Bau'. Rubrics are labels that qualify smaller sections within a composition. The sections defined by rubrics usually correspond to literary units, like strophes or stanzas.

In the absence of explicitly interpretative texts, we know little about the criteria applied to the assignment of these compositions to the various types. Some types of composition are fairly coherent in terms of formal features and thematic domains. The *adab* and *tigi* compositions are very consistent structurally, and both are hymns addressed to a deity usually also containing praise for a ruler. Other types display a larger diversity both formally and thematically. (The *balbale* and *šir-namgala* compositions in this volume illustrate this point.) The fact that these compositions were nevertheless classified together suggests that formal and thematic features were only two among a set of criteria applied by the scribes. Other criteria which relate to the performance of these compositions and which unfortunately cannot be recovered from the texts alone must also have played an important role in the generic assignation.

The complex nature of native generic assignation is also reflected in the meaning of the subscripts which appear to highlight different aspects of the performance. The labels *adab*, *tigi*, and perhaps *kuŋar* derive from the names of musical instruments—various types of drums—accompanying the performance of the compositions. Genre names derived from musical instruments are also known from the European tradition; the name of the lyric genre derives ultimately from the Greek name of the lyre (*lyra*) used as an accompanying instrument. Other subscripts may refer to the performers (*šir-namgala*, lit. 'a song characteristic of the cult of the *gala* priests'), or to the emotions invoked by the composition (*šir-šag-ḫula*, lit. 'song of a joyful heart'). More often, however, the meaning of the subscripts is obscure (*šir-gida*, lit. 'long song'; *šir-namursaĝa*, lit. 'song of warrior quality'; *šir-namšub*, lit. 'incantation song'), or even unknown (*balbale*, *ululumama*).

An interesting hint at the contemporary perception of the subscripts can be found in the composition commemorating king Ur-Namma's death (*The death of Ur-Namma*, Group A, line 187), where the dead monarch says in his self-lament:

My *tigi*, *adab*, flute, and *zamzam* songs have been turned into laments because of me.

This sentence suggests that subscripts may have been conventionally associated with different ways of performance which in turn evoked different sentiments. In particular the quotation suggests that the sentiments associated with the subscripts listed in the first part of this sentence were incompatible with the sentiments of mourning.

Rubrics divide up the compositions into smaller sections. Their exact significance eludes us. They are commonly thought to be related to the way accompanying music was performed. Some authors, however, argue that some of them (for example, the *kirugu*) may instead mark phases in the cultic event associated with the performance of the compositions. Without pertinent textual sources the interpretations must be contingent on the etymology of the labels. The meaning of the rubrics is, though, obscure or uncertain in most cases (*sa-gida*, lit. 'long or tense string'; *sa-ĝara*, lit. 'set string'; *ĝišgiĝal* 'counterpart'; *kirugu*, perhaps 'bowing down') so this method cannot produce reliable results without other evidence.

Some of the rubrics (e.g. *kirugu*, *ĝišgiĝal*) are also regularly used in compositions that do not end with subscripts (see, for example, *The lament for Sumer and Urim*, Group D).

FURTHER READING

Kilmer, A. D., 'Musical Practice in Nippur', in M. de J. Ellis (ed.), *Nippur at the Centennial* (University Museum: Philadelphia, 1992), pp. 101–12.

Tinney, S. J., *The Nippur Lament: Royal Rhetoric and Divine Legitimation in the Reign of Išme-Dagan of Isin (1953–1935 BC)* (University Museum: Philadelphia, 1996), pp. 11–18.

Vanstiphout, H. L. J., ' "I can put anything in its right place": Generic and Typological Studies as Strategies for the Analysis and Evaluation of Mankind's Oldest Literature', in B. Roest and H. L. J. Vanstiphout (eds.), *Aspects of Genre and Type in Pre-Modern Literary Cultures* (Styx: Groningen, 1999), pp. 71–99.

OTHER COMPOSITIONS WITH GENERIC SUBSCRIPTS INCLUDE

Group A An *adab* to An for Lipit-Eštar
Group B Dumuzid's dream (*šir-kalkal*)
Ploughing with the jewels (*kuŋar*)
Dumuzid and Enkimdu (*balbale*)
A love song for Šu-Suen (*balbale*)
Group D A *balbale* to Nanna
A *šir-namgala* to Nanna
Group E An *adab* to Nergal for Šu-ilišu
Ninurta's exploits (*šir-gida*)
Ninurta's return to Nibru (*šir-gida*)
A *balbale* to Ninurta
Group F A *tigi* to Nintud-Aruru
A *balbale* to Inana and Dumuzid

An *adab* to Bau for Išme-Dagan

The goddess Bau (also called here by the name Šuḫalbi) was a daughter of the supreme god An. This hymn to her was composed on behalf of Išme-Dagan, king of the city of Isin. It takes the form of an *adab*, with a *sa-gida* (30 lines) followed by a one-line *ŋišgiŋal* of the *sa-gida*, then a *sa-ŋara* (27 lines) followed by a final three-line *uru*.

In the *sa-gida*, Bau is praised for her medical skills. The hymn recounts how Enlil (also called Nunamnir here) gave Bau her authority and rank as a food stewardess of his temple E-kur in Nibru (also called Dur-an-ki). Her father An married her to Enlil's son Niŋirsu, giving her status in Niŋirsu's temple E-ninnu at Ŋirsu in the city-state of Lagaš. Specifically, she was assigned the shrine E-ŋalga-sud of the temple Tar-sirsir. In her turn, Bau has blessed king Išme-Dagan, who is also described here as a son of the god Enlil.

(Throughout the period of this literature, many kings of Urim, Isin, Larsa, and Babylon were deified in their own lifetimes.)

The *sa-g̃ara* tells how Bau has introduced Išme-Dagan into the presence of Enlil in his shrine E-namtila at Isin, with the result that Enlil too has bestowed a blessing on the king. Finally, in the *uru*, Bau grants long life to Išme-Dagan at Enlil's behest.

Translation

1–8   Lady, imbued with fearsomeness, whose greatness is recognized in heaven and on earth, perfect in nobility! Mother Bau, foremost among ladies, warrior . . . ! Powerful goddess, who perfectly controls the august divine powers, proud one, . . . great intelligence! . . . , true woman, wise lady who has been made knowledgeable from birth! Daughter of An, expert, eloquent, who holds everything in her hand! Lady, great doctor of the black-headed people, who keeps people alive, and brings them to birth. Šuḫalbi, incantation priestess of the numerous people, . . . ! Merciful, compassionate one of the Land, lady of justice!

9–19   Enlil, the king of all the foreign countries, Nunamnir, the lord who determines the fates, decreed something of great importance in the shrine Nibru, in Dur-an-ki: he made you exalted in the shining E-kur, ... You are the strong spread-net of Nunamnir. *Anguba* priestess, who provides the E-kur with food, you are in charge of the wine. You are Enlil's exalted daughter-in-law, you are the one who stands next to him with the libation water (?). Because you prostrated yourself humbly with supplications, Nunamnir, the prince of all the foreign countries, entrusted to you the exalted office of accountant of heaven and earth, and exalted you, giving you the rank of lady of the shrine which brought the seeds of mankind forth.

20–6   Your own father, An, the highest god, clothed you in the *ma* garment. He gave you the warrior of Enlil, Ning̃irsu, as your husband. He bestowed on you the E-ninnu, the holy city, the shrine which brought forth the seeds of mankind. He has set up your lofty throne-dais in Lagaš, in G̃irsu, the mooring post of the Land, in E-g̃alga-sud, your beloved residence, in Tar-sirsir, the temple of ladyship; and now all the gods of the land of Lagaš bow down before your august residence.

27–30   Supreme lady, whose divine powers are untouchable, daughter of

An, omniscient great lady, young woman, mother Bau, you have looked favourably on the young man of handsome form, prince Išme-Dagan, the son of Enlil; you have determined for him a good fate once and for all.

31 *Sa-gida.*

32 It is mother Bau who is to give prince Išme-Dagan, the son of Enlil, a life of numerous days.

33 *Ĝišĝiĝal* of the *sa-gida.*

34–42 You introduced prince Išme-Dagan, clasping to his breast a white lamb and a sheep of auspicious omens, into the E-namtila, Enlil's temple, and made him stand at the royal offering place of life. Then you saluted the Great Mountain, Enlil, and told him: 'Father Enlil, great lord of all the foreign countries, determine the fate of Išme-Dagan, call him by name!' Enlil, the king of all the foreign countries, looked encouragingly upon him, beaming radiantly; and determined a fate for Išme-Dagan:

43–60 'Prince Išme-Dagan, as your fate, you shall be given a throne which concentrates all divine powers, an enduring legitimate crown and a sceptre which maintains the people and keeps them united. The Tigris and the Euphrates shall bring abundance, carp-filled waters for you, their yield shall be long-lasting for you. Their banks shall grow vegetation for you, they shall bring (?) you rejoicing. The irrigated orchards shall yield (?) syrup and wine for you. The fertile arable tracts shall grow dappled grain for you; grain piles shall be heaped up for you. Cattle-pens shall be built, sheepfolds shall be enlarged for you. Your name shall be exalted as king; you shall be elevated as prince. All the foreign countries from below as far as the uplands shall bring tribute for you. You shall shine radiantly in the grand main courtyard like sunlight. Your food offerings shall never cease in the shining E-kur.' This is how Enlil determined his fate. From the E-kur he gave huge strength to the king. He has been made lordly; Enlil's words made him a man without rival. He directed his steps proudly there and entered the august palace, the royal residence. As he took his seat on the shining holy throne-dais, the palace . . . .

61 *Sa-ĝara.*

62–4 Good woman, daughter of An, Enlil has called for you! . . . the holy shining throne-dais . . . told you; young woman, mother Bau, the daughter of An, Enlil has called for you! . . . the holy shining throne-dais . . . told you: 'Bestow on Išme-Dagan, the son of Enlil, a life of numerous days!'

65 Its *uru*.

66 An *adab* of Bau.

A *balbale* to Ninĝišzida

This song-like hymn is addressed to the god Ninĝišzida, a son of the god Ninazu and the goddess Ningirida. It is described as a *balbale* and is in a single section of 36 lines.

After a reference to the god's infancy, when he was suckled by Ningirida (such references to the childhood of deities are rare in Sumerian literature), the hymn praises four different aspects of Ninĝišzida: his association with fields and meadows (and thus alluding to fertility); his relationship with snakes and dragons (as a deity of the Underworld); his connection with troops and battles (in his role as a warrior god); and finally his expertise as a purification priest.

Within the composition, the god Enki sings a *šir-namšub* song to Ninĝišzida (22–4), and then officially determines a destiny for him (28–31). The hymn ends by praising both Ninĝišzida and his patron Enki, who has bestowed authority and status on him.

Translation

1–10 Hero, lord of field and meadow, lion of the distant mountains! Ninĝišzida, who brings together giant snakes and dragons! Great wild bull who, in the murderous battle, is a flood that . . . ! Beloved by his mother, he to whom Ningirida gave birth from her luxurious body, who drank the good milk at her holy breast, who sucked in lion's spittle, who grew up in the Abzu! August purification priest who holds the holy *ešda* vessels, checker of tablets, who secures justice . . . ! King, wild bull with tall limbs (?), who directs speech aright, and who hates wickedness! Mighty power, whom no one dares stop when he spreads confusion! Mighty Ninĝišzida, whom no one dares stop when he spreads confusion!

11–15 The troops are constantly at your service. Shepherd, you understand how to keep a check on the black-headed. The sheep and lambs come to seek you out, and you understand how to wield the sceptre over the goats and kids, into the distant future. Ninĝišzida, you understand how to wield the sceptre, into the distant future.

16–24 The merciful king° entrusted you from your birth with your words of prayer. He let you have life and creation. Prince endowed with attractiveness, Ninĝišzida, when taking your seat on the throne-dais in an elevated location, lord, god, youth, right arm—clothed in your . . . , with the shining sceptre grasped in your hands—then . . . performs a *šir-namšub* song to you, addressing you intimately: '(*1 line missing*) You bring calming of the heart to . . . who calls out . . . words. You fall upon the many . . . and you burn them like fire.'

FIG. 30. 'Ninĝišzida, who brings together giant snakes and dragons!'—Gudea is led by his personal god Ninĝišzida on a fragmentary stone stela from Ĝirsu

25–36 The king who is the lord of broad understanding° has determined a good destiny for you on your elevated throne-dais; the god who loves justice° has spoken these favourable words: 'Foremost one, leader of the assembly, glory of . . . , king endowed with awesomeness, sun of the masses, advancing in front of them! Who can rival you in the highest heaven? What can equal you?' Hero who, after surveying the battle, goes up to the high mountains! Ninĝišzida, who, after

surveying the battle, goes up to the high mountains! King, you who
carry out commands in the great Underworld, you who carry out the
Underworld's business! Any youth who has a personal god is at your
disposal, there where your commands are issued. O king, honeyed
mouth of the gods! Praise be to Enki! Ninğišzida, son of Ninazu!
Praise be to father Enki!
37 A *balbale* of Ninğišzida.

Notes

16–24 'The merciful king': Enki.
25–36 'The king who is the lord of broad understanding': Enki; 'the god who loves
justice': probably Utu.

A *kunğar* to Inana and Dumuzid

This *kunğar* is a marriage song of the goddess Inana and her lover Dumuzid.
It is composed in two almost equal sections, of which the first is a 24-line
sa-gida and the second an unlabelled 22 lines. It is characterized by a song-
like style, with repetitions, simple syntax, and absence of any explanatory
context. As is often the case, the words of a song are included within the composition (see *A balbale to Ninğišzida* for instance).

In the *sa-gida*, an unidentified man brings herbs, dates, water, and
precious stones for Inana. She chooses a variety of precious stones, jewellery,
and perfumes, and hangs or attaches them all over her body: on her buttocks,
head, nape, hair, ear, ear-lobes (?), face, nose, mouth, navel, hips, thighs,
genitals, and toes.

In the second section, Dumuzid (also called the shepherd or servant of the
god Enlil, and the servant or herdsman of the god An) meets Inana at the
door leading to her *ğipar* shrine in her temple E-ana at Unug. Inana sings a
message to be delivered to her father An, also worshipped at Unug, to the
effect that the decorated marriage-bed should now be prepared for her. The
'man of her heart'—Dumuzid, called here Ama-ušumgal-ana—should be
brought into her presence so that they can take their pleasure together.

Translation

1–10 . . . he who cools, who cools . . . . He who uproots the grass for holy
Inana, who uproots . . . . He who gathers the dates, . . . the date palm.

He who gathers the dates for holy Inana, . . . the date palm. Let him bring her water, let him bring her water, and black emmer wheat. With the water let him bring Inana a heap, and white emmer wheat. The man brings, the man brings, he brings a heap of stones to choose from. The man brings to the maiden Inana, he brings a heap of stones to choose from. He gathers the lapis lazuli from the top of the heap. He gathers the lapis lazuli for Inana from the top of the heap.

11–24 She chooses the buttocks beads and puts them on her buttocks. Inana chooses the head stones and puts them on her head. She chooses the lumps of translucent lapis lazuli and puts them on the nape of her neck. She chooses the golden genitals and puts them on the hair of her head. She chooses the ribbons (?) of gold for the ears and puts them on her ears. She chooses the burnished bronze and puts it in her ear lobes (?). She chooses that which drips with honey and puts it on her face. She chooses that of the outer shrine and puts it on her nose. She chooses the . . . and puts it on her mouth. She chooses the beautiful . . . ring and puts it in her navel. She chooses a well of honey and fresh water and puts it on her hips. She chooses bright alabaster and puts it on her thighs. She chooses black . . . willow (?)° and puts it on her genitals. She chooses ornate sandals and puts them on her toes.

25 *Sa-gida.*

26–31 The lord meets her for whom lapis lazuli was gathered from the heap. Dumuzid meets Inana for whom lapis lazuli was gathered from the heap. The shepherd of An, the servant of Enlil, the lord meets her. The servant of An, the herdsman of Enlil, Dumuzid meets her. The lord meets her at the lapis lazuli door which stands in the *ĝipar* shrine. Dumuzid meets her at the narrow door which stands in the storehouse of E-ana.

32–6 When she turns from the top of the heap, when Inana turns from the top of the heap, may the woman enter (?) with her songs, decorated (?). The maiden, singing, sends a messenger to her father. Inana, dancing from joy, sends a messenger to her father:

37–47 'Let them . . . for me into my house, my house. Let them . . . into my house, my house for me, the queen. Let them . . . for me into my *ĝipar* shrine. Let them erect for me my flowered bed. Let them spread it for me with herbs like translucent lapis lazuli. For me let them bring in the man of my heart. Let them bring in to me my Ama-ušumgal-ana. Let them put his hand in my hand, let them put his

heart by my heart. As hand is put to head, the sleep is so pleasant. As
heart is pressed to heart, the pleasure is so sweet.'
48 A *kuŋĝar* of Inana.

Note

11–24 Instead of '. . . willow' 1 MS has: 'fleece (?)'.

A *šir-gida* to Ninisina

The goddess Ninisina was a daughter of An and Uraš, and the spouse of
Pabilsaĝ (himself a son of Enlil). This substantial and complex composition
in the form *šir-gida* (lit. 'long song'), consisting of one uninterrupted section
of 135 lines, praises several diverse aspects of Ninisina. Direct speech by the
goddess is used to create literary variety.

First to be extolled are her medical and surgical skills, which she has been
granted by Enki and has transmitted in turn to her son Damu, god of the
town of Ĝirsi (15–35). Her skills in performing incantations are also praised,
as she intercedes with An and Enlil on behalf of the personal gods of individual humans plagued by demons (36–60).

We then hear how Ninisina invented the jewellery of *šuba* stones, which
have an explicit sexual symbolism, for the goddess Inana (see *Ploughing with
the jewels*, Group B) (61–73). For human mothers, she acts as a divine
midwife (74–82); in this context she evokes her own birth resulting from sex
between her parents An and Uraš.

Ninisina herself praises the antiquity and opulence of her temple beside
the Kirsig watercourse in the city of Isin, where she is worshipped along with
Pabilsaĝ. She recounts her adventures as a warrior goddess in Enlil's service
(lines 105–20), to whom she praises herself in the closing lines (121–35).

Translation

1–14 . . . who has taken her seat on an exalted dais, . . . , imbued with awesomeness, an amazing sight, . . . Ninisina, joyously fresh, . . . ,
gathering up the divine powers, she announces the rites. . . . Ninisina
. . . with intricate skill. . . . , ministering with intricate skill, she
gathers up the divine powers; Ninisina, ministering with intricate
skill, she gathers up the divine powers. She takes in her hands the
august divine powers. She attaches the incrustations to the great

garment, while speaking favourable words. She tests the surgical lancet; Ninisina sharpens the scalpel. She has made perfect the divine powers of medicine, and hands them over to her son, the king of Ĝirsi, the kindly Damu:

15–26 'My son, pay attention to everything medical! Damu, pay attention to everything medical!' He takes the bandages and wipes them; he treats the bandages with embrocation, and softens the plaster that had been put on them. He mops up the blood and suppuration, and places a warm hand on the horrid wound. My lady, the midwife of the mothers of the Land, is the chief doctor of the black-headed; Ninisina, the daughter of An, hands this all over to her son, the king of Ĝirsi, the kindly Damu:

27–35 'My son, pay attention to everything medical! Damu, pay attention to everything medical! You will be praised for your diagnoses.' Holy Ninisina performs for him her role as incantation priest, which Enki bestowed on her from the princely Abzu. Because of the anxiety and intestinal disease which pursue mankind, this person writhes like a . . . snake, hissing like a snake in waste ground, always calling out anew: 'My heart! My stomach!'

36–45 My lady performs the incantations perfectly. Ninisina speaks the incantation formula over them and they become better. She performs the incantation with ghee, and pours it into her great bowl, bringing it along in her cooling hands. She makes the illness leave this person's body like wind. Like a raging fire of esparto grass, it dies out of its own accord. The personal gods of mankind stand before her pleading and praying; at their request, holy Ninisina intercedes before An and Enlil for them at his highest cult place:

46–51 'The evil demons and the evil demonesses who beset mankind, Dimme and Dim-mea who enter by night, Namtar and Asag who will not leave a man alone, stand before the man. He is robbed of sleep (?). His god who smites all.' (*1 line unclear*)

52–60 That man calls a dream interpreter, wishing to have knowledge of the future. The man for whom the demonic illness has been too great utters pleas to holy Ninisina, utters prayers to her: 'My lady, I come to do homage to you!' Then your incantation descends onto the man, and you will treat him like a youth who has a protective deity. Afterwards, when you have stretched out your finger over him, he will himself praise you fittingly and call upon your name favourably!

61–73 My lady searched intensively on her own (?), concerned herself with things that otherwise one does not bother with, directed her attention to things that otherwise one does not do. Proudly she . . . the rank of Mistress, and my lady took away all the divine powers established for it. At that time, the jewellery of *šuba* stones did not exist; no jewellery of *šuba* stones was worn on the neck. Ninisina invented it: it was she who ploughed with the *šuba* stones, she who made them into seeds. For (?) the goddess, the great Mistress of heaven°, she invented the jewellery of *šuba* stones. Radiating terrifying splendour as she grasped it, she placed it joyously on her head.

74–82 To create offspring for thousands of young women, to make things in order like a potter, to cut the umbilical cord, to determine destinies, to place a hand on the door of the Niĝin-ĝar°, . . . , to let the human child scream loud and long after it is received in the embrace, to turn its belly downwards and to turn it upside down, to . . . the office of Mistress, to treat it quickly, to wash . . .—after she has made all these great divine powers appear gloriously, and my lady has spoken praise . . . in addition, Ninisina praises herself fittingly:

83–9 'I am the lady, the youthful woman, the great strength of Enlil! I am the beautiful woman Ninisina, daughter of holy An! My father An the king, shepherd of the gods, sat me in the Land on a holy dais. My mother Uraš, the lady of the gods, had momentous sex with An, relaxing in the holy bedchamber; my place of engendering by holy An was a holy place.

90–104 'My house is the house of Isin, the cosmic border of heaven and earth, a fragrant cedar forest whose perfume does not diminish; its interior is a mountain established in plenteousness. Before the land of Dilmun ever existed, my house was created from a date palm. Before the land of Dilmun ever existed, Isin was created from a date palm. Its dates are like a great linen garment that hangs on a tree, heaped up into piles. The Anuna, the great gods, eat together with me. My house is a place of healing, full of opulence, the place of the formation of the Land. At night it shines to me like the moonlight; in the noonday heat it shines to me like the sunlight. My husband, lord Pabilsaĝ, the son of Enlil, lies inside with me . . . , enjoying his rest there. My watercourse is the Kirsig watercourse, which produces plenty for eating, which spreads out over the wheat; in it the flowing water always rises high for me. Its banks make syrup and wine grow there, and make their produce rich for me.

105–20 'The heart of the Great Mountain Enlil became fearsome: he frowned at the enemy land, and cursed the rebel land. My father Enlil dispatched me to the rebel land, the enemy land that he had frowned at—me, the young woman, me, the strong heroine—I went there. I made the shepherd of the rebel land there grasp Enlil's words well in his ears. He became frightened at me and became silent (?) in my presence, after I had stormed (?) in his ear for him. Now no one knows him there in the destroyed city, no one finds the shepherd there in his pastures. After I had destroyed it like water, drowned it like the harvest, after I had grabbed him as a threshing sledge grabs barley, after I had set him ablaze like esparto grass, I struck him with the mace and killed him. I announced the news to my father Enlil in Nibru.

121–35 'I am the lady who sits upon terrifying divine powers! I am she who is endowed from holy heaven with the office of incantation priestess! I am she who withdraws the first-fruits from the palace, I am she who has received the divine powers from the most elevated dais. I am mighty, I am the forceful one of An and Uraš, I am the great lady of the gods! My terror is fearsome as it weighs on the Land; my terrifying splendour burdens all the foreign lands. No man anticipates my commands. I am the lady, I am heroic, I am youthful, I am the powerful one of the Land! The heavens fold themselves in my presence like a mourning garment; the earth is more and more submerged as if by the water of a flood when I am present. I am the neck-stock of the Land which grips mankind. I am she who hastens like a north wind storm into the midst of the people! I am she who hears prayer and pleading!' Praise be to holy Ninisina!

136 A *šir-gida* of Ninisina.

Notes

61–73 'the great Mistress of heaven': Inana.
74–82 'Niĝin-ĝar': a part of Ninisina's temple at Isin.

A *šir-namgala* to Ninisina for Lipit-Eštar

This hymn to Ninisina, composed on behalf of Lipit-Eštar, king of Isin, is in the form *šir-namgala* (lit. 'a song characteristic of the cult of the *gala* priests'). The surviving content of this song, in comparison with some others, seems relatively lightweight. Although its poetic style is not very elaborate, it must be borne in mind that this was probably compensated for by its musical form.

At least two *kirugus*, nearly half the composition, must be missing from the beginning, since the preserved text begins with a two-line *šagbatuku* followed by the third *kirugu* (10 lines) and its one-line *ĝišgiĝal*. Then the fourth *kirugu* (8 lines) precedes a two-line *ĝišgiĝal* and a further brief two-line section.

In the preserved portion of the composition, Enlil (also called Nunamnir here) instructs Ninisina that Lipit-Eštar should be the provider who will sustain the economy and life of his city. The goddess in return intercedes with Enlil to grant the king long life. Enlil duly blesses Lipit-Eštar, appointing Ninurta (Uta-ulu) to be his divine helper in battle.

Translation

(Unknown number of lines missing)

1-2 He° told her, Ninisina, the great daughter of An, the great daughter-in-law, . . . : 'That Lipit-Eštar should be your provider—so let it be!'

3 *Šagbatuku*.

4-13 Ninisina (?) paid attention to Enlil's utterance. She answered with humility: 'Father Enlil, god whose name is manifest, . . . , Enlil; lord . . . , your divine powers are the most . . . , your instructions are the most precious (?). For the trustworthy shepherd . . . , . . . lord Lipit-Eštar (*2 lines unclear*) He has settled the people . . . , he (?) has made the Land feel content. You looked upon him with your life-giving gaze: now decree him a true fate!'

14 3rd *kirugu*.

15 Nunamnir, bestow upon prince Lipit-Eštar a long life of many days!

16 Its *ĝišgiĝal*.

17-24 The Great Mountain Enlil paid attention to the words spoken by Ninisina. He blessed the king and decreed his fate: 'Lipit-Eštar, you whom I have called by name, shall be elevated among the people. May the living look to you as to their own fathers and mothers! May the strong one who cares for E-kur, the ruler of the august shrine, Uta-ulu, be your help on the battlefield! May he collect your enemies like small birds for you; may he spread them out like sheaves for you!'

25 4th *kirugu*.

26-7 Nunamnir, the lord whose order cannot be altered, has made the name of prince Lipit-Eštar exalted among the numerous people.

28 Its *ğišğiğal.*

29–30 I, Enlil, am elevated in heaven, and am the lord of all the divine powers on earth. The good fate I have decreed to Lipit-Eštar is something which can never be changed!

31 A *šir-namgala* of Ninisina.

Note

1–2 'He': probably Enlil.

A *šir-namšub* to Utu

This unusual hymn, addressed to the sun-god Utu, also a god of justice, is in the form *šir-namšub* (lit. 'incantation song'). It consists of probably ten *kirugu*s, whose lengths are apparently deliberately patterned:

1st *kirugu*	7 lines	6th *kirugu*	6 lines
2nd *kirugu*	15 lines	7th *kirugu*	5 lines
3rd *kirugu*	16 lines	8th *kirugu*	4 lines
4th *kirugu*	17 lines	9th and 10th *kirugu*s	25 lines together
5th *kirugu*	7 lines	(text damaged)	

The first *kirugu* introduces Utu's family: his divine grandparents Enlil and Ninlil; his spouse Šerida; and finally the paired ancestors Enmul and Ninmul and the *enki* and *ninki* deities. The second *kirugu* elaborates the first, and prays for the long life of an unidentified 'righteous man'.

In the third *kirugu*, the god Nuska, Enlil's minister, pours out beer for his master. Parts of this section seem to be addressed directly to Enlil. In the fourth, the righteous man has made bread and beer offerings to Enlil; the theme of beer offerings recurs throughout the hymn, which may be connected to a ritual. The fifth *kirugu* addresses Utu, praising his beneficent gaze.

In the sixth *kirugu*, a speaker in the first person (perhaps the 'righteous man') prays for sustenance in return for the cleansed offerings he makes. In the seventh and eighth *kirugu*s, which are both preserved only in a fragmentary condition, the god Utu is directly addressed. The remainder of the poem is badly damaged.

The repeated use of untranslatable exclamatory utterances (*elalu*, *auamma*, *alliliamma*, *ulili*) perhaps lend the composition the character of a magical incantation. It is likely that Enlil is present in this hymn as the supreme deity from whom Utu derives his authority as a judge; Utu is then empowered to bestow long life and prosperity on the righteous among mankind.

Translation

1–7 Whoever has eaten good bread has also drunk good beer, in the house where the righteous man has filled the bowls with liquor—the lord of the storehouse, the Great Mountain Enlil; the lady of the storehouse, great mother Ninlil; youthful Utu, lord of the mountain; Šerida, youthful leader of battle; the *enki* and *ninki* deities; Enmul and Ninmul.

8 1st *kirugu*.

9–18 Unto distant days, indeed forever, stand by the righteous man who gives you bread, O exalted one, O exalted one, O exalted one—*elalu*! Unto distant days, indeed forever, stand by the most righteous of men who gives you bread, O lord of the storehouse, Great Mountain Enlil! O lady of the storehouse, great mother Ninlil! O youthful Utu, lord of the mountain! O Šerida, youthful leader of battle! O exalted one, O exalted one, O exalted one—*elalu*!

19–23 May the righteous man have a long life, indeed forever! May the most righteous of men have a long life, indeed forever! Stand by him, O exalted one, O exalted one, O exalted one—*elalu*!

24 2nd *kirugu*.

25–33 *Auamma!*—in the house—*ulili*! *Alliliamma!*—in the house—*ulili*! Pour out beer for him, pour out liquor for him, O minister, pour out liquor for your lord, O Nuska, pour out liquor for Enlil! Beer has now been poured out: let me give you this beer to drink. Liquor has now been poured out: let me give you this liquor to refresh yourself. O lord, eat and drink! May it be acceptable (?) to you! O Enlil, eat and drink! May it be acceptable (?) to you!

34–40 As you eat, flax comes into being, grain comes into being. As you drink, early floods come into being in the rivers. As you eat, mottled grain comes into being in the fields. Accept what the righteous man has brought to you! Accept the flour that the most righteous man has brought to you! He has paid homage to you. He says to you: 'Eat', he says to you: 'Drink'.

41 3rd *kirugu*.

42–50 The beer for the *bur-gia* offerings has been filled to overflowing.

Among the offerings of the house, at the place where the huge bowls have been stood under the heavens, where bread has been offered by pure hands, at the house where the righteous man has offered prayers, where the most righteous of men has offered prayers, where the god of the man has offered prayers, where lord Enki has offered prayers, there the righteous man has filled to overflowing the beer for the *bur-gia* offerings.

51–8 The righteous man, the most righteous of men, has filled them to overflowing. O lord of the storehouse, Great Mountain Enlil, he has filled them to overflowing. O lady of the storehouse, great mother Ninlil, he has filled them to overflowing. The most righteous of men has . . . the bowls with your beer. May this bronze vessel increase his long life. When Nibru had been fully built, when . . . had been . . . , when the brickwork of this house had been . . . , the living spouse . . . , the seed of the house, the seed . . . .

59 4th *kirugu.*

60–6 Gaze upon him, gaze upon him! O Utu, gaze upon him, gaze upon him! O wild bull of the E-babbar, gaze upon him, gaze upon him! O bearded one, son born to Ningal, . . . , gaze upon him! When you gaze upon the bulls in the cattle-pen, bulls fill the cattle-pen. When you gaze upon the sheep in the fold, sheep fill the fold. When you have gazed upon the man, ...

67 5th *kirugu.*

68–73 I will clear away the sparrows' droppings from the malt for you. I will clear away the mouse droppings from the grain for you. I will clear away the beaked locusts from the grain for you. May the lord eat this produce—he has eaten . . . . May the hero, youthful Utu, drink—he has drunk . . . . May youthful Utu . . .—he will give it to me to eat; may he . . .—he will give it to me to drink.

74 6th *kirugu.*

75–9 The beer . . . your seat in the brewery. Over your brewing vats . . . . The good minister . . . the *gala* priest. The minister of the good house . . . . Youthful Utu . . . .

80 7th *kirugu.*

81–4 When the heart . . . , the precious seed . . . . The holy offerings . . . . Youthful Utu . . . .

85 8th *kirugu.*

86–110 Ulili . . . ! Enlil . . . . (*2 lines missing; 21 lines fragmentary*)

111 . . . *kirugu.*°

Note

111 This composition is inscribed on a tablet whose colophon specifies it as a *šir-namšub* of Utu.

A *šir-namursaĝa* to Inana for Iddin-Dagan

This remarkable composition is extraordinarily vivid and has an almost narrative style. It is addressed to the goddess Inana (the Mistress [of heaven]; Ninegala; the planet Venus, Ninsiana) on behalf of Iddin-Dagan, king of the city of Isin. It appears to relate to the cult of the goddess at Isin.

The hymn is composed in the form *šir-namursaĝa* (lit. 'a song of warrior quality') and consists of 10 *kirugu*s of varying lengths (respectively 16, 14, 9, 14, 9, 18, 22, 15, 33, and 68 lines). The first *kirugu* is followed by a one-line *ĝišgiĝal*, the eighth by a four-line *ĝišgiĝal* and a one-line *šagbatuku*, and the tenth by a two-line *ĝišgiĝal*. As the climax approaches, the sections become longer.

The first section praises the goddess as the planet Venus, prominent in the skies. *Kirugu*s 2–6 describe a procession of the votaries of Inana occurring monthly at the new moon. To the accompaniment of drums and *alĝar* instruments, male prostitutes, wise women, drummers (some bearing weapons), priestesses, and *kurĝara* priests with their swords spilling blood (probably their own) process as the goddess, in her form as evening star, looks on with pleasure. The procession theme continues in the background in *kirugu*s 6 to 10. In the seventh, people and animals honour the goddess. In the eighth, she judges good and evil, as her votaries bring their suits before her. In the ninth, people sacrifice to Inana/Ninegala everywhere, making offerings of sacrificed animals, dairy products, fruits, cakes, and beers. They also sing to her.

The last and longest section describes a sacred marriage ritual. When the people have assembled, a dais is erected for the goddess. As described here, the king stays with her at the New Year on the day of this ritual. A bed is prepared for her, and she bathes and perfumes herself. She and the king lie down together and make love. The king makes offerings to Inana in her temple Egal-maḫ in the city of Isin. She embraces him and sits besides him on the throne dais. A banquet with music follows. The king is referred to as Ama-ušumgal-ana, a name of Dumuzid, Inana's divine beloved. The people celebrate and sing songs praising Inana.

It is difficult to know what to make of this vivid description. It seems impossible to tell whether it describes a ritual performance in which the king's wife or a priestess was thought to be transfigured into the goddess during the ritual. Or is it a transcendental description of a ritual which in reality involved only the king, temporarily elevated to the role of Inana's husband?

Translation

1–16 I shall greet her who descends from above, her who descends from above, I shall greet the Mistress who descends from above, I shall greet the great lady of heaven, Inana! I shall greet the holy torch who fills the heavens, the light, Inana, her who shines like daylight, the great lady of heaven, Inana! I shall greet the Mistress, the most awesome lady among the Anuna gods; the respected one who fills heaven and earth with her huge brilliance; the eldest daughter of Suen, Inana! For the young lady I shall sing a song about her grandeur, about her greatness, about her exalted dignity; about her becoming visible at evening; about her filling the heaven like a holy torch; about her stance in the heavens, as noticeable by all lands, from the south to the highlands, as that of Nanna or of Utu; about the greatness of the Mistress of heaven!

17 1st *kirugu.*

18 Her descending is that of a warrior.

19 *Ĝišgiĝal.*

20–33 When standing in the heavens she is the good wild cow of An, on earth she instils respect; she is the lady of all the lands. She received the divine powers in the Abzu, in Eridug; her father Enki presented them to her. He placed the lordship and kingship in her hands. She takes her seat on the great dais with An; she determines the fates in her Land with Enlil. Monthly, at the new moon, the gods of the Land gather around her so that the divine powers are perfected. The great Anuna gods, having bowed before them, stand there with prayers and supplications and utter prayers on behalf of all the lands. My lady decrees judgments in due order for the Land.° Her black-headed people parade before her.

34 2nd *kirugu.*

35–43 Making silver *alĝar* instruments sound for her, they parade before her, holy Inana. I shall greet the great lady of heaven, Inana! Making holy *ub* and holy *lilis* drums sound for her, they parade before her,

holy Inana. I shall greet the great lady of heaven, Inana! Beating (?)
holy *balaĝ* and holy *lilis* drums for her, they parade before her, holy
Inana. I shall greet° the eldest daughter of Suen°, Inana!

44 3rd *kirugu*.

FIG. 31. 'They parade before her, holy Inana'—
musicians on an Old Babylonian terracotta plaque

45–58 Combing (?) their hair (?) for her, male prostitutes parade before her,
holy Inana. Their locks of hair at the back are adorned for her with
coloured bands (?); they parade before her, holy Inana. Clothed (?) in
the leather (?) of divinity, they parade before her, holy Inana. The
trustworthy man° and the proud lady, the doyenne of the great wise
women, parade before her, holy Inana. Those who are in charge (?)
of beating (?) the soothing *balaĝ* drums parade before her, holy
Inana. Each girded with a sword belt, the strength of battle, they
parade before her, holy Inana. Grasping a spear, the strength of
battle, in their hands, they parade before her, holy Inana.

59 4th *kirugu*.

60–8 Dressed with men's clothing on the right side, they parade before
her, holy Inana. I shall greet the great lady of heaven, Inana! Adorned
(?) with women's clothing on the left side, they parade before her,
holy Inana. I shall greet the great lady of heaven, Inana! Competing
with skipping ropes of (?) coloured cords for her, they parade before
her, holy Inana. I shall greet the eldest daughter of Suen°, Inana!

69 5th *kirugu.*

70–81 Young men in neck-stocks sing to her and parade before her, holy
Inana. Young women, coiffured *šugia* priestesses, parade before her,
holy Inana. . . . sword and dagger for her, they parade before her, holy
Inana. With daggers in their hands, . . . *kurǧara* priests parade before
her, holy Inana. Those who cover their swords with gore spatter
blood as they parade before her, holy Inana. Blood is poured on the
dais standing in the *guena* hall, as *tigi, šem,* and *ala* drums are made
to sound loudly.

82–7 The Mistress stands alone in the pure heavens. From the midst of
heaven my lady looks with joy at all the lands and the black-headed
people, who are as numerous as sheep°.° I praise the lady of the
evening, Inana, the august one, the young lady, Inana. The lady of
the evening reaches the borders of heaven!°

88 6th *kirugu.*

89–105 When at evening, the radiant star, the Venus star, the great light
which fills the holy heavens, the lady of the evening, descends from
above like a warrior, the people in all the lands lift their gaze to her.
The men purify themselves, the woman cleanse themselves. The
oxen toss (?) their heads in their yoke. The sheep stir up dust in their
pens. Because of my lady, the numerous beasts of Šakkan, the
creatures of the plain, the four-legged animals under the broad
heavens°, the orchards and gardens, the plots, the green reed-beds,
the fish of the deep, the birds of heaven, all hasten to their sleeping
places. All the living creatures and the numerous people bend the
knee before her. When called for (?) by my lady, the matriarchs
plentifully provide food and drink, and my lady refreshes herself in
her Land. There is play in the Land, which is made festive. The
young men take pleasure in their spouses.

106–10 From the midst of heaven my lady looks down with joy. They parade
before her, holy Inana. The lady of the evening, Inana, is august; I
praise the young lady, Inana. The lady of the evening, her grandeur
reaches the borders of heaven!

111 7th *kirugu.*

112–21 At night the skilled and beautiful one (?), the joy of An, the ornament
of broad heaven, appears like moonlight; in the heat of the noon she
appears like sunlight. After the storehouses of the Land have been
filled with fine food, and all the lands and the black-headed people
have assembled°, those who sleep on the roofs and those who sleep

by the walls step up before her with . . . and bring her their cases. Then she makes her orders known, and identifies the evil. She judges the evil as evil and destroys the wicked. She looks with favour on the just and determines a good fate for them.

122-6 From the midst of heaven my lady looks down with joy. They parade before her, holy Inana. The lady exalted as high as the heaven, Inana, is august! I praise the young woman, Inana. The lady exalted as high as the heaven, her grandeur reaches the borders of heaven.

127 8th *kirugu*.

128-31 The beautiful lady, the joy of An, has descended from above like a warrior. She carries there what befits the . . . of heaven. She takes counsel with An in his lofty place. Among youths and heroes°, may she be alone chosen!

132 *Ĝišgiĝal*.

133 She is mighty, she is respected, she is exalted, she is august and great, she is surpassing in youthfulness.

134 *Šagbatuku*.

135-41 As the lady, admired by the Land, the lone star, the Venus star, the lady elevated as high as the heaven, descends from above like a warrior, all the lands tremble before her . . . . The faithful black-headed people bow to her. The young man travelling on the road directs himself by her. The oxen raise their heads in their yoke to her.° With her the storehouses of the Land prosper.

142-9 Everybody hastens to holy Inana. For my lady in the midst of heaven the best of everything is prepared (?). In the pure places of the plain, at its good places, on the roofs, on the rooftops, the rooftops of the dwellings (?), in the sanctuaries (?) of mankind, incense offerings like a forest of aromatic cedars are transmitted to her. They sacrifice *alum* sheep, long-haired sheep, and fattened sheep for her. They purify the earth for the Mistress, they carry out purification rites for her°.

150-62 They fill the tables of the Land with ghee, dates, cheese, and seven sorts of fruits as first-fruit offerings for her. They pour dark beer for her, they pour light beer for her. Dark beer, emmer beer, and emmer beer for my lady bubble in the *šagub* jar and the *lamsari* vat for her. From pastes of honey mixed with ghee°, they bake date-syrup cakes for her. They pour out early-morning beer, flour, flour in honey, honey, and wine of sunrise for her. The personal gods of the people also attend upon her with food and drink. They provide the Mistress with food in the holy place, the pure place°.

163–7 From the midst of heaven my lady looks down with joy. They parade before her, holy Inana. Inana, the lady exalted as high as the heaven is august! I praise the young lady, Inana. The lady exalted as high as the heaven, her grandeur reaches the borders of heaven!

168 9th *kirugu.*

169–80 When the black-headed people have assembled in the palace, the house that advises the Land, the neck-stock of all the foreign countries, the house of the river of ordeal, a dais is set up for Ninegala. The divine king stays there with her. At the New Year, on the day of the rites, in order for her to determine the fate of all the countries°, so that during the day (?) the faithful servants can be inspected, so that on the day of the disappearance of the moon the divine powers can be perfected, a bed is set up for my lady. Esparto grass is purified with cedar perfume and arranged on that bed for my lady, and a coverlet is smoothed out on the top (?) of it.

181–6 In order to find sweetness in the bed on the joyous coverlet, my lady bathes her holy thighs. She bathes them for the thighs of the king; she bathes them for° the thighs of Iddin-Dagan. Holy Inana rubs herself with soap; she sprinkles oil and cedar essence on the ground.

187–94 The king goes to her holy thighs with head held high,° he goes to the thighs of Inana with head held high. Ama-ušumgal-ana lies down beside her and caresses her holy thighs°. After the lady has made him rejoice with her holy thighs on the bed, after holy Inana has made him rejoice with her holy thighs on the bed, she relaxes (?) with him on her bed: 'Iddin-Dagan, you are indeed my beloved!'

195–202 To pour libations, to carry out purification rites, to heap up incense offerings, to burn juniper resin (?), to set out food offerings, to set out offering-bowls, he goes into her Egal-maḫ. She embraces her beloved spouse, holy Inana embraces him. She shines like daylight on the great throne dais° and makes the king position himself next (?) to her like the sun.

203–16 Abundance and celebration are prepared before her in plenty. He arranges a rich banquet for her. The black-headed people line up before her. With instruments loud enough to drown out the south wind storm, with sweet-sounding *algar* instruments, the glory of the palace, and with harps, the source of joy for mankind, musicians perform songs which delight her heart. The king sees to what is eaten and drunk, Ama-ušumgal-ana sees to what is eaten and drunk. The palace is in festive mood, the king is joyous. The people spend the day amid plenteousness. Ama-ušumgal-ana stands in great joy. May his days be long on the splendid throne! He proudly (?) occupies the royal dais.

217–22 They praise my lady on my behalf (?) with the hymns of heaven and earth: 'You are the Mistress born together with heaven and earth.' In the holy place, the pure place, they celebrate the Mistress in songs: 'Joy of the black-headed people, ornament of the assembly, Inana, eldest daughter of Suen, lady of the evening, it is sweet to praise you!'

223–5 From the midst of heaven my lady looks down with joy. They parade before her, holy Inana. Inana, the lady elevated as high as the heavens, is august!°

226 10th *kirugu*.

227–8 She is mighty, she is respected, she is exalted, she is august and great, she is surpassing in youthfulness!

229 *Ĝišgiĝal*.

230 A *šir-namursaĝa* of Ninsiana.

Notes

20–33 After 'in due order for the Land.' 2 MSS add 1 line: 'Inana decides verdicts for the Land together with Enlil.'

35–43 After 'greet' 1 MS adds: 'in (?) her grandeur, in (?) her greatness, in (?) her exalted dignity as she becomes visible at evening,'. Instead of 'the eldest daughter of Suen' some MSS have: 'the great lady of heaven'.

45–58 Instead of 'man' 1 MS has: 'king'.

60–8 Instead of 'the eldest daughter of Suen' 1 MS has: 'the great lady of heaven'.

82–7 Instead of 'sheep' 1 MS has: 'ewes'; after 'sheep.' some MSS add 1 line: 'They parade before her, holy Inana.' Instead of 'The lady of the evening reaches the borders of heaven!' 1 MS has: 'The lady exalted as high as the heaven, Inana, is august!'

89–105 Instead of 'under the broad heavens' 1 MS has: 'of the broad high (?) plain'.

112–21 After 'assembled' 1 MS adds: 'and the storehouses of the Land have been made full (?)'.

128–31 Instead of 'youths and heroes' some MSS have: 'heroic youths'.

135–41 After 'yoke to her.' 2 MSS add: 'The melody of the song of those tending the cattle resounds . . . on the plain. The farmer . . . the cattle . . . their yoke in the Land.'

142–9 Instead of 'carry out purification rites for her' some MSS have: 'celebrate her in songs'.

150–62 After 'honey mixed with ghee' some MSS add 1 line: 'From . . . mixed with ghee'. Instead of 'They provide the Mistress with food in the holy place, the pure place' some MSS have: 'They purify the earth for the Mistress, they celebrate her in songs'.

169–80 Instead of 'in order for her to determine the fate of all the countries' 1 MS has: 'in order for the life of all the countries to be attended to'.

181–6 Instead of 'she bathes them for' some MSS have: 'with head held high she goes to'.

187–94 After 'with head held high,' some MSS add: 'she goes to the thighs of Iddin-Dagan,'; instead of 'caresses her holy thighs' some MSS have: '(*says:*) "O my holy thighs! O my holy Inana!"'

195–202 Instead of 'the great throne dais' 1 MS has: 'the throne at one side (?)'.

223–5 Instead of 'Inana, the lady elevated as high as the heavens, is august!' some MSS have: 'The lady of the evening, her grandeur reaches the borders of heaven!'

A *šir-šag-ḫula* to Damgalnuna

According to the subscript of this hymn addressed to the goddess Damgalnuna, it was composed in the form *šir-šag-ḫula* (lit. 'song of a joyful heart'). As the tablet is rather badly damaged, only four discontinuous segments remain, one of which preserves the end of the hymn. The beginning is missing altogether.

In the surviving portion, Damgalnuna is extolled as the wife of Enki (Nudimmud), who is also praised. Typically as a great goddess, she is called 'rampant wild cow'—a term of praise, not abuse! She is said to act as a midwife for the great gods, an allusion to her identification with the birth goddess Nintud.

Translation

(*Unknown number of lines missing*)

A1–9 The great prince Enki, . . . heaven and earth, . . . cherishes you. Bride of Enki who determines fates favourably, great wild cow, exceptional in appearance, pre-eminent forever! Your husband, the great lord Nudimmud who makes perfect the borders of the Land, the lord on whom An the king has bestowed perceptiveness; the wise adviser, the sage lord whose command is foremost, who is skilful in everything, the majestic leader who pleases (?) Enlil's heart; whose divine powers cannot be withstood, he of deep understanding, called by an auspicious name, reaching decisions . . . who is knowledgeable about giving birth, . . . , (*unknown number of lines missing*)

B1–8 An the king . . . . Rampant wild cow, ... Life and living . . . .

Mankind .... The established first-fruit offerings .... Pleasing the
spirit and ... the heart, ... Living and a long life .... In the house
where beer is poured out, ... the oil of cedars .... (*unknown number
of lines missing*)

C1–3 The churn (?) .... The great prince Enki .... The house (?) ....
(*unknown number of lines missing*)

D1–5 The divine powers of the Abzu .... The good .... Outstanding
among ladies, your praise .... You never cease being the wife of your
Eridug, the mountain of abundance. She is the birth-giver of the
great gods, she is their goddess.

D6 A *šir-šag-ḫula* of Damgalnuna.

A *tigi* to Enki for Ur-Ninurta

This hymn is addressed to the god Enki (Nudimmud; also called 'the junior
Enlil') on behalf of Ur-Ninurta, king of the city of Isin. It is composed in the
form *tigi*, consisting of a *sa-gida* (20 lines) followed by a two-line *ĝišgiĝal*,
followed by a *sa-ĝara* (10 lines) and a final section of 12 lines. The structure is
similar to that of *An adab to Bau for Išme-Dagan*, although the proportions
are different.

In the first section, the poet praises Enki for his magical skills, advice,
guardianship of the divine powers, and water provision (rivers and rain). His
powers are derived from the gods An and Enlil.

In the *sa-ĝara*, Enki is again praised for his guardianship of the divine
powers in the Abzu (subterranean waters). The Abzu is both the god's realm
and the shrine where he is worshipped; it is so powerful that it even casts a
shadow over the E-kur, the shrine of the god Enlil (and here also An) in the
city of Nibru.

In the final section, Enki is asked directly to bless Ur-Ninurta so he will be
wise, splendid, and successful and will bring offerings to the E-kur shrine;
then Enlil will give him long life.

Translation

1–12 Lord of complex divine powers, who establishes umderstanding,
whose intentions are unfathomable, who knows everything! Enki, of
broad wisdom, august ruler of the Anuna, wise one who casts spells,

who provides words, who attends to decisions, who clarifies verdicts, who dispenses advice from dawn to dusk! Enki, lord of all true words, I will praise you. Your father, An the king, the lord who caused human seed to come forth and who placed all mankind on the earth, has laid upon you the guarding of the divine powers of heaven and earth, and has elevated you to be their prince. An, king of the gods, has instructed you to keep open the holy mouths of the Tigris and Euphrates, to fill them with splendour, to make the dense clouds release plentiful water and make them rain all over the fields, to make Ezina lift her head in the furrows, to make vegetation . . . in the desert, and to make orchards and gardens ripe with syrup and vines grow as tall as forests.

13–20 Enlil, the lord who creates everything, has bestowed on you his august, proud, and greatly awe-inspiring name: you are the junior Enlil. Throughout heaven and earth he alone is divine, and you are his younger brother. He has placed in your hands the power like him to decide destinies of both the south and the uplands. A good decision that comes forth from your mouth is exceptionally power-ful. Sa-bara°, you concern yourself with the sustenance of the people who are widely settled as far as the borders of the mountains: you are their true father. Lord, all together they praise your greatness like the greatness of their protective deities.

21 *Sa-gida.*

22–3 Nudimmud, let your holy word and august command be a source of honour for Ur-Ninurta, and let him have no rivals.

24 *Ĝišgiĝal.*

25–34 August lord, you excel in heaven and earth, and you have made your name shine forth. Enki, you have gathered up all the divine powers that there are, and stored them in the Abzu. You have made praise-worthy the divine powers, exceeding all other divine powers, of your holy dwelling which you have chosen in your heart—the Abzu, the august shrine . . .—as well as its divine plans. Its shadow covers all lands from east to west, and its terrifying splendour rests upon the holy heavens like dense thunderclouds. It fills with terror E-kur, the holy dwelling of An and Enlil. Therein, equipped with the sceptre, you fashion the numerous seeds (?) . . . for the assigned divine powers of the great gods; to create mankind and to preserve them alive is in your power, father Enki, when you take your seat on the dais where you decide destinies.

35 *Sa-ǧara.*

36–47 May Ur-Ninurta, the king in whom Enlil trusts, open up your house of wisdom in which you have gathered knowledge in plenty, and then be the great ruler of the black-headed. Make terrifying splendour befitting his godhead issue from him, the lion of kingship, in everything that he does, for as long as he lives. May you present him with weighty tribute from the upper and the lower seas, and let Ur-Ninurta bring it into the glorious E-kur. May Enlil look upon him joyously, and add to his period of rule blissful days and years of joy and life. Father Enki, inspiring terrible awe, surpassing description, may the Anuna, your divine brothers, rejoice over you. Son of An, possessor of august honour, it is sweet to praise you!

48 A *tigi* of Enki.

Note

13–20 'Sa-bara': a name of Enlil as judge.

An *ululumama* to Suen for Ibbi-Suen

The forms of the moon-god varied throughout the month, from youthful Suen to father Nanna; he was also known as Ašimbabbar (see the Introduction to Group D). Suen was also the patron god of the city of Urim; this hymn is directed to him on behalf of Ibbi-Suen, last king of the Third Dynasty of Urim. It is composed in a single uninterrupted section of about 54 lines, although the preserved text is damaged by a break on the tablet.

The moon-god shines over Urim, the principal city of Sumer. He is the son of Ninlil and Enlil (Nunamnir), who are worshipped in the city of Nibru, where their temples the E-kur and Ki-ur are located. In Sumerian religious thought, all subsidiary authority derives from a higher authority and ultimately from the most supreme deities. Suen is thus credited with interceding with his father Enlil, who has bestowed royal authority on Ibbi-Suen from the sacred, authoritative centre Nibru (see the Introduction to Group C). He will also ensure the continuing prosperity of Urim.

The hymn is addressed both to the moon-god and to the king Ibbi-Suen (whose downfall is vividly depicted in *The lament for Sumer and Urim*, Group D).

Translation

A1–8 Great lord, light holding his head high in the vault of the sky, . . . brilliance, Suen, powerful dragon from the high mountains shedding light on the people, light of the remote heavens, crown . . . , joy of the father who begot him! Impressive son born of Ninlil, respected in the E-kur, visible even at midday, youthful Suen, . . . light of heaven, whose majestic radiance is visible even at midday, light who illuminates the black-headed people, Father Nanna, emerging from the remote (?) . . . , understanding well how to make the night pleasant! Respected prince who, when he appears, is the glorious radiance of the heavens!

FIG. 32. 'He has filled the heart with joy, my Ibbi-Suen!'—
the king depicted on a cylinder seal belonging to one
of his senior officials

A9–16 At the foundations of heaven and earth, Father Nanna appears in the night-time over Urim, the foremost city of Sumer, whose divine powers can never be altered. He has called the name, he has filled the heart with joy, my Ibbi-Suen! At the shrine Nibru, whose interior is a mountain of abundance, the dwelling-place of the Ki-ur, he spreads his majestic light from above over the land in princely style, in the august courtyard, the unceasing . . . of its majestic light determining great destinies. Suen offers a prayer in the assembly hall to the father who begot him, the great . . . of heaven and earth, lord Nunamnir:

A17–20 'Canal inspector, prince on the dais, prince with life-giving divine powers! There shall be no end to the butter and the milk of the cow in the cattle-pen—the shrine Urim, which you have chosen in your heart, the august royal dwelling-place, the encouragement of the Land! It shall have an abundance of butter, fish, birds, births, copper, and gold!'

A21–32   The divine powers of the city which was responsible for the emergence of human seed cannot be altered, my Ibbi-Suen! He has made its kingship shine forth; he prolongs life! He has strengthened for you the foundations of its great dais, and has made you take your seat proudly upon it. He has made the divine powers of its kingship come forth; great power emerges from there. Those august commands cannot ever be changed, my Ibbi-Suen! You, Ašimbabbar, have caused respect for the king to shine forth throughout the whole of heaven and earth. For Nanna . . . the just man chosen in the holy heart, my Ibbi-Suen, . . . august . . . shine forth like a god. Suen . . . his command . . . the E-kur; An and Enlil, who determine the destiny of the land, the Great Mountain Enlil . . . (*1 line unclear; approximately 7 lines missing*)

B1–15   The destiny which has been determined . . . . Ašimbabbar . . . . He has made the divine powers of kingship . . . shine forth . . . with head high . . . , Nanna-Suen . . . , the noble manifest lord . . . in heaven and earth, source of trust, son of Ninlil, ornament of . . . , Nanna, lord with a holy mouth (?) and with an august name, encouragement of the Land! Prince endowed with charm, chosen in my holy heart, my Ibbi-Suen! Among the numerous people his name reaches far abroad, . . . the decision of the Land. You know well how to benefit the reign and to increase abundance; direct your attention to the great storehouses! Father Nanna, . . . is given to the one you have chosen in your heart, you noble lord who . . . the good seed, impressive with your divine powers, making . . . decisions together with Enlil, unique bull, manifest lord! Praise be to Suen!

B16   An *ululumama* of Suen.

I. SCRIBES AND LEARNING

Without the scribes, of course, no Sumerian literature would have been recorded or preserved for posterity. Sumerian literature was by definition chosen, written, remodelled by a few highly literate individuals—and it thus reflects their concerns, beliefs, and interests. It is not surprising, then, that scribal characters, and notions of literacy and numeracy, loom large in the Sumerian literary corpus.

Nisaba, patron goddess of scribes, accountants, and administrators, has frequent bit-parts in many narratives and myths: she is an essential figure in the world of the gods, without whom accounts would not be kept, nor crops harvested—without whom the civilized order of the world would dis-integrate (see *A hymn to Nisaba*). She reflects the scribal class's view of itself as central to the running of cities and the Land. Curiously, her divine spouse Ḫaia, who was believed to share many of her attributes and abilities, is a very minor figure within the literary corpus (see *A hymn to Ḫaia for Rīm-Sîn*).

Literacy and numeracy feature regularly too: in *Sargon and Ur-Zababa* (Group A), for instance, the plot turns on a tablet sealed in a clay envelope, while in both *A praise poem of Šulgi* and *A praise poem of Lipit-Eštar* (both Group J) the king boasts: 'I am a knowledgeable/proficient scribe of Nisaba.' In *The herds of Nanna* (Group D) the moon-god's cows are enumerated as if in a shepherd's annual account. Other compositions, though, portray knowledge and wisdom as something that is passed down orally from father to son (see *The instructions of Šuruppag*).

Although a literary composition about oral transmission may seem to be paradoxical or perverse, it is simply a reflection of the scribes' everyday reality: patterns of preservation of tablets suggest strongly that our manuscript sources are not the traces of a copied literary tradition but one of telling, listening, and memorization. Ironically, many of the tablets preserving the world's oldest literary tradition are ephemera: they were produced as part of the memorization process and were never intended to last (see the Introduction).

Narratives about scribes (see *A supervisor's advice to a young scribe*) and fictional letters from scribes (see *Letter from Nabi-Enlil to Ilum-puzura*) have often been used as primary historical sources for scribal schooling. The humour in them, however, suggests that they may have been more like the *St Trinian's* films or Harry Potter stories. Their point is perhaps not how realistically they portray the scribal school (which is one thing that no scribe needs telling) but rather how much they deviate from humdrum reality in order to poke fun at the stupid and the pompous. More recently, archaeologically based studies of school houses such as House F in Nibru (see Introduction) have allowed us to temper the highly coloured literary images with important evidence of physical setting and curriculum (see Group J). With their fictionality acknowledged the school narratives remain an important window into the scribes' world; but rather than showing us the reality of scribal education they tell us much about how the scribes liked to view themselves and the educational process. Pride in the profession, disdain for the incompetent or self-important, and a sharp sense of humour are all celebrated and passed on to the next generation.

FURTHER READING

Alster, B., *Proverbs of Ancient Sumer: The World's Oldest Proverb Collections* (CDL Press: Bethesda, Md., 1997) edits and translates the known corpus of Sumerian proverbs.

Michalowski, P., 'Nisaba', *Reallexikon der Assyriologie*, 9 (2001), 575–9 surveys what is known about the goddess of scribes.

Nissen, H. J., Damerow, P., and Englund, R. K., *Archaic Bookkeeping: Writing and Techniques of Economic Administration in the Ancient Near East* (University of Chicago Press: Chicago, 1993) is a fascinating window onto the humdrum world of most Sumerian scribes.

Vanstiphout, H. L. J., 'Sumerian Canonical Compositions, C. Individual Focus, 6. School Dialogues', in W. W. Hallo (ed.), *The Context of Scripture*, I: *Canonical Compositions from the Biblical World* (Brill: London/New York/, 1997, pp. 588–93) gives lively English translations of some other Sumerian compositions set in scribal schools.

OTHER COMPOSITIONS ON THIS THEME INCLUDE

Group A   Enmerkar and En-suḫgir-ana
           Sargon and Ur-Zababa
Group C   Enlil and Sud
Group D   The herds of Nanna
Group E   Ninurta's exploits
Group G   Enki and the world order

Group J   A praise poem of Šulgi
           A praise poem of Lipit-Eštar
           The song of the hoe
           The Keš temple hymn

A supervisor's advice to a young scribe

This dialogue is one of several related compositions which purport to describe the lives of scribes and their trainees. Here, an older man patronizingly lectures a recent scribal school graduate on his own exemplary educational career. He tells his apprentice what an obedient, hard-working student he was, under his excellent teacher, and exhorts the young man to follow his own example, perhaps quoting proverbs to make his point (3–28). The young man is not impressed, however: he berates his supervisor for talking down to him and vigorously outlines his own accomplishments as a scribe (29–53). The older man backs down, acknowledging at last that the younger man is ready in his turn to become a teacher (54–72), and invokes the blessing of Nisaba, patron goddess of scribes.

Such compositions have often been used as primary evidence for the working conditions and professional attitudes of Old Babylonian scribes. But the archaeological evidence from scribal schools such as House F shows that this work and others like it were copied by the trainee scribes in the process of their education. In fact, one tablet from House F in Nibru contains both the first 20 lines of this work and a mathematical exercise. This means we need to think quite carefully about how the students themselves interpreted them. Did they recognize in these dialogues a true picture of school life, or some humorous heightened reality which bore only tangential similarity to their own experiences and feelings? The nuances of humour are very hard to recover from Sumerian literature, yet they seem to be present here, for instance in pointedly contrasting pairs of words, such as 'The *learned* scribe *humbly* answered' and 'Your *charming* ditty delivered in a *bellow*' (29–35). The dialogue structure of the composition also links it to the Debate genre (see *The debate between Sheep and Grain* and *The debate between Bird and Fish*, both Group G) in which the vigorous nature of the exchanges often descends into gutter humour and slapstick. The school poems, in this light, may not be the serious documentary sources we have taken them to be after all.

Translation

1–2 (*The supervisor speaks:*) 'One-time member of the school, come here to me, and let me explain to you what my teacher revealed.

3–8 'Like you, I was once a youth and had a mentor. The teacher assigned a task to me—it was man's work. Like a springing reed, I leapt up and put myself to work. I did not depart from my teacher's instructions, and I did not start doing things on my own initiative. My mentor was delighted with my work on the assignment. He rejoiced that I was humble before him and he spoke in my favour.

9–15 'I just did whatever he outlined for me—everything was always in its place. Only a fool would have deviated from his instructions. He guided my hand on the clay and kept me on the right path. He made me eloquent with words and gave me advice. He focused my eyes on the rules which guide a man with a task: zeal is proper for a task, time-wasting is taboo; anyone who wastes time on his task is neglecting his task.

16–20 'He did not vaunt his knowledge: his words were modest. If he had vaunted his knowledge, people would have frowned. Do not waste time, do not rest at night—get on with that work! Do not reject the pleasurable company of a mentor or his assistant: once you have come into contact with such great brains, you will make your own words more worthy.

21–6 'And another thing: you will never return to your blinkered vision; that would be greatly to demean due deference, the decency of mankind. The heart is calm in . . . , and sins are absolved. An empty-handed man's gifts are respected as such. Even a poor man clutches a kid to his chest as he kneels. You should defer to the powers that be and . . .—that will calm you.

27–8 'There, I have recited to you what my teacher revealed, and you will not neglect it. You should pay attention—taking it to heart will be to your benefit!'

29–35 The learned scribe humbly answered his supervisor: 'I shall give you a response to what you have just recited like a magic spell, and a rebuttal to your charming ditty delivered in a bellow. Don't make me out to be an ignoramus—I will answer you once and for all! You opened my eyes like a puppy's and you made me into a human being. But why do you go on outlining rules for me as if I were a shirker? Anyone hearing your words would feel insulted!

FIG. 33. 'I chivvy them around like sheep'—
an Old Babylonian terracotta plaque

36–41 'Whatever you revealed of the scribal art has been repaid to you. You put me in charge of your household and I have never served you by shirking. I have assigned duties to the slave girls, slaves, and subordinates in your household. I have kept them happy with rations, clothing, and oil rations, and I have assigned the order of their duties to them, so that you do not have to follow the slaves around in the house of their master. I do this as soon as I wake up, and I chivvy them around like sheep.

42–9 'When you have ordered offerings to be prepared, I have performed them for you on the appropriate days. I have made the sheep and banquets attractive, so that your god is overjoyed. When the boat of your god arrives, people should greet it with respect. When you have ordered me to the edge of the fields, I have made the men work there. It is challenging work which permits no sleep either at night or in the heat of day, if the cultivators are to do their best at the field-borders. I have restored quality to your fields, so people admire you. Whatever your task for the oxen, I have exceeded it and have fully completed their loads for you.

50–3 'Since my childhood you have scrutinized me and kept an eye on my behaviour, inspecting it like fine silver—there is no limit to it! Without speaking grandly—as is your shortcoming—I serve before

you. But those who undervalue themselves are ignored by you—
know that I want to make this clear to you.'

54–5 (*The supervisor answers:*) 'Raise your head now, you who were
formerly a youth. You can turn your hand against any man, so act as
is befitting.'

56–9 (*The scribe speaks:*) 'Through you who offered prayers and so blessed
me, who instilled instruction into my body as if I were consuming
milk and butter, who showed his service to have been unceasing, I
have experienced success and suffered no evil.'

60–72 (*The supervisor answers:*) 'The teachers, those learned men, should
value you highly.° You who as a youth sat at my words have pleased
my heart. Nisaba has placed in your hand the honour of being a
teacher. For her, the fate determined for you will be changed and so
you will be generously blessed.° May she bless you with a joyous
heart and free you from all despondency. . . . at whatever is in the
school, the place of learning. The majesty of Nisaba . . . silence. For
your sweet songs even the cowherds will strive gloriously. For your
sweet songs I too shall strive and shall . . . . They should recognize
that you are a practitioner (?) of wisdom. The little fellows should
enjoy like beer the sweetness of decorous words: experts bring light
to dark places, they bring it to closes and streets.'

73–4 Praise be to Nisaba who has brought order to . . . and fixed districts
in their boundaries, the lady whose divine powers are divine powers
that have no rival!

Note

60–72 After 'value you highly.' 2 MSS add 3 lines: 'They should . . . in their houses
and in prominent places. Your name will be hailed as honourable for its
prominence. For your sweet songs even the cowherds will strive gloriously.' 1
of the 2 MSS adds 2 more lines which correspond to ll. 67 and 68 in this
edition: 'For your sweet songs I too shall strive and shall . . . . The teacher will
bless you with a joyous heart.' Instead of 'For her, the fate determined for you
will be changed and so you will be generously blessed.' 1 MS has: 'You were
created by Nisaba! May you . . . upwards.'

Letter from Nabi-Enlil to Ilum-puzura

This fictional letter, known from at least three copies, is supposedly from a scribe called Nabi-Enlil to one Ilum-puzura, who seems to have put his sons' or pupils' names down for the wrong school. Nabi-Enlil reports that he visited that school a few years earlier, somewhere outside Nibru, and was shocked: the house was too small and the teacher—himself apparently Nabi-Enlil's former teacher—woefully ignorant. It came nowhere near to the standards of schooling expected at Nibru (6–16). Nabi-Enlil himself, however, would be happy to take on Ilum-puzura's boys. He would offer them a whole range of Sumerian material to learn, fully up to the Nibru standard even though he is based at Isin (17–22). Meanwhile, Ilum-puzura should continue the boys' elementary education by having them memorize the standard word lists *izi* 'fire' and *lu* 'man', named after their first lines. The final metaphorical exhortation, 'In the future, you should not eat weeds!', appears to mean, 'You should not settle for less than the best!'

Studies of the school tablets found at House F and other scribal schools in Nibru show that *izi* and *lu* were regularly taught there. Elementary education was about learning how Sumerian and the cuneiform sign system worked, and involved for the most part the memorization of long standardized lists of signs, words, and phrases, in chunks of 10–30 lines at a time. Because the students used one particular tablet type both to learn short extracts of new exercises and to revise longer passages of ones learned earlier, it has been possible to piece together a common sequence or curriculum of elementary exercises at Nibru. Both *lu* and *izi*, being long and difficult exercises, belonged to the penultimate educational phase, just before the students moved on to writing whole sentences of Sumerian in the form of proverbs (see *Proverbs: collection 25*). Only after proverbs did they move on to Sumerian literary works such as those translated here.

Translation

1–5 Say to Ilum-puzura: thus speaks Nabi-Enlil the scribe, son of Saĝ-Enlil. What is this that you have done? The boys should smell the scent of Nibru!

6–14 Three years ago I returned to the man. There where they lived, in the master's house—in the first place, in my opinion it was not pleasant and, further, it was cramped; I told Pī-Ninurta. Because it was my master's house, I did not open my mouth. Now listen—there where they are living, it is not a proper scribal school. He cannot teach the education of a scribe there. He cannot recite even twenty or thirty incantations, he cannot perform even ten or twenty praise songs. But in his presence, in my master's house, I cannot open my mouth.

15–16 Don't you know that the scribal school in Nibru is unique? I told you that . . . is ignorant; but afterwards you neglected my words.

17–22 If they learn the scribal art at my hands, then Nibru will be built in Isin and take the duty upon itself! I will teach them the incantations, the praise songs, inscriptions, standard Sumerian, . . . and . . . , as far as the liturgical literature. I will set it on a foundation equal to Nibru and set a value on them . . . of a talent of silver.

23–7 You should definitely not be negligent about . . . , and not withhold from the boys the explanation of words, and put obstacles in the way of scribal training. They should get to know the . . . , the word lists *izi* and *lu*. . . . in the future, you should not eat weeds!

Proverbs: collection 25

In the eighteenth-century city of Nibru, proverbs comprised the final stage of elementary scribal education. Some collections were widely copied: one, now known as Collection 2+6, is over 300 lines long and is attested on over 150 different tablets. Some of those tablets are small and round with only one two- or three-line proverb written in good handwriting on the front (presumably by a teacher or advanced student) and again on the back rather more clumsily, presumably by a pupil who was learning it for the first time. Another, much larger standard tablet type typically bears 10–20 lines (5–10 proverbs) on the rectangular obverse, again in two copies: the model to be copied on the left, and the student's attempt(s) to replicate it on the right. On the back of such tablets the student typically copied out a much longer extract from an earlier exercise or from an earlier part of the proverb collection. The third type of tablet is typically a rather smaller rectangle, bearing the student's copy alone of a similar-sized extract—5 to 10 proverbs. Finally, there are large multi-columned tablets containing the whole of a collection, or significant fractions of it, which students appear to have written out on completing that stage of their education. The entries in the collections are typically separated by a double horizontal line.

Much less is understood about the typology and functions of similar tablets from other cities, such as Unug, Susa, and Urim. Collection 25 is known from just two sources, one of which is perhaps from Larsa. In common with other Sumerian proverb collections, it also contains small fables and parables (1, 4). Some take the theme of 'palaces', the employing agency for many scribes (8–12), while others may be paradoxes (1–5, 7), but the meanings of many remain obscured in cultural and linguistic difficulties.

Translation

1–4 1. It became cloudy, but it did not rain. It rained, but no one undid their belt. Although the Tigris was on its high tide, no water reached the arable lands. It rained on the riverbank, but the dry land did not get any of it.

5–6 2. The *en* priest eats fish and eats leeks; but cress makes him ill.

7–8 3. The lord cursed Unug, but he himself was cursed by the lady of E-ana°.

9–15 4. Nanni cherished his old age. He had not finished the building of Enlil's temple. He . . . the building of the wall of Nibru. He had abandoned the building of the E-ana, ... He had captured Simurrum, but had not managed to carry off (?) its tribute. Mighty kingship was not bestowed upon him. Was not Nanni thus brought to the Underworld with a depressed heart?

16–20 5. Although the number of unhappy days is endless (?), yet life is better than death . . . . When I . . . (*2 lines fragmentary*)

21–2 6. Into a plague-stricken city one has to be driven like a pack-ass.

23–4 7. A house built by a righteous man is destroyed by a treacherous man.

25–6 8. The palace is a slippery place, where one slips. Watch your step when you decide to go home!

27 9. The palace bows down, but only of its own accord.

28 10. The palace—one day a lamenting mother, the next day a mother giving birth.

29–30 11. Even the palace cannot avoid the wasteland. Even a barge cannot avoid straw. Even a nobleman cannot avoid corvée work.

31–4 12. What flows in is never enough to fill it, and what flows out can never be stopped—don't envy the king's property!

35–6 13. When a man sailing downstream encounters a man whose boat is travelling upstream, an inspection is an abomination to Suen.

Note

7–8 'the lady of E-ana': Inana.

The instructions of Šuruppag

The instructions of Šuruppag is an early example of a genre known as Mirrors for Princes, widely attested in Middle Eastern literature. Such works take the form of advice given to a young man, usually of royal blood, by an older male. In this case the introduction (1–13) situates the advice-giving in the distant past. The speaker is one Šuruppag, son of Ubara-Tutu, and the advisee his son Zi-ud-sura. Šuruppag is more commonly found in Sumerian literature as the name of a city and Ubara-Tutu as its ruler. In the Sumerian King List (ETCSL 2.1.1), for instance, Ubara-Tutu is portrayed as the last ruler of Sumer before the primordial flood:

> 30–9   Then Zimbir fell (?) and the kingship was taken to Šuruppag. In Šuruppag, Ubara-Tutu became king; he ruled for 18,600 years. 1 king; he ruled for 18,600 years. In 5 cities 8 kings; they ruled for 241,200 years. Then the flood swept over.

Zi-ud-sura, on the other hand, is found in the Sumerian *Flood story* (Group G) as the king who survives the flood, by building an ark-like boat onto which he loads animals and plants. Even in the first-millennium Babylonian *Epic of Gilgameš*, attested a millennium and more later than *The instructions of Šuruppag*, the flood survivor—under the Akkadian name Ūt-napištim—is described as the son of Ubara-Tutu, king of Šuruppag.

The advice itself comprises three long streams of proverb-like aphorisms, each of which ends: 'Šuruppag gave these instructions to his son. Šuruppag, the son of Ubara-Tutu, gave these instructions to his son Zi-ud-sura.' The first section (14–72), addressed directly to 'you', is primarily concerned with relationships with other people; the second (83–142) and third (153–276) are predominantly in the third person and have no overarching theme. The composition ends with praise to the goddess Nisaba (278–80).

The instructions of Šuruppag was widely copied by trainee scribes in Old Babylonian Nibru. A version is also known from the Early Dynastic city of Abu Salabikh.

Translation

> 1–8   In those days, in those far remote days, in those nights, in those far-away nights, in those years, in those far remote years, at that time the wise one who knew how to speak in elaborate words lived in the Land; Šuruppag, the wise one, who knew how to speak with elaborate words lived in the Land. Šuruppag gave instructions to his son;

Šuruppag, the son of Ubara-Tutu, gave instructions to his son Zi-ud-sura:

9–13 My son, let me give you instructions: you should pay attention! Zi-ud-sura, let me speak a word to you: you should pay attention! Do not neglect my instructions! Do not transgress the words I speak! The instructions of an old man are precious; you should comply with them!

14 You should not buy a donkey which brays; it will split (?) your midriff (?).

15–18 You should not locate a field on a road; . . . . You should not plough a field at° a path; . . . . You should not make a well in your field: people will cause damage on it for you. You should not place your house next to a public square: there is always a crowd (?) there.

19–20 You should not vouch for someone: that man will have a hold on you; and you yourself, you should not let somebody vouch for you°.

21 You should not make an inspection (?) on a man: the flood (?) will give it back (?) to you.

22–7 You should not loiter about where there is a quarrel; you should not let the quarrel make you a witness. You should not let (?) yourself . . . in a quarrel. You should not cause a quarrel; . . . . the gate of the palace . . . . Stand aside from a quarrel, . . . you should not take (?) another road.

28–31 You should not steal anything; you should not . . . yourself. You should not break into a house, you should not wish for the money chest (?). A thief is a lion, but after he has been caught, he will be a slave. My son, you should not commit robbery; you should not cut yourself with an axe.

32–4 You should not make a young man best man. You should not . . . yourself. You should not play around with a married young woman: the slander could be serious. My son, you should not sit alone in a chamber with a married woman.

35–8 You should not pick a quarrel; you should not disgrace yourself. You should not . . . lies; . . . . You should not boast; then your words will be trusted. You should not deliberate for too long (?); you cannot bear . . . glances.

39–41 You should not eat stolen food with anyone°. You should not sink (?) your hand into blood. After you have apportioned the bones, you will be made to restore the ox, you will be made to restore the sheep.

42–3 You should not speak improperly; later it will lay a trap for you.

44–6 You should not scatter your sheep into unknown pastures. You should not hire someone's ox for an uncertain . . . . A safe . . . means a safe journey.

47 You should not travel during the night: it can hide both good and evil.

48 You should not buy an onager: it lasts (?) only until the end of the day.

49 You should not have sex with your slave girl: she will chew you up (?).

50 You should not curse strongly: it rebounds on you.

51–2 You should not draw up water which you cannot reach°: it will make you weak. (*1 line unclear*)

53 You should not drive away a debtor: he will be hostile towards you.

54–7 You should not establish a home with an arrogant man: he will make your life like that of a slave girl. You will not be able to travel through any human dwelling without be being shouted at: 'There you go! There you go!'

58–9 You should not undo the . . . of the garden's reed fence; 'Restore it! Restore it!' they will say to you.

60 You should not provide a stranger (?) with food; you should not wipe out (?) a quarrel.

61–2 My son, you should not use violence (?); . . . . You should not commit rape on someone's daughter; the courtyard will learn of it.

63–4 You should not drive away a powerful° man; you should not destroy the outer wall. You should not drive away a young man; you should not make him turn against the city.

65–6 The eyes of the slanderer always move around as shiftily as a spindle. You should never remain in his presence; his intentions (?) should not be allowed to have an effect (?) on you.

67 You should not boast in beer halls° like a deceitful man°.

68–72 Having reached the field of manhood, you should not jump (?) with your hand. The warrior is unique, he alone is the equal of many; Utu is unique, he alone is the equal of many. With your life you should always be on the side of the warrior; with your life you should always be on the side of Utu.

73–5 Šuruppag gave these instructions to his son. Šuruppag, the son of Ubara-Tutu, gave these instructions to his son Zi-ud-sura.

76–8 A second time, Šuruppag gave instructions to his son. Šuruppag, the son of Ubara-Tutu, gave instructions to his son Zi-ud-sura:

79–82 My son, let me give you instructions: you should pay attention! Zi-ud-sura, let me speak a word to you: you should pay attention! Do not neglect my instructions! Do not transgress the words I speak!°

83–91 The beer-drinking mouth . . . . My little one . . . . The beer-drinking mouth . . . . Ninkasi . . . . (*5 lines unclear*)

92–3 Your own man will not repay (?) it for you. The reed-beds are . . . , they can hide (?) slander.

94–6 The palace is like a mighty river: its middle is goring bulls; what flows in is never enough to fill it, and what flows out can never be stopped.

97–100 When it is about someone else's bread, it is easy to say: 'I will give it to you', but the time of actual giving can be as far away as the sky. If you go after the man who said: 'I will give it to you', he will say: 'I cannot give it to you—the bread has just been finished up.'

101–2 Property is something to be expanded (?); but nothing can equal my little ones.

103–5 The artistic mouth recites words; the harsh mouth brings litigation documents; the sweet mouth gathers sweet herbs.

106–8 The garrulous° fills (?) his bread bag; the haughty one brings an empty bag and can fill his empty mouth only with boasting.

109 Who works with leather will eventually (?) work with his own leather.

110 The strong one can escape (?) from anyone's hand.

111–14 The fool loses something. When sleeping, the fool loses something. 'Do not tie me up!' he pleads; 'Let me live!' he pleads.

115–17 The imprudent decrees fates; the shameless one piles up (?) things in another's lap: 'I am such that I deserve admiration.'

118 A weak wife is always seized (?) by fate.

119–23 If you hire a worker, he will share the bread bag with you; he eats with you from the same bag, and finishes up the bag with you. Then he will quit working with you and, saying 'I have to live on something', he will serve at the palace.

124–5 You tell your son to come to your home; you tell your daughter to go to her women's quarters.

126 You should not pass judgment when you drink beer.

127 You should not worry unduly about what leaves the house.

128–30 Heaven is far, earth is most precious, but it is with heaven that you multiply your goods, and all foreign lands breathe under it.

131–3 At harvest time, at the most priceless time, collect like a slave girl, eat like a queen; my son, to collect like a slave girl, to eat like a queen, this is how it should be.

FIG. 34. 'At harvest time . . . collect like a slave
girl'—a female agricultural worker on a fragmentary
Early Dynastic plaque

134–42   Who insults can hurt only the skin; the greedy eyes (?), however, can
kill. The liar, shouting, tears up his garments. Insults bring (?) advice
to the wicked. To speak arrogantly is like an abscess: a herb that
makes the stomach sick. (*1 line unclear*) My words of prayer bring
abundance. Prayer is cool water that cools the heart. Only (?) insults
and stupid speaking receive the attention of the Land.

143–5   Šuruppag gave these instructions to his son. Šuruppag, the son of
Ubara-Tutu, gave these instructions to his son Zi-ud-sura.

146–8   A third time, Šuruppag gave instructions to his son. Šuruppag, the
son of Ubara-Tutu, gave instructions to his son Zi-ud-sura:

149–52   My son, let me give you instructions: you should pay attention! Zi-
ud-sura, let me speak a word to you: you should pay attention! Do
not neglect my instructions! Do not transgress the words I speak!°

153   You should not beat a farmer's son: he has constructed (?) your
embankments and ditches.

154–64   You should not buy a prostitute: she is a mouth that bites. You
should not buy a house-born slave: he is a herb that makes the
stomach sick. You should not buy a free man: he will always lean
against the wall. You should not buy a palace slave girl: she will
always be the bottom of the barrel (?). You should rather bring down
a foreign slave from the mountains, or you should bring somebody
from a place where he is an alien; my son, then he will pour water for
you where the sun rises and he will walk before you. He does not

belong to any family, so he does not want to go to his family; he does not belong to any city, so he does not want to go to his city.° He will not . . . with you, he will not be presumptuous with you.

165–7   My son, you should not travel alone eastwards. Your acquaintance should not . . . .

168–9   A name placed on another one . . . ; you should not pile up a mountain on another one.

170–1   Fate is a wet bank; it can make one slip.

172–4   The elder brother is indeed like a father; the elder sister is indeed like a mother. Listen therefore to your elder brother, and you should be obedient to your elder sister as if she were your mother.

175–6   You should not work using only your eyes; you will not multiply your possessions using only your mouth.

177   The negligent one ruins (?) his family.

178–80   The need for food makes some people ascend the mountains; it also brings traitors and foreigners, since the need for food brings down other people from the mountains.

181–2   A small city provides (?) its king with a calf; a huge city digs (?) a house plot (?).

183–8   . . . is well equipped. The poor man inflicts all kinds of illnesses on the rich man. The married man is well equipped; the unmarried makes his bed in a haystack (?). He who wishes to destroy a house will go ahead and destroy the house; he who wishes to raise up will go ahead and raise up.

189–92   By grasping the neck of a huge ox, you can cross the river. By moving along (?) at the side of the mighty men of your city, my son, you will certainly ascend (?).

193–201   When you bring a slave girl from the hills, she brings both good and evil with her. The good is in the hands; the evil is in the heart. The heart does not let go of the good; but the heart cannot let go of the evil either. As if it were a watery place, the heart does not abandon the good. Evil is a store-room . . . .° May the boat with the evil sink in the river! May his waterskin split in the desert!

202–3   A loving heart maintains a family; a hateful heart destroys a family.

204–7   To have authority, to have possessions and to be steadfast are princely divine powers. You should submit to the respected; you should be humble before the powerful. My son, you will then survive (?) against the wicked.

208–12   You should not choose a wife during a festival. Her inside is illusory

(?); her outside is illusory (?). The silver on her is borrowed; the lapis lazuli on her is borrowed.° The dress on her is borrowed; the linen garment on her is borrowed. With . . . nothing (?) is comparable.

213–14 You should not buy a . . . bull. You should not buy a vicious bull; . . . a hole (?) in the cattle-pen . . . .

215 One appoints (?) a reliable woman for a good household.

216–17 You should not buy a donkey at the time of harvest. A donkey which eats . . . will . . . with another donkey.

218–19 A vicious donkey hangs its neck; however, a vicious man, my son, ...

220 A women with her own property ruins the house.

221 A drunkard will drown the harvest.

222–34 A female burglar (?) . . . ladder; she flies into the houses like a fly. A she-donkey . . . on the street. A sow suckles its child on the street. A woman who pricked herself begins to cry and holds the spindle which pricked (?) her in her hand. She enters every house; she peers into all streets. . . . she keeps saying: 'Get out!' She looks around (?) from all parapets. She pants (?) where there is a quarrel. (*2 lines unclear*)

235–41 Marry (?) . . . whose heart hates (?). My son, . . . (*4 lines unclear*) A heart which overflows with joy . . . .

242–4 Nothing at all is to be valued, but life should be sweet. You should not serve things; things should serve you. My son, ...

245 You should not . . . grain; its . . . are numerous.

246–7 You should not abuse a ewe; otherwise you will give birth to a daughter. You should not throw a lump of earth into the money chest (?); otherwise you will give birth to a son.

248–9 You should not abduct a wife; you should not make her cry (?). The place where the wife is abducted to . . . .

250–1 'Let us run in circles (?), saying: "Oh, my foot, oh, my neck!" Let us with united forces (?) make the mighty bow!'

252–3 You should not kill a . . . , he is a child born of . . . . You should not kill . . . like . . . ; you should not bind him.

254 The wet-nurse in the women's quarters determines the fate of their lord.

255–60 You should not speak arrogantly to your mother; that causes hatred for you. You should not question the words of your mother and your personal god. The mother, like Utu, gives birth to the man; the father, like a god, makes him bright (?). The father is like a god: his words are reliable. The instructions of the father should be complied with.

261 Without suburbs a city has no centre either.

262-3 My son, a field situated at the bottom of the embankments, be it wet or dry, is nevertheless a source of income.

264 It is inconceivable (?) that something is lost forever.

265 ... of Dilmun ....

266-71 To get lost is bad for a dog; but terrible for a man°. On the unfamiliar way at the edge of the mountains, the gods of the mountains are man-eaters. They do not build houses there as men do; they do not build cities there as men do. (*1 line unclear*)

272-3 For the shepherd, he stopped searching, he stopped bringing back the sheep. For the farmer (?), he stopped ploughing the field. (*1 line unclear*)

274-6 This gift of words is something which soothes the mind ... ; when it enters the palace, it soothes the mind .... The gift of many words ... stars.

277 These are the instructions given by Šuruppag, the son of Ubara-Tutu.

278-80 Praise be to the lady who completed the great tablets, the maiden Nisaba, that Šuruppag, the son of Ubara-Tutu, gave his instructions!

Notes

15-18 After 'a field at' 1 MS adds: 'a road or'.

19-20 After 'vouch for you' 1 MS adds: ': that man will despise (?) you.'

39-41 Instead of 'anyone' 1 MS has: 'a thief'.

51-2 Instead of 'reach' 1 MS has: 'grasp'.

63-4 Instead of 'powerful' 1 MS has: 'strong'.

67 Instead of 'beer halls' 1 MS has: 'breweries'. After 'a deceitful man' 1 MS adds: ': then your words will be trusted.'

79-82 After 'Do not transgress the words I speak!' 1 MS adds 1 line: 'The instructions of an old man are precious; you should comply with them!'

106-8 Instead of 'garrulous' 1 MS has: 'liar'.

149-52 After 'Do not transgress the words I speak!' some MSS add 1 line: 'The instructions of an old man are precious; you should comply with them!'

154-64 After 'go to his city.' 1 MS adds 2 lines: 'He cannot knock at the door of ... , he cannot enter ....'

193-201 After 'Evil is a store-room ....' 1 MS adds: '(*2 lines unclear*)'.

208-12 Instead of 'The silver on her is borrowed; the lapis lazuli on her is borrowed.' 1 MS has: '... ; the jewellery on her is borrowed, the jewellery on her is borrowed.'

266–71 Instead of 'To get lost is bad for a dog; but terrible for a man.' 1 MS has: 'An unknown place is terrible; to get lost is shameful (?) for a dog.' See *Lugalbanda in the mountain cave* (Group A), lines 151–70.

A hymn to Nisaba

This hymn describes the great goddess Nisaba as patron deity of scribes and accountants. She carries a lapis lazuli tablet, the colour of the night sky, from which she reads the future through celestial omens. Without her, harvests could not be calculated nor bread and beer offerings apportioned. The first section (1–13) directly addresses Nisaba, describing her many attributes and functions, and relating her especially to the god Enlil. The following lines (14–35) narrate her appointment of an *en* priest as chief administrator to help her in the management of temple assets. She dwells in the city of Ereš in the House of Stars (E-mulmul), also known as the Lapis Lazuli House (E-zagin). This last is also the name of a temple in the mythical eastern city of Aratta (see *Enmerkar and En-suḫgir-ana*, Group A). In the third part of the composition Enki, the god of wisdom, blesses and praises her (36–55).

Although this particular hymn is formally dedicated not to Nisaba but to her patron Enki, seven other compositions presented in this book are dedicated to her. Four belong to the curricular grouping now known as the Decad (Group J), while the other three were also found on dozens of tablets in the Nibru school House F:

Group A Enmerkar and En-suḫgir-ana
Group I   A supervisor's advice to a young scribe
              The instructions of Šuruppag
Group J   A praise poem of Šulgi
              The song of the hoe
              Inana and Ebiḫ
              Gilgameš and Ḫuwawa

The hymn to Nisaba itself belongs to a further curricular grouping known as the Tetrad, which comprises four hymns in simple Sumerian which were occasionally used as a stepping stone between the elementary curriculum and the Decad. Eight of the first nine lines of the hymn are also attested on a stone tablet from late third-millennium Lagaš, while several much older compositions from Šuruppag and Abu Ṣalabikh are dedicated to Nisaba as well.

Translation

1–6 Lady coloured like the stars of heaven, holding° a lapis lazuli tablet!
Nisaba, great wild cow born of Uraš, wild sheep nourished on good
milk among holy alkaline plants, opening the mouth for seven . . .
reeds! Perfectly endowed with fifty great divine powers, my lady,
most powerful in E-kur!

7–13 Dragon emerging in glory at the festival, Aruru° of the Land, . . .
from the clay, calming . . .°, lavishing fine oil° on the foreign lands,
engendered in wisdom by the Great Mountain°! Good woman, chief
scribe of An, record-keeper of Enlil, wise sage of the gods!

14–20 In order to make barley and flax grow in the furrows, so that
excellent corn can be admired; to provide for the seven great throne-
daises by making flax shoot forth and making barley shoot forth at
the harvest, the great° festival of Enlil—in her great princely role she
has cleansed her body and has put° the holy priestly garment on her
torso.

21–6 In order to establish bread offerings where none existed, and to pour
forth great libations of alcohol, so as to appease the god of grandeur,
Enlil, and to appease merciful Kusu and Ezina, she will appoint a
great *en* priest, and will appoint a festival; she will appoint a great *en*
priest of the Land.

27–35 He° approaches the maiden Nisaba in prayer. He has organized pure
food-offerings; he has opened up Nisaba's house of learning, and
has placed the lapis lazuli tablet on her knees, for her to consult
the holy tablet of the heavenly stars. In Aratta he has placed E-zagin
at her disposal. You have built up Ereš in abundance, founded
from little . . . bricks, you who are granted the most complex
wisdom!

36–50 In the Abzu, the great crown of Eridug, where sanctuaries are
apportioned, where elevated . . . are apportioned—when Enki, the
great princely farmer of the awe-inspiring temple, the carpenter of
Eridug, the master of purification rites, the lord of the great *en*
priest's precinct, occupies E-Engur, and when he builds up the Abzu
of Eridug; when he takes counsel in Ḫal-an-kug, when he splits with
an axe the house of boxwood; when the sage's hair is allowed to hang
loose, when he opens the house of learning, when he stands in the
street of the door of learning; when he finishes (?) the great dining-
hall of cedar, when he grasps the date-palm mace, when he strikes (?)

the priestly garment with that mace, then he utters seven . . . to Nisaba, the supreme nursemaid:

51–5 'O Nisaba, good woman, fair woman, woman born in the mountains°! Nisaba, may you be the butter in the cattle-pen, may you be the cream in the sheepfold, may you be keeper of the seal in the treasury, may you be a good steward in the palace, may you be a heaper up of grain among the grain piles and in the grain stores!'

56–57 Because the Prince° cherished Nisaba, O Father Enki, it is sweet to praise you!

Notes

1–6   Instead of 'holding' 3 MSS have: 'perfectly endowed with'.
7–13   'Aruru': mother goddess. Instead of '. . .' 1 MS has: 'the region with cool water'. Instead of 'fine oil' 3 MSS have: 'plenty'. 'Great Mountain': an epithet of Enlil.
14–20   Instead of 'great' 1 MS has: 'august'. Instead of 'put' 1 MS has: 'draped'.
27–35   'He': Enki (?)—or the *en* priest.
51–5   Instead of 'in the mountains' 1 MS has: 'by the mountains'.
56–7   'the Prince': Enki.

A hymn to Ḫaia for Rīm-Sîn

Ḫaia has a much lower profile in Sumerian literature than his divine spouse Nisaba, patron goddess of scribes and accountants. This hymn is formally divided into one long *uru* and a short *ǧišǧiǧal* at the end. The first 28 lines describe him as the god Enlil's father-in-law and accountant at Nibru, as well as being associated with the temple of the moon-god at Urim. From line 29 onwards the third-person epithets are replaced by direct address to Ḫaia as 'you'. In lines 49–57 Ḫaia is asked to bless Rīm-Sîn, king of Larsa, in exchange for which Ḫaia's praise will be sung. The *ǧišǧiǧal* echoes that request.

In the 1940s a temple to Ḫaia was excavated in the small Old Babylonian city of Šaduppûm, now in the suburbs of Baghdad. It was located right by the main gate of the city wall, and was easily distinguishable from the surrounding buildings. Its façade was elaborately decorated with niches and buttresses, and the imposing steps to the entrance were flanked by life-sized terracotta lions. An entrance area led directly onto the main courtyard with a large well in the centre and a row of administrative offices running off the courtyard to the right. Directly ahead was the cella or shrine, marked like the entrance by monumental steps and ornate wall decoration. The niche in

which the statue of Ḫaia would have been displayed was directly opposite—
and could even have been visible from the street when the temple doors were
open.

Translation

1–8   Lord, perfect in august wisdom and recognized for his mighty
counsel, Ḫaia, who holds the great tablets, who enriches wisdom
with wisdom! Accountant of Ḫal-an-kug, having the final overview
of the arts of Nisaba's house of wisdom; palace archivist of heaven
and earth, who keeps count of every single assignment, who holds a
holy reed-stylus and covers the great tablets of destiny with writing!
Wise one, who prompts holy An with words and attention at the
appropriate times; seal-holder of Father Enlil! He who brings forth
the holy objects from the treasure-house of E-kur; ornament of the
Abzu shrine, wearing his hair loose for lord Nudimmud!

9–20   Ḫaia, linen-clad priest of E-unir, who stocks the holy animal-fatten-
ing pens; learned scholar of the shrine E-kiš-nugal, whose august
name is great, whose mind is discerning; who dwells in the great
dining-hall alongside the maiden Ningal! Fair of features, beloved
spouse of Nun-bar-še-gunu and augustly renowned father-in-law of
Father Enlil the Great Mountain; junior administrator, possessor of
wisdom, acknowledged in heaven and earth, who receives the tribute
for the gods, the abundance of mountains and seas! Interpreter of the
obscurity of Enlil's (?) words, skilful one who steers the august
princely divine powers, with . . . girt at his side! Formed (?) with a
broad heart, holding in his hands the holy divine plans of the temple
of Eridug, Ḫaia, who wears the ceremonial robe during pure
lustrations of the *engur*! Indagara, administrator who performs the
opening of the mouth for the gods in the heavens and in the
Underworld, and who is versed in the meaning of obscure tablets;
craftsman of the great gods!

21–8   He who fixes the standards on their pegs, planner (?) who artfully
excavates (?) the soil of the Land, who decorates the floor and makes
the dining-hall attractive for Anšar and the Great Mountain! Tall
and with head high, he whose utterances from the Abzu shrine are
favourable, who carefully holds the pure white loaves of the house of
the gods! Kusu and Indagara, without whom heaven would not be
pure nor earth bright, continual providers of the great meals of An
and Enlil in their grand dining-hall! He who gazes upon the holy

precinct, upon lord Nudimmud; he who holds the holy bronze vessels, who makes hearts rejoice and soothes spirits!

29–38 My king, I shall praise your eminence in song! Haia, I will declare your greatness perpetually! Who among the gods is fitted like you for the holy divine powers? Your beloved spouse is the maiden Nisaba, the great queen of queens. Ninlil, who was born of her holy womb, the august wife of Nunamnir, sits with her on the dais of E-kur with head raised high, uniquely entitled to behave as queen of the gods, the peerless goddess. In the Abzu shrine, Enki has bestowed his incantations of life on you, great breed-bull, who are recognized for your right understanding, who constantly care for the gods, Haia, you who operate effectively the assigning of divine powers, who mark out the cult places.

39–42 You appoint the high priest for the ĝipar shrine and install him there as its caretaker. You make the shepherd of the Land hold in his hands the august sceptre until distant days. Haia, you are the god of the Land who gives ear to the prayers of all the people. You make the king hold the widespread people in his hands for the great gods.

43–8 When Father Enki comes forth from the Abzu, he assigns (?) its greatness to you, Haia. You cause the people who are in its midst to lift their necks towards heaven; you make its population pass their days in rejoicing. You keep all its people forever contented. You establish festivals in the houses of the great gods; you spread splendour.

49–57 Leader, leader (?) of the gods, complete the great fates of the people. Look favourably upon the king with your gracious gaze that is full of life. Duly grant a joyous reign of long days to prince Rīm-Sîn, marking its years on the tablet of life, forever unalterable. May An and Enlil love the shepherd Rīm-Sîn in the office of high priest. The singers will make your praise resound sweetly in their mouths; Haia, the singers will make your praise resound sweetly in their mouths. Lord of heaven and earth, king of the Abzu, its praise is august. Father Enki, king of the Abzu, it is sweet to praise you!

58 Its *uru*.

59 Haia, god of the Land, who loves the words 'Give me life!', extend your broad arms round prince Rīm-Sîn.

60 Its ĝišĝiĝal.

A hymn to Ninkasi

This short hymn is addressed to Ninkasi, the goddess of beer. It consists of paired couplets in which the first two-line phrase is repeated, the repetition prefaced by Ninkasi's name. Lines 1–12 outline her relationship to the deities Ninḫursaĝa, Enki, and Ninti (Damgalnuna, Enki's spouse), and the remaining 36 lines describe how she brews beer.

First barley or emmer wheat was malted, by letting it sprout (21–8). This malted grain was made into beer bread with honey, dates, and other flavourings (13–16). The bread was then mixed with hulled grain and warmed to a mash (17–20) which was then cooled on reed mats (29–32). The mash was mixed with water in a large vat, to which sweeteners were added to activate fermentation (33–40). The resulting beer was filtered into a collecting jar below (41–8).

Beer was a staple in Mesopotamia and its surroundings from prehistoric times, as the fermentation process was an effective method of killing bacteria and waterborne disease. Its manufacture was recorded and controlled by scribes even in the earliest written records, from the late fourth millennium BCE. Beer was consumed by people at all levels of society and offered to gods and to the dead in libation rituals. The hero Lugalbanda sings Ninkasi's praise at the beginning of *Lugalbanda and the Anzud bird* (Group A).

Translation

1–4 Given birth by the flowing water . . . , tenderly cared for by Ninḫursaĝa! Ninkasi, given birth by the flowing water . . . , tenderly cared for by Ninḫursaĝa!

5–8 Having founded your town upon wax, she completed its great walls for you. Ninkasi, having founded your town upon wax, she completed its great walls for you.

9–12 Your father is Enki, the lord Nudimmud, and your mother is Ninti, the queen of the Abzu. Ninkasi, your father is Enki, the lord Nudimmud, and your mother is Ninti, the queen of the Abzu.

13–16 It is you who handle the . . . and dough with a big shovel, mixing, in a pit, the beer bread with sweet aromatics. Ninkasi, it is you who handle the . . . and dough with a big shovel, mixing, in a pit, the beer bread with sweet aromatics.

17–20 It is you who bake the beer bread in the big oven, and put in order the piles of hulled grain. Ninkasi, it is you who bake the beer bread in the big oven, and put in order the piles of hulled grain.

21–4 It is you who water the earth-covered malt; the noble dogs guard it even from the potentates (?). Ninkasi, it is you who water the earth-covered malt; the noble dogs guard it even from the potentates (?).

25–8 It is you who soak the malt in a jar; the waves rise, the waves fall. Ninkasi, it is you who soak the malt in a jar; the waves rise, the waves fall.

29–32 It is you who spread the cooked mash on large reed mats; coolness overcomes . . . . Ninkasi, it is you who spread the cooked mash on large reed mats; coolness overcomes . . . .

33–6 It is you who hold with both hands the great sweetwort, brewing it with honey and wine. Ninkasi, it is you who hold with both hands the great sweetwort, brewing it with honey and wine.

37–40 (*1 line fragmentary*) You . . . the sweetwort to the vessel. Ninkasi, ... You . . . the sweetwort to the vessel.

41–4 You place the fermenting vat, which makes a pleasant sound, appropriately on top of a large collector vat. Ninkasi, you place the fermenting vat, which makes a pleasant sound, appropriately on top of a large collector vat.

FIG. 35. 'It is you who pour the filtered beer out of the collector vat'—banqueters sharing a jar of beer on an Early Dynastic cylinder seal from Urim

45–8 It is you who pour the filtered beer out of the collector vat; it is like the onrush of the Tigris and the Euphrates. Ninkasi, it is you who pour the filtered beer out of the collector vat; it is like the onrush of the Tigris and the Euphrates.

J. THE DECAD, A SCRIBAL CURRICULUM

The Decad is the clearest example we have of a curricular grouping of Sumerian literary compositions. As its name suggests, there are ten works in the group. Evidence for its existence comes from a variety of sources.

First, there are two ancient catalogues of Sumerian literary works, one excavated at Nibru (*Literary catalogue from Nibru*), and one unprovenanced but strikingly similar to the first, which both start by listing the members of the Decad in the same order. Another one, from Sippar, shares the first nine of those entries. Second, several large tablets and four-sided clay prisms contain sequences of two or more Decad compositions in identical order to the catalogues.

The catalogues and 'collective' tablets prove the existence of a fixed sequence of ten literary works which clearly has no overriding thematic principles. It starts with two very different royal hymns of self-praise, one focused on a particular event and the other very generally on the attributes of good kingship. Then comes *The song of the hoe*, an extraordinary extended play on the syllable *al* 'hoe'. Three hymns to major deities and temples follow: to Inana, ostensibly by En-ḫedu-ana, daughter of king Sargon the Great; to Enlil and his temple E-kur; and to the great temple at Keš. Continuing the temple thread, *Enki's journey to Nibru* is a narrative centred around the construction of his temple E-Engur in Eridug, then *Inana and Ebiḫ* moves us firmly to the realm of mythical battles. A hymn to the minor goddess Nungal, patron deity of prisons (which once again is as much about a building as a deity), is followed by an epic adventure which pits Gilgameš and his servant Enkidu against Ḫuwawa, spirit of the cedar forests.

What the Decad members do have in common is length—all are between 100 and 200 lines long—and an absence of formal divisional and generic labels that appear to mark out the hymnic genres (see Group H). And they were very widely copied: nearly 80 manuscripts, on average, are known for each Decad composition, compared to a small handful for most Sumerian literary works. Some 80 per cent of known Decad tablets are from Nibru, and a third of those—a quarter of the total—are from the scribal school now called House F (see the Introduction to this book). This is the clinching evidence for the Decad as a *curricular* sequence as opposed to some other sort of grouping: even within House F it stands out as having some twenty manuscript sources for each composition compared to an overall average of eight tablets per work across the house as a whole.

Two other curricular sequences of Sumerian literary works are known. The four-member Tetrad, including *A hymn to Nisaba* (Group I), sometimes served as a bridge between elementary scribal education and Sumerian literary studies, and is well attested from Unug and Isin as well as Larsa. The 'House F Fourteen', as its name suggests, is another group of literary works well attested at House F (with around eighteen manuscript sources each) and partially represented in the ancient catalogues, but which did not have the same currency as the Decad, even within Nibru.

FURTHER READING

Tinney, S. J., 'On the Curricular Setting of Sumerian Literature', *Iraq*, 59 (1999), 159–72, presents the evidence for the existence of the Tetrad and Decad.
Vanstiphout, H. L. J., 'How Did they Learn Sumerian?' *Journal of Cuneiform Studies*, 31 (1979), 118–26, analyses a Sumerian literary work (which we now know belongs to the Tetrad) in purely pedagogical terms.
Veldhuis, N., 'Sumerian Proverbs in their Curricular Context', *Journal of the American Oriental Society*, 120 (2000), 383–99, shows how proverbs fit into elementary education at Nibru.

OTHER COMPOSITIONS KNOWN TO BELONG TO CURRICULAR GROUPINGS INCLUDE

Group A Gilgameš, Enkidu, and the Underworld
Group B Dumuzid's dream
Group C The cursing of Agade
Group E Ninurta's exploits
Group G The debate between Sheep and Grain
Group I A supervisor's advice to a young scribe
The instructions of Šuruppag
A hymn to Nisaba

Literary catalogue from Nibru

About a dozen ancient Sumerian literary catalogues are known, which list the incipits, or first lines, of a large number of compositions. While some seem to have had a library function, recording the tablets kept in a particular basket, room, or building, others such as this one are more clearly curricular. It has 62 entries, divided into six groups of about 10 by horizontal rulings on the tablet. The first section comprises the curricular grouping known as the Decad, which is presented in this chaper, while all but seven (shown in italics) of the other 52 entries are identifiable as Sumerian literary works well known from Nibru. Eighteen of them (shown in bold) are translated elsewhere in this book; many of the others can be found on the ETCSL website under the (modern) catalogue numbers given.

Some thematic groupings are visible within the catalogue: the last member of the Decad, *Gilgameš and Ḫuwawa*, attracts other Gilgameš tales (11–14); many of the debate poems (25, 27–30) and city laments (32–4) are grouped together. Three of the four Lugalbanda narratives are listed together (38–40, 48), as are some of the hymns to Inana (41, 44, 45). Finally, the school narratives and debates (really arguments) between scribes are clustered with diatribes against individuals (50–2, 54–62).

Translation

1 **I, the king, (was a hero) already in the womb**	A praise poem of Šulgi
I am a king treated with respect	A praise poem of Lipit-Eštar
Not only did the lord (make the world appear) in its correct form	The song of the hoe
Lady of all the divine powers	The exaltation of Inana
5 **Enlil('s commands are) by far (the loftiest)**	Enlil in the E-kur
The princely one	The Keš temple hymn
In those remote days	Enki's journey to Nibru
Goddess of the fearsome divine powers	Inana and Ebiḫ
House, furious storm of heaven and earth	A hymn to Nungal

10 **Now the lord (once decided to set) off) for the mountain where the man lives**	Gilgameš and Ḫuwawa

(I will sing the song) of the man of battle	Gilgameš and the Bull of Heaven (ETCSL 1.8.1.2)
Envoys of Aga	Gilgameš and Aga (ETCSL 1.8.1.1)
Gudam (. . .) the city	The tale of Gudam (?) (ETCSL 1.3.4)
So come on now	Gilgameš and Ḫuwawa, version B (ETCSL 1.8.1.5.1)
15 Great matriarch	Išbi-Erra E (ETCSL 2.5.1.5)
My fish, (I have built you) a home!	The home of the fish, Group G
When, upon the hill of heaven and earth	The debate between Sheep and Grain, Group G
(After Enlil's) frown	The cursing of Agade, Group C
Grieve, O countryside!	Dumuzid's dream, Group B
20 **In those remote days**	Gilgameš, Enkidu, and the Underworld, Group A

In those remote days	The instructions of Šuruppag, Group I
There is a city	Enlil and Ninlil, Group C *or* Nanše A (ETCSL 4.14.1)
Lady of good divine powers **There is a city**	Enlil and Ninlil, Group C *or* Nanše A (ETCSL 4.14.1)
25 O the Hoe, the Hoe	The debate between Hoe and Plough (ETCSL 5.3.1)
The king, (to make) his name (famous) for all time	Šulgi hymn B (ETCSL 2.4.2.02)
In those ancient days	The debate between Bird and Fish, Group G
The great Ki-ur	The debate between Tree and Reed (ETCSL 5.3.4)
An (lifted his head) in pride	The debate between Winter and Summer (ETCSL 5.3.3)
30 **(What do they say) in the reed-beds whose growth is good?**	The heron and the turtle, Group G

The pelican (?) (came forth) from the holy reed-beds	Nanše hymn C (ETCSL 4.14.3)
(He has abandoned) his cattle-pen	The lament for Urim (ETCSL 2.2.2)
After the cattle-pen (had been built) for the foremost divine powers	The lament for Nibru (ETCSL 2.2.4)
To overturn the appointed times	The lament for Sumer and Urim, Group D
35 *City of good divine powers*	
Furious storm of Sumer	
Furious storm on the horizon	
When in ancient days heaven (was separated) from earth	Lugalbanda in the mountain cave, Group A
Lugalbanda	Lugalbanda and the Anzud bird, Group A
40 **Brickwork (rising out) from the pristine mountain**	Enmerkar and En-suḫgir-ana, Group A

From the great heaven (she set her mind) on the great below	Inana's descent to the Underworld, Group B
Grandiloquent lord of heaven and earth	Enki and the world order, Group G
Green young reeds	
The mistress who, having all the great divine powers	Inana and Šu-kale-tuda, Group F
45 **Great light, heavenly lioness**	Inana hymn D (ETCSL 4.07.4)
Great lord, wearing the crown in Kulaba	
The princely one	
City, majestic bull	Enmerkar and the lord of Aratta (ETCSL 1.8.2.3)
O, E-unir	The temple hymns (ETCSL 4.80.1)

50 **Where did you go?**	*Eduba* A (ETCSL 5.1.1)
Come here to me	A supervisor's advice to a young scribe (*Eduba* C), Group I
Come, let's test each other!	Dialogue 1 (ETCSL 5.4.01)
Old Man Cultivator	The farmer's instructions (ETCSL 5.6.3)
Where do you come from?	*Eduba* B (ETCSL 5.1.2)
55 Where do you come from?	Dialogue 5 (ETCSL 5.4.05)

Do you know Sumerian?	*Eduba* D (ETCSL 5.1.4)
Why (. . .) instructions	*Eduba* R (ETCSL 5.1.6)
Young one, today	Dialogue 2 (ETCSL 5.4.02)
(Well, fellow student, what shall we write today) on the back of our tablets?	Dialogue 3 (ETCSL 5.4.03)
60 (. . .) fool	Diatribe B (ETCSL 5.4.11)
His reasoning, his following	Diatribe A (ETCSL 5.4.10)
Good seed of a dog	Diatribe C (ETCSL 5.4.12)

A praise poem of Šulgi

Šulgi was the king of Urim for nearly 50 years of the 21st century BCE. Under his leadership Urim's territory grew to encompass all of Sumer and beyond; the size of its bureaucracy, army, and taxation regime grew with it.

Some twenty-five hymns are known praising Šulgi, or praising deities on his behalf. This example is a hymn of self-praise, written as if Šulgi is speaking about himself. Its main intent is to describe a great physical feat, portraying Šulgi as both mighty and devout.

Šulgi outlines his physical prowess in general terms, by means of comparison with powerful wild animals, interspersing this with an enumeration of his relationship to the main deities of Sumer (1–25). He then describes the planning and inauguration of an improved road system between his capital city Urim and the religious centre of Nibru some 120 miles north (26–87). To celebrate its opening, Šulgi says that he himself made the epic journey on foot, from Nibru to Urim and back. Running past throngs of admiring subjects, he reaches Urim at daybreak and celebrates with a ceremony and festival. On the return leg, he battles through fierce storms to enter Nibru at sunset for further festivity and offerings. He ends with a wish that he and his deeds be remembered and glorified (88–101).

Animal and bird imagery permeates this hymn. Šulgi mostly likens himself to a lion ('a fierce-looking lion, begotten by a dragon'; 'the lion, never failing in his vigour'; 'like a lion, spreading fearsomeness', 'like a fierce lion'), but creatures which are renowned for their endurance or speed are also summoned up. Equids are the subject of the third paragraph, while the ass image is also used later in the composition: 'I galloped like an ass in the desert'; 'trotting like a solitary wild ass'. Šulgi is also 'like a mountain kid hurrying to its habitation' or like the mythical Anzud bird 'lifting its gaze to the mountains'. 'Like a pigeon anxiously fleeing from a . . . snake, I spread my wings' is intended to conjure up swiftness of response rather than fear; elsewhere Šulgi compares himself to predatory raptors: 'I arose like an owl (?), like a falcon.'

Translation

1–6   I, the king, was a hero already in the womb; I, Šulgi, was born to be a mighty man. I am a fierce-looking lion, begotten by a dragon. I am the king of the four regions; I am the herdsman and shepherd of the black-headed people. I am a respected one, the god of all the lands.

7–15   I am a child born of Ninsumun. I am the choice of holy An's heart. I am the man whose fate was decided by Enlil. I am Šulgi, the beloved of Ninlil. I am he who is cherished by Nintud. I am he who was endowed with wisdom by Enki. I am the powerful king of Nanna. I am the growling lion of Utu. I am Šulgi, who has been chosen by Inana for his attractiveness.

16–18   I am a mule, most suitable for the road. I am a horse, whose tail waves on the highway. I am a stallion of Šakkan, eager to run.°

19–25   I am a knowledgeable scribe of Nisaba; I have perfected my wisdom just as my heroism and my strength°. Reliable words can reach (?) me. I cherish righteousness but do not tolerate wickedness. I hate anyone who speaks wickedly.

26–35   Because I am a powerful man who enjoys using his thighs, I, Šulgi, the mighty king, superior to all, strengthened (?) the roads, put in order the highways of the Land. I marked out the *danna*° distances, built lodging houses there. I planted gardens by their side and established resting-places°, and installed in those places experienced men. Whichever direction one comes from, one can refresh oneself at their cool sides; and the traveller who reaches nightfall on the road can seek haven there as in a well-built city.

36–41   So that my name should be established for distant days and never fall into oblivion, so that my praise should be uttered° throughout the Land, and my glory should be proclaimed in the foreign lands, I, the fast runner, summoned my strength and, to prove my speed, my heart prompted me to make a return journey from Nibru to brick-built Urim as if it were only the distance of a *danna*.

42–7   I, the lion, never failing in his vigour, standing firm in his strength, fastened the small *niğlam* garment firmly to my hips. Like a pigeon anxiously fleeing from a . . . snake, I spread my wings; like the Anzud bird lifting its gaze to the mountains, I stretched forward my legs. The inhabitants of the cities which I had founded in the land lined up for me; the black-headed people, as numerous as ewes, looked at me with sweet admiration.

FIG. 36. 'I, Šulgi, who make everything abundant'—Šulgi makes a libation on a cylinder seal dedicated for his life by the governor of Nibru

48–59 I entered the E-kiš-nugal like a mountain kid hurrying to its habitation, when Utu spread broad daylight over the countryside. I filled with abundance the temple of Suen, a cattle-pen which yields plenty of fat. I had oxen slaughtered there; I had sheep offered there lavishly°. I caused *šem* and *ala* drums to resound there and caused *tigi* drums to play there sweetly.° I, Šulgi, who make everything abundant, presented there food-offerings and after, like a lion, spreading fearsomeness from (?) the royal offering-place, I bent down (?) and bathed in flowing water; I knelt down and feasted in the Egal-maḫ of Ninegala.

60–9 Then I arose like an owl (?), like a falcon to return to Nibru in my vigour. But a storm shrieked, and the west wind whirled around. The north wind and the south wind howled at each other. Lightning together with the seven winds vied with each other in the heavens. Thundering storms made the earth quake, and Iškur roared in the broad heavens. The rains of heaven mingled° with the waters of the earth. Small and large hailstones drummed on my back.

70–8 I, the king, however, did not fear, nor was I terrified. I rushed forth like a fierce lion. I galloped like an ass in the desert. With my heart full of joy, I ran (?) onward. Trotting like a solitary wild ass, I traversed a distance of fifteen *danna*° by the time Utu was to set his face toward his house; my *saĝursaĝ* priests looked at me with admiration.° I celebrated the *eše*š festival in both Nibru and Urim on the same day!

79–83 I drank beer in the palace founded by An with my brother and companion, the hero Utu. My singers praised me with songs accompanied by seven *tigi* drums. My spouse, the maiden Inana, the lady, the joy of heaven and earth, sat with me at the banquet.

84–7 Truly I am not boasting! Wherever I look to, there I go; wherever my heart desires, there I reach.° An placed firmly a legitimate and lofty° crown on my head.

88–94 In the lustrous E-kur, I seized the holy sceptre and I lifted my head towards heaven on a shining dais, a throne with firm foundation. I consolidated my kingship, subdued the foreign lands, fortified the Land of Sumer. May my name be proclaimed among the well-guarded people of the four regions! May they praise it in holy hymns about me! May they glorify my majesty, saying:

95–101 'The one provided with lofty royal power; the one given heroism, power, and happy life by Suen of the E-kiš-nuĝal; the one endowed with superior strength by Nunamnir; Šulgi, the destroyer of foreign lands, the fortifier of the Land, the purification priest of heaven and earth, who has no rival; Šulgi, who is cared for by the respected child of An!'

102 Praise be to Nisaba!°

Notes

16–18 Instead of 'I am a stallion of Šakkan, eager to run.' 1 MS has: 'I am a donkey of Šakkan, who loves running.'

19–25 Instead of 'my strength' 1 MS has: 'my distinction'.

26–35 A *danna* is equivalent to about 11 kilometres. Instead of 'I planted gardens by their side and established resting-places' 1 MS has: 'I established gardens (?) and resting-places by their side'.

36–41 Instead of 'uttered' 1 MS has: 'spread'.

48–59 Instead of 'offered there lavishly' some MSS have: 'butchered there'. Instead of 'and caused *tigi* drums to play there sweetly.' 1 MS has: 'I . . . the *balaĝ* drummer (?).'

60–9 Instead of 'mingled' 1 MS has: 'competed'.

70–8 Fifteen *danna* is equivalent to over 160 kilometres. Instead of 'my *saĝursaĝ* priests looked at me with admiration.' 1 MS has: '. . . numerous (?) . . . ; I prayed in the . . . of Enlil and Ninlil.'

84–7 After 'reach.' 1 MS adds at least 10 lines: 'By the life of my father holy Lugalbanda, and Nanna the king of heaven and earth, I swear that the words written on my tablet are . . . . (*at least 4 lines missing or unclear*) . . . since the days of yore, since . . . , no king of Sumer as great as I has existed for the people.' Instead of 'legitimate and lofty' some MSS have 'golden'; 1 MS has: 'good silver'; 1 MS has: 'silver'.

101–2 Instead of ' "Šulgi, who is cared for by the respected child of An!" Praise be to Nisaba!' 1 MS has: 'Šulgi, be praised (?) by An's respected son!'

A praise poem of Lipit-Eštar

This hymn of self-praise is composed as if king Lipit-Eštar of Isin himself were speaking. The refrain 'I am Lipit-Eštar' splits the composition into nine unequal parts, each on a different theme of his exemplary attributes of king-ship.

After a brief introduction (1–2) the king describes his physical prowess and good looks, in terms reminiscent of Šulgi (above) (3–17). We then read of the divine support he enjoys—from An, Enlil and Ninlil, Nintud, Nanna, Ninurta (Uta-ulu), Enki, Inana, Nisaba, and Utu (18–42). Lipit-Eštar then presents himself as a great provider, for both humankind (43–50) and the gods in their temples (51–70). Against enemies he is the strongest of warriors (71–9) but to his own people he is a wise judge and a role-model of good behaviour (80–97). For the goddess Inana he is a virile sexual partner (98–104).

All of these tropes of good kingship can be found in other royal praise poems—*A praise poem of Šulgi* is a case study in both piety and bodily athleticism; *A love song for Šu-Suen* (Group B) has Inana lusting for the king; *An adab to Nergal for Šu-ilišu* (Group E) is addressed to the warrior god Nergal for help in battle—but no other paints such a clear and rounded portrait of the ideal ruler as *A praise poem of Lipit-Eštar*. This may have been one of the reasons for its durability within the school canon; in Nibru it was copied until at least the 1740s, some two centuries after the king's reign. Its scholastic function then was probably not so much to memorialize a long-dead ruler from a long-defunct dynasty but to instil into the trainee scribes the values and ideals of Mesopotamian kingship—which apparently did not include modesty!

Translation

1–2 I am a king treated with respect, good offspring from the womb. I am Lipit-Eštar, the son of Enlil.

3–17 From the moment I lifted my head like a cedar sapling, I have been a man who possesses strength in athletic pursuits. As a young man I grew very muscular (?). I am a lion in all respects°, having no equal. I am a gaping dragon, a source of great awe for the soldiers. I am like the Anzud bird, peering about in the heart of the mountains. I am a wild bull whom nobody dares oppose in its anger. I am a bison, sparkling with beautiful eyes, having a lapis lazuli beard; I am . . . . With my kind eyes and friendly mouth, I lift people's spirits. I have a most impressive figure, lavishly endowed with beauty. I have lips appropriate for all words. As I lift my arms, I have beautiful fingers. I am a very handsome young man, fine to admire. I am Lipit-Eštar, king of the Land.

18–22 I am the good shepherd of the black-headed. I am the foremost in the foreign countries, and exalted in the Land. I am a human god, the lord of the numerous people. I am the strong heir of kingship. Holding my head high, I am established in my position.

23–32 I am An's purification priest with purified hands. An placed the great and good crown firmly on my head. Enlil gave the sceptre to me, his beloved son, in the Ki-ur. I am what makes Ninlil happy: she determined a good fate in the Ga-ĝiš-šua. I have been made excellently beautiful by Nintud, the joyful woman, in brick-built Keš. I am one looked on favourably by Nanna: he spoke to me affirmatively in Urim.

33–42 Uta-ulu imbued me, the man of his heart, with great awesomeness in E-šumeša. I am he on whom Enki has bestowed wisdom: he gave me kingship in Eridug. As the beloved husband of Inana, I lift my head high in the place Unug. I am a proficient scribe of Nisaba. I am a young man whose word Utu confirms. I am the perfection of kingship. I am Lipit-Eštar, Enlil's son.

43–50 I am he who makes an abundant crop grow, the life of the Land. I am a farmer, piling up his grain-piles. I am a shepherd making fat and milk abundant in the cattle-pen. I am he who makes the fish and birds grow bigger in the marshes. I am a river of plenty, bringing flowing water. I am he who increases the splendour of the great mountains. I have been given enormous strength by Enlil. I am Lipit-Eštar, his young man who respects him.

51–61 I am the provider of the gods. I am he who cares unceasingly for the E-kur. I am the king clutching a kid to the breast as a gift. I pray in all humility. I am a king standing in prayer. I am he who speaks friendly words to appease Enlil. I am he whose prayers make Ninlil happy. I am he who serves Nuska indefatigably. I am he who is ever praying (?) at the Ki-ur. Bestowing many things, I am perfect for the foundation°. I am one who always hurries, but whose knees never tire.

62–70 Bringing first-fruits, I do not pass by the E-babbar. I am he who records abundance for Nibru. I serve Keš as its purification priest. I am first-rate fat and first-rate milk for Urim. I am indefatigable with respect to Eridug. I am he who increases the food offerings for the place Unug. I am he to whom life was given in the E-kur. I am he who desires liveliness for his city. I am Lipit-Eštar, the shepherd of all foreign lands.

71–9 I, the king, am like pounding waves in battle. Girded in manliness, I never loosen my harness. I am he who sharpens his dagger. In battle I flash like lightning. A firm foundation, I repulse the troops. I am a saĝkal stone, a pešpeš stone. I am a siege shield, a screen for the army. A clear-eyed warrior, I make the troops firm. I am Lipit-Eštar, Enlil's son.

80–92 Like a waterskin with cool water, I am life for the young men. Keeping my eyes on the road, I am the protection° of the soldiers. I am a king who, as he sits, is fitted for the throne. I am possessed of a weighty persona for speaking. I am one with a far-reaching mind and intellect, examining requests. I do not hurry over anything, but research its background. I have a far-reaching heart and broad wisdom. I am a stone that brings . . . out of the Land. I am one that has truth in his mouth. I am one who never destroys a just person. I am a judge who, in making a decision, weighs his words fairly. I am one who is well acquainted with giving orders to the foreign lands. I have established justice in Sumer and Akkad, and made the Land feel content.

93–7 What of my truthful things can be thrown away? I, prince Lipit-Eštar, keep the people on a straight path. As regards my integrity: in what respect have I ever been idle? I am a strong person who has brought distinction to everything. I am Lipit-Eštar, Enlil's son.

98–104 In my royal palace, my holy and good residence, my spouse holy
Inana made firm the foundation of my throne. She will embrace me
forever and eternally. I will spend all day for the Mistress in the good°
bedchamber that fills the heart with joy! I am Lipit-Eštar, the powerful heir.

105–8 I am the king that makes justice prominent. May my name be called
on in all the foreign lands! I am Lipit-Eštar, Enlil's son. It is sweet to
praise me!

Notes

3–17 Instead of 'in all respects' 3 MSS have: 'to the extremes (?)'.
51–61 Instead of 'foundation' 1 MS has: 'city (?)'.
80–92 Instead of 'the protection' 1 MS has: 'the aid (?)'.
98–104 Instead of 'good' 1 MS has: 'lapis lazuli'.

The song of the hoe

In this composition, the word *al* 'hoe' is used as often as possible, as well as
many nouns or verb forms beginning with—or merely containing—the
syllable *al* (occasionally also *ar*). In that sense we could think of it as a long
series of puns, or perhaps a tongue-twister; but it is also a sort of one-sided
Debate poem (see Group G) which surveys the hoe's usefulness to gods and
humankind alike; and then again it is also a kind of creation account.

The narrative starts with the god Enlil separating heaven from earth and
linking the two at Dur-an-ki, the sacred term for Nibru (1–7). He does this,
we are told, with a primordial hoe made of precious materials (8–17)—for
how can one create the world without the right tools to hand? Now Enlil sets
to creating people; as in other Mesopotamian creation myths he uses clay as
the raw materials, so once again he needs the hoe (18–27). The people
themselves take up the hoe in order to build the temples of the Land (28–58).
The hoe can be used for other purposes too: as a weapon (59–70) and to bury
the dead (71–82). This passage contains several allusions to the Gilgameš
narratives, including Enkidu's return from the Underworld (see *Gilgameš,
Enkidu, and the Underworld*, Group A) and Gilgameš rowing across the
waters of death. Then comes an enumeration of all sorts of other objects with
names encompassing the sound *al* (83–93) and a summary of all the useful
building and agricultural tasks one can do with the hoe (94–106). Both
Nisaba and the hoe are praised at the end of the composition.

The Mesopotamian hoe was more like a mattock than a modern garden hoe. Its wide blade was at right angles to the shaft, which meant it could be used like a pick to break up earth, as well as to till and smooth it. As scribal students in Nibru were mostly affluent urbanites destined for careers in temple administration it is unlikely that any of them would have ever seen the business end of a hoe. The composition should perhaps be seen as at once reminding the young men that the foundations of institutional prosperity rest on manual labour, while distancing them from it through elaborate intellectual word games and clever origin myths.

Translation

1–7   Not only did the lord make the world appear in its correct form—the lord who never changes the destinies which he determines: Enlil, who will make the human seed of the Land come forth° from the earth°—and not only did he hasten to separate heaven from earth, and hasten to separate earth from heaven, but, in order to make it possible for humans to grow in Where Flesh Came Forth°, he first suspended° the axis of the world at Dur-an-ki.

8–17   He did this with the help of the hoe (*al*)—and so daylight broke forth (*aled*). By distributing (*altare*) the shares of duty he established daily tasks, and for the hoe (*al*) and the carrying-basket wages were even established. Then Enlil praised his hoe (*al*), his hoe (*al*) wrought in gold, its top inlaid with lapis lazuli, his hoe (*al*) whose blade was tied on with a cord, which was adorned with silver and gold, his hoe (*al*), the edge of whose point (?) was a plough of lapis lazuli, whose blade was like a battering ram standing up to a great (*gal*) wall°. The lord evaluated the hoe (*al*), determined its future destiny and placed a holy crown on its head . . . .

18–27   Here, in Where Flesh Came Forth, he set this very hoe (*al*) to work;° he had it place the first model of mankind in the brick mould. His Land started to break through the soil towards Enlil. He looked with favour at his black-headed people. Now the Anuna gods stepped forward to him, and did (*g̃al*) obeisance to him. They calmed Enlil with a prayer, for they wanted to demand (*al-dug*) the black-headed people from him. Ninmena, the lady who had given birth to the ruler, who had given birth to the king, now set (*alg̃ag̃a*) human reproduction going.

28–34   The leader of heaven and earth, lord Nunamnir, named the important persons and valued (*kal*) persons. He . . . these persons, and recruited them to provide for the gods. Now Enki praised Enlil's hoe (*al*), and the maiden Nisaba was made responsible for keeping records of the decisions. And so people took (*ĝal*) the shining hoes (*al*), the holy hoes (*al*), into their hands.

35–42 The E-kur, the temple of Enlil, was founded by the hoe (*al*). By day it was building (*aldue*) it, by night it caused the temple to grow (*almumu*). In well-founded Nibru, the hero Ninurta entered into the presence of Enlil in the inner chamber of the *Tummal*—the *Tummal*, the bread basket (?)° of mother Ninlil—the innermost chamber of the *Tummal*, with regular food deliveries. Holy Ninisina entered into the presence of Enlil with black kids and fruit offerings for the lord.

43–5 Next comes the Abzu, with the lions before it, where the divine powers may not be requested (*al-dug*): the hoe wielder (?) (*altar*), the good man, lord Nudimmud was building (*aldue*) the Abzu, Eridug having been chosen as the construction site (*altar*).

46–8 The mother of the gods, Ninḫursaĝa, had the mighty (?) (*altar*) light of the lord live with her in Keš; she had Šul-pa-eda, no less, help her with the construction work (*altar*).

49–51 The shrine E-ana was cleaned up by means of the hoe (*al*) for the lady of E-ana, the good cow (*immal*)°. The hoe (*al*) deals with ruin mounds, the hoe (*al*) deals with weeds.

52–5 In the city of *Zabalam*, the hoe (*al*) is Inana's workman (?). She determined the destiny of the hoe (*al*), with its projecting lapis lazuli beard°. Utu was ready to help her with her building project (*altar*); it is the renowned (?) building project (*altar*) of youthful Utu.

56–8 The lady with broad (*daĝal*) intelligence, Nisaba, ordered the measuring of the E-ana for a construction project (*altar*), and then designed her own E-ḫamun for construction (*altar*).

59–70 The king who measured up the hoe (*al*) and who passes (*zal*) his time in its tracks, the hero Ninurta, has introduced working with the hoe (*altar*) into the rebel (*bal*) lands. He subdues (*alĝaĝa*) any city that does not obey its lord. Towards heaven he roars (*algigi*) like a storm, earthwards he strikes (*alĝaĝa*) like a dragon (*ušumgal*). Šara sat down on° Enlil's knees, and Enlil gave him what he had desired (*al-dug*): he had mentioned the mace, the club, arrows and quiver, and the hoe (*al*)°. Dumuzid is the one who makes the upper land fertile (*allumlum*). Gibil made his hoe (*al*) raise its head towards the heavens—he caused the hoe (*al*), sacred indeed, to be refined with fire. The Anuna were rejoicing (*alḫulḫuledeš*).

71–82 The temple of Ĝeštin-ana resembled drum sticks (?) (*alĝarsur*), the drum sticks (?) (*alĝarsur*) of mother Ĝeštin-ana that make a pleasant sound. The lord° bellowed at his hoe (*al*) like a bull. As for the grave (*irigal*): the hoe (*al*) buries people, but dead people are also brought up from the ground by the hoe (*al*). With the hoe (*al*), the hero honoured by An, the younger brother of *Nergal*, the warrior Gilgameš is as powerful as a hunting net. The° son of Ninsumun is pre-eminent with oars (*ĝisal*). With the hoe (*al*) he is the great barber (*kindagal*) of the watercourses. In the chamber° of the shrine, with the hoe (*al*) he is the minister (*sukkal*). The wicked (*ḫulĝal*) . . . are sons of the hoe (*al*); they are born in sleep from heaven.

83–93 In the sky there is the *altirigu* bird, the bird of the god. On the earth there is the hoe (*al*): a dog in the reed-beds, a dragon (*ušumgal*) in the forest. On the battlefield, there is the *dur-allub* battle-axe. By the city wall there is the battle-net (*alluḫab*). On the dining-table there is the bowl (*maltum*). In the waggon shed, there is the sledge (*mayaltum*). In the donkey stable there is the cupboard (*argibil*). The hoe (*al*)!— the sound of the word is sweet: it also occurs (*munĝal*) on the hillsides: the tree of the hillsides is the *allanum* oak. The fragrance of the hillsides is the *arganum* balm. The precious stone of the hillsides is the *algameš* steatite.

94–106 The hoe (*al*) makes everything prosper, the hoe makes everything flourish. The hoe (*al*) is good barley, the hoe (*al*) is a hunting net°. The hoe (*al*) is brick moulds, the hoe (*al*) has made people exist (*ĝal*). It is the hoe (*al*) that is the strength of young manhood. The hoe (*al*) and the basket are the tools for building cities. It builds (*aldue*) the right kind of house, it cultivates (*alĝaĝa*) the right kind of fields. It is you, hoe, that extend (*dagal*) the good agricultural land! The hoe (*al*) subdues for its owner (*lugal*) any agricultural lands that have been recalcitrant (*bal*) against their owner (*lugal*), any agricultural lands that have not submitted to their owner (*lugal*). It chops the heads off the vile esparto grasses, yanks them out at their roots, and tears at their stalks. The hoe (*al*) also subdues (*alĝaĝa*) the *ḫirin* weeds.

107–9 The hoe (*al*), the implement whose destiny was fixed by Father Enlil—the renowned hoe (*al*)! Praise be to Nisaba!

Notes

1–7 Instead of 'forth' 3 MSS have: 'up'. Instead of 'earth' 2 MSS have: 'chamber'. Instead of 'Where Flesh Came Forth' (the name of a cosmic location) 2 MSS have: 'Where Flesh Grew'. Instead of 'suspended' 2 MSS have: 'raised'.

8–17 Instead of 'standing up to a great (*gal*) wall' 1 MS has: 'born for a great (*gal*) person (?)'.

18–27 Instead of 'in Where Flesh Came Forth, he set this very hoe (*al*) to work;' 1 MS has: 'in Where Flesh Grew the unassailable (?)'.

35–42 Instead of 'bread basket (?)' 1 MS has: '. . . masterpiece (?)'.

49–51 Instead of 'cow (*ummal*)' 2 MSS have: 'woman'.

52–55 Instead of 'beard' 1 MS has: 'tooth'.

59–70 Instead of 'sat down on' 1 MS has: 'got onto'. Instead of 'he had mentioned the mace, the club, arrows and quiver, and the hoe (*al*)' 3 MSS have: 'he desired (*al-dug*) the mace, the club, arrows and quiver'.

71–82 'The lord': Enlil. After 'The' 1 MS adds: 'sage'. Instead of 'chamber' 1 MS has: 'place'.

94–106 Instead of 'a hunting net' 1 MS has: 'an overseer'.

The exaltation of Inana

Like *A hymn to Inana* (Group B), this hymn is supposedly by En-ḫedu-ana, as *en* priestess of the moon-god Nanna-Suen in Urim during the reign of Sargon the Great.

The first part (1–65) is a powerful prayer to Inana, which never once mentions her by name. We can infer that she and no other goddess is the object of worship because she is said to hold the *me* or divine powers, as in many of the myths about Inana (1–12). Further she is portrayed as violent and vengeful, all-powerful even in relation to the other gods (13–59).

At the start of the second part (66–138) En-ḫedu-ana introduces herself as a faithful yet deserted servant of Inana (66–73). She asks the moon-god to intercede to An on her behalf (74–80), regarding an individual called Lugalane who has destroyed E-ana—and perhaps captured Unug (81–90). No historical corroboration for this event is known, and it is obscurely presented within the narrative. The gods have deserted En-ḫedu-ana but she is praying for revenge (91–108) and for Inana and Nanna to relent (109–38). In the short concluding section it is as if this prayer has already been answered: the gods have forgiven En-ḫedu-ana and restored her to their good books.

While there is enough textual and archaeological evidence to establish

En-ḫedu-ana's historicity—she really was the *en* priestess of Nanna-Suen during the reign of Sargon the Great—there are no strong grounds for attributing this hymn, or any other currently known, to her personal authorship. At best we can say that En-ḫedu-ana had a scribe, known to us by his cylinder seal, and that it is possible, even likely, that hymns were composed on her behalf—perhaps including a precursor of this one. At worst it should be pointed out that all the manuscript sources are from the second millennium BCE, mostly from the eighteenth century, some six centuries after she lived. And all of those, as far as we can determine, were found in school settings, not in cultic ones. The linguistic features of the surviving sources show no traces of Old Sumerian: if they are based on an original third-millennium composition they have all been thoroughly revised and updated, making it impossible to posit what that putative original might have looked like. It is nevertheless intriguing that En-ḫedu-ana survived in scribal literature, perhaps as part of the continuing fascination with the dynasty of her father Sargon the Great (see *Sargon and Ur-Zababa*, Group A; *The cursing of Agade*, Group C).

Translation

1–12 Lady of all the divine powers, resplendent light, righteous woman clothed in radiance, beloved of An and Uraš! Mistress of heaven, with the great pectoral jewels, who loves the good headdress befitting the office of *en* priestess, who has seized all seven of its divine powers! My lady, you are the guardian of the great divine powers! You have taken up the divine powers, you have hung the divine powers from your hand. You have gathered up the divine powers, you have clasped the divine powers to your breast. Like a dragon you have deposited venom on the foreign lands. When like Iškur you roar at the earth, no vegetation can stand up to you. As a flood descending upon (?) those foreign lands, powerful one of heaven and earth, you are their Inana.

13–19 Raining blazing fire down upon the Land, endowed with divine powers by An, lady who rides upon a beast, whose words are spoken at the holy command of An! The great rites are yours: who can fathom them? Destroyer of the foreign lands, you confer strength on the storm. Beloved of Enlil, you have made awesome terror weigh upon the Land. You stand at the service of An's commands.

20–33 At your battle-cry, my lady, the foreign lands bow low. When humanity comes before you in awed silence at the terrifying radiance and tempest, you grasp the most terrible of all the divine powers. Because of you, the threshold of tears is opened, and people walk along the path of the house of great lamentations. In the van of battle, all is struck down before you. With your strength, my lady, teeth can crush flint. You charge forward like a charging storm. You roar with the roaring storm, you continually thunder with Iškur. You spread exhaustion with the storm-winds, while your own feet remain tireless. With the lamenting *balaǧ* drum a lament is struck up.

34–41 My lady, the great Anuna gods fly from you to the ruin mounds like scudding bats. They dare not stand before your terrible gaze. They dare not confront your terrible countenance. Who can cool your raging heart? Your malevolent anger is too great to cool. Lady, can your mood be soothed? Lady, can your heart be gladdened? Eldest daughter of Suen, your rage cannot be cooled!

42–59 Lady supreme over the foreign lands, who can take anything from your province? Once you have extended your province over the hills°, vegetation there is ruined. Their great gateways° are set afire. Blood is poured into their rivers because of you, and their people must drink it°. They must lead their troops captive before you, all together. They must scatter their elite regiments for you, all together. They must stand their able-bodied young men at your service, all together. Tempests have filled the dancing-places of their cities. They drive their young men before you as prisoners. Your holy command has been spoken over the city which has not declared 'The foreign lands are yours!', wherever they have not declared 'It is your own father's!'; and it is brought back under your feet. Responsible care is removed from its sheepfolds. Its woman no longer speaks affectionately with her husband; at dead of night she no longer takes counsel with him, and she no longer reveals to him the pure thoughts of her heart. Impetuous wild cow, great daughter of Suen, lady greater than An, who can take anything from your province?

60–5 Great queen of queens, issue of a holy womb for righteous divine powers, greater than your own mother, wise and sage, lady of all the foreign lands, life-force of the teeming people: I will recite your holy song! True goddess fit for divine powers, your splendid utterances are magnificent. Deep-hearted, good woman with a radiant heart, I will enumerate your divine powers° for you!

FIG. 37. 'I, En-ḫedu-ana, the *en* priestess'—
En-ḫedu-ana and her retinue on a fragmentary
stone plaque from Urim

66–73 I, En-ḫedu-ana, the *en* priestess, entered my holy *ĝipar* shrine in your service. I carried the ritual basket, and intoned the song of joy. But funeral offerings were° brought, as if I had never lived there. I approached the light, but the light was scorching hot to me. I approached that shade, but I was covered with a storm. My honeyed mouth became venomous. My ability to soothe moods vanished.

74–80 Suen, tell An about Lugal-ane and my fate! May An undo it for me! As soon as you tell An about it, An will release me. The woman will take the destiny away from Lugal-ane; foreign lands and flood lie at her feet. The woman too is exalted, and can make cities tremble. Step forward, so that she will cool her heart for me.

81–90 I, En-ḫedu-ana, will recite a prayer to you. To you, holy Inana, I shall give free vent to my tears like sweet beer! I shall say to her: 'Your decision!'° Do not be anxious about Ašimbabbar. In connection with the purification rites of holy An, Lugal-ane has altered everything of his, and has stripped An of the E-ana. He has not stood in awe of the greatest deity. He has turned that temple, whose attractions were inexhaustible, whose beauty was endless, into a destroyed temple. While he entered before me as if he was a partner, really he approached out of envy.

91–108 My good divine wild cow, drive out the man, capture the man! In the place of divine encouragement, what is my standing now? May An extradite the land which is a malevolent rebel against your Nanna! May An smash that city! May Enlil curse it! May its plaintive child not be placated by his mother! Lady, with the laments begun, may your ship of lamentation be abandoned in hostile territory. Must I die because of my holy songs? My Nanna has paid no heed to me°. He has destroyed me utterly in renegade territory. Ašimbabbar has certainly not pronounced a verdict on me. What is it to me if he has pronounced it? What is it to me if he has not pronounced it? He stood there in triumph and drove me out of the temple. He made me fly like a swallow from the window; I have exhausted my life-strength. He made me walk through the thorn bushes of the mountains. He stripped me of the rightful crown° of the *en* priestess. He gave me a knife and dagger, saying to me: 'These are appropriate ornaments for you.'

109–21 Most precious lady, beloved by An, your holy heart is great; may it be assuaged on my behalf! Beloved spouse of Ušumgal-ana, you are the great lady of the horizon and zenith of the heavens. The Anuna have submitted to you. From birth you were the junior queen: how supreme you are now over the Anuna, the great gods! The Anuna kiss the ground with their lips before you. But my own trial is not yet concluded, although a hostile verdict encloses me as if it were my own verdict. I did not reach out my hands to the° flowered bed. I did not reveal the pronouncements of Ningal to anybody. My lady beloved of An, may your heart be calmed towards me, the brilliant *en* priestess of Nanna!

122–38 It must be known! It must be known! Nanna has not yet spoken out! He has said: 'He is yours!' Let it be known that you are lofty as the heavens! Let it be known that you are broad as the earth! Let it be known that you destroy the rebel lands! Let it be known that you roar at the foreign lands! Let it be known that you crush heads! Let it be known that you devour corpses like a dog! Let it be known that your gaze is terrible! Let it be known that you lift your terrible gaze! Let it be known that you have flashing eyes! Let it be known that you are unshakeable and unyielding! Let it be known that you always stand triumphant! That Nanna has not yet spoken out, and that he has said 'He is yours!' has made you greater, my lady; you have become the greatest! My lady beloved by An, I shall tell of all your rages°! I have heaped up the coals in the censer, and prepared the purification rites. The E-ešdam-kug shrine awaits you. Might your heart not be appeased towards me?

139–43 Since it was full, too full for me, great exalted lady, I have recited this song for you. May a singer repeat to you at noon that which was recited to you at dead of night: 'Because of your captive spouse, because of your captive child, your rage is increased, your heart unassuaged.'

144–54 The powerful lady, respected in the gathering of rulers, has accepted her offerings from her. Inana's holy heart has been assuaged. The light was sweet for her, delight extended over her, she was full of fairest beauty. Like the light of the rising moon, she exuded delight. Nanna came out to gaze at her properly, and her mother Ningal blessed her. The door posts greeted her. Everyone's speech to the mistress is exalted. Praise be to the destroyer of foreign lands, endowed with divine powers by An, to my lady enveloped in beauty, to Inana!

Notes

42–59 Instead of 'Once you have extended your province over the hills' 2 MSS have: 'If you frown at the mountains'. Instead of 'great gateways' 1 MS has: 'palaces'. Instead of 'must drink it' 2 MSS have: 'could not drink'.

60–5 Instead of 'your divine powers' 2 MSS have: 'good divine powers'; 1 MS has: 'holy divine powers'.

66–73 Instead of 'funeral offerings were' 1 MS has: 'my ritual meal was'.

81–90 Instead of ' "Your decision!" ' some MSS have: ' "Greetings!" '.

91–108 Instead of 'paid no heed to me' 1 MS has: 'has not decided my case'. Instead of 'crown' 1 MS has: 'garment'.

109–21 Instead of 'the' 1 MS has: 'my'.

122–38 Instead of 'rages' 1 MS has: 'daises'.

Enlil in the E-kur

This hymn praises the E-kur, Enlil's great temple in Nibru, as much as it does Enlil himself. The structure alternates between third-person descriptions (1–64, 100–30) and direct addresses to the deity (65–99, 131–71). Images of righteousness (18–25), festivity (44–55), visual brilliance (65–73), awesomeness (74–83), fatefulness (100–8), and justice (139–55) are dominant for much

of the poem. In one extraordinary passage (109–30) the poet tries to imagine
the world without Enlil: he concludes that nothing at all would exist. His
consort Ninlil receives praise too, almost as an afterthought (156–66).

In Sumerian cosmology, Enlil's sanctuary Dur-an-ki was conceptualized
as the bond between heaven and earth—which is what the name itself
signifies. Its great stepped tower, still prominent in the desert landscape
today, must have been a dominant, awe-inspiring landmark in ancient times
too. The southern Mesopotamian plain is extraordinarily flat, being formed
only from the alluvium of the Tigris and Euphrates rivers with little or
no stone outcrops for much of its duration. Enlil himself often carries the
sobriquet Great Mountain, while E-kur literally means 'mountain house'.
Some have seen in this nomenclature Sumerian origins in mountainous
territory, but one could argue just as strongly that mountains might be
imbued with even more power and splendour for being so alien to the
southern Mesopotamian landscape. The mountain in question is presumably none other than the artificially constructed ziggurrat tower, a
development of the temple on platform of the late fourth millennium. Cultic
platforms and ziggurrats were built for many reasons: to cover over decom-
missioned temples without destroying their foundations prior to rebuilding;
to give temples and cultic places height and prominence in the landscape
over many miles; and as conspicuous consumption of labour and materials
for non-utilitarian ends as a display of wealth, power, and piety. While
almost all cities had temples and ziggurrats, Nibru came to be seen as a
particularly holy place—never a political capital but always desirable as the
possession of it meant endorsement from the great Enlil himself.

Translation

1–9 Enlil's commands are by far the loftiest, his words° are holy, his
utterances are immutable! The fate he decides is everlasting, his
glance makes the mountains anxious, his . . . reaches (?) into the
interior of the mountains. All the gods of the earth bow down to
Father Enlil, who sits comfortably on the holy dais, the lofty dais°, to
Nunamnir, whose lordship and princeship are most perfect. The
Anuna gods enter° before him and obey his instructions faithfully.

10–17 The mighty lord, the greatest in heaven and earth, the knowledgeable judge, the wise one of wide-ranging wisdom, has taken his seat
in the Dur-an-ki, and made the Ki-ur, the great place, resplendent
with majesty. He has taken up residence in Nibru, the lofty bond (?)
between heaven and earth. The front of the city is laden with terrible

fearsomeness and radiance, its back is such that even the mightiest god does not dare to attack, and its interior is the blade of a sharp dagger, a blade of catastrophe. For the rebel lands it is a snare, a trap, a net.

18-25 It cuts short the life of those who speak too mightily. It permits no evil word to be spoken in judgment (?). . . . , deception, inimical speech, hostility, impropriety, ill-treatment, wickedness, wrong-doing, looking askance (?), violence, slandering, arrogance, licentious speech (?), egotism, and boasting are abominations not tolerated within the city.

26-34 The borders of Nibru form a great net, within which the eagle spreads wide its talons. The evil or wicked man does not escape its grasp. In this city endowed with steadfastness, for which righteousness and justice have been made a lasting possession, and which is clothed (?) in pure clothing on the quay, the younger brother honours the older brother and treats him with human dignity; people pay attention to a father's word, and submit themselves to his protection; the child behaves humbly and modestly towards his mother and attains a ripe old age.

35-43 In the city, the holy settlement of Enlil, in Nibru, the beloved shrine of father Great Mountain, he has made the dais of abundance, the E-kur, the shining temple, rise from the soil; he has made it grow on pure land as high as a towering mountain. Its prince, the Great Mountain, Father Enlil, has taken his seat on the dais of the E-kur, the lofty shrine. No god can cause harm to the temple's divine powers. Its holy hand-washing rites are everlasting like the earth. Its divine powers are the divine powers of the Abzu: no one can look upon them.

44-55 Its interior is a wide sea which knows no horizon. In its . . . glistening as a banner (?), the bonds and ancient divine powers are made perfect. Its words are prayers, its incantations are supplications. Its word is a favourable omen . . . , its rites are most precious. At the festivals, there is plenty of fat and cream; they are full of abundance. Its divine plans bring joy and rejoicing, its verdicts are great. Daily there is a great festival, and at the end of the day there is an abundant harvest. The temple of Enlil is a mountain of abundance; to reach out, to look with greedy eyes, to seize are abominations in it.

56-64 The *lagar* priests of this temple whose lord has grown together with it are expert in blessing; its *gudug* priests of the Abzu are suited for°

lustration rites; its *nueš* priests are perfect in the holy prayers. Its great farmer is the good shepherd of the Land, who was born vigorous on a propitious day. The farmer, suited for the broad fields, comes with rich offerings; he does not . . . into the shining E-kur.

65–73 Enlil, when you marked out the holy settlements, you also built Nibru, your own city. You (?) . . . the Ki-ur, the mountain, your pure place. You founded it in the Dur-an-ki, in the middle of the four quarters of the earth. Its soil is the life of the Land, and the life of all the foreign countries. Its brickwork is red gold, its foundation is lapis lazuli. You made it glisten on high° in Sumer as if it were the horns of a wild bull. It makes all the foreign countries tremble with fear. At its great festivals, the people pass their time in abundance.

74–83 Enlil, holy Uraš is laden with charm for you; you are greatly suited for the Abzu, the holy throne°; you refresh yourself in the deep Underworld, the holy chamber. Your presence spreads awesomeness over the E-kur, the shining temple, the lofty dwelling. Its fearsomeness and radiance reach up to heaven, its shadow stretches over all the foreign lands, and its crenellation reaches up to the midst of heaven. All lords and sovereigns regularly supply holy offerings there, approaching Enlil with prayers and supplications.

84–92 Enlil, if you look upon the shepherd favourably, if you elevate the one truly called in the Land, then the foreign countries are in his hands, the foreign countries are at his feet! Even the most distant foreign countries submit to him. He will then cause enormous incomes and heavy tributes, as if they were cool water, to reach the treasury. In the great courtyard he will supply offerings regularly. Into the E-kur, the shining temple, he will bring (?) . . . .

93–9 Enlil, faithful shepherd of the teeming multitudes, herdsman, leader of all living creatures, has manifested his rank of great prince, adorning himself with° the holy crown. As the Wind of the Mountain (?) occupied the dais, he spanned the sky as the rainbow. Like a floating cloud, he moved alone (?).

100–8 He alone is the prince of heaven, the dragon of the earth. The lofty god of the Anuna himself determines the fates. No god can look upon him. His great minister and commander° Nuska learns his commands and his intentions from him, consults with him and then executes his far-reaching instructions on his behalf. He prays to him with holy prayers (?) and divine powers (?).

109–23 Without the Great Mountain Enlil, no city would be built, no settlement would be founded; no cattle-pen would be built, no sheepfold would be established; no king would be elevated, no lord would be given birth; no high priest or priestess would perform extispicy; soldiers would have no generals or captains; no carp-filled waters would . . . the rivers at their peak; the carp would not . . . come straight up (?) from the sea, they would not dart about. The sea would not produce all its heavy treasure, no freshwater fish would lay eggs in the reed-beds, no bird of the sky would build nests in the spacious land; in the sky the thick clouds would not open their mouths; on the fields, dappled grain would not fill the arable lands, vegetation would not grow lushly on the plain; in the gardens, the spreading trees° of the mountain would not yield fruits.

124–30 Without the Great Mountain Enlil, Nintud would not kill, she would not strike dead; no cow would drop its calf in the cattle-pen, no ewe would bring forth a . . . lamb in its sheepfold; the living creatures which multiply by themselves would not lie down in their . . .°; the four-legged animals would not propagate, they would not mate.

131–8 Enlil, your ingenuity takes one's breath away! By its nature it is like entangled threads which cannot be unravelled, crossed threads which the eye cannot follow. Your divinity can be relied on. You are your own counsellor and adviser, you are a lord on your own. Who can comprehend your actions? No divine powers are as resplendent as yours. No god can look you in the face.

139–55 You, Enlil, are lord, god, king. You are a judge who makes decisions about heaven and earth. Your lofty word is as heavy as heaven, and there is no one who can lift it. The Anuna gods . . . at your word. Your word is weighty in heaven, a foundation on the earth. In the heavens, it is a great . . . , reaching up to the sky. On the earth it is a foundation which cannot be destroyed. When it relates to the heavens, it brings abundance: abundance will pour from the heavens. When it relates to the earth, it brings prosperity: the earth will produce prosperity. Your word means flax, your word means grain. Your word means the early flooding, the life of the lands. It makes the living creatures, the animals (?) which copulate and breathe joyfully in the greenery. You, Enlil, the good shepherd, know their ways (?). . . . the sparkling stars.

156–66 You married Ninlil, the holy consort, whose words are of the heart, her of noble countenance in a holy *ma* garment, her of beautiful shape and limbs, the trustworthy lady of your choice. Covered with allure, the lady who knows what is fitting for the E-kur, whose words of advice are perfect, whose words bring comfort like fine oil for the heart, who shares° the holy throne, the pure throne with you, she takes counsel and discusses matters with you. You decide the fates together at the place facing the sunrise. Ninlil, the lady of heaven and earth, the lady of all the lands, is honoured in the praise of the Great Mountain.

167–71 Prominent one whose words are well established, whose command and support are things which are immutable, whose utterances take precedence, whose plans are firm words, Great Mountain, Father Enlil, your praise is sublime!

Notes

1–9   Instead of 'words' 1 MS has: 'commands'. Instead of 'dais' some MSS have: 'Engur'. Instead of 'enter' some MSS have: 'stand'.

56–64   After 'suited for' 1 MS adds: 'your'.

65–73   Instead of 'made it glisten on high' 1 MS has: 'raised its glistening top'.

74–83   Instead of 'throne' 1 MS has: 'Engur'.

93–9   Instead of 'adorning himself with' 1 MS has: 'putting on'.

100–8   Instead of 'commander' 1 MS has: 'chief barber'.

109–23   Instead of 'spreading trees' 1 MS has: 'forests'.

124–30   Instead of 'lie down in their . . .' 1 MS has: 'sit within . . .'.

156–66   Instead of 'shares' 1 MS has: 'sits on'.

The Keš temple hymn

With *The instructions of Šuruppag*, *The Keš temple hymn* is one of the oldest known works of Sumerian literature, with a version known from the mid-third-millennium city of Abu Ṣalabikh. By the time the Decad was current in scribal schools some eight centuries later Keš was apparently no longer a major settlement, though presumably its temple of Nintud, the birth goddess, still functioned. Its location is uncertain today. In this composition Nintud is equated with both Aruru and Ninḫursaĝa (see *A tigi to Nintud-Aruru*, Group F) and she has a warrior son, Ašgi.

The hymn is formally divided into eight 'houses', each of which ends with a trio of rhetorical questions: 'Will anyone else bring forth something as great as Keš? Will any other mother ever give birth to someone as great as its hero

Ašgi? Who has ever seen anyone as great as its lady Nintud?' In the first house, Enlil compares the Keš temple favourably with his E-kur (see *Enlil in the E-kur*). The second, third, and sixth houses capture its awe-inspiring physical appearance in powerful metaphors and similes. The fourth describes the offerings it receives, the fifth lists its divine inhabitants, and the seventh its priestly functionaries. The eighth captures its attractive splendour and frightening awesomeness with the refrain 'Draw near—but do not draw near!'

Enlil in the E-kur and *Enki's journey to Nibru* both incorporate extended praise to the temples in which their chief protagonists reside.

Translation

1–9 The princely one, the princely one came forth from the house. Enlil, the princely one, came forth from the house. The princely one came forth royally from the house. Enlil lifted his glance over all the lands, and the lands raised themselves to Enlil. The four corners of heaven became green for Enlil like a garden. Keš was positioned there for him with head uplifted, and as Keš lifted its head among all the lands, Enlil spoke the praises of Keš.

10–20 Nisaba was its decision-maker (?); with its words she wove it intricately like a net. Written on tablets it was held in her hands: 'House, platform of the Land, important fierce bull! House Keš, platform of the Land, important fierce bull! Growing as high as the hills, embracing the heavens, growing as high as E-kur, lifting its head among the mountains! Rooted in the Abzu°, verdant like the mountains! Will anyone else bring forth something as great as Keš? Will any other mother ever give birth to someone as great as its hero Ašgi? Who has ever seen anyone as great as its lady Nintud?'

21 The first house.

22–30 Good house, built in a good location, house Keš,° built in a good location, floating in the heavens like a princely barge, like a holy barge furnished with a . . . gate, like the boat of heaven, the platform of all the lands! . . . from the riverbank like a . . . boat cabin! House roaring like an ox, bellowing loudly like a breed-bull! House in whose interior is the power of the Land, and behind which is the life of Sumer!

31–43 House, great enclosure, reaching to the heavens, great, true house, reaching to the heavens! House, great crown reaching to the heavens, house, rainbow reaching to the heavens! House whose platform extends into the midst of the heavens, whose foundations are fixed in the Abzu, whose shade covers all lands! House founded by An, praised by Enlil, given an oracle by mother Nintud! House Keš, green in its fruit! Will anyone else bring forth something as great as Keš? Will any other mother ever give birth to someone as great as its hero Ašgi? Who has ever seen anyone as great as its lady Nintud?

44 The second house.

45–57 House, 10 *šar°* at its upper end, 5 *šar* at its lower end; house, 10 *bur°* at its upper end, 5 *bur* at its lower end! House, at its upper end a bison, at its lower end a stag; house, at its upper end a wild sheep, at its lower end a deer; house, at its upper end a dappled wild sheep, at its lower end a beautiful deer! House, at its upper end green like a bee-eater (?), at its lower end floating on the water like a pelican! House, at its upper end rising like the sun, at its lower end spreading like the moonlight; house, at its upper end a warrior mace, at its lower end a battle-axe; house, at its upper end a mountain, at its lower end a spring! House, at its upper end threefold indeed! Will anyone else bring forth something as great as Keš? Will any other mother ever give birth to someone as great as its hero Ašgi? Who has ever seen anyone as great as its lady Nintud?

58 The third house.°

59–73 It is indeed a city, it is indeed a city! Who knows its interior? The house Keš is indeed a city! Who knows its interior? The heroes make their way straight into its interior and perform its oracle rites perfectly. Frisking cattle are gathered at the house in herds. The house consumes many cattle; the house consumes many sheep. (*1 line unclear*) Those who sit on daises bow their necks before it. It wears a crown to vie with the boxwood tree, it spreads out to vie with the poplar . . . ; it is° as green as the hills! Will anyone else bring forth something as great as Keš? Will any other mother ever give birth to someone as great as its hero Ašgi? Who has ever seen anyone as great as its lady Nintud?

74 The fourth house.

75–86 House given birth by a lion, whose interior the hero has embellished (?)! House Keš, given birth by a lion, whose interior the hero has embellished (?)! The heroes make their way straight into its interior. Ninḫursaḡa sits within like a great dragon. Nintud the great mother assists at births there. Šul-pa-eda the ruler acts as lord. Ašgi the hero consumes the contents of the vessels (?). Urumaš, the great herald of the plains, dwells there too. Stags are gathered at the house in herds. Will anyone else bring forth something as great as Keš? Will any other mother ever give birth to someone as great as its hero Ašgi? Who has ever seen anyone as great as its lady Nintud?

87   The fifth house.

FIG. 38. 'Ninḫursaǧa sits within like a great dragon'—
a goddess, perhaps Ninḫursaǧa, depicted on a fragmentary
Early Dynastic stone vessel

88–102   House positioned over its foundations like a storm, like white bulls standing about on the plain; house founded by the prince, in praise on the *tigi* drum! House in whose interior is the power of the Land, and behind which is the life of Sumer°; at whose gate is a lion reclining on its paws, at whose gate is the ruler who decides cases (?)! House at whose door is the Great Mountain without adversary; at whose bolt° is a great frisking wild bull°! Whose well-founded storehouse is a corner of heaven, a corner of earth°; whose terrace is supported by *laḫama* deities; whose princely° wall . . . the shrine of Urim! Will anyone else bring forth something as great as Keš? Will any other mother ever give birth to someone as great as its hero Ašgi? Who has ever seen anyone as great as its lady Nintud?

103   The sixth house.°

104–15 The holy house whose . . . is the shrine, the holy house Keš, whose
. . . is the shrine; the house whose lords are the Anuna gods, whose
nueš priests are the sacrificers of E-ana! In the house the king places
stone bowls in position; the good *en* priest . . . holds the lead-rope
dangling. The *atu* priest holds the staff; the . . . brings the . . . waters.
The . . . takes his seat in the holy place; the *enkum* priests bow down
. . . . The *pašeš* priests beat the drumskins; they recite powerfully,
powerfully.

116–26 The bull's horn is made to growl; the drumsticks (?) are made to
thud. The singer cries out° to the *ala* drum; the grand sweet *tigi*
drum is played for him°. The house is built; its nobility is good! The
house Keš is built; its nobility is good! Its lady has taken a seat in its
. . . . Ninḫursaĝa, its lady, has taken her seat in its . . . . Will anyone
else bring forth something as great as Keš? Will any other mother
ever give birth to someone as great as its hero Ašgi? Who has ever seen
anyone as great as its lady Nintud?

127 The seventh house.

128–33 Draw near, man, to the city, to the city—but do not draw near!
Draw near, man, to the house Keš, to the city—but do not draw
near! Draw near, man, to its hero Ašgi—but do not draw near! Draw
near, man, to its lady Nintud—but do not draw near! Praise be to
well-built Keš, O Ašgi! Praise be to cherished Keš and Nintud!

134 The eighth house.

Notes

10–20 Instead of 'Rooted in the Abzu' 2 MSS have: 'Colourful as the Abzu'.

22–30 After 'house Keš,' some MSS add: 'good house,'.

45–57 10 *šar* is equivalent to just under 4,000 hectares; 10 *bur* is about 65 hectares.

58 After this line 1 MS adds: 'House . . . inspiring great awe, called with a mighty
name by An; house . . . whose fate is grandly determined by the Great
Mountain Enlil! House of the Anuna gods possessing great power, which gives
wisdom to the people; house, reposeful dwelling of the great gods! House,
which was planned together with the plans of heaven and earth, . . . with the
pure divine powers; house which underpins the Land and supports the
shrines! House, mountain of abundance which passes the days in glory; house
of Ninḫursaĝa which establishes the life of the Land! House, great hillside
worthy of the purification rites, altering (?) all things; house without whom no
decisions are made! House, good . . . carrying in its hands the broad Land;
house which gives birth to countless peoples, seed which has sprouts! House
which gives birth to kings, which determines the destinies of the Land; house
whose royal personages are to be revered! Will anyone else bring forth

something as great as Keš? Will any other mother ever give birth to someone as great as its hero Ašgi? Who has ever seen anyone as great as its lady Nintud? The . . . house.'

59–73 After 'it is' 1 MS adds: 'growing'.

88–102 Instead of 'is the life of Sumer' some MSS have: 'it is filled with life'. Instead of 'bolt' some MSS have: 'bar'. After 'wild bull' some MSS add: ', at whose bolt is a beast . . . a man'; 1 MS adds instead: ', at whose . . . is an awe-inspiring lion'. Instead of 'Whose well-founded storehouse is a corner of heaven, a corner of earth' 1 MS has: 'Whose storehouse established as a household . . .'. After 'princely' 1 MS adds: 'great'.

103 After this line 1 MS (which uses a different numbering of the sections) adds: 'House imbued with radiance, . . . excellence! House . . . ! Lord Nudimmud in heaven and earth . . . brickwork of the Land, brickwork . . . grandly in the Abzu. Terrace, relaxing abode, . . . holy splendour . . . of the people! House which is seemly for the foreign lands! Will anyone else bring forth something as great as Keš? Will any other mother ever give birth to someone as great as its hero Ašgi? Who has ever seen anyone as great as its lady Nintud? The eighth house.'

116–26 Instead of 'cries out' 1 MS has: 'declaims'. Instead of 'the grand sweet *tigi* drum is played for him' some MSS have: 'the sweet *tigi* drum is well tuned'.

Enki's journey to Nibru

Enki, god of wisdom, was god of the freshwater ocean, the Abzu or Engur, which was believed to exist under the Land. His primary temple was thus at Eridug deep in the marshes in the far south of Mesopotamia. Eridug was considered to be the oldest city, the first to be inhabited before the Flood (see *The Flood story*, Group G). Excavations at Eridug have confirmed that ancient belief—and a small temple with burned offerings and fish bones was found in the lowest levels, dating to some time in the early fifth millennium BCE.

Enki's journey to Nibru is in four parts, only one of which concerns the journey itself. In the first section (1–17) Enki oversees the construction of his temple E-Engur, as also described briefly in *Enki and the world order* (Group G), lines 285–98. When it is completed Enki's minister Isimud delivers a long hymn of praise to the temple (18–70). Then Enki embarks on his barge (see *Šulgi and Ninlil's barge*, Group C) to visit Enlil and his entourage at Nibru (71–116), where he lays on a boozy celebration (there is no food: only alcohol is consumed—see *A hymn to Ninkasi*, Group I). The composition ends with Enlil toasting Enki and his marvellous new abode (117–29).

For another divine journey see *Nanna-Suen's journey to Nibru* (Group D).

Translation

1–8 In those remote days, when the fates were determined; in a year when An brought about abundance, and people broke through the earth like herbs and plants—then the lord of the Abzu, king Enki, Enki, the lord who determines the fates, built up his temple entirely from silver and lapis lazuli. Its silver and lapis lazuli were the shining daylight. Into the shrine of the Abzu he brought joy.

9–17 An artfully made bright crenellation rising out from the Abzu was erected for lord Nudimmud. He built the temple from precious metal, decorated it with lapis lazuli, and covered it abundantly with gold. In Eridug, he built the house on the bank. Its brickwork makes utterances and gives advice. Its eaves roar like a bull; the temple of Enki bellows. During the night the temple praises its lord and offers its best for him.

18–25 Before lord Enki, Isimud the minister praises the temple; he goes to the temple and speaks to it. He goes to the brick building and addresses it: 'Temple, built from precious metal and lapis lazuli; whose foundation pegs are driven into the Abzu; which has been cared for by the prince in the Abzu! Like the Tigris and the Euphrates, it is mighty and awe-inspiring (?). Joy has been brought into Enki's Abzu.

26–32 'Your lock has no rival. Your bolt is a fearsome lion. Your roof beams are the bull of heaven, an artfully made bright headgear. Your reed-mats are like lapis lazuli, decorating the roof-beams. Your vault is a bull° raising its horns. Your door is a lion who seizes a man°. Your staircase is a lion coming down on a man.

33–43 'Abzu, pure place which fulfils its purpose! E-Engur! Your lord has directed his steps towards you. Enki, lord of the Abzu, has embellished your foundation pegs with cornelian. He has adorned you with . . . and (?) lapis lazuli. The temple of Enki is provisioned with holy wax (?); it is a bull obedient to its master, roaring by itself and giving advice at the same time. E-Engur, which Enki has surrounded with a holy reed fence! In your midst a lofty throne is erected, your door-jamb is the holy locking bar of heaven.

44–8 'Abzu, pure place, place where the fates are determined—the lord of wisdom, lord Enki,° Nudimmud, the lord of Eridug, lets nobody look into its midst. Your *abgal* priests let their hair down their backs.

49–61 'Enki's beloved Eridug, E-Engur whose inside is full of abundance! Abzu, life of the Land, beloved of Enki! Temple built on the edge, befitting the artful divine powers! Eridug, your shadow extends over the midst of the sea! Rising sea without a rival; mighty awe-inspiring river which terrifies the Land! E-Engur, high citadel (?) standing firm on the earth! Temple at the edge of the Engur, a lion in the midst of the Abzu; lofty temple of Enki, which bestows wisdom on the Land; your cry, like that of a mighty rising river, reaches (?) king Enki.

62–7 'He made the lyre, the *algar* instrument, the *balag̃* drum with the drumsticks (?)°, the *ḫarḫar*, the *sabitum*, and the . . . *miritum* instruments offer their best for his holy temple. The . . . resounded by themselves with a sweet sound. The holy *algar* instrument of Enki played for him on his own and seven singers sang°.

68–70 'What Enki says is irrefutable; . . . is well established (?).' This is what Isimud spoke to the brick building; he praised the E-Engur with sweet songs°.

71–82 As it has been built, as it has been built; as Enki has raised Eridug up, it is an artfully built mountain which floats on the water. His shrine (?) spreads (?) out into the reed-beds; birds brood° in its green orchards laden with fruit. The *suḫur* carp play among the honey-herbs, and the *eštub* carp dart among the small *gizi* reeds. When Enki rises, the fishes rise before him like waves. He has the Abzu stand as a marvel, as he brings joy into the Engur.

83–92 Like the sea, he is awe-inspiring; like a mighty river, he instils fear. The Euphrates rises before him as it does before the fierce south wind. His punting pole is Niraḫ; his oars are the small reeds. When Enki embarks, the year will be full of abundance. The ship departs of its own accord, with tow rope held (?) by itself. As he leaves the temple of Eridug, the river gurgles (?) to its lord: its sound is a calf's mooing, the mooing of a good cow.

93–5 Enki had oxen slaughtered, and had sheep offered there lavishly. Where there were no *ala* drums, he installed some in their places; where there were no bronze *ub* drums, he dispatched some to their places.

96–103 He directed his steps on his own to Nibru and entered the *giguna*, the shrine of Nibru. Enki reached for (?) the beer, he reached for (?) the liquor. He had liquor poured into big bronze containers, and had emmer-wheat beer pressed out (?). In *kukuru* containers which make the beer good he mixed beer-mash. By adding date-syrup to its taste (?), he made it strong. He . . . its bran-mash.

104–16 In the shrine of Nibru, Enki provided a meal for Enlil, his father. He seated An at the head of the table and seated Enlil next to An. He seated Nintud in the place of honour and seated the Anuna gods at the adjacent places (?). All of them were drinking and enjoying beer and liquor. They filled the bronze *aga* vessels to the brim and started a competition, drinking from the bronze vessels of Uraš. They made the *tilimda* vessels shine like holy barges. After beer and liquor had been libated and enjoyed, and after . . . from the house, Enlil was made happy in Nibru.

117–29 Enlil addressed the Anuna gods: 'Great gods who are standing here! Anuna, who have lined up in the place of assembly! My son, king Enki, has built up the temple! He has made Eridug rise up (?)° from the ground like a mountain! He has built it in a pleasant place, in Eridug, the pure place, where no one is to enter—a temple built with silver and decorated with lapis lazuli, a house which tunes the seven *tigi* drums properly, and provides incantations; where holy songs make all of the house a lovely place—the shrine of the Abzu, the good destiny of Enki, befitting the elaborate divine powers; the temple of Eridug, built with silver: for all this, praise be to Father Enki!

Notes

26–32 Instead of 'bull' some MSS have: 'wild bull'. Instead of 'seizes a man' 1 MS has: 'is awe-inspiring'.

44–8 After 'lord Enki,' 1 MS adds 1 line: 'the lord who determines the fates,'.

62–7 Instead of 'the lyre, the *algar* instrument, the *balaĝ* drum with the drumsticks (?)' some MSS have: 'the lyre, the *algar* instrument, the *balaĝ* drum of your *sur* priests'; 1 MS has: 'your lyre and *algar* instrument, the *balaĝ* drum with the drumsticks (?)'; 1 MS has: 'the lyre, the *algar* instrument, the *balaĝ* drum and even the plectrum (?)'. Instead of 'singers sang' some MSS have: '*tigi* drums resounded'.

68–70 Instead of 'with sweet songs' 1 MS has: 'duly'.

71–82 After 'birds brood' 1 MS adds: 'at night'.

117–29 Instead of 'rise up (?)' 1 MS has: 'come out'.

Inana and Ebiḫ

The myth of *Inana and Ebiḫ* shows Inana in warrior mode. It starts with a hymn to the goddess as 'lady of battle' (1–24). Then Inana describes how the mountains of Ebiḫ refused to bow down to her, and the revenge she wants to take (25–52). She recounts the incident and her desires to An, the supreme deity, and asks for his assistance (53–111). An doubts her ability to overcome Ebiḫ (112–30), so Inana storms out and attacks it in a furious rage (131–59). She then triumphantly recounts what she has done (160–81). The composition ends with praise for both Inana—and for Nisaba in her role as scribal deity (see Group I): she has nothing at all to do with the narrative.

The poem focuses on the idea of the destruction of the 'rebel lands': the mountainous region to the north-east of the Land, tentatively identified with the Jebel Hamrin range in modern Iraq. The rebel lands were home to the nomadic, barbaric tribes who loom large in Sumerian literature as forces of destruction and chaos, sometimes let loose on the land by the gods (see *The cursing of Agade*, Group C, and *The lament for Sumer and Urim*, Group D) and sometimes as here needing to be brought under divine control themselves. No doubt nomadic incursions, particularly at times of economic stress, were as terrifying and destabilizing as the literature depicts, but mountains could also be portrayed as areas of safety or beauty (121–6, and see *Lugalbanda in the mountain cave*, Group A). There is also a vast amount of documentary evidence to show that in times of stability the sedentary and nomadic populations of the Land and its neighbours were economically interdependent and peacefully coexistent.

Translation

1–6   Goddess of the fearsome divine powers, clad in terror, riding on the great divine powers, Inana, made complete by the strength of the holy *ankar* weapon, drenched in blood, rushing around in great battles, with shield resting on the ground (?), covered in storm and flood, great lady Inana, knowing well how to plan conflicts, you destroy mighty lands with arrow and strength and overpower lands.

7–9   In heaven and on earth you roar like a lion and devastate the people. Like a huge wild bull you triumph over lands which are hostile. Like a fearsome lion you pacify the insubordinate and unsubmissive with your gall.

10–22   My lady, on your acquiring the stature of heaven, maiden Inana, on your becoming as magnificent as the earth, on your coming forth like Utu the king and stretching your arms wide, on your walking in heaven and wearing fearsome terror, on your wearing daylight and brilliance on earth, on your walking in the mountain ranges and bringing forth beaming rays, on your bathing the *girin* plants of the mountains (in light), on your giving birth to the bright mountain, the mountain, the holy place, on your . . . , on your being strong with the mace like a joyful lord, like an enthusiastic (?) lord, on your exulting in such battle like a destructive weapon—the black-headed people ring out in song and all the lands sing their song sweetly.

23–4 I shall praise the lady of battle, the great child of Suen, maiden Inana.

25–32 (*Inana announced:*) 'When I, the goddess, was walking around in heaven, walking around on earth, when I, Inana, was walking around in heaven, walking around on earth, when I was walking around in Elam and Subir, when I was walking around in the Lulubi mountains, when I turned towards the centre of the mountains, as I, Inana, approached the mountain it showed me no respect, as I, Inana, approached the mountain it showed me no respect, as I approached the mountain range of Ebiḫ it showed me no respect.

33–6 'Since they showed me no respect, since they did not put their noses to the ground for me, since they did not rub their lips in the dust for me, I shall personally fill the soaring mountain range with my terror.

37–40 'Against its magnificent sides I shall place magnificent battering-rams, against its small sides I shall place small battering-rams. I shall storm it and start the "game" of holy Inana. In the mountain range I shall start battles and prepare conflicts.

41–4 'I shall prepare arrows in the quiver. I shall . . . slingstones with the rope. I shall begin the polishing of my lance. I shall prepare the throw-stick and the shield.

45–8 'I shall set fire to its thick forests. I shall take an axe to its evil-doing. I shall make Gibil, the purifier, bare his holy teeth at its watercourses. I shall spread this terror through the inaccessible mountain range Aratta.

49–52 'Like a city which An has cursed, may it never be restored. Like a city at which Enlil has frowned, may it never again lift its neck up. May the mountain tremble when I approach. May Ebiḫ give me honour and praise me.'

53–8 Inana, the child of Suen, put on the garment of royalty and girded herself in joy. She bedecked her forehead with terror and fearsome radiance. She arranged cornelian rosettes around her holy throat. She brandished the seven-headed *šita* weapon vigorously to her right and placed straps of lapis lazuli on her feet.

59–61 At dusk she came forth regally and followed the path to the Gate of Wonder. She made an offering to An and addressed a prayer to him.

62–4 An, in delight at Inana, stepped forward and took his place. He filled the seat of honour of heaven.

65–9 (*Inana announced:*) 'An, my father, I greet you! Lend your ear to my words. You have made me terrifying among the deities in heaven. Owing to you my word has no rival in heaven or on earth. You have given me the . . . and the *šilig* weapon, the *antibal* and *mansium* emblems.

70–9 'To set the socle in position and make the throne and foundation firm, to carry the might of the *šita* weapon which bends like a *mubum* tree, to hold the ground with the sixfold yoke, to extend the thighs with the fourfold yoke, to pursue murderous raids and widespread military campaigns, to appear to those kings in the . . . of heaven like moonlight, to shoot the arrow from the arm and fall on fields, orchards and forests like the tooth of the locust, to take the harrow to rebel lands, to remove the locks from their city gates so the doors stand open—King An, you have indeed given me all this, and . . . .

80–2 'You have placed me at the right hand of the king in order to destroy rebel lands: may he, with my aid, smash heads like a falcon in the foothills of the mountain, King An, and may I . . . your name throughout the land like a thread.

83–8 'May he destroy the lands as a snake in a crevice. May he make them slither around like a *saĝkal* snake coming down from a mountain. May he establish control over the mountain, examine it and know its length. May he go out on the holy campaign of An and know its depth. The gods . . . , since the Anuna deities have . . . .

89–95 'How can it be that the mountain did not fear me in heaven and on earth, that the mountain did not fear me, Inana, in heaven and on earth, that the mountain range of Ebiḫ, the mountain, did not fear me in heaven and on earth? Because it showed me no respect, because it did not put its nose to the ground, because it did not rub its lips in the dust, may I fill my hand with the soaring mountain range and hand it over to my terror.

96–9 'Against its magnificent sides let me place magnificent battering rams, against its small sides let me place small battering rams. Let me storm it and start the "game" of holy Inana. In the mountain range let me set up battle and prepare conflicts.

100–3 'Let me prepare arrows in the quiver. Let me . . . slingstones with the rope. Let me begin the polishing of my lance. Let me prepare the throw-stick and the shield.

104–7 'Let me set fire to its thick forests. Let me take an axe to its evil-doing. Let me make Gibil, the purifier, bare his holy teeth at its watercourses. Let me spread this terror through the inaccessible mountain range Aratta.

108–11 'Like a city which An has cursed, may it never be restored. Like a city at which Enlil has frowned, may it never again lift its neck up. May the mountain tremble when I approach. May Ebiḫ give me honour and praise me.'

112–15 An, the king of the deities, answered her: 'My little one demands the destruction of this mountain—what is she taking on? Inana demands the destruction of this mountain—what is she taking on? She demands the destruction of this mountain—what is she taking on?

116–20 'It has poured fearsome terror on the abodes of the gods. It has spread fear among the holy dwellings of the Anuna deities. It has poured its terror and ferocity over this land. It has poured the mountain range's radiance and fear over all the lands. Its arrogance extends grandly to the centre of heaven.

121–6 'Fruit hangs in its flourishing gardens and luxuriance spreads forth. Its magnificent trees are themselves a source of wonder to the roots of heaven. In Ebiḫ . . . lions are abundant under the canopy of trees and bright branches. It makes wild rams and stags freely abundant. It stands wild bulls in flourishing grass. Deer couple among the cypress trees of the mountain range.

127–30 'You cannot pass through its terror and fear. The mountain range's radiance is fearsome. Maiden Inana, you cannot oppose it.' Thus he spoke.

131–7 The mistress, in her rage and anger, opened the arsenal and pushed on the lapis lazuli gate. She brought out magnificent battle and called up a great storm. Holy Inana reached for the quiver. She raised a towering flood with evil silt. She stirred up an evil raging wind with potsherds.

138–43 My lady confronted the mountain range. She advanced step by step. She sharpened both edges of her dagger. She grabbed Ebiḫ's neck as if ripping up esparto grass. She pressed the dagger's teeth into its interior. She roared like thunder.

144–51 The rocks forming the body of Ebiḫ clattered down its flanks. From its sides and crevices great serpents spat venom. She damned its forests and cursed its trees. She killed its oak trees with drought. She poured fire on its flanks and made its smoke dense. Inana established authority over the mountain. Holy Inana did as she wished.

152–9 She went to the mountain range of Ebiḫ and addressed it: 'Mountain range, because of your elevation, because of your height, because of your attractiveness, because of your beauty, because of your wearing a holy garment, because of your reaching up to heaven, because you did not put your nose to the ground, because you did not rub your lips in the dust, I have killed you and brought you low.

160–5 'As with an elephant I have seized your tusks. As with a great wild bull I have brought you to the ground by your thick horns. As with a bull I have forced your great strength to the ground and pursued you savagely. I have made tears the norm in your eyes. I have placed laments in your heart. Birds of sorrow are building nests on these flanks.'

166–70 For a second time, rejoicing in her fearsome terror, she spoke out righteously: 'My father Enlil has poured my great terror over the centre of the mountains. On my right side he has placed a weapon. On my left side a . . . is placed. My anger, a harrow with great teeth, has torn the mountain apart.

171–5 'I have built a palace and done much more. I have put a throne in place and made its foundation firm. I have given the kurĝara priests a dagger and prod. I have given the gala priests ub and lilis drums. I have changed the headgear of the pilipili priests.

176–81 'In my victory I rushed towards the mountain. In my victory I rushed towards Ebiḫ, the mountain range. I went forward like a surging flood, and like rising water I overflowed the dam. I imposed my victory on the mountain. I imposed my victory on Ebiḫ.'

182–3 For destroying Ebiḫ, great child of Suen, praise be to maiden Inana!

184 Praise be to Nisaba!

A hymn to Nungal

Little mentioned in Sumerian literature (one of the dead Ḫuwawa's auras is assigned to her in *Gilgameš and Ḫuwawa*), Nungal was considered to be a daughter of Ereškigala, queen of the Underworld (see *Inana's descent to the Underworld*, Group B). This hymn falls into two equal parts: a powerful depiction of Nungal's prison-temple and the sufferings of its inmates (1–61), followed by Nungal's own description of it as a house 'built on compassion' (62–121). It thus encapsulates the eternal tension between imprisonment as punishment and as rehabilitation. The outsider (the anonymous narrator of the first half of the composition) sees the prison as terrifying and dehumanizing. The insider (Nungal) argues, on the contrary, that it can 'snatch men from the jaws of destruction' (line 82).

This is one of the most menacing and unsettling compositions in the Sumerian literary corpus, posing difficult questions about the nature of justice and hinting darkly at the fate of criminals and transgressors in early Mesopotamia—for while the legal process is well recorded in law-codes and court records, the operation of prisons themselves is virtually undocumented. As a curricular composition it sent a message to the scribes in training that it was their duty to uphold a just and fair legal system while showing what was in store if they did not.

Translation

1–11 House, furious storm of heaven and earth, battering its enemies; prison, jail of the gods, august neck-stock of heaven and earth! Its interior is evening light, dusk spreading wide; its awesomeness is frightening. Raging sea which mounts high, no one knows where its rising waves flow. House, a pitfall waiting for the evil one; it makes the wicked tremble! House, a net whose fine meshes are skilfully woven, which gathers up people as its booty! House, which keeps an eye on the just and on evildoers; no one wicked can escape from its grasp. House, river of the ordeal which leaves the just ones alive, and chooses the evil ones! House, with a great name, Underworld, mountain where Utu rises; no one can learn its interior! Big house, prison, house of capital offences, which imposes punishment! House, which chooses the righteous and the wicked; An has made its name great!

12–26 House whose foundations are laden with great awesomeness! Its gate

is the yellow evening light, exuding radiance. Its stairs are a great
open-mouthed dragon, lying in wait for men. Its door jamb is a great
dagger whose two edges . . . the evil man. Its architrave is a scorpion
which quickly dashes from the dust; it overpowers everything. Its
projecting pilasters are lions; no one dares to rush into their grasp. Its
vault is the rainbow, imbued with terrible awe. Its hinges are an eagle
whose claws grasp everything. Its door is a great mountain which
does not open for the wicked, but does open for the righteous man,
who was not brought in through its power. Its bars are fierce lions
locked in stalwart embrace. Its latch is a python, sticking out its
tongue and hissing. Its bolt is a horned viper, slithering in a wild
place. House, surveying heaven and earth, a net spread out! No evildoer can escape its grasp, as it drags the enemy around.

27–31 Nungal, its lady, the powerful goddess whose aura covers heaven and
earth, resides on its great and lofty dais. Having taken a seat in the
precinct of the house, she controls the Land from there. She listens
to the king in the assembly and clamps down on his enemies; her
vigilance never ends.

32–9 Great house! For the enemy it is a trap laying in wait, but giving good
advice to the Land; fearsome waves, onrush of a flood that overflows
the river banks°. When an individual is brought in, he cannot resist
its aura. The gods of heaven and earth bow down before its place
where judgments are made. Ninegala takes her seat high on its lapis
lazuli dais. She keeps an eye on the judgments and decisions, distinguishing true and false. Her battle-net of fine mesh is indeed cast
over the land for her; the evildoer who does not follow her path will
not escape her arm.

40–7 When a man of whom his god disapproves (?) arrives at the gate of
the great house, which is a furious storm, a flood which covers everybody, he is delivered into the august hands of Nungal, the warden of
the prison; this man is held by a painful grip like a wild bull with
spread (?) forelegs. He is led to a house of sorrow, his face is covered
with a cloth, and he goes around naked. He . . . the road with his foot,
he . . . in a wide street. His acquaintances do not address him, they
keep away from him.

48–54 Even a powerful man cannot open up its door; incantations are
ineffective (?). It opens to a city in ruins, whose layout is destroyed.
Its inmates, like small birds escaped from the claws of an owl, look to
its opening as to the rising of sun. Brother counts for brother the days

of misfortune, but their calculations get utterly confused. A man does not recognize his fellow men; they have become strangers. A man does not return the password of his fellow men, their looks are so changed.

55–61 The interior of the temple gives rise to weeping, laments and cries. Its brick walls crush evil men and give rebirth to just men. Its angry heart causes one to pass the days in weeping and lamentation. When the time arrives, the prison is made up as for a public festival; the gods are present at the place of interrogation, at the river ordeal, to separate the just from the evildoers; a just man is given rebirth. Nungal clamps down on her enemy, so he will not escape her clutches.

62–74 Then the lady is exultant; the powerful goddess, holy Nungal, praises herself: 'An has determined the fate for me, the lady; I am the daughter of An. Enlil too has provided me with an eminent fate, for I am his daughter-in-law. The gods have given into my hands the divine powers of heaven and earth. My own mother, Ereškigala, has allotted to me her divine powers. I have set up my august dais in the Underworld, the mountain where Utu rises. I am the goddess of the great house, the holy royal residence. I speak with grandeur to Inana, I am her heart's joy. I assist Nintud at the place of child-delivery (?); I know how to cut the navel-cord and know the favourable words when determining fates. I am the lady, the true stewardess of Enlil; he has heaped up possessions for me. The storehouse which never becomes empty is mine; . . . .

75–82 'Mercy and compassion are mine. I frighten no one. I keep an eye upon the black-headed people: they are under my surveillance. I hold the tablet of life in my hand and I register the just ones on it. The evildoers cannot escape my arm; I learn their deeds. All countries look to me as to their divine mother. I temper severe punishments; I am a compassionate mother. I cool down even the angriest heart, sprinkling it with cool water. I calm down the wounded heart; I snatch men from the jaws of destruction.

83–94 'My house is built on compassion; I am a life-giving (?) lady. Its shadow is like that of a cypress tree growing in a pure place. Birtum the very strong, my spouse, resides there with me. Taking a seat on its great and lofty dais, he gives mighty orders. The guardians of my house and the fair-looking protective goddesses . . . . My chief superintendent, Ig-alim, is the neck-stock of my hands. He has been promoted to take care of my house; .... My messenger does not forget anything: he is the pride of the palace. In the city named after (?) Enlil, I recognize true and false. Ninḫarana brings the news and puts it before me. My chief barber sets up the bed for me in the house imbued with awesomeness. Nezila arranges joyous° occasions (?).

95–105 'When someone has been brought into the palace of the king and this man is accused of a capital offence, my chief prosecutor, Nindimgul, stretches out his arm in accusation (?). He sentences that person to death, but he will not be killed; he snatches the man from the jaws of destruction and brings him into my house of life and keeps him under guard. No one wears clean clothes in my dusty (?) house. My house falls upon the person like a drunken man. He will be listening for snakes and scorpions in the darkness of the house. My house gives birth to a just person, but exterminates a false one. Since there are pity and tears within its brick walls, and it is built with compassion, it soothes the heart of that person, and refreshes his spirits.

106–16 'When it has appeased the heart of his god for him; when it has polished him clean like silver of good quality, when it has made him shine forth through the dust; when it has cleansed him of dirt, like silver of best quality . . . , he will be entrusted again into the propitious hands of his god. Then may the god of this man praise me appropriately forever! May this man praise me highly; may he proclaim my greatness! The uttering of my praise throughout the Land will be breathtaking! May he provide . . . butter from the pure cattle-pen, and bring the best of it for me! May he provide fattened sheep from the pure sheepfold, and bring the best of them for me! Then I will never cease to be the friendly guardian of this man. In the palace, I will be his protector; I shall keep watch over him there.'

117–21 Because the lady has revealed her greatness; because she has provided the prison, the jail, her beloved dwelling, with awesome radiance, praise be to Nungal, the powerful goddess, the neck-stock of the Anuna gods, whose . . . no one knows, foremost one whose divine powers are untouchable!

Notes

32–9 Instead of 'that overflows the river banks' 1 MS has: 'which never stops raging, huge and overflowing (?)'.
83–94 After 'joyous' 1 MS adds: 'and valued (?)'.

Gilgameš and Ḫuwawa

The last and longest member of the Decad was the scribal students' first literary encounter with the legendary hero Gilgameš (see *Gilgameš, Enkidu, and the Underworld*, Group A). It is an extraordinarily well-crafted composition in three scenes, each 60 lines long (though with many variant additional lines; see the notes) and a 20-line epilogue.

In a foreshadowing of the explicit concern with mortality in the Babylonian *Epic of Gilgameš*, the hero states at the outset that he is looking for a great adventure to make him famous, 'since a man cannot pass beyond the final end of life' (line 4). His desire is to go to the cedar forests (of the Lebanon), in reality a journey of about two months up the Euphrates and across the Syrian desert. Gilgameš and Enkidu pray to Utu for permission and assistance in their journey and recruit a cohort of single young men to come with them.

Once in the forest they start to fell trees, but Gilgameš and his followers are suddenly overcome by sleep; only Enkidu manages to resist. When Enkidu finally rouses him, Gilgameš is furious, desperate to know who has done this to him. Enkidu counsels caution but Gilgameš is spoiling for a fight.

But when they find Ḫuwawa, the monstrous guardian of the cedar forest, his powerful divine auras mean that they cannot get anywhere near him. Gilgameš tricks the lonely and gullible Ḫuwawa out of them one by one by promising to be his friend and offering all sorts of implausible gifts. (Most of these are preserved only in sources from places other than Nibru, and are given in the notes to the composition.) Then, unfair to the last, he sneaks up behind Ḫuwawa and punches him in the face. Ḫuwawa, hurt more emotionally than physically, pleads with Gilgameš and Enkidu in turn to take pity and let him go. But when a war of words develops between Enkidu and Ḫuwawa, Enkidu's patience snaps and he chops off the monster's head. Ironically, then, it is not the hero Gilgameš who kills Ḫuwawa in the end, but his sensible servant who has all along been advising restraint.

When they take Ḫuwawa's head as an offering to Enlil, he is furious with them for abusing Ḫuwawa's trust, and hands out the dead monster's auras to various terrifying and dangerous places.

Translation

1–3 Now the lord once decided to set off for the mountain where the man lives; lord Gilgameš decided to set off for the mountain where the man lives. He spoke to his slave Enkidu:

4–7 'Enkidu, since a man cannot pass beyond the final end of life, I want to set off into the mountains, to establish my renown there. Where renown can be established there, I will establish my renown; and where no renown can be established there, I shall establish the renown of the gods.'

8–12 His slave Enkidu answered him: 'My lord, if today you want to set off into the mountains, Utu should know about it from us.° Utu, youthful Utu, should know about it from us. A decision that concerns the mountains is Utu's business. A decision that concerns the Mountains of Cedar-felling is the business of youthful Utu. Utu should know about it from us.'

13–16 Gilgameš prepared° a white kid. He clasped a brown kid, a sacrificial animal, close to his breast.° In his hand he held a holy staff before his nose, as he addressed Utu of heaven:

17–18 'Utu, I want to set off into the mountains! May you be my helper! I want to set off into the Mountains of Cedar-felling! May you be my helper!'

19–20 From heaven Utu replied to him: 'Young man, you are noble already in your own right—but what would you want with the mountains?'

21–33 'Utu, I have something to say to you—a word in your ear! I greet you—please pay attention! In my city people are dying, and hearts are full of distress. People are lost—that fills me with° dismay. I craned my neck over the city wall: corpses in the water make the river almost overflow. That is what I see. That will happen to me too—that is the way things go. No one is tall enough to reach heaven; no one can reach wide enough to stretch over the mountains. Since a man cannot pass beyond the final end of life, I want to set off into the mountains, to establish my renown there. Where renown can be established there, I will establish my renown; and where no renown can be established there, I shall establish the renown of the gods.'

34–47 Utu accepted his tears as a fitting gift. As befits a compassionate person, he turned to him full of compassion: 'Now there are seven warriors, sons of a single mother. The first, their eldest brother, has lion's paws and eagle's talons. The second is a . . . snake, ... The

third is a dragon snake, ... The fourth blazes with fire .... The fifth
is a ... snake, ... The sixth° beats at the flanks of the mountains like
a battering flood°. The seventh ... flashes like lightning, and no one
can deflect it°.° They should guide you through the mountain
valleys!' The warrior, youthful Utu, gave these seven to Gilgameš.°
The feller of cedars was filled with joy; lord Gilgameš was filled with
joy.

48–51 In his city he had the horn sounded for single men; similarly for two
together he made them call out. 'Let him who has a household go to
his household! Let him who has a mother go to his mother! Let
bachelor males, types like me,° join me at my side!'

52–60 Whoever had a household went to his household. Whoever had a
mother went to his mother. Bachelor males, types like him—there
were fifty—joined him at his side. He made his way to the black-
smith's, and had them cast ... weapons and axes, the strength of
warriors. Then he made his way to the deeply shaded plantations,
where he had ebony trees felled, and ḫalub trees, apricot trees, and
box trees. He ... to his fellow-citizens who were going with him.°
The first, their eldest brother, has lion's paws and eagle's claws. They
will guide him through the mountain valleys.

61 He crossed the first mountain range, but his intuition did not lead
him to find the cedars there.°

62–7 When he had crossed the seventh mountain range, there his
intuition led him to find the cedars. He did not need to ask, nor did
he have to search any further. Lord Gilgameš began to chop at the
cedars, while Enkidu lopped off their branches, ... to Gilgameš.°
... stacked them in piles.° He loosed his terrors against .... °

68–75 Gilgameš ... was overcome by sleep, and it affected Enkidu ... as a
powerful longing. His fellow-citizens who had come with him flailed
around at his feet like puppies. Enkidu awoke from his dream,
shuddering from his sleep. He rubbed his eyes; there was eery silence
everywhere. He touched Gilgameš, but could not rouse him. He
spoke to him, but he did not reply.

76–84 'You who have gone to sleep, you who have gone to sleep! Gilgameš,
young lord of Kulaba, how long will you sleep for? The mountains
are becoming indistinct as the shadows fall across them; the evening
twilight lies over them. Proud Utu is already on his way to the bosom
of his mother Ningal. Gilgameš, how long will you sleep for? The
sons of your city who came with you should not have to wait at the

foot of the hills. Their own mothers should not have to twine string in the square of your city.'

85–9 He thrust that into his right ear; he covered him with his aggressive words as if with a cloth°. He gathered° in his hand a cloth with thirty shekels of oil on it and smothered° it over Gilgameš's chest. Then Gilgameš stood up like a bull on the great earth. Bending his neck downwards, he yelled at him:

90–1 'By the life of my own mother Ninsumun and of my father, holy Lugalbanda! Am I to become again as if I were slumbering still on the lap of my own mother Ninsumun?'

92–5 A second time he spoke to him: 'By the life of my own mother Ninsumun and of my father, holy Lugalbanda! Until I discover whether that person was a human or a god, I shall not direct back to the city my steps which I have directed to the mountains.'

96–7 The slave, trying to ameliorate the situation, trying to make life appear more attractive, answered his master:

98–106 'My master, you have not yet really seen that person, he should not vex you.—But he vexes me—me, who have seen him before. His pugnacious mouth is a dragon's maw; his face is a lion's grimace. His chest is like a raging flood; no one dares approach° his brow, which devours the reed-beds.° Travel on, my master, up into the mountains!—but I shall travel back to the city. If I say to your mother about you "He is alive!", she will laugh. But afterwards I shall say to her about you "He is dead!", and she will certainly weep over you°.'°

107–16 'Look, Enkidu, two people together will not perish! A grappling-pole does not sink! No one can cut through a three-ply cloth! Water cannot wash someone away from a wall! Fire in a reed house cannot be extinguished! You help me, and I will help you—what can anyone do against us then? When it sank, when it sank, when the Magan boat sank, when the Magilum Barge sank, then at least the life-saving grappling-pole of the boat was rescued°! Come on, let's get after him and get a sight of him!'

117–19 'If we go after him, there will be terror! There will be terror. Turn back! Is it advisable? Is it advisable? Turn back!'

120 'Whatever you may think—come on, let's get after him!'

121–5 Before a man can approach within even sixty *nindan*°, Ḫuwawa has already reached his house among the cedars. When he looks at someone, it is the look of death. When he shakes his head at someone, it is a gesture full of reproach.° 'You may still be a young

man, but you will never again return to the city of your mother who
bore you!'

126–9 Fear and terror spread through his° sinews and his feet. He could not
move (?) his feet on the ground; the big toenails of his feet stuck . . .
to the path (?). At his side . . . .

130–5 (*Ḫuwawa addressed Gilgameš:*) 'So come on now, you heroic
bearer of a sceptre of wide-ranging power! Noble glory of the
gods, angry bull standing ready for a fight! Your mother knew
well how to bear sons, and your nurse knew well how to nourish
children on the breast! Don't be afraid, rest your hand on the
ground!'

136–9 Gilgameš rested his hand on the ground, and addressed Ḫuwawa:
'By the life of my own mother Ninsumun and of my father, holy
Lugalbanda! No one really knows where in the mountains you live;
they would like to know where in the mountains you live. Here, I
have brought you En-me-barage-si, my big sister, to be your wife in
the mountains.'

140–4 And again he addressed him: 'By the life of my mother Ninsumun
and of my father, holy Lugalbanda! No one really knows where in the
mountains you live; they would like to know where in the mountains
you live. Here, I have brought you Ma-tur, my little sister, to be your
concubine in the mountains. Just hand over your terrors to me! I
want to become your kinsman!'

145–8 Then Ḫuwawa handed over to him his first terror. Gilgameš's
fellow-citizens who had come with him began to lop off the branches
and bundle them together, so as to lay them down at the foot of the
hills.°

149–51 When Ḫuwawa had finally handed over to him his seventh terror,
Gilgameš found himself beside Ḫuwawa. He went up to him
gradually° from behind, as one does with a . . . snake. He made as if
to kiss him, but then punched him on the cheek with his fist.

152 Ḫuwawa bared his teeth at him°.

153–7 He tugged at Gilgameš's hand.° 'I want to talk to Utu! Utu, I never
knew a mother who bore me, nor a father who brought me up! I was
born in the mountains—you brought me up! Yet Gilgameš swore to
me by heaven, by earth, and by the mountains.'

158–60 Ḫuwawa clutched at Gilgameš's hand, and prostrated himself before
him. Then Gilgameš's noble heart took pity on him. Gilgameš
addressed Enkidu°:

161–2 'Enkidu, let the captured bird run away home! Let the captured man return to his mother's embrace!'

163–74 Enkidu replied to Gilgameš°: 'Come on now, you heroic bearer of a sceptre of wide-ranging power! Noble glory of the gods, angry bull standing ready for a fight! Young lord Gilgameš, cherished in Unug, your mother knew well how to bear sons, and your nurse knew well how to nourish children!—One so exalted and yet so lacking in understanding° will be devoured by fate without him ever understanding that fate. The very idea that a captured bird should run away home, or a captured man should return to his mother's embrace!—Then you yourself would never get back to the mother-city that bore you!°'

175–7 Ḫuwawa addressed Enkidu: 'Enkidu, you speak such hateful° words against me to him! You hireling, who are hired for your keep! You who follow along after him—you speak such hateful words to him.°'°

178–80 As Ḫuwawa spoke like that to him, Enkidu, full of rage and anger, cut his throat. He put° his head in a leather bag.

181–6 They entered before Enlil. After they had kissed the ground before Enlil, they threw the leather bag down, tipped out his head, and placed it before Enlil. When Enlil saw the head of Ḫuwawa, he spoke angrily to Gilgameš:°

FIG. 39. 'As Ḫuwawa spoke like that to him, Enkidu,
full of rage and anger, cut his throat'—the scene as depicted
on an Old Babylonian terracotta plaque from Urim

187–92 'Why did you act in this way? . . . did you act . . . ?° He should have
sat before you!° He should have eaten the bread that you eat, and
should have drunk the water that you drink! He should have been
honoured . . . you!'°

193–200 He gave Ḫuwawa's first aura to the fields.° He gave his second aura
to the rivers. He gave his third aura to the reed-beds. He gave his
fourth aura to the lions. He gave his fifth aura to the palace°. He gave
his sixth aura to the forests°. He gave his seventh aura to Nungal. . . .
his terror . . . .°

201–2 Mighty one, Gilgameš, who is cherished!° Praise be to Nisaba!°

Notes

8–12 After 'from us.' 1 MS adds: 'If you want to set off into the Mountains of Cedar-
felling, Utu should know about it from us.'

13–16 Instead of 'prepared' 2 MSS have: 'took hold of'. Instead of 'He clasped a
brown kid, a sacrificial animal, close to his breast.' 1 MS has: 'He . . . a brown
kid.'

21–33 After 'with' 1 MS adds: 'wretched'.

34–47 After 'sixth' 1 MS adds: ', a shackle that . . . the rebel lands in the hills,'. Instead
of 'like a battering flood' 1 MS has: 'floodwater that destroys all'. Instead of
'it' 1 MS has: 'its power'. After that phrase 1 MS adds 4 fragmentary lines;
another adds instead 6 lines: '(2 lines fragmentary) . . . kingship . . . . Nisaba has
bestowed . . . on you in addition. They . . . , and know the routes on earth.
They will help you find the . . . of the way.' Instead of 'The warrior, youthful
Utu, gave these seven to Gilgameš.' 3 MSS have: 'These seven the warrior,
youthful Utu, gave to lord Gilgameš.'

48–51 After 'types like me,' 4 MSS add: '—fifty of them—'.

52–60 After 'going with him.' 1 MS adds: 'Warriors, sons of a single mother . . . .'.

61 Instead of 'but his intuition did not lead him to find the cedars there' 1 MS has:
'the cedars did not catch his attention'. The same MS adds: 'He crossed the
second mountain range, but the cedars did not catch his attention. He crossed
the third mountain range, but the cedars did not catch his attention. He
crossed the fourth mountain range, but the cedars did not catch his attention.
He crossed the fifth mountain range, but the cedars did not catch his attention. He crossed the sixth mountain range, but the cedars did not catch his
attention.' Another MS adds instead: '(*unknown number of lines missing*) He
crossed the third mountain range, but his intuition did not lead him to find
the cedars there. He crossed the fourth mountain range, but his intuition did
not lead him to find the cedars there. He crossed the fifth mountain range,
but his intuition did not lead him to find the cedars there. He crossed the
sixth mountain range, but his intuition did not lead him to find the cedars
there.'

62–7   Instead of 'while Enkidu lopped off their branches, . . . to Gilgameš.' 1 MS has:
'while Enkidu . . . their branches, and his fellow-citizens . . . .'. 1 MS adds here:
'to . . . , Enkidu . . . .' After 'in piles.' 1 MS adds: 'Ḫuwawa . . . .' Instead of
'while Enkidu lopped off their branches, . . . to Gilgameš. . . . stacked them in
piles. He loosed his terrrors against . . . .' 1 MS has: 'while Enkidu cut up the
timbers, and the widows' sons who had come with him heaped them up in
piles. Since, because of the . . . , Ḫuwawa had been scared in his lair by
Gilgameš, he began to radiate his terrors . . . .'

85–9   After 'cloth' 1 MS adds: ', laid them out like linen'. Instead of 'gathered' 3 MSS
have: 'picked up'. Instead of 'smothered' 1 MS has: 'rubbed'.

98–106   Instead of 'dares approach' 1 MS has: 'can escape from'. After 'reed-beds.' 2
MSS add 1 line: 'A man-eating lion, he never wipes away the blood from his
slaver.' 1 MS adds instead 5 lines: '(*1 line fragmentary*) . . . a lion eating a corpse,
he never wipes away the blood (*3 lines fragmentary*)'. Instead of 'over you' 1 MS
has: 'bitterly'. 1 MS adds here: '. . . replied to . . . :'.

107–16   Instead of 'was rescued' 1 MS has: 'was not allowed to sink'.

121–5   Sixty *nindan* is equivalent to about 360 metres. After 'reproach' 1 MS adds:
'When he speaks to someone, he certainly does not prolong his words:'.

126–9   Instead of 'his' 1 MS has: 'Gilgameš's'.

145–8   Several MSS preserve a more elaborate, but repetitive, narrative built on
the pattern of lines 145–8. Some preserve the repetitions in an extremely
abbreviated form. No MS known to be from Nibru preserves the additional
lines. One MS of unknown origin adds at least 53 lines (and another fragmentary MS of unknown origin gives an abbreviated version of these, always
replacing 'terror' by 'aura'):

A–K   And again he addressed him: 'By the life of my mother Ninsumun and of my
father, holy Lugalbanda! No one really knows where in the mountains you
live; they would like to know where in the mountains you live. Here, I have
brought to the mountains for you . . . . Couldn't I get close to you and your
family? Just hand over your terrors to me! I want to become your kinsman!'
Then Ḫuwawa handed over to him his second terror. Gilgameš's fellow-
citizens who had come with him began to lop off the branches and bundle
them together, so as to lay them down at the foot of the hills.

L–V   And a third time he addressed him: 'By the life of my mother Ninsumun and
of my father, holy Lugalbanda! No one really knows where in the mountains
you live; they would like to know where in the mountains you live. Here, I
have brought to the mountains for you some *eša* flour—the food of the
gods!—and a waterskin of cool water. Couldn't I get close to you and your
family? Just hand over your terrors to me! I want to become your kinsman!'
Then Ḫuwawa handed over to him his third terror. Gilgameš's fellow-citizens
who had come with him began to lop off the branches and bundle them
together, so as to lay them down at the foot of the hills.

W–FF   And a fourth time he addressed him: 'By the life of my mother Ninsumun and of my father, holy Lugalbanda! No one really knows where in the mountains you live; they would like to know where in the mountains you live. Here, I have brought to the mountains for you some big shoes for your big feet. Couldn't I get close to you and your family? Just hand over your terrors to me! I want to become your kinsman!' Then Ḫuwawa handed over to him his fourth terror. Gilgameš's fellow-citizens who had come with him began to lop off the branches and bundle them together, so as to lay them down at the foot of the hills.

GG–PP And a fifth time he addressed him: 'By the life of my mother Ninsumun and of my father, holy Lugalbanda! No one really knows where in the mountains you live; they would like to know where in the mountains you live. Here, I have brought to the mountains for you some tiny shoes for your tiny feet. Couldn't I get close to you and your family? Just hand over your terrors to me! I want to become your kinsman!' Then Ḫuwawa handed over to him his fifth terror. Gilgameš's fellow-citizens who had come with him began to lop off the branches and bundle them together, so as to lay them down at the foot of the hills.

QQ–AAA And a sixth time he addressed him: 'By the life of my mother Ninsumun and of my father, holy Lugalbanda! No one really knows where in the mountains you live; they would like to know where in the mountains you live. Here, I have brought you rock-crystal, *nir* stone, and lapis lazuli—from the mountains. Couldn't I get close to you and your family? Just hand over your terrors to me! I want to become your kinsman!' Then Ḫuwawa handed over to him his sixth terror. Gilgameš's fellow-citizens who had come with him began to lop off the branches and bundle them together, so as to lay them down at the foot of the hills.

149–51 Instead of 'went up to him gradually' 1 MS has: . . . .'.

152 At the end of this line 1 MS adds: ', furrowing his brows at him'. 2 MSS from Urim add 8 lines: 'Ḫuwawa addressed Gilgameš: "Hero, . . . to act falsely!" The two of them . . . on him . . . . the warrior from his dwelling. . . . said to him: "Sit down!" . . . Ḫuwawa from his dwelling. . . . said to him: "Sit down!" The warrior sat down and began to weep, shedding tears. Ḫuwawa sat down and began to weep, shedding tears. Ḫuwawa . . . plea . . . to Gilgameš.' 2 other MSS add 2 lines: 'He threw a halter over him as over a captured wild bull. He tied up his arms like a captured man.' 1 MS adds 1 further line: 'Ḫuwawa wept, ...'

153–7 Instead of 'He tugged at Gilgameš's hand.' 4 MSS have: ' "Gilgameš, let me go!" '

158–60 Instead of 'Gilgameš addressed Enkidu' 3 MSS have: 'He addressed his slave Enkidu'.

163–74 Instead of 'Enkidu replied to Gilgameš' 2 MSS have: 'His slave Enkidu replied'. Instead of 'understanding' 1 MS has: 'judgment'. After 'bore you!' 1 MS adds: 'A captured warrior set free! A captured high priestess . . . to the *ĝipar* shrine! A captured *gudug* priest restored to his wig of hair! . . . ever, ever . . . ? (*2 lines fragmentary*) . . . his attention to his words . . . .'

175–7 After 'hateful' 1 MS adds: 'hostile'. Instead of 'you speak such hateful words to him.' 2 MSS have: 'why do you speak such hateful words to him?' 1 MS adds two fragmentary lines here.

178–80 Instead of 'Enkidu, full of rage and anger,' 2 MSS from Nibru have: 'they'. Instead of 'He put' the same 2 MSS from Nibru have: 'They put'; 1 other MS has: 'He chucked'.

181–6 Instead of these lines 1 MS has: 'They brought it before Enlil and Ninlil. When Enlil approached (?), . . . went out the window (?), and Ninlil went out . . . . When Enlil with Ninlil had returned (?),'.

187–92 Instead of '. . . did you act . . . ?' 1 MS has: 'Was it commanded that his name should be wiped from the earth?' Instead of 'He should have sat before you!' 1 MS has: 'He should have sat . . . , ...' Instead of ' "He should have been honoured . . . you!" ' 1 MS has: ' "Ḫuwawa—he . . . honoured!" '; 1 other MS has: 'From his seat, Enlil assigned Ḫuwawa's heavenly auras to . . . .'

193–200 The MS tradition for these lines is extremely confused about the order in which the various auras are assigned; the sequence presented here is a compromise. Instead of 'palace' 1 MS has: 'debt slaves'. Instead of 'forests' 1 MS has 'hills'. Instead of '. . . his terror . . .' 1 MS or possibly 2 MSS have: '. . . the rest of the auras . . . Gilgameš . . . .'

201–2 Instead of 'Mighty one, Gilgameš, who is cherished!' 1 MS has: 'Praise be to the mighty one, Gilgameš! Praise be to Enkidu!' Instead of these lines 1 MS has: 'Ḫuwawa, . . . ! . . . cherished, . . . ! Praise be to Enkidu . . . !'

OTHER THEMATIC GROUPINGS

DEATH AND THE UNDERWORLD

Group A   Gilgameš, Enkidu, and the Underworld
           The death of Ur-Namma
Group B   Inana's descent to the Underworld
           Dumuzid's dream
Group E   The dedication of an axe to Nergal
           An *adab* to Nergal for Šu-ilišu
Group H   An *adab* to Bau for Išme-Dagan

DESTINY AND JUDGMENT

Group A   Gilgameš, Enkidu, and the Underworld
           The building of Ningirsu's temple (extract)
           An *adab* to An for Lipit-Eštar
           The death of Ur-Namma
Group B   Inana's descent to the Underworld
           A hymn to Inana
Group C   Enlil and Nam-zid-tara
           The cursing of Agade
Group E   Ninurta's exploits
Group F   Inana and Šu-kale-tuda
Group G   Enki and the world order
Group H   A *balbale* to Ningišzida
           A *šir-namgala* to Ninisina for Lipit-Eštar
           A *šir-namursaĝa* to Inana for Iddin-Dagan
           An *ululumama* to Suen for Ibbi-Suen
Group J   The song of the hoe
           Enlil in the E-kur
           A hymn to Nungal

DREAMS

Group A   Lugalbanda in the mountain cave
           Sargon and Ur-Zababa
           The building of Ningirsu's temple (extract)
Group B   Dumuzid's dream
Group C   The cursing of Agade

ENKI AND DAMGALNUNA

Group A	Gilgameš, Enkidu, and the Underworld
	The death of Ur-Namma
Group B	Inana's descent to the Underworld
Group D	The lament for Sumer and Urim
Group G	Enki and the world order
	The debate between Sheep and Grain
	The debate between Bird and Fish
	The heron and the turtle
Group H	A *balbale* to Ningišzida
	A *šir-šag-ḫula* to Damgalnuna
	A *tigi* to Enki for Ur-Ninurta
Group I	A hymn to Nisaba
	A hymn to Ḫaia for Rīm-Sîn
Group J	The song of the hoe
	Enki's journey to Nibru

COMPOSITIONS WITH GENERICALLY MARKED SECTIONS

Group A	An *adab* to An for Lipit-Eštar
Group C	Šulgi and Ninlil's barge
Group D	The lament for Sumer and Urim
	A *šir-namgala* to Nanna
Group E	An *adab* to Nergal for Šu-ilišu
	A hymn to Numušda for Sîn-iqīšam
Group F	A *tigi* to Nintud-Aruru
Group H	An *adab* to Bau for Išme-Dagan
	A *kungar to* Inana and Dumuzid
	A *šir-namgala* to Ninisina for Lipit-Eštar
	A *šir-namšub* to Utu
	A *šir-namursaga* to Inana for Iddin-Dagan
Group J	The Keš temple hymn

JOURNEYS

Group A	Enmerkar and En-suḫgir-ana
	Lugalbanda in the mountain cave
	Lugalbanda and the Anzud bird
	Gilgameš, Enkidu, and the Underworld
	Sargon and Ur-Zababa
	The building of Ningirsu's temple (extract)

Group B	Inana's descent to the Underworld
Group C	Enlil and Ninlil
	Šulgi and Ninlil's barge
Group D	Nanna-Suen's journey to Nibru
Group E	Ninurta's return to Nibru
Group F	Lu-diĝira's message to his mother
Group G	Enki and the world order
Group J	A praise poem of Šulgi
	Enki's journey to Nibru
	Gilgameš and Ḫuwawa

MINOR GODDESSES

Group A	The building of Ninĝirsu's temple (extract)
Group D	The lament for Sumer and Urim
	The herds of Nanna
Group F	A *tigi* to Nintud-Aruru
Group G	The debate between Sheep and Grain
	The home of the fish
Group H	An *adab* to Bau for Išme-Dagan
	A *šir-gida* to Ninisina
	A *šir-namgala* to Ninisina for Lipit-Eštar
Group I	A hymn to Nisaba
	A hymn to Ninkasi
Group J	The song of the hoe
	A hymn to Nungal

NIBRU

Group B	Inana and Išme-Dagan
Group C	Enlil and Ninlil
	The cursing of Agade
Group D	A *balbale* to Nanna
	Nanna-Suen's journey to Nibru
Group E	Ninurta's return to Nibru
Group F	Lu-diĝira's message to his mother
Group H	An *adab* to Bau for Išme-Dagan
	An *ululumama* to Suen for Ibbi-Suen
Group J	A praise poem of Šulgi
	A praise poem of Lipit-Eštar
	Enlil in the E-kur
	Enki's journey to Nibru

TEMPLES AND RITUAL

Group A	The building of Ninĝirsu's temple (extract)
Group B	Inana and Išme-Dagan
Group C	Enlil and Nam-zid-tara
	The cursing of Agade
Group D	The lament for Sumer and Urim
	A *balbale* to Nanna
Group E	The dedication of an axe to Nergal
Group H	An *adab* to Bau for Išme-Dagan
	A *kunĝar to* Inana and Dumuzid
	A *šir-gida* to Ninisina
	A *šir-namursaĝa* to Inana for Iddin-Dagan
Group J	A praise poem of Šulgi
	A praise poem of Lipit-Eštar
	The song of the hoe
	The exaltation of Inana
	Enlil in the E-kur
	The Keš temple hymn
	Enki's journey to Nibru
	A hymn to Nungal

UNUG

Group A	Enmerkar and En-suḫgir-ana
	Lugalbanda in the mountain cave
	Lugalbanda and the Anzud bird
	Gilgameš, Enkidu, and the Underworld
Group J	A praise poem of Lipit-Eštar
	Gilgameš and Ḫuwawa

URIM

Group A	The death of Ur-Namma
Group B	A love song for Šu-Suen
Group D	The lament for Sumer and Urim
Group F	A lullaby for a son of Šulgi
Group G	The heron and the turtle
Group H	An *ululumama* to Suen for Ibbi-Suen
Group J	A praise poem of Šulgi

UTU THE SUN-GOD

Group A	Lugalbanda in the mountain cave
Group B	Inana's descent to the Underworld
	Dumuzid's dream
	Dumuzid and Enkimdu
Group D	The lament for Sumer and Urim
Group F	A *balbale* to Inana and Dumuzid
Group G	The Flood story
Group H	A *šir-namšub* to Utu

WARFARE AND CONFLICT

Group A	Enmerkar and En-suḫgir-ana
	Lugalbanda and the Anzud bird
	The death of Ur-Namma
Group B	Dumuzid's dream
	Inana and Išme-Dagan
	A hymn to Inana
Group D	The lament for Sumer and Urim
Group E	An *adab* to Nergal for Šu-ilišu
	A hymn to Numušda for Sîn-iqīšam
	Ninurta's exploits
	Ninurta's return to Nibru
Group F	Inana and Šu-kale-tuda
Group G	The debate between Sheep and Grain
	The debate between Bird and Fish
	The heron and the turtle
Group H	A *šir-gida* to Ninisina
	A *šir-namursaĝa* to Inana for Iddin-Dagan
Group I	A supervisor's advice to a young scribe
	The instructions of Šuruppag
Group J	A praise poem of Lipit-Eštar
	The exaltation of Inana
	Inana and Ebiḫ
	Gilgameš and Ḫuwawa

INDEX OF COMPOSITIONS BY
ETCSL CATALOGUE NUMBER

GLOSSARY OF SUMERIAN NAMES

Abba-šušu a minor deity, in the entourage of Inana in *Inana and Šu-kale-tuda* (Group F)

Abzu the freshwater underworld, home of the god Enki; a name for Enki's temple in Eridug

Adab a Sumerian city to the east of Šuruppag, modern name Bismaya

Aga a legendary king of Kiš, son of En-me-barage-si, adversary of Gilgameš

Agade the capital city of king Sargon, possibly in the area of modern-day Baghdad, exact location unknown

Agrun-kug the goddess Ningal's sanctuary in Urim, literally 'Sacred bedroom'

Akkad the land to the north of Sumer; territorial state whose capital was Agade, *c*.2350–2230 BCE

Akkadians the people of the land of Akkad

Akšak a Sumerian city on the Tigris river, exact location unknown

Alamuš the minister of the moon-god Nanna-Suen

Ama-ĝeštin-ana another name for Ĝeštin-ana, the sister of Dumuzid the shepherd-god

Amaš-e-kug the goddess Inana's temple in Kisiga, literally 'Pure sheepfold'

Ama-ušumgal-ana another name for the shepherd-god Dumuzid

An the supreme deity, very distant from the affairs of humans

Ansiga-ria the minister of the lord of Aratta in *Enmerkar and En-suhgir-ana* (Group A)

Anšan an Elamite city far to the east of Sumer, modern Tall i-Malyan in south-west Iran; also the area ruled by that city

Anšar a primordial deity, involved in the creation of the world and the gods

Anuna a collective name for the gods

Anzagar the goddess Inana's temple in the city of Akšak , literally 'Tower'

Anzud a mythical creature, half lion, half eagle; in modern scholarship sometimes called Anzu, Imdugud, or the Thunderbird

Arali a name for the Underworld

Aratta a legendary city far to the east of Sumer

Aruru sometimes depicted as a birth goddess, identified with Nintud; sometimes as a fierce and frightening deity

Asag a powerful demon, defeated by Ninurta in *Ninurta's exploits* (Group E)

Asarluhi the god of Kuara near Eridug; associated with magic; considered to be the son of the god Enki and his spouse Damgalnuna

Ašgi a warrior god, son of Nintud, local to the cult at Keš

Ašimbabbar a name for the moon-god: also known as Nanna and Suen; possibly to be read as Dilimbabbar

Aššu a settlement on a river, location unknown

Azimua another name for the goddess Ninazimua, divine spouse of Ninğišzida

Babylon a city to the north of Sumer, seat of the First Dynasty of Babylon (*c.*1894–1595 BCE), which defeated the Dynasties of Isin and Larsa to rule over the entire Land under king Ḫammurabi (ruled *c.*1792–1750 BCE), father of Samsu-iluna

Bad-tibira a Sumerian city, near Larsa

Bagara the god Ninğirsu's temple in Lagaš

Barag-dur-ğara the goddess Inana's shrine in Nibru

Bau an important goddess of the Lagaš-Ğirsu region; divine spouse of Zababa or else Ninğirsu; worshipped in the temples E-ğalga-sud and E-Iri-kug (also called Tar-sir-sir)

Belili the old woman in whose house the shepherd-god Dumuzid hides in *Dumuzid's dream* (Group B)

Bēliš-tikal King Ur-Zababa's chief smith in *Sargon and Ur-Zababa* (Group A)

Birtum the goddess Nungal's divine spouse

Bison one of the seven Slain Heroes defeated by the god Ninurta and one of his trophies in the battle against the Asag demon

Dagan a West Semitic grain god, worshipped especially along the upper Euphrates; occurs in the names of Iddin-Dagan and Išme-Dagan, kings of Isin

Damgalnuna the god Enki's divine spouse

Damu a god of healing, son of the goddess Ninisina

Dilmun the Sumerian name for Bahrain and perhaps the surrounding area, on the Gulf coast

Dim-me and Dim-mea a pair of evil female demons who cause illnesses

Dimpikug, Dimpimekug two names for a female deity or demon in the entourage of the god Ninğišzida

(Warrior) Dragon one of the seven Slain Heroes defeated by the god Ninurta and one of his trophies in the battle against the Asag demon

Du-ašaga an unidentified location where rushes grow in *Nanna-Suen's journey to Nibru* (Group D)

Dubla-maḫ the court of judgment at Urim, dedicated to the moon-god Nanna-Suen

Dumuzid the shepherd-god, lover of the goddess Inana and brother of the goddess Ğeštin-ana; who is sent to the Underworld as Inana's substitute

Dumuzid-abzu the goddess of the village Kinirša near Lagaš; no connection with the shepherd-god Dumuzid.

Dumuzid-ušumgal-ana another name for the shepherd-god Dumuzid

Dur-an-ki a name of Nibru as centre of the universe, literally 'Bond of heaven and earth'; a name of Inana's sanctuary at Nibru

Dur-ğišnimbar another name for Nibru

Durtur the divine mother of the shepherd-god Dumuzid and his sister Ğeštin-ana

E-ana the goddess Inana's temple in Unug, literally 'House of heaven'

Early Dynastic Period a period of cultural commonality and political conflict between independent Sumerian city states, *c.*3000–2350 BCE

E-babbar the sun-god Utu's temple in Larsa, literally 'Shining house'

Ebiḫ a mountain range to the north-east of Sumer, thought to be the Jebel Hamrin

Ebla a city in Syria, modern Tell Mardikh, 55 km south-west of modern Aleppo

E-danna a secondary temple of the moon-god Nanna-Suen on the outskirts of Urim, perhaps 'House at the end of a *danna*' (*c*.11 km)

E-Dilmuna a temple of the goddess Inana in Urim, literally 'House of Dilmun'

E-Engur another name for E-abzu, Enki's temple in Eridug, literally 'House of fresh water'

E-ešdam-kug a temple of the goddess Inana in Ğirsu, literally 'House, sacred brothel'

Egal-maḫ a temple of the goddess Ninegala-Inana in Urim; also the name of the goddess Ninisina's temple in Isin; literally 'August palace'

E-gida the god Ninazu's temple in Enegir, literally 'Long house'

E-ğalga-sud a shrine of the goddess Bau in the temple Tar-sirsir in Ğirsu

E-ḫamun a temple of the goddess Nisaba

E-ḫuš a sanctuary of Ninğirsu in Lagaš-Ğirsu, literally 'Fearsome house'

E-Iri-kug another name for Tar-sirsir, the temple of the goddess Bau in Iri-kug, the sacred quarter of Ğirsu

E-kiš-nuğal the moon-god Nanna-Suen's temple in Urim

E-kur the god Enlil's temple in Nibru, literally 'Mountain house'

Elam the region to the east of Sumer, now south-west and south-central Iran

Elamites the inhabitants of Elam

E-maḫ the god Šara's temple in Umma, literally 'August house'; also the sanctuary of the god Enki's temple in Eridug and another name of Eš-maḫ

E-mešlam the god Nergal's temple in Kutha, literally 'House, warrior of the Underworld'

E-mud-kura a shrine in the E-kiš-nuğal temple of Nanna in Urim, literally 'House, creator of the mountains'

E-muš-kalama the temple of Dumuzid and Inana in Bad-tibira, literally 'House, face of the land'

E-namtila the god Enlil's sanctuary in his temple E-kur in Nibru, literally 'House of life'

En-Batibira perhaps a name of the goddess Aruru

Enbilulu the divine canal inspector, offspring of Enlil and Ninlil

Enegir a settlement on the canal between Larsa and Urim

Engur another name for the Abzu

En-ḫedu-ana a daughter of king Sargon (*c*.2350 BCE), high priestess of the mood-god Nanna-Suen at Urim

E-ninnu(-anzud-babbar) the god Ninğirsu's temple at Ğirsu, literally 'House of the fifty (divine powers): the white Anzud bird'

Enki the god of wisdom and cunning, whose main temple was at Eridug and who was thought to reside in the Abzu

Enkidu the hero Gilgameš's servant

Enkimdu a farming deity, sometime rival of the shepherd-god Dumuzid

Enlil the father of the gods, whose main temple was the E-kur, in Nibru

En-me-barage-si an Early Dynastic king of Kiš who became mythologized as the father of Gilgameš's adversary Aga; whom Gilgameš offers jokingly as a bride to the monster Ḫuwawa

Enmerkar a mythical king of Unug, father of the hero Lugalbanda

En-me-šara Enlil's uncle in *Enlil and Nam-zid-tara* (Group C)

Enmul a male ancestor deity, partner of Ninmul

En-suḫĝir-ana a mythical king of Aratta; adversary of Enmerkar, king of Unug

E-nutura a temple of the goddess Ninḫursaĝa

E-puḫruma a cultic location; literally 'Assembly house'

Ereš a Sumerian city in the region of Nibru, exact location unknown

Ereškigala the goddess of the Underworld, sister of Inana

Eridug a city in the far south of Sumer, main cult centre of the god Enki, believed by the Sumerians to be the first city; modern name Abu Shahrain; also called Eridu in modern scholarship

E-sig-meše-du the goddess Inana's temple in Isin, literally 'House, brickwork worthy of the divine powers'

E-sikil a temple of the goddess Inana in Kiš, literally 'Pure house'

E-šag-ḫula the goddess Inana's temple in Kazallu; literally 'House of a joyful heart'

E-šara the goddess Inana's temple in Adab, literally 'House of the universe'

Eš-maḫ the god Nuska's temple in Nibru, literally 'Exalted house'

Eštar the Akkadian name for the goddess Inana, also written Ištar; found in the names Lipit-Eštar, Šat-Eštar, and Šimat-Eštar

E-šumeša the god Ninurta's temple in Nibru

E-temen-ni-guru the ziggurrat terrace attached to E-kiš-nuĝal, the moon-god Nanna-Suen's temple in Urim; literally 'House, foundation platform clad in terror'

E-Ulmaš the goddess Inana's temple at Ulmaš in Agade

E-unir the ziggurrat attached to the god Enki's temple in Eridug

Euphrates the westernmost river of the Sumerian plain, running from high in the Taurus mountains many hundreds of miles to the north, into the Gulf sea; in antiquity the Euphrates and Tigris did not meet

E-zagin the goddess Nisaba's temple in Ereš; also the name of the goddess Inana's temple in the mythical city of Aratta; literally 'Lapis lazuli house'

Ezina(-Kusu) deified grain (female), also known in modern scholarship as Ašnan

Gaeš a settlement to the east of Urim, a cult centre of the moon-god Nanna-Suen

Ganzer the gate into the Underworld

Gate of Wonder a cultic location in *Inana and Ebiḫ* (Group J)

Gayau a minor deity of cattle, associated with the moon-god Nanna

Gibil deified fire

Giguna the goddess Inana's temple in Zabalam

Gilgameš a mythical heroic adventurer, king of Unug, master of Enkidu

Gu-aba a sea port in the state of Lagaš, cult centre of the goddess Ninmarki

Gubin a name for the Zagros mountains to the east of Sumer, home of the Gutian people

Gudea a ruler of the city-state of Lagaš, in south-east Sumer in the late twenty-second century BCE; considered to immediately precede or overlap the beginning of the reign of Ur-Namma of Urim

Gud-gal-ana the divine spouse of the Underworld goddess Ereškigala, literally 'Great bull of heaven'

Gu-edina fertile land near the Sumerian cities of Umma and Lagaš

Gutians a nomadic people of the mountains to the north-east of Sumer, archetypical barbaric invaders who threaten the stability and prosperity of the Land

Gutium the collective name for the Gutian people

Gypsum a type of stone; one of the seven Slain Heroes defeated by the god Ninurta and one of his trophies in the battle against the Asag demon

Ĝa-bur the goddess Ningublaga's temple in Ki-abrig, literally 'Chamber of stone jars'

Ĝa-ĝiš-šua the goddess Ninlil's sanctuary in her temple Ki-ur in Nibru, literally 'Chamber of the stool'

Ĝatumdug a protective goddess particular to the city-state of Lagaš

Ĝeštin-ana a goddess, sister of the shepherd-god Dumuzid, who agrees to spend half the year in the Underworld as Dumuzid's substitute

Ĝeštin-dudu the goddess Ĝeštin-ana's girlfriend

Ĝirsi an unknown location

Ĝirsu the northernmost town of the city-state of Lagaš in south-eastern Sumer, modern name Telloh

Ĝišbanda the cult centre of the god Ninĝišzida, to the east of Enegir between Urim and Larsa

Holy Mound a cosmic location where the gods determine destinies, and where they were thought to have lived before the world was created

Ḫaia a minor god of scribal arts, spouse of the much more important goddess Nisaba

Ḫal-an-kug another name for the god Enki's temple E-Engur in Eridug, literally 'Holy secret of heaven'

Ḫamazu a legendary city in Iran; also known as Ḫamazi; home of the sorcerer Ur-ĝirnuna in *Enmerkar and En-Suḫgir-ana* (Group A)

Ḫarali a mythical location

Ḫursaĝ-galama the god Enlil's sanctuary on the ziggurrat of his temple in Nibru, literally 'Skilfully built mountain'

Ḫursaĝ-kalama a temple of the goddess Inana in Kiš, literally 'Mountain of the Land'

Ḫušbisag the divine spouse of the Underworld deity Namtar

Ḫuwawa the divine guardian of the Lebanese cedar forests, killed by Gilgameš and Enkidu

Ibbi-Suen the fifth king of the Third Dynasty of Urim, ruled c.2029–2004 BCE

Ibgal the goddess Inana's temples in both Umma and Lagaš

Iddin-Dagan the third king of the Dynasty of Isin, ruled c.1953–1935 BCE

Id-kura literally 'River of the Underworld'; setting for an encounter between Enlil and Ninlil in *Enlil and Ninlil* (Group C)

Ig-alim a minor deity; offspring of the goddess Bau and servant of the goddess Nungal

Igigi a collective name for the great gods

Igi-ḫeĝala one of the god Enki's attendants, with Ka-ḫeĝala; literally 'Eyes of abundance'

Igi-sigsig the father of the gardener's boy Šu-kale-tuda in *Inana and Šu-kale-tuda* (Group F)

Ilum-puzura the recipient of the *Letter from Nabi-Enlil to Ilum-puzura* (Group I)

Inana the most important goddess of Sumer, sometimes seen as the daughter of An (at Unug) or (as the star Venus, under the name Ninsiana) daughter of the moon-god Nanna-Suen and sister of the sun-god Utu; she was worshipped for her sexual relations with her lover Dumuzid and others, and for her warlike aspect; there were important temples to her at Unug, Zabalam, Kiš, and Agade as well as elsewhere; equated with the Akkadian goddess Eštar or Ištar

Indagara another name for the god Ḫaia

Inim-kur-dugdug a minor deity, in the entourage of Inana in *Inana and Šu-kale-tuda* (Group F)

Isimud a minor deity, two-faced minister to the god Enki

Isin a city to the south of Nibru, seat of the Dynasty of Isin which (with Larsa) was one of the successor states to the Third Dynasty of Urim in the early second millennium BCE (*c.*2017–1794) and which continued to promote Sumerian court literature

Iškur the god of thunderstorms, hail, and flood

Išme-Dagan the fourth king of the Dynasty of Isin (*c.*1953–1935 BCE), who commissioned a great deal of high-quality royal praise poetry

Ištar the Akkadian name for the goddess Inana, also written Eštar

Ištaran the god of the city of Der, east of the Tigris river, whose minister was the snake god Niraḫ; also with a shrine in the E-ninnu temple in Ĝirsu

Ka-ḫeĝala an attendant of the god Enki, with Igi-ḫeĝala; literally 'Mouth of abundance'

Kazallu a city to the north of Sumer, between Babylon and Zimbir; cult centre of the divine couple Numušda and Namrat

Keš an important cult centre in the heart of Sumer, whose location is today uncertain

Ki-abrig the cult centre of the deity Ningublaga to the east of Gišbanda, between Urim and Larsa

Kinirša the cult centre of the goddess Dumuzid-abzu between Ĝirsu and Lagaš

Kiritaba a settlement, location uncertain

Kirsig a canal near Isin

Kisala a canal near Nibru

Kisiga a settlement in the far south of Sumer, south-east of Urim; a cult centre of Dumuzid and Inana

Kiš a city to the north of Sumer, just to the east of Babylon; cult centre of Inana and Zababa in their temple Ḫursaĝ-kalama

Ki-ur the goddess Ninlil's shrine within the temple E-kur in Nibru, literally 'Levelled place'

Kuara a Sumerian city to the north-west of Eridug; cult centre of Asarluḫi and Nineḫama

Ku-bireš(-dildareš) a mythical location to which Dumuzid escapes in *Dumuzid's dream* (Group B)

Kug-nuna a forested place in *Nanna-Suen's journey to Nibru* (Group D)

Kulaba the cultic area of the city of Unug, often used to mean Unug in its entirety

Kulla a minor deity of bricks and brick-making

Kun-satu the god Numušda's temple in Kazallu, literally 'Threshold of the mountain'

Kusu another name for the grain goddess Ezina

Lagaš a city-state in the east of Sumer, whose capital was Ĝirsu, seat of Gudea's dynasty; home to a particular, local set of deities; the modern name of the site is al-Hiba

Lā'ibum Sargon's father in *Sargon and Ur-Zababa* (Group A)

Langi a source of juniper trees in *Nanna-Suen's journey to Nibru* (Group D)

Larag a mythical antediluvian city, exact location unknown; associated with the god Pabilsaĝ

Larsa a Sumerian city to the south-east of Unug; seat of the Dynasty of Larsa, with Isin one of the successor states to the Third Dynasty of Urim in the early second millennium (*c*.2025–1763 BCE); cult centre of the sun-god Utu

Lipit-Eštar the fifth ruler of the Dynasty of Isin (*c*.1934–1924 BCE), some of whose praise poetry had a long afterlife in Sumerian scribal schools

Lord Saman-ana one of the seven Slain Heroes defeated by the god Ninurta and one of his trophies in the battle against the Asag demon

Lu-diĝira the protagonist of *Lu-diĝira's message to his mother* (Group F)

Lugal-anbara with Ud-ane and Lugal-kur-dub, in the entourage of the god Ninurta

Lugal-ane the priestess En-ḫedu-ana's adversary in *The exaltation of Inana* (Group J)

Lugalbanda a legendary hero and king of Unug, son of Enmerkar and father of Gilgameš

Lugal-kur-dub with Ud-ane and Lugal-ane, in the entourage of the god Ninurta

Lugal-Marda the principal god of Marda to the south of Kiš; divine spouse of Ninzuana

Lugal-šuba the father of Nibruta-lu, protagonist of *The dedication of an axe to Nergal* (Group E and Introduction)

Lugal-zage-si a king of Umma and Unug, overthrown by Sargon of Agade in the mid-twenty-fourth century BCE

Lulal a warrior god in the entourage of Inana; worshipped especially at the E-muš-kalama temple in Bad-tibira

Lulubi a nomadic tribe from the Zagros mountains, to the north-east of Sumer

Magan the Sumerian name for the Oman peninsula; an important source of copper ore, and entrepôt for trade in ivory, cornelian, and other goods

Magilum Barge one of the seven Slain Heroes defeated by the god Ninurta and one of his trophies in the battle against the Asag demon

Mardu a nomadic people from the Syrian desert, sometimes called Amurru or Amorites; often portrayed as dangerous to settled Sumerian life.

Marḫaši a region of the Iranian plateau, to the east of Elam; source of various exotic stones and other trade goods

Maš-gula a cowherd in *Enmerkar and En-suḫgir-ana* (Group A)

Ma-tur Gilgameš's little sister, jokingly offered in marriage to the monster Ḫuwawa in *Gilgameš and Ḫuwawa* (Group J); literally 'Little fig'

Meluḫa the Sumerian name for the Harappan civilization of the Indus Valley, an important source of ivory, cornelian, gold, and other high-value trade goods, which came by sea via the Gulf

Meluḫans the inhabitants of Meluḫa

Mermaid one of the seven Slain Heroes defeated by the god Ninurta and one of his trophies in the battle against the Asag demon

Mešlamta-eda another name for the god Nergal

Mountains of Cedar Felling the Lebanese cedar forests, a prestigious source of building timber for Sumer; Gilgameš's destination in *Gilgameš and Ḫuwawa* (Group J)

Mušdama a deity of house-building, in the entourage of the god Enlil

Nabi-Enlil the sender of the *Letter from Nabi-Enlil to Ilum-puzura* (Group I)

Namena-tuma the minister of Enmerkar, king of Unug, in *Enmerkar and En-suḫgirana* (Group A)

Namma a creator goddess, associated with the Abzu or Engur; found in the royal name Ur-Namma

Namrat the warrior god Numušda's divine spouse, worshipped at the city of Kazallu

Namtar an Underworld deity, minister of the goddess Ereškigala, who decrees the fates of the dead

Nam-zid-tara a *gudug* priest and protagonist of *Enlil and Nam-zid-tara* (Group C)

Nanibgal another name for the goddess Nisaba

Nanna the moon-god, also known as Suen and Ašimbabbar; worshipped especially in the E-kiš-nuĝal temple in Urim; spouse of the goddess Ningal, father of the sun-god Utu and the goddess Inana

Nanni a legendary ruler of Nibru

Nanše a marsh goddess, associated with birds and fish, worshipped especially at Niĝin in the state of Lagaš; mother of Ninmarki

Naram-Suen the third ruler of the Dynasty of Agade, ruled *c*.2254–2218, grandson of king Sargon

Nergal a warrior and Underworld deity, sometimes depicted as the spouse of the goddess Ereškigala; worshipped especially in the temple E-mešlam in Kuta; also called Mešlamta-eda

Neti the divine doorkeeper of the Underworld

Nezila a minor deity, in the entourage of the goddess Nungal

Nibru an important city and cult centre in the north of Sumer, where the large majority of the manuscript sources for Sumerian literature have been found; centre of worship for the gods Enlil, Ninlil, and Ninurta; also known as Nippur in modern scholarship

Nibruta-lu the protagonist of *The dedication of an axe to Nergal* (Group E and Introduction)

Niĝin a settlement in the state of Lagaš, near Gu-aba; cult centre of the goddess Nanše

Niĝin-dua a canal connecting the cities of Ĝirsu and Niĝin

Niĝin-ĝar-kug the goddess Inana's temple in Šuruppag

Niĝir-sig a minor deity, captain of Enki's barge

Ninazimua an Underworld scribal goddess, divine spouse of the god Ninĝišzida

Ninazu an Underworld deity worshipped at Enegir, between Urim and Larsa; divine spouse of the goddess Ningirida, father of the god Ninĝišzida

Nindimgul a minor god of law, minister of the goddess Nungal

Ninegala a goddess often identified with Inana, literally 'Lady of the palace'

Nineḫama a minor goddess worshipped at Kuara, perhaps the spouse of the god Asarluḫi

Ningal the moon-god Nanna-Suen's divine spouse and mother of the sun-god Utu; worshipped in the shrine Agrun-kug in Urim

Ningikuga a minor goddess in the entourage of Enki, often identified with Ningal

Ningirida an Underworld goddess worshipped at Enegir, between Urim and Larsa; divine spouse of the god Ninazu, and mother of the god Ninĝišzida

Ningublaga a cattle god, son of the moon-god Nanna-Suen, worshipped in the Gabur temple in Ki-abrig

Ninguenaka another name for the goddess Ninkasi

Ninĝirsu the most important deity of the state of Lagaš, a warrior like Ninurta

Ninĝišzida an Underworld and warrior deity, son of the god Ninazu and goddess Ningirida, spouse of the goddess Ninazimua; personal deity of Gudea, the ruler of Lagaš

Ninḫarana a goddess in the entourage of the goddess Nungal, literally 'Lady of the highway'

Ninḫursaĝa an important birth goddess with cult centres at Adab and Keš; at Keš considered to be the spouse of Šul-pa-eda but also equated sometimes with Ninmaḫ and Aruru

Niniagar the goddess of the city of Ki-abrig; divine spouse of Ningublaga; housekeeper of Nanna's temple E-kiš-nuĝal in Urim

Ninilduma a minor deity, patron god of carpenters, worshipped especially in the Zabalam area

Ninisina the goddess of medicine and healing, spouse of the minor god Pabilsaĝ and mother of Damu; chief deity of the city of Isin, where she was worshipped at the temple Egal-maḫ

Ninkarnuna a minor deity, in the entourage of the god Ninurta

Ninkasi the patron goddess of beer and brewing; also known as Ninguenaka

Ninlil the great god Enlil's divine spouse, sometimes equated with the goddess Sud; she had her own temple Ki-ur in the E-kur temple complex in Nibru and was also worshipped at nearby Tummal

Ninmaḫ 'Exalted lady', another name for the birth goddess Nintud

Ninmarki the goddess of the port of Gu-aba, worshipped in the temple E-abšaga-la; daughter of the goddess Nanše

Ninmena 'Lady of the crown', another name for the birth goddess Nintud

Ninmug the patron goddess of metalworking, sister of the god Enki

Ninmul a female ancestor deity, partnered with Enmul

Ninmutum a canal in the city of Nibru

Ninnibru the warrior god Ninurta's divine spouse, literally 'Lady of Nibru' (Ninurta's main cult centre)

Ninsiana a name for the goddess Inana as the star Venus

Ninsikila another name for the goddess Damgalnuna, spouse of the god Enki

Ninsumun the deified hero Lugalbanda's divine spouse and mother of the legendary hero Gilgameš, literally 'Lady wild cow'

Ninšubura the goddess Inana's (female) minister, who organizes her escape from the Underworld

Ninti another name for the goddess Damgalnuna, spouse of the god Enki

Nintud an important birth goddess, sometimes equated with Ninḫursaǧa; also known by the names Ninmaḫ and Ninmena

Ninunuga a name for Sud, goddess of the city of Šuruppag

Ninurta an important warrior god and agricultural deity whose main cult centre was the E-šumeša at Nibru

Ninzuana the goddess of the city of Marda; divine spouse of Lugal-Marda

Niraḫ a snake god and minister of the god Ištaran, often associated with boats, and worshipped especially at the city of Der

Nisaba an important goddess of grain, accounting, and scribal education, worshipped especially at Ereš in the temple E-zagin; daughter of An and Uraš, mother of the goddess Sud, and spouse of the god Ḫaia; also known as Nun-bar-še-gunu and Nanibgal

Nudimmud another name for the great god Enki

Numušda a warrior god of the city of Kazallu to the north of Sumer, whose temple was Kun-satu; spouse of the goddess Namrat and son of Nanna-Suen and Ningal

Nunamnir another name for the great god Enlil

Nuna-Nanna a canal running through the city of Urim

Nun-bar-še-gunu another name for the goddess Nisaba

Nunbir-tum a canal running through the city of Nibru

Nungal a goddess who was the patron deity of prisons, daughter of the Underworld goddess Ereškigala and spouse of the minor god Birtum, son of Enlil; she had a shrine within the E-kur temple in Nibru and was also worshipped in Lagaš-Ǧirsu

Nuska the son and minister of the great god Enlil, also associated with fire and light

Pabilsaǧ the goddess Ninisina's divine spouse, associated with the antediluvian city of Larag; sometimes identified with the warrior gods Ninurta and Ninǧirsu

Palm-tree King one of the seven Slain Heroes defeated by the god Ninurta and one of his trophies in the battle against the Asag demon

Rīm-Sîn the ninth king of the Dynasty of Larsa, ruled *c.*1822–1763 BCE until defeated by king Ḫammurabi of Babylon

Saba a distant, mountainous land in *Ninurta's exploits* (Group E)

Sa-bara a name of the great god Enlil as judge

Saǧ-buru wise woman who defeats the sorcerer Ur-ǧirnuna on behalf of Enmerkar in *Enmerkar and En-suḫgir-ana* (Group A)

Saǧ-Enlil Father of Nabi-Enlil, sender of the *Letter from Nabi-Enlil to Ilum-puzura* (Group I)

Sala a canal running through the city of Nibru

Samsu-iluna the seventh king of the Dynasty of Babylon, ruled *c.*1749–1712 BCE, son of king Ḫammurabi

Sargon the first king of the Dynasty of Agade, ruled *c.*2334–2279 BCE, who conquered the entire Land; father of the priestess En-ḫedu-ana and grandfather of king Naram-Suen

Seven-headed Serpent one of the seven Slain Heroes defeated by the god Ninurta and one of his trophies in the battle against the Asag demon

Sig-kur-šaga another name for the E-maḫ temple of the god Šara in Umma

Silu-igi (?) the boatman whom Enlil disguises himself as in *Enlil and Ninlil* (Group C); pronunciation uncertain

Simurrum a city between the Diyala and Tigris rivers to the north of Sumer

Sîn the Akkadian version of Suen, a name of the moon-god; found in the royal names Sîn-iqīšam and Rīm-Sîn

Sîn-iqīšam the seventh ruler of the Dynasty of Larsa, ruled *c.*1840–1836 BCE

Sirara a district of the city of Niĝin in the Lagaš-Ĝirsu region, containing Nanše's temple of the same name

Sirsir a divine boatman, in the entourage of the god Enki

Six-headed Wild Ram one of the seven Slain Heroes defeated by the god Ninurta and one of his trophies in the battle against the Asag demon

Strong Copper one of the seven Slain Heroes defeated by the god Ninurta and one of his trophies in the battle against the Asag demon

Subir a land in northern Mesopotamia

Sud the goddess of the city of Šuruppag and daughter of Nisaba; equated with Ninlil through marriage to Enlil

Suen another name for the moon-god Nanna; known in Akkadian as Sîn

Surungal after the Tigris and Euphrates, the major watercourse running through Sumer; perhaps a canalized channel of the Euphrates

Šakkan the protective deity of the wild animals of the Sumerian plains; also an Underworld god through the association of the Underworld and the desert

Šara a warrior god and son of the goddess Inana, in her entourage; worshipped at the E-maḫ temple in Umma

Šar-gaz a divine weapon belonging to the warrior god Ninurta, literally 'Crushes a myriad'

Šar-ur a divine mace belonging to the warrior god Ninurta, literally 'Mows down a myriad'

Šat-Eštar Lu-diĝira's mother in *Lu-diĝira's message to his mother* (Group F); sometimes called Šimat-Eštar

Šerida the sun-god Utu's divine spouse

Šimaški a region to the north-east of Sumer and north of Elam, in the Iranian highlands

Šimat-Eštar another name for Šat-Eštar, Lu-diĝira's mother in *Lu-diĝira's message to his mother* (Group F)

Šu-galam a gateway and cultic site in the temple E-ninnu in Ĝirsu, probably the major entrance into the shrine

Šuḫalbi another name for the goddess Bau

Šu-ilišu the second ruler of the Dynasty of Isin, ruled *c.*1984–1975

Šu-kale-tuda 'Spotty', the gardener's boy who rapes the goddess Inana in *Inana and Šu-kale-tuda* (Group F)

Šulgi the second ruler of the Third Dynasty of Urim, ruled *c*.2094–2047 BCE; responsible for its transformation from city-state to empire; son of Ur-Namma and father of Šu-Suen; patron of high-quality praise poetry

Šul-pa-eda a minor deity of the cult of Keš, where he was considered to be the spouse of the goddess Ninḫursaĝa

Šuni-dug a minor deity in the entourage of the moon-god Nanna

Šuruppag a city in the heart of Sumer, one of those thought to have existed before the Flood; modern name Fara; also the name of a mythical king, perhaps the city personified; sometimes known in modern scholarship as Šuruppak

Šu-Suen the fourth king of the Third Dynasty of Urim, ruled *c*.2037–2029 BCE; a son of king Šulgi

Tar-sirsir the goddess Bau's temple in Iri-kug in Ĝirsu; also known as E-Iri-kug

Tidnum a hostile nomadic people from the Zagros mountains, sometimes associated with the Mardu people.

Tigris a major river running from Anatolia through Iraq to the east of Sumer, down to the Gulf; too fast-flowing and prone to flooding in antiquity to be as navigable or manageable as the Euphrates

Tiraš a shrine of the god Ninĝirsu near Lagaš

Tummal the goddess Ninlil's cult centre, downstream from Nibru

Tutub a city in the Diyala valley to the north-east of Sumer; modern Khafaje

Ubara-Tutu a mythical king of Šuruppag; alternatively father of the mythical king Šuruppag, father of Zi-ud-sura.

Ub-šu-unkena a shrine in the temple E-ninnu in Ĝirsu

Ud-ane with Lugal-anbara and Lugal-kur-dub, in the entourage of the god Ninurta

Ulmaš an area of the city of Agade, where Inana's temple E-Ulmaš was located

Umma a Sumerian city, between Adab and Ĝirsu, cult centre of the god Šara

Underworld the dark and uncomfortable dwelling place of the dead, ruled by the goddess Ereškigala

Unug a major city in the centre of Sumer, cult centre of An and Inana, also known as Uruk (and in the Bible as Erech); modern name Warka; according to legend, home of the heroes Gilgameš, Lugalbanda, and Enmerkar; the cultic district was named Kulaba

Uraš a goddess, divine spouse of the supreme deity An; mother of the goddesses Ninisina and Nisaba (there was also a male deity Uraš, patron deity of the city of Dilbat, who does not feature in these compositions)

Ur-edina a shepherd in *Enmerkar and En-suḫgir-ana* (Group A)

Ur-ĝirnuna the sorcerer from Ḫamazu who cast spells on behalf of the lord of Aratta in *Enmerkar and En-suḫgir-ana* (Group A)

Urim a major city in the south of Sumer; seat of the great Third Dynasty of Urim (*c*.2112–2004 BCE) which ruled the whole of the Land; cult centre of the moon-god Nanna-Suen

Ur-Namma the first ruler of the Third Dynasty of Urim, ruled *c*.2112–2095 BCE; father of king Šulgi

Ur-Ninurta the sixth ruler of the Dynasty of Isin, ruled *c.*1923–1896 BCE

Urumaš a minor deity of the cult at Keš

Ur-Zababa a historically attested king of Kiš in the mid-third millennium BCE, who according to legend employed the young Sargon of Agade as his cupbearer

Ušumgal-ana an epithet of the shepherd-god Dumuzid

Uta-ulu another name for the warrior god Ninurta

Uttu the goddess of weaving

Utu the sun-god, worshipped especially at Larsa and Zimbir; in both cities his temple was named E-babbar ('Shining house'); also identified with the Akkadian sun-god Šamaš and the West Semitic Samsu; spouse of the goddess Šerida

Zababa a warrior god and patron of the city of Kiš, where his divine spouse was considered to be Inana; worshipped at the temple E-mete-ursaĝ

Zabalam a Sumerian city between Adab and Umma, a cult centre of the goddess Inana

Zabu a mountainous region in Elam to the east of Sumer

Zangara the god of dreams

Zimbir a city to the north of Babylon, also known in modern scholarship as Sippar or Sippir; cult centre of the sun-god Utu; modern name Abu Habba

Zi-ud-sura a mythical king of Šuruppag and survivor of the Flood; also known in modern scholarship as Ziusudra and by the Akkadian names Ūt-napištim and Atra-ḫasīs

Zubi a mountainous region somewhere to the east of Sumer, thought to be a source of tin